D1726395

European Yearbook of International Economic Law

EYIEL Monographs - Studies in European and International Economic Law

Volume 37

EYIEL Monographs is a subseries of the European Yearbook of International Economic Law (EYIEL). It contains scholarly works in the fields of European and international economic law, in particular WTO law, international investment law, international monetary law, law of regional economic integration, external trade law of the EU and EU internal market law. The series does not include edited volumes. EYIEL Monographs are peer-reviewed by the series editors and external reviewers.

Sven Nikolai Pauls

EU Sustainable Finance and International Trade Law

Legality and Propagation of EU Sustainable Finance Regulation under GATS and Free Trade Agreements

 Springer

Sven Nikolai Pauls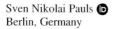
Berlin, Germany

ISSN 2364-8392   ISSN 2364-8406   (electronic)
European Yearbook of International Economic Law
ISSN 2524-6658   ISSN 2524-6666   (electronic)
EYIEL Monographs - Studies in European and International Economic Law
ISBN 978-3-031-73852-4   ISBN 978-3-031-73853-1   (eBook)
https://doi.org/10.1007/978-3-031-73853-1

This Springer imprint is published by the registered company Springer Nature Switzerland AG
The registered company address is: Gewerbestrasse 11, 6330 Cham, Switzerland

If disposing of this product, please recycle the paper.

To Cristina and my family

Acknowledgements

This book is based on my dissertation, which was accepted at the Faculty of Law of the Georg-August-Universität Göttingen in March 2024.

The research, drafting, and publication process—in and out of the Covid-19 pandemic—was a challenging journey and I am grateful to my supervisor Prof. Dr. Dr. h.c. Peter-Tobias Stoll for his academic and methodological guidance. His advice, feedback, and interdisciplinary approach have proved to be cornerstones along the way. I would also like to acknowledge Prof. Dr. Eckart Bueren, Dipl.-Volkswirt, whose publication on Sustainable Finance provided a concise introduction to the relevant aspects of European law.

I am also grateful to Agata Daszko for meticulously reviewing the dissertation and to my fellow doctoral students at the Department for International Economic and Environmental Law for providing me with valuable feedback and motivation.

I would like to use this opportunity to especially thank my wife Cristina for her tireless encouragement—and my parents and my brother for their support and faith in me throughout the years. This book is dedicated to them.

Contents

List of Abbreviations

AAAA	Addis Ababa Action Agenda
AIF	Alternative Investment Fund
BIT	Bilateral Investment Agreement
CARIFORUM	Caribbean Forum
CBA	Carbon border adjustment
CETA	Comprehensive Economic and Partnership Agreement
CMU	Capital Market Union
CRA	Credit rating agency
CSR	Corporate social responsibility
DSU	Dispute Settlement Understanding
EBA	European Banking Authority
EC	European Community *or* European Communities, *respectively*
ECB	European Central Bank
EEC	European Economic Community
EFRAG	European Financial Reporting Advisory Group
EFSD	European Fund for Sustainable Development
EFSI	European Fund for Strategic Investments
EIB	European Investment Bank
EIOPA	European Insurance and Occupational Pensions Authority
EIP	External Investment Plan
EPA	Economic Partnership Agreement
ESA	European Supervisory Authority
ESG	Environmental Social Governance
ESM	European Stability Mechanism
ETS	Emission trading system
EU	European Union
EU GBS	EU Green Bond Standard
Euratom	European Atomic Energy Community
EURIBOR	European Interbank Offered Rate
FCA	Financial Conduct Authority

FDI	Foreign Direct Investment
FSB	Financial Stability Board
FTA	Free trade agreement
G20	Group of Twenty
G7	Group of Seven
GATS	General Agreement on Trade in Services
GATT	General Agreement on Tariffs and Trade
GFSG	*See SFSG*
ICAAP	Internal Capital Adequacy Assessment Process
ICMA	International Capital Markets Association
IFRS	International Financial Reporting Standards
IISD	International Institute for Sustainable Development
ILO	International Labour Organization
IOSCO	International Organization of Securities Commissions
IPCC	Intergovernmental Panel on Climate Change
ISO	International Organization for Standardization
KID	Key information document
KPI	Key performance indicator
Libor	London Interbank Offered Rate
MC	Ministerial conference
MDG	Millennium Development Goal
MFF	Multiannual financial framework
NFI	Nonfinancial information
NFR	Nonfinancial reporting
NGFS	Network for Greening the Financial System
ODA	Official development assistance
OECD	Organization for Economic Cooperation in Europe
PEPP	Pan-European personal pension product
PRIIP	Packaged retail and insurance-based investment products
Rio+20	*See UNCSD*
RTS	Regulatory technical standard
SDG	Sustainable Development Goal
SFSG	Sustainable Finance Study Group
SI	Significant institution
SMA	European Securities and Markets Authority
SRA	Sustainability rating agency
SREP	Supervisory Review and Evaluation Process
SRI	Sustainable and responsible investment
SSM	Single Supervisory Mechanism
TBT	Technical barriers to trade
TCA	Trade and Cooperation Agreement
TCFD	Task Force on Climate-related Financial Disclosures
UK	United Kingdom of Great Britain and Northern Ireland
UN	United Nations

UN CPC	UN Central Product Classification
UNCSD	UN Conference on Sustainable Development
UNEP	UN Environment Programme
UNEP FI	UNEP Finance Initiative
UNFCCC	UN Framework Convention on Climate Change
UN PAGE	UN Partnership for Action on Green Economy
WTO	World Trade Organization

.

Chapter 1
Introduction

In 2015, United Nations (*UN*) Member States adopted the 2030 Agenda[1] putting forward seventeen Sustainable Development Goals (*SDGs*), marking the moment when the necessity of change towards sustainability was recognized by and for the international community.

In the 2030 Agenda, UN Member States claim that an *"important use of international public finance [. . .] is to catalyse additional resource mobilization from other sources, public and private"*. Already in the 2012 'The future we want' Outcome Document, UN Member States had recognized *"the importance of mobilizing funding from a variety of sources, public and private, bilateral and multilateral, including innovative sources of finance, to support nationally appropriate mitigation actions [. . .]."*[2] Consequently, the necessary changes in infrastructure and the economy as a whole, had to be undertaken and financed. Separate negotiation rounds at UN level, most notably the UN Financing for Development conferences, took up the task of outlining both traditional and alternative ways of financing the SDGs, resulting in the adoption of the 2015 Addis Ababa Action Agenda on Financing for Development (*AAAA*).[3]

The conceptual base of financing the SDGs can be summarized as *Sustainable Finance*. This entails a wide range of regulatory instruments. As described above, the challenge of ensuring financial backing for the achievement of the Millennium

---

[1] General Assembly Resolution 70/1, Transforming our World: The 2030 Agenda for Sustainable Development. 25 September 2015. A/RES/70/1.

[2] General Assembly Resolution 66/288, The future we want. 27 July 2012. A/RES/66/288, p. 191; The UN Conference on Sustainable Development (*UNCSD* or *Rio+20*) was held from 20 to 22 June 2012 in Rio de Janeiro, Brazil.

[3] Addis Ababa Action Agenda of the Third International Conference on Financing for Development (Addis Ababa Action Agenda), The final text of the outcome document adopted at the Third International Conference on Financing for Development (Addis Ababa, Ethiopia, 13–16 July 2015) and endorsed by the General Assembly in its resolution 69/313 of 27 July 2015. 15 July 2015.

© The Author(s), under exclusive license to Springer Nature Switzerland AG 2024
S. N. Pauls, *EU Sustainable Finance and International Trade Law*, EYIEL Monographs - Studies in European and International Economic Law 37, https://doi.org/10.1007/978-3-031-73853-1_1

Development Goals (*MDGs*) and the SDGs has been discussed for several years already. Financing their implementation through private capital,[4] however, is a method that gathered increased attention only recently.

The Goals underline the urgency of a swift and comprehensive transformation towards ecologically and socially sustainable ways of living, trading, and producing. This accounts both for the economic and political spheres. From a regulatory perspective, these changes can be understood as a shift within the very aim of economic regulation, the focus of which changed from mere economic prosperity and fair competition towards a comprehensive policy guided by environmental, social, and governance (*ESG*) factors. The SDGs aim to embed sustainability deep into all parts of a UN Member State's policy frameworks.

International trade law as a policy field inherently international, as the SDGs themselves, was affected by this shift. In an international context, trade and investment and the respective legal regimes are where the three ESG factors of sustainable development interrelate most. This interrelation between sustainable development and international trade law has been a much-discussed topic in academic literature and jurisprudence for years.

There are, however, also profound similarities in the concepts of the global financial markets and sustainable development. Both are future-oriented and, particularly long-term investments, are likely to follow sustainable investment strategies.[5] This cluster can be complemented by the concept of Sustainable Finance and the cross-border trade in financial services. Both correlate with sustainable development and global financial markets in their international nature and the cases to which they apply.

This book aims to contribute to the understanding of the interrelation between international trade law and Sustainable Finance. It primarily intends to answer two interrelated questions: Are current or future Sustainable Finance provisions legal under, in other words *consistent* with, international trade law? Which role can international trade law play in the propagation and justification of Sustainable Finance policy?

This book's assessment of the interrelation between Sustainable Finance and international trade law will rely on the European Union's (*EU*) Sustainable Finance legislation as an example. This accounts both for the potential inconsistency of the EU's Sustainable Finance measures *under* international trade law and its propagation and justification *through* international trade law.

This choice of example is due to the crucial role the EU played throughout the international policy-setting process of sustainable development depicted above. The European Commission (the *Commission*) was at the forefront of not only the Rio + 20 negotiations but also the Paris Summit and the, previously separately negotiated, 2030 Agenda. It had a significant influence on these processes. Its

---

[4]The term *private capital* will be used in this book as to the understanding of all funds except and in contrast to public financial resources.

[5]Bueren (2019), p. 826.

recently envisaged leadership role in international sustainable development negotiations also translates into internal regulatory adaption of the externally set goals.[6] Furthermore, the Commission is one of the first governmental institutions to not only mainstream sustainable development into virtually all its regulatory action, it is also at the very forefront of drafting Sustainable Finance legislation.

The subsequent chapters will provide a brief overview of the concept of Sustainable Finance (1.1) and the structure of this book (1.2).

1.1   Sustainable Finance

The international agreements on sustainable development set out a regime of rules and benchmarks, by which parties to these agreements are bound. These rules aim to ensure sustainable human development and environmental protection. Transforming them into national legislation and real-life impact requires national governments not only to introduce new laws but to fund projects, research, and infrastructure. Global investments necessary for the transition towards a sustainable economy in line with the SDGs are estimated to be between $5 trillion and $7 trillion per annum.[7]

Parties realized promptly that these funds could not originate exclusively from tax resources. The discussion turned towards private capital as a source of funding for sustainable development. This private capital was already available but needed to be rechanneled towards sustainable investment alternatives. This was the core aim of the concept that would later become known as *Sustainable Finance*.

EU Sustainable Finance covers a wide range of prudential and fiscal legislative acts covering the financial sector and beyond. The legislation implemented within the EU will be detailed in Chap. 2. However, there are some general categories of instruments identifiable focusing only on the EU's particular approach (each a *Sustainable Finance instrument*).

For instance, Sustainable Finance can be understood either as prudential legislation introduced by a legislator to foster sustainability-led investment decision-making by market participants; or it can be understood as the decision-making itself. Therefore, on the one hand, the legislator may either create incentives for investment into sustainable economic activity, for example, by issuing sustainability labels, granting relief in capital requirements, or raising awareness for ESG issues. He could also impede the acquisition or market access of unsustainable financial services or financial service suppliers, for instance, by adjusting its trade policy, market access screening, licensing, or credit rating requirements.

On the other hand, a government may decide to use its public funds and own resources to create these incentives. For instance, it could leverage investments into sustainable economic activities, or invest itself—either directly or through public

---

[6]Cf. Sect. 4.1.1.
[7]UNCTAD (2014), p. xi.; Cf. UN PAGE (2018), p. 10.

investment funds. Further options involve sustainable public procurement or public-private partnerships, or introducing impediments. This could be achieved by divesting from unsustainable economic activities.

There have been numerous industry-led initiatives that set out voluntary standards on sustainability-led investment decision-making by market participants. Examples are the UN Environment Programme (*UNEP*) Finance Initiative's (*UNEP FI*) *Principles for Responsible Banking* as a public-private partnership,[8] the *UNEP Global Reporting Initiative,* and its *Financial Services Sector Supplements,*[9] or the stewardship concept.[10] There also have been several industry-led sustainability labels and several stock exchanges introduced rules. These usually govern financial services and products being traded on their platforms,[11] for instance, the *UN Sustainable Stock Exchange Initiative.*[12]

Although the landmark agreements on sustainable development reached in 2015 moved Sustainable Finance into the international spotlight, the concept existed before. There had been plenty of sustainable financial services and products on the market. Regulation governing it was drawn up on a national level by countries such as France and China.[13] The concept of Sustainable Finance is also embedded in the EU Treaties, for instance in Art. 3.3 and Art. 21 TEU.[14]

The roots of Sustainable Finance can be traced back to the late 1960s, where civil rights movements and activists urged private investments to be withdrawn from companies engaged in Vietnam or apartheid South Africa. As a result, Sustainable Finance can be seen as rooted in corporate social responsibility (*CSR*). However, in the wake of the 1972 Club of Rome report,[15] the 1987 Brundtland report,[16] and environmental catastrophes, the international attention increasingly shifted the focus from CSR aspects towards environmental concerns.[17] Consequently, the focus of Sustainable Finance changed in favor of environmentally sustainable finance, too.[18] As shown above, Sustainable Finance is a broad concept and to achieve its aim of fostering the SDGs, it has to be translated into detailed policy proposals. However, to assess these proposals, the scope of this concept must be defined.

---

[8]PRI are the former UN Principles for Responsible Investment that include six procedural and substantial goals that require its members to take into account ESG factors when taking an investment decision, cf. EBA (2019), p. 19; Bueren (2019), p. 841.

[9]Bueren (2019), p. 841.

[10]Bueren (2019), p. 829.

[11]Bueren (2019), p. 844.

[12]Bueren (2019), p. 832.

[13]Bueren (2019), p. 815.

[14]Consolidated version of the Treaty on European Union [2012] OJ C 326/13; Cf. European Commission (2018a), p. 1.

[15]Meadows et al. (1972).

[16]United Nations (1987).

[17]Bueren (2019), pp. 828, 838; Hush (2018), p. 99.

[18]Bueren (2019), p. 816.

A variety of definitions of Sustainable Finance exist depending on the perspective taken and the approach chosen.[19]

The Commission defines Sustainable Finance as "*the process of taking due account of environmental and social considerations in investment decision-making, leading to increased investments in longer-term and sustainable activities*".[20] The Commission's definition thus encompasses the investor's perspective. It does not, however, explicitly include the regulator's perspective. The regulator would intend to influence the investor's decision-making process in favor of sustainable investment alternatives.

More broadly, the European Banking Authority (*EBA*) defines Sustainable Finance from the regulator's perspective. It comprehends Sustainable Finance as "*financing and related institutional and market arrangements that contribute to the achievement of strong, sustainable, balanced and inclusive growth, through supporting directly and indirectly the framework of the Sustainable Development Goals*".[21]

Adding to the two possible vertical perspectives (those of an investor and the regulator), Sustainable Finance can also be defined horizontally. Risk-assessment considerations concerning investments and stability of financial system account for the risks posed by, for instance, climate change.[22] This is contrasted by economic considerations which frame sustainable activities as a long-term investment. The concomitant moral high ground is seen as little more than good business practice and marketing opportunity.

The risk-assessment considerations are usually summarized under two terms: *sustainability risks* and *transition risks*. Art. 1(22) Sustainability Disclosures Regulation[23] defines the former as "*an environmental, social or governance event or condition that, if it occurs, could cause an actual or a potential material negative impact on the value of the investment*". The latter that is *transition* risks, describe the risk of a loss in value of an investment due to the shift towards a more sustainable economy and financial system. Investments affected by such transition risks are referred to as *stranded assets*.[24] The European Insurance and Occupational Pensions Authority (*EIOPA*) uses the term *sustainability factors* for describing both, climate change-related opportunities and sustainability risks.[25]

Ultimately, Sustainable Finance also intends to prevent a potential threat to financial stability caused by a negative impact on the investment's value. Preventing

---

[19] Bueren (2019), p. 816.

[20] European Commission (2018a), p. 2.

[21] EBA (2019), p. 4.

[22] Cf. e.g. EBA (2019), p. 15.

[23] Regulation (EU) 2019/2088 of the European Parliament and of the Council of 27 November 2019 on sustainability-related disclosures in the financial services sector [2019] OJ L 317/1; Originally proposed in European Commission (2018b).

[24] For a description of *transition risks* cf. Bueren (2019), p. 872.

[25] EIOPA (2019b), p. 6; EIOPA, however, mostly focuses on sustainability risks.

financial instability (*resilience*) particularly was a lesson learned from the 2007–2008 financial crisis. Achieving such resilience is both precondition and desirable result of effectively implementing financial sustainability in the financial sector.

Sustainability risks can be exemplified by a loss in value of an investment due to an investment decision-making process geared towards short-term profits instead of paying due regard to sustainability-based considerations. Such way of decision-making could pose a threat to the financial system. In other words, profit-oriented investment decisions are likely to insufficiently consider sustainability considerations. Such investments usually have a short investment horizon. This phenomenon is referred to as *short-termism*, or as the *"tragedy of the horizon"*.[26] Short-termism stands in contrast to so-called *long-termism*, which in turn plays a central role in Sustainable Finance. The importance and economic benefit of long-termism and sustainability in investment considerations are regularly pointed out.[27] Fostering long-term decision-making feeds into various parts of financial regulation. It is mentioned throughout the various instruments of Sustainable Finance described in Chap. 2.

In similar terms to the Commission and EIOPA, the Commission's High-Level Expert Group on Sustainable Finance (*HLEG*)[28] defined Sustainable Finance as encompassing two imperatives. The goal of Sustainable Finance is to *"improve the contribution of finance to sustainable and inclusive growth as well as the mitigation of climate change"*. Furthermore, Sustainable Finance would *"strengthen financial stability by incorporating [ESG] factors into investment decision-making. Both imperatives are pressing, given the rising climate-related risks and degradation in the environment and other sustainability areas"*.[29] Thus, the HLEG's definition is characterized by its focus on the aim of Sustainable Finance.

As binding legislation addressing Sustainable Finance is still sparse, nonbinding, voluntary and industry-led self-governance are flourishing. Set on corporate and sectoral levels, there are numerous initiatives, sustainability labels, and voluntary self-regulatory bodies in the EU and abroad.[30] Each has a unique definition of Sustainable Finance but one that is usually rooted in CSR. These initiatives increasingly shift towards adopting the broader concept of sustainable development into their wider standards. Two of the most notable nonbinding standards are the Equator Principles introducing a minimum standard agreed upon by several international investment banks[31] and the International Capital Markets Association's (*ICMA*) Green Bond Principles.[32] Yet another initiative, the European Sustainable

---

[26] Carney (2015); Cf. HLEG (2018), p. 2; Cf. JRC (2019), p. 45.

[27] Cf. e.g. European Commission (2018a), p. 2.

[28] For a description of HLEG, cf. Chap. 2.

[29] HLEG (2018), p. 6.

[30] For an overview, cf. Bueren (2019), p. 837.

[31] Bueren (2019), p. 840; Cf. Equator Principles Association (2020).

[32] ICMA (2018); Bueren (2019), p. 829.

Investment Forum, defines sustainable and responsible investment (*SRI*) as "*a long-term oriented investment approach which [. . .] combines fundamental analysis and engagement with an evaluation of ESG factors in order to better capture long term returns for investors, and to benefit society by influencing the behavior of companies.*"[33]

It can be concluded that certain elements of Sustainable Finance are common to the above-mentioned definitions. First, Sustainable Finance aims at supporting the SDGs. It thus does not only have its roots but also derives its conceptual base from the UN sustainable development agenda. Conceptually, Sustainable Finance shares the same sense of urgency and internationalism that is rooted in the UN sustainable development agreements. It can also be understood as a means of implementing sustainable development. Or, as Gabriel Bernardino, EIOPA's Chairman, stated, sustainable development and Sustainable Finance are "*two sides of the same coin*".[34] Thus, despite their differences, both concepts correlate strongly and must be interpreted with respect to each other.[35] Adding to this, it must be noted that both Sustainable Finance and sustainable development share the use of and relate to the three ESG factors.

To achieve its aim, Sustainable Finance possesses prudential and fiscal instruments rechanneling private capital into more sustainable economic activities and investment alternatives.[36] This rechanneling of private capital takes place in an economic environment characterized by a competition-based market economy and short-term profit. Therefore, it is likely to create plenty of room for conflicts. These conflicts particularly arise between the legitimate interest of market participants in free and fair competition, and the regulator's interventions in favor of sustainable financial services. Plus, Sustainable Finance aims to protect the financial sector and indirectly, the real economy, from sustainability risks and transitional risks. This aim can cumulatively be summed up as ensuring financial stability.

The definition of Sustainable Finance used in this book, the methodology of analyzing the interrelation between Sustainable Finance and international trade law, and the structure of this book will be described in the following section (1.2).

---

[33] Bueren (2019), p. 816; EuroSIF (2016), p. 9.

[34] EIOPA (2018), p. 1; C.f. also, EIOPA (2019a).

[35] For a closer discussion on the interrelation between the concepts of Sustainable Development and Sustainable Finance, cf. Sects. 3.3.4 and 5.2.

[36] Apart from its definition, a core challenge in drafting Sustainable Finance policy is setting the scope of economic activities that are considered sustainable and thus, desirable. These considerations are not relevant at this point, but they are at the core of the implementation of Sustainable Finance and its impact on international trade law. Thus, they will be assessed in Sects. 2.1 and 3.3.4.

1.2   Methodology and Structure of this Book

This book's assessment of the interrelation between Sustainable Finance and international trade law will be based on a broad understanding of the concept of Sustainable Finance. Sustainable Finance will be understood as instruments for the implementation of sustainable development in financial services regulation. Sustainable Finance, therefore, encompasses all financial service suppliers. It aims at rechanneling investments into such economic activities in which ESG factor-based decision-making is considered at least of equal importance to other criteria, such as profit maximization. Additionally, such activities shall support at least one of the ESG factors whilst not significantly harming the remaining two.

For the vertical scope of this book, it will focus on Sustainable Finance regulation at EU level, without taking into account national regulatory advances in recent years. This is due to the pioneering role of the EU in respect of both, the concepts of sustainable development and Sustainable Finance. The EU assumed this role not only at the drafting stage of international agreements but also at the implementation stage.

As shown in the previous section, the definition and scope of application of Sustainable Finance vary depending on the jurisdiction and the respective institutional and regulatory framework. Therefore, the regulation does not build on the underlying concept, but both logical steps intertwine. Thus, the latter evolves by the adaption of the former due to the necessity of swift structural change towards sustainable development. However, to enable a more comprehensive analysis of EU Sustainable Finance under international trade law, this book will consider international trade law both as a related policy field—and as a conceptual source for Sustainable Finance policy. Therefore, this book takes a three-step analytical approach:

> definition of the scope of EU Sustainable Finance,
>   assessment of EU Sustainable Finance's legality under international trade law,
>   identification of actual and possible channels of propagation and justification through international trade law.

Defining the scope of the assessment under international trade law and determining the legal provisions it will be based on, Chap. 2 specifies the EU's existing Sustainable Finance legislation and categorizes them into *instruments* of Sustainable Finance. These instruments either follow a prudential approach to rechannelling private capital (2.1), or a fiscal approach by using the EU's public financial resources (2.2). Hence, the term *instruments* used in this book aims to categorize Sustainable Finance *legislation* (or *regulation*), which in turn refers to all EU level 1, level 2, and level 3 legislative and administrative acts. In contrast, the expression Sustainable Finance *measures* is only used for assessing these instruments under international trade law.[37] This is followed by a chapter on current EU regulatory processes, which

---

[37] Cf. Sect. 3.2.

are set to be introduced or materialize in the upcoming years. This includes proposals for further Sustainable Finance regulation voiced by working groups and panels within the EU (2.3).

Based on this overview of Sustainable Finance regulation in the EU, this regulation will be assessed regarding its consistency with international trade law (Chap. 3), in particular with the General Agreement on Trade in Services (*GATS*).[38]

Consistency or *inconsistency* of EU Sustainable Finance measures in this book refer to a measure's potential legality or illegality under the EU's international trade law obligations, respectively. The terms are used in an analogous manner by the Appellate Body, which refers to *inconsistency* when determining the breach of an obligation under WTO law.[39] The GATS uses the terms *consistency, inconsistent, and conformity.*[40]

The consistency test under GATS conducted in Chap. 3 is particularly important considering the transparency requirements of Art. III(3) GATS. It requires that the Council for Trade in Service be informed "*of the introduction of any new, or any changes to existing, laws, regulations or administrative guidelines which significantly affect trade in services covered by its specific commitments under [GATS].*" In respect thereof, the assessment of EU Sustainable Finance regulation distinguishes between existing regulation and regulatory processes and proposals.

Existing EU Sustainable Finance regulation will be assessed first (3.2) focusing on its consistency with the GATS disciplines. Subsequently, the same assessment will be conducted regarding prospective EU Sustainable Finance regulation and its consistency with GATS (3.3). This includes the question, whether the GATS framework limits the EU's policy space to introduce such legislation.

This assessment is complemented with an analysis covering the varying channels and instruments available to the EU for the propagation of Sustainable Finance into bilateral and multilateral frameworks (Chap. 4). This is particularly through the provision of expertise in international working groups, expert panels, and other types of entities of international cooperation (*international fora*; 4.1). It also comprises the propagation and justification through trade negotiations under the GATS framework (4.2). The meaning of *justification*—for the purposes of this book— invokes the notion of a variety of counterbalancing measures against potential restrictions to EU Sustainable Finance. Justification not only comprises the General Exceptions in Art. XIV GATS and the policy exemptions in Recital 4 GATS and para. 2(a) GATS Annex on Financial Services but it, for instance, also refers to the framing and interpretation of international trade law disciplines and other activities conducive to protecting the policy space of EU Sustainable Finance.

Thereinafter (Chap. 5), the potential influence of the EU's free trade agreements (*FTAs*) will be assessed in respect of their incorporation of sustainability (5.1). It

---

[38] General Agreement on Trade in Services, Marrakesh Agreement Establishing the World Trade Organization, Annex 1B. 15 April 1994. U.N.T.S. 1867 (1994).

[39] Cf. e.g. WTO DSB (2016) *Argentina – Measures Relating to Trade in Goods and Services*, Appellate Body report, para. 6.169; Cf. WTO (2020), p. 4; Cf. Sect. 3.2.4.1.

[40] Cf. e.g. Art. II(2), Art. V(7)(a), Art. VI(5)(b), and Art. XIV(c) to (e) GATS respectively.

further comprises the corresponding sustainability and environmental chapters in EU FTAs (5.2), and the feasibility of sustainable development or prudential carve-out clauses for Sustainable Finance measures (5.3). In parallel with Chap. 4, it will also address the propagation and justification through EU FTAs (5.4). This includes proposals for FTA clauses that would ensure sufficient policy space for the EU in Sustainable Finance within future FTAs or revisions of existing FTAs. The assessment conducted in Chap. 5 further comprises the international trade law provisions adopted in connection with the United Kingdom's (*UK*) withdrawal from the EU.[41]
This is followed by concluding remarks (Chap. 6).

Legislation

General Agreement on Trade in Services, Marrakesh Agreement Establishing the World Trade Organization, Annex 1B. 15 April 1994. U.N.T.S. 1867 (1994)
Directive 2009/138/EC of the European Parliament and of the Council of 25 November 2009 on the taking-up and pursuit of the business of Insurance and Reinsurance (Solvency II) [2009] OJ L 335/1
General Assembly Resolution 66/288, The future we want. 27 July 2012. A/RES/66/288
Consolidated version of the Treaty on European Union [2012] OJ C 326/13
Addis Ababa Action Agenda of the Third International Conference on Financing for Development (Addis Ababa Action Agenda), The final text of the outcome document adopted at the Third International Conference on Financing for Development (Addis Ababa, Ethiopia, 13–16 July 2015) and endorsed by the General Assembly in its resolution 69/313 of 27 July 2015. 15 July 2015
General Assembly Resolution 70/1, Transforming our World: The 2030 Agenda for Sustainable Development. 25 September 2015. A/RES/70/1
Regulation (EU) 2019/2088 of the European Parliament and of the Council of 27 November 2019 on sustainability-related disclosures in the financial services sector [2019] OJ L 317/1

References

Bibliography

Bueren E (2019) Sustainable Finance. Zeitschrift für Unternehmens- und Gesellschaftsrecht 48(5): 813–875. https://doi.org/10.1515/zgr-2019-0022. Accessed 19 Dec 2021

---

[41] For an overview of these provisions, cf. the introduction to Chap. 5.

Carney M (2015) Breaking the tragedy of the horizon – climate change and financial stability, speech at Lloyd's of London. 29 September 2015. https://www.bankofengland.co.uk/speech/2015/breaking-the-tragedy-of-the-horizon-climate-change-and-financial-stability. Accessed 19 Dec 2021

Hush ER (2018) Where no man has gone before: the future of sustainable development in the comprehensive economic and trade agreement and new generation free trade agreements. Colum J Environ Law 43(1):93–180. https://ssrn.com/abstract=3373398. Accessed 8 May 2024

Meadows DH et al (1972) Club of Rome, The Limits to growth, A report for the Club of Rome's project on the predicament of mankind. Potomac Associates, Washington, DC. https://collections.dartmouth.edu/content/deliver/inline/meadows/pdf/meadows_ltg-001.pdf. Accessed 19 Dec 2021

Documents

EBA (2019) EBA Action Plan on sustainable finance. https://eba.europa.eu/sites/default/documents/files/document_library//EBA%20Action%20plan%20on%20sustainable%20finance.pdf. Accessed 8 May 2024

EIOPA (2018) Summary of EIOPA's roundtables on sustainable finance. 22 June 2018. https://www.eiopa.europa.eu/sites/default/files/publications/advice/summary_eiopa_first_roundtable_sustainable_finance_june_2018.pdf. Accessed 19 Dec 2021

EIOPA (2019a) Summary of EIOPA's roundtables on sustainable finance. 23 January 2019. https://www.eiopa.europa.eu/sites/default/files/publications/advice/summary_eiopa_second_roundtable_sustainable_finance_jan._2019.pdf. Accessed 19 Dec 2021

EIOPA (2019b) Technical advice on the integration of sustainability risks and factors in Solvency II and the Insurance Distribution Directive. 30 April 2019. https://www.eiopa.europa.eu/sites/default/files/publications/advice/technical_advice_for_the_integration_of_sustainability_risks_and_factors.pdf. Accessed 19 Dec 2021

Equator Principles Association (2020) The Equator Principles, A financial industry benchmark for determining, assessing and managing environmental and social risk in projects. July 2020. https://equator-principles.com/wp-content/uploads/2020/05/The-Equator-Principles-July-2020-v2.pdf. Accessed 19 Dec 2021

European Commission (2018a) Communication from the Commission, Action Plan: Financing Sustainable Growth. 8 March 2018. COM(2018) 97 final. https://eur-lex.europa.eu/legal-content/EN/TXT/PDF/?uri=CELEX:52018DC0097&from=EN. Accessed 19 Dec 2021

European Commission (2018b) Proposal for a Regulation of the European Parliament and of the Council on disclosures relating to sustainable investments and sustainability risks and amending Directive (EU) 2016/2341. 24 May 2018. COM(2018) 354 final, 2018/0179 (COD). https://eur-lex.europa.eu/legal-content/EN/TXT/PDF/?uri=CELEX:52018PC0354&from=DE. Accessed 19 Dec 2021

EuroSIF (2016) European SRI Study 2016. http://www.eurosif.org/wp-content/uploads/2016/11/SRI-study-2016-HR.pdf

HLEG (2018) Final report of the High-Level Expert Group on Sustainable Finance. 31 January 2018. https://ec.europa.eu/info/publications/180131-sustainable-finance-report_en. Accessed 19 Dec 2021

ICMA (2018) Green bond principles, voluntary process guidelines for issuing green bonds. 14 June 2018. https://www.icmagroup.org/assets/documents/Regulatory/Green-Bonds/June-2018/Green-Bond-Principles%2D%2D-June-2018-140618-WEB.pdf. Accessed 19 Dec 2021

JRC (2019) Development of EU Ecolabel criteria for Retail Financial Products, Technical Report 2.0, Draft proposal for the product scope and criteria. 20 December 2019. https://susproc.jrc.ec.

europa.eu/Financial_products/docs/20191220_EU_Ecolabel_FP_Draft_Technical_Report_2-0. pdf. Accessed 19 Dec 2021

UN PAGE (2018) International Investment Agreements and Sustainable Development: Safeguarding Policy Space and Mobilizing Investment for a Green Economy. https://www. greengrowthknowledge.org/sites/default/files/downloads/resource/international_investment_ agreements_sustainable_development_1.pdf. Accessed 8 May 2024

UNCTAD (2014) World Investment Report 2014, https://unctad.org/system/files/official- document/wir2014_en.pdf. Accessed 19 December 2021

United Nations (1987) Report of the World Commission on Environment and Development. 4 August 1987. A/42/427. https://sustainabledevelopment.un.org/content/documents/5987our- common-future.pdf. Accessed 19 December 2021

WTO (2020) Analytical Index GATS – Article XIV (Jurisprudence). https://www.wto.org/english/ res_e/publications_e/ai17_e/gats_art14_jur.pdf. Accessed 8 May 2024

Jurisprudence

WTO DSB (2016) Argentina – Measures Relating to Trade in Goods and Services, Appellate Body report, 14 April 2016, WT/DS453/AB/R

Chapter 2
Sustainable Finance Legislation in the EU

This chapter will describe the existing EU regulation governing Sustainable Finance.[1] To make the numerous regulations more tangible for assessment, they will be arranged into *instruments*. Under the regulatory approach chosen, these instruments are subdivided into two categories. Prudential instruments use prudential regulation to rechannel private capital (2.1). Fiscal instruments use the EU's public financial resources to create incentives for private market participants (2.2).[2] Although the integrated nature of EU Sustainable Finance regulation does not always allow for a robust differentiation between prudential and fiscal instruments, a subdivision highlights the two differing aims and makes the instruments more accessible.[3] This will be complemented by a description of current regulatory processes and proposals concerning EU Sustainable Finance (2.3).

Describing EU Sustainable Finance regulation, it is paramount to point out the ambiguity of the underlying aims of sustainability in financial regulation in general. Sustainability, for example, as set out in the concept of long-termism (Sect. 1.1), may aim at protecting the stability of the financial system on the one hand. On the other hand, sustainability in financial regulation may also focus on the ESG factors and the furtherance of sustainable development as a wider policy objective. In the past, Sustainable Finance was a niche in EU capital markets regulation.[4] In the aftermath of the 2007–2008 financial crisis, the EU Commission adopted a variety of new legislation governing financial markets while first focusing on the issue of short-termism. Later, with the increasing scope of regulation in the field, the EU incrementally used the broader concept of ESG-based sustainability to define new rules

---

[1] EU legislation was considered up to and including 3 June 2024.

[2] For a comprehensive list of EU Sustainable Finance instruments, cf. Table 2.1.

[3] A different approach for the categorization of Sustainable Finance instruments was taken by Busch et al. by drawing out five broad categories: *"Public incentives, standardization, disclosure, corporate governance and financial regulation"*, cf. Busch et al. (2018), p. 15.

[4] Bueren (2019), p. 813.

S. N. Pauls, *EU Sustainable Finance and International Trade Law*, EYIEL Monographs - Studies in European and International Economic Law 37, https://doi.org/10.1007/978-3-031-73853-1_2

Table 2.1 List of regulatory instruments in sustainable finance. Source: Own Research

Instrument	Sub-chapter	Description	Personal Scope (of the Instrument)	Implementation (EU Legislation)
Taxonomy	2.1.1	Uniform set of criteria to define sustainable economic activity	All financial market participants	Taxonomy Regulation; EuSEF Regulation; ELTIF Regulation; HLEG Final Report; TEG Taxonomy Technical Report
Labeling	2.1.2	Labels for sustainable financial services and products	Product manufacturers	EU Ecolabel for financial products
Green Bond Standard	2.1.3	Label for ecologically sustainable bonds	Issuers of designated green bonds and EU Green Bonds	TEG Green Bond Standard Report; HLEG Green Bond Supplement
Benchmarks	2.1.4	Labels and transparency provisions for EU PABs, EU CTBs, and sustainability-related benchmarks	Providers of EU PABs and EU CTBs and designated sustainability-related benchmarks	Climate BMR
Credit Rating	2.1.5	Rules for sustainability-related credit ratings and sustainability ratings	Credit rating agencies and providers of sustainability ratings	–
Transparency	2.1.6	Disclosure, reporting, and accountancy standards on ESG factors	All financial market participants	Sustainability Disclosures Regulation, SRD II, Amending Regulations to MiFID II and PRIIPs
Capital Requirements	2.1.7	E.g., a Green Supporting Factor in calculating the capital requirements	Financial institutions or investment firms	Similar in Recital 44 CRR, Solvency II DelReg
Fiduciary and Advisory Duties	2.1.8	The fiduciary is obligated to consider ESG factors in investment decision	Fiduciaries and investment advisors	Art. 41 (1)(b) PEPP Regulation Art. 1(2) MiFID II DelReg
Corporate Governance	2.1.9	ESG-based corporate governance and remuneration policies	All financial market participants	–
Shareholder Engagement	2.1.10	Increased ESG-related engagement of shareholders	All publicly traded financial institutions	–
Awareness	2.1.11	Raising awareness for sustainability	All financial market participants	–

(continued)

Table 2.1 (continued)

Instrument	Sub-chapter	Description	Personal Scope (of the Instrument)	Implementation (EU Legislation)
		regarding private investors		
Leveraging and Blending	2.2	Leveraged or blended funding of sustainable economic activity	All financial market participants	–
Targeted Funding and Public-Private Partnerships	2.2	Direct funding or partnerships concerning sustainable economic activity	All financial market participants	–
Public Procurement and Divestment	2.2	ESG-aware public procurement and divestment of public funds	All financial market participants	–
Trade Policy and Border Screening	2.2	ESG factors in trade policy and establishment of e.g. carbon border adjustments	Third country financial market participants	–

for the financial markets.[5] An important assumption was that since the financial system had experience in responding to the 2007–2008 financial crisis, it could, too, play a significant role in addressing climate change mitigation.[6]

The EU's focus on Sustainable Finance as a broader concept and in particular environmental protection and climate change mitigation increased with the adoption of the Paris Agreement and the 2030 Agenda. The rechanneling of private capital is seen as a key instrument in achieving the EU climate targets by the year 2030. As described in Sect. 1.1, this is due to an estimated annual investment gap in public funds of about €180 billion.[7] The Commission estimates that an additional €260 billion of investments per annum is required to achieve the 2030 targets. This would at least partly need to be covered by private capital.[8] The Commission thus expects that private capital is key to funding the transition towards a more sustainable economy.[9] Another estimate sets out necessary additional energy and infrastructure investments at about €175 billion to €290 billion per annum to reach the climate change mitigation targets.[10]

---

[5] Bueren (2019), p. 854.

[6] Cf. e.g. European Commission (2018a), p. 1.

[7] European Commission (2018a), p. 2; The European Investment Bank (*EIB*) even estimates an investment gap of up to €270 billion annually, cf. EIB (2016); Cf. TEG (2019c), pp. 11 et seq.

[8] European Commission (2019c), pp. 15; European Commission (2020c), p. 3; European Commission (2019a).

[9] European Commission (2019c), pp. 16 et seq.

[10] TEG (2019c), p. 13.

Thus in recent years, in order to rechannel private capital towards more sustainable investment alternatives, the Commission saw financial stability, transparency, and long-termism as the adequate policies to be adopted as a part of the capital markets union (*CMU*).[11] In its 2017 mid-term report on the CMU, the Commission pointed out that a "*deep re-engineering of the financial system*" was necessary to conduct this rechanneling and to ensure that the EU's 2030 Agenda commitments are met.[12] To achieve such *deep re-engineering*, the EU issued several agendas and action plans. They depict the Commission's approach to the implementation of Sustainable Finance within the different fields of financial regulation. Usually at the beginning of such drafting processes, the Commission or the EU specialized agencies set up a working group or expert panel—or these agencies issue technical advises and reports themselves. The most notable ones are the HLEG, the Technical Expert Group on Sustainable Finance (*TEG*), and the technical advices by the European Supervisory Authorities[13] (*ESAs*) the Commission's Joint Research Center (*JRC*).

The Commission created the HLEG in October 2016.[14] It was tasked with drafting policy recommendations aimed at rechanneling capital flows towards sustainable investments and protecting the stability of the financial system against sustainability risks.[15] The HLEG initiated its work in January 2017, publishing an interim report in July 2017.[16] Its final report was published in January 2018.[17] It entailed eight key recommendations,[18] eight cross-cutting recommendations,[19] eight recommendations concerning financial institutions and specific sectors,[20] and four social and broader environmental sustainability recommendations.[21] Its focus was mainly on environmental aspects.[22] The HLEG Final Report highlighted two imperatives of Sustainable Finance: The contribution of private funding towards the goal of sustainability and, *vice versa*, the enhancement of financial stability through the

---

[11] European Commission (2018a), p. 1.

[12] Cf. European Commission (2017a), p. 9; TEG (2019c), p. 11.

[13] There are three ESAs within the institutional framework of the EU: The European Banking Authority (*EBA*), the European Securities and Markets Authority (*ESMA*) and the European Insurance and Occupational Pensions Authority (*EIOPA*).

[14] European Commission (2016b), Art. 1; European Commission (2018a), p. 1; HLEG (2018a), p. 6; TEG (2019c), p. 13; JRC (2019c), p. 2.

[15] European Commission (2016b), Art. 2; HLEG (2018a), p. 6.

[16] HLEG (2018a).

[17] HLEG (2018a); Cf. JRC (2019c), p. 2.

[18] HLEG (2018a), pp. 15–44; TEG (2019c), p. 13.

[19] HLEG (2018a), pp. 45–66.

[20] HLEG (2018a), pp. 67–84.

[21] HLEG (2018a), pp. 85–94.

[22] Bueren (2019), p. 854; European Commission (2018a), p. 1.

inclusion of ESG factors.[23] The HLEG Final Report[24] created the conceptual basis upon which subsequent EU Sustainable Finance regulations were drafted.[25]

This refers to the Commission's Sustainable Finance Action Plan of March 2018.[26] It incorporated the HLEG Interim Report's[27] and HLEG Final Report's[28] recommendations and environmental focus.[29] The Sustainable Finance Action Plan states three policy goals: The rechanneling of private capital towards more sustainable investment alternatives, the management of financial risk rooted in environmental issues, and increased transparency and long-termism in finance and industry.[30]

The inclusion or mainstreaming of environmental and social sustainability considerations into investment risk assessments is another policy goal outlined in the Sustainable Finance Action Plan. By mainstreaming these considerations, the risk rooted in the effects of climate change and, for instance, social inequality would be recognized in risk assessments. This could lead to both, more sustainable investment decisions and a more resilient financial system.[31]

Finally, corporate transparency on sustainability performance is seen as key to ensuring well-informed and long-term investment assessments. For investors to take environmental and social considerations into account, long-termism must be the driving incentive in the investment assessment. This also encompasses addressing current market dynamics favoring short-term, high-yield investments.[32] The Sustainable Finance Action Plan furthermore introduced ten measures of which the first eight aim at regulating capital markets.[33]

Subsequently, in July 2018, the Commission set up the TEG. It consisted of representatives from civil society, academia, and the finance and business sector. It was mandated to propose a technical classification and an EU Green Bond Standard (*EU GBS*), as recommended by the HLEG Final Report and outlined in the Sustainable Finance Action Plan.[34] The TEG presented its Climate-related Disclosures Report in January 2019,[35] its Green Bond Standard Report and Taxonomy Report

---

[23] European Commission (2018a), p. 1.

[24] HLEG (2018a).

[25] Bueren (2019), p. 814.

[26] European Commission (2018a).

[27] HLEG (2017).

[28] HLEG (2018a).

[29] HLEG (2018a), p. 7; Bueren (2019), p. 855; European Commission (2018a), p. 1.

[30] European Commission (2018a), p. 2; JRC (2019c), p. 2.

[31] European Commission (2018a), p. 3.

[32] European Commission (2018a), pp. 3 et seq.

[33] Bueren (2019), p. 855; JRC (2019c), p. 2.

[34] Bueren (2019), p. 857; European Commission (2018a), p. 4; HLEG (2018a), p. 19.

[35] TEG (2019a).

in June 2019,[36] and its Climate Benchmarks Report in September 2019.[37] Each of these reports indicated a significant advance in the drafting of Sustainable Finance policy in the EU.

More recently, the Commission's 2020 European Green Deal[38] announced a Renewed Sustainable Finance Strategy building *inter alia* upon the Commission's 2018 Sustainable Finance Action Plan. It would take into account the increased climate action targets reflected in the European Green Deal and current challenges due to the Covid-19 pandemic.[39] Adding to this, many of the publications on Sustainable Finance by international fora can also be attributed to the Commission, seeing as they had either been co-drafted by the EU, its institutions, or its specialized agencies or been referenced by EU Sustainable Finance regulations. These references and inter-linkages will be described with regard to the respective EU legislation below.[40]

2.1 Prudential Instruments

This chapter describes those EU Sustainable Finance instruments that utilize prudential regulation to achieve the rechanneling of private capital towards sustainable investment alternatives. This approach usually materializes in the amendment of existing regulations, for instance, the amendment of the BMR by the Climate BMR.[41] In some cases, however, stand-alone legislation was passed to implement Sustainable Finance into an existing field of prudential legislation such as the Sustainability Disclosures Regulation.[42]

---

[36] TEG (2019b); TEG (2019c); Cf. JRC (2019c), pp. 88 et seq.

[37] TEG (2019d).

[38] European Commission (2019c).

[39] European Commission (2020c), p. 4.

[40] For a complete chronological table of international reports on Sustainable Finance, in which the EU directly or indirectly took part, cf. Sect. 4.1.2.

[41] Regulation (EU) 2016/1011 of the European Parliament and of the Council of 8 June 2016 on indices used as benchmarks in financial instruments and financial contracts or to measure the performance of investment funds and amending Directives 2008/48/EC and 2014/17/EU and Regulation (EU) No 596/2014 [2016] OJ L 171/1; Regulation (EU) 2019/2089 of the European Parliament and of the Council of 27 November 2019 amending Regulation (EU) 2016/1011 as regards EU Climate Transition Benchmarks, EU Paris-aligned Benchmarks and sustainability-related disclosures for benchmarks [2019] OJ L 317/17.

[42] Regulation (EU) 2019/2088 of the European Parliament and of the Council of 27 November 2019 on sustainability-related disclosures in the financial services sector [2019] OJ L 317/1.

2.1.1 Taxonomy

Precondition and key to the operationalization of Sustainable Finance policies is defining which financial services and thus which underlying economic activities and which financial service suppliers are to be deemed *sustainable*. As set out above, Sustainable Finance regulation may rely rather on considerations about the stability of the financial system, or the furtherance of any combination of the ESG factors. These general assumptions as to whether an economic activity will be deemed sustainable, however, do not allow for quantification and operationalization.

This gap would need to be filled by the introduction of a general taxonomy. A taxonomy is a scheme for categorizing not only financial service suppliers but economic activities in general. It would thus allow for other Sustainable Finance instruments to be drafted and applied based upon it.[43] Such taxonomy was described as "*a list of economic activities assessed and classified based on their contribution to EU sustainability related policy objectives*".[44] The industry-led Network for Greening the Financial System (*NGFS*)[45] drew up three major tasks a taxonomy would need to accomplish: These are to prevent *greenwashing*,[46] to provide criteria for the certification of environmentally sustainable assets, and finally to facilitate the inclusion of sustainability risks in risk analysis.[47] Besides, the HLEG Final Report lists examples of potential uses for the taxonomy: Measuring financial flows, asset identification, and allocation, measuring portfolio exposure and calculating revenue, and providing rules on investor engagement and disclosure.[48]

As of 2017, there was no uniform taxonomy on sustainability criteria in the EU. Market participants had to rely on industry-led initiatives. The latter, however, would not necessarily be aligned with the EU's sustainability targets.[49] The considerable risk of greenwashing through an absence of uniform classification criteria was met by the creation of sustainability labels for financial services and products by the EU Member States. This, in turn, posed a risk of fragmentation.[50]

The introduction of such a unified taxonomy serving as a source for the definition of sustainable economic activities is the first action set out in the Commission's Sustainable Finance Action Plan. This proposal had been based on the HLEG Final Report's first recommendation.[51] It is aimed at providing the base for further elaboration of standards, labels, prudential requirements, and benchmarks as a

---

[43] European Commission (2018a), p. 4.

[44] TEG (2019c), p. 10.

[45] For further detail regarding the NGFS, cf. Sect. 4.1.2 and the NGFS website, cf. https://www.ngfs.net/, accessed 26 May 2024.

[46] This is to say wrongly attributing the term *green* or *sustainable* to a service.

[47] NGFS (2019b), p. 33.

[48] HLEG (2018a), p. 16.

[49] TEG (2019c), p. 14.

[50] TEG (2019c), p. 14.

[51] HLEG (2018a), pp. 13, 15; TEG (2019c), p. 13.

"technically robust classification system".[52] The Commission set up the TEG to elaborate a proposal for a technical classification, which eventually was presented in the TEG Taxonomy Technical Report.[53]

After the Commission's May 2018 original Proposal on a Taxonomy Regulation[54] from which the EP's legislative resolution of March 2019 deviated significantly[55] and a December 2019 final compromise[56] the Taxonomy Regulation was published in January 2020.[57] It sets out universal criteria on the definition of sustainability in respect of financial products and financial market participants.[58] It is intended to serve as the central point of reference and definition as to all financial market regulations concerning sustainability.[59]

The core definition of the Taxonomy Regulation is the definition of the term *environmentally sustainable investment*. It is fulfilled if an investment funds an environmentally sustainable economic activity.[60] Significantly this demonstrates that the Taxonomy Regulation implemented the TEG's focus on environmentally sustainable activities.[61] This environmental focus is common among EU Sustainable Finance regulations and proposals.[62]

Another core term of the EU taxonomy is defined in Art. 3(a) to (d) Taxonomy Regulation. It defines *ecologically sustainable economic activities* as being supportive of at least one of the environmental objectives in Art. 9 Taxonomy Regulation (*positive list*). Additionally, it must not cause significant harm to any of the environmental objectives in Art. 9 Taxonomy Regulation (*blacklist*). It must further respect the minimum safeguards deriving from the ILO conventions as of Art. 18 Taxonomy Regulation and correspond with the technical screening criteria established under Art. 10(3) Taxonomy Regulation.[63] Such positive or *supportive*, and negative or *no significant harm* criteria are common to the terminology of sustainable economic activity. They had been used, for instance, in the Green

---

[52] HLEG (2018a), pp. 13, 15; Bueren (2019), p. 859; European Commission (2018a), p. 4.

[53] Bueren (2019), p. 857; European Commission (2018a), p. 4; HLEG (2018a), p. 19; Cf. in the introduction to Chap. 2.

[54] European Commission (2018e).

[55] Bueren (2019), p. 857; European Parliament (2019).

[56] European Council (2019).

[57] Regulation (EU) 2020/852 of the European Parliament and of the Council of 18 June 2020 on the establishment of a framework to facilitate sustainable investment, and amending Regulation (EU) 2019/2088 [2020] OJ L 198/13.

[58] Art. 1(1) Regulation (EU) 2020/852.

[59] Art. 4 Regulation (EU) 2020/852.

[60] Art. 2(1) Regulation (EU) 2020/852; Cf. EIOPA (2019b), p. 5.

[61] Cf. e.g. European Council (2019), Art. 5; There was considerable criticism against this focus on ecological aspects, cf. Bueren (2019), p. 860.

[62] Cf. e.g. EIOPA (2019b), p. 6.

[63] Bueren (2019), p. 858.

Bond Principles and the TEG Taxonomy Technical Report. The latter, in turn, built upon the Commission's Proposal on a Taxonomy Regulation.[64]

Art. 10 Taxonomy Regulation sets out the term *substantial contribution to climate change mitigation* by referring to certain actions of a market participant. This includes the improvement of its energy efficiency or the increase in the use of sustainable materials. Art. 11 Taxonomy Regulation, in turn, defines the *substantial contribution to climate change adaption* as a risk reduction measure by the relevant market participant. The substantial contribution to the other environmental objectives mentioned in Art. 9 Taxonomy Regulation are defined by Art. 12 et seqq. Taxonomy Regulation. Correspondingly, the term of *do no significant harm* is defined in Art. 17 Taxonomy Regulation. The ESAs see a strong link between the *do no significant harm* in the Taxonomy Regulation and the Sustainability Disclosures Regulation.[65]

With these criteria, the Taxonomy Regulation's standard is much stricter than the one previously in use by the Green Bond Principles. This is both in respect of the recognized economic activities and the social minimum standards.[66] With its limited scope, the Taxonomy Regulation is believed to have the ability to tackle the fact that in practice social and governance considerations are the least considered of the three ESG factors.[67] However, the Taxonomy Regulation may only provide the legislative basis for the introduction of an actual EU taxonomy in the form of a classification scheme. This classification scheme would quantify the requirements of *substantial contribution* and *no significant harm*. Art. 19(1) Taxonomy Regulation calls for so-called *technical screening criteria* as a core element of the EU taxonomy. These technical screening criteria are meant to operationalize the aforementioned requirements.[68] Concerning the classification of *activities contributing substantially to the climate objectives*, the criteria were set out in the TEG Taxonomy Technical Report published in June 2019. It takes a sector-specific approach by proposing technical screening criteria on each economic sector's activities to be considered sustainable.[69]

Such technical screening criteria have been adopted in the form of the Climate Delegated Act and the Disclosures Delegated Act in December 2021. The Climate Delegated Act sets out the *"technical screening criteria for determining the conditions under which an economic activity qualifies as contributing substantially to climate change mitigation and for determining whether that economic activity*

---

[64] Cf. TEG (2019c), p. 19; The TEG's approach to the taxonomy saw four decisive factors defining a sustainable economic activity: It has to contribute significantly and do no significant harm to the environmental objectives, comply with ILO minimum standards and with technical screening criteria, cf. TEG (2019c), pp. 10, 19.

[65] ESMA (2020), p. 9.

[66] Bueren (2019), p. 861.

[67] Bueren (2019), p. 861.

[68] Cf. Recitals 38 et seqq. Regulation (EU) 2020/852.

[69] TEG (2019c), p. 23.

causes no significant harm to any of the other environmental objectives".[70] The
Disclosures Delegated Act sets out the sustainability disclosures obligations for
non-financial undertakings, asset managers, credit institutions, investment firms,
insurance undertakings, and disclosures rules common to all financial undertakings.[71] In November 2023, these Delegated Acts were complemented by the Environmental Delegated Act, which sets out the technical screening criteria related to
the sustainable use and protection of water and marine resources, related to the
transition to a circular economy, related to pollution prevention and control, and
related to the protection and restoration of biodiversity and ecosystems.[72]

However, concerns have been raised in Sustainable Finance literature on the
binary categorization undertaken by the Taxonomy Regulation as regards the sustainability of economic activities.[73] With most companies conducting multiple
economic activities simultaneously—with a differing sustainability rating each—
the percentual evaluation approach taken by the Taxonomy Regulation may run the
risk of impeding the taxonomy's effective implementation.[74] With a view towards

---

[70] Commission Delegated Regulation (EU) 2021/2139 of 4 June 2021 supplementing Regulation
(EU) 2020/852 of the European Parliament and of the Council by establishing the technical
screening criteria for determining the conditions under which an economic activity qualifies as
contributing substantially to climate change mitigation or climate change adaptation and for
determining whether that economic activity causes no significant harm to any of the other environmental objectives (Text with EEA relevance) [2021] OJ L 44271, Art. 1; The Commission
Delegated Regulation (EU) 2021/2139 has been amended by Commission Delegated Regulation
(EU) 2022/1214 of 9 March 2022 amending Delegated Regulation (EU) 2021/2139 as regards
economic activities in certain energy sectors and Delegated Regulation (EU) 2021/2178 as regards
specific public disclosures for those economic activities (Text with EEA relevance) [2022] OJ L
188/1; The Commission Delegated Regulation (EU) 2021/2139 has been further amended by the
Commission Delegated Regulation (EU) 2023/2485 of 27 June 2023 amending Delegated Regulation (EU) 2021/2139 establishing additional technical screening criteria for determining the
conditions under which certain economic activities qualify as contributing substantially to climate
change mitigation or climate change adaptation and for determining whether those activities cause
no significant harm to any of the other environmental objectives [2023] OJ L 2023/2485.

[71] Commission Delegated Regulation (EU) 2021/2178 of 6 July 2021 supplementing Regulation
(EU) 2020/852 of the European Parliament and of the Council by specifying the content and
presentation of information to be disclosed by undertakings subject to Articles 19a or 29a of
Directive 2013/34/EU concerning environmentally sustainable economic activities, and specifying
the methodology to comply with that disclosure obligation (Text with EEA relevance) [2021] OJ L
443/9, Art. 2–7.

[72] Commission Delegated Regulation (EU) 2023/2486 of 27 June 2023 supplementing Regulation
(EU) 2020/852 of the European Parliament and of the Council by establishing the technical
screening criteria for determining the conditions under which an economic activity qualifies as
contributing substantially to the sustainable use and protection of water and marine resources, to the
transition to a circular economy, to pollution prevention and control, or to the protection and
restoration of biodiversity and ecosystems and for determining whether that economic activity
causes no significant harm to any of the other environmental objectives and amending Commission
Delegated Regulation (EU) 2021/2178 as regards specific public disclosures for those economic
activities, OJ L 2023/2486, Art. 1–4.

[73] Bueren (2019), p. 861.

[74] Bueren (2019), p. 861.

investments by insurance companies, however, EIOPA states that the EU taxonomy will facilitate the sector's investment into sustainable, long-term assets. It would then match insurance-specific long-term liabilities.[75]

Apart from the Taxonomy Regulation, there are other classification systems. Some refer to the Taxonomy Regulation as a source of defining sustainable economic activities, like the JRC's proposal for an EU Ecolabel for the definition of a *green economic activity*.[76] Some use a separate set of criteria, like the Sustainability Disclosures Regulation.

Art. 2(17) Sustainability Disclosures Regulation defines *sustainable investment* using three criteria. To be considered a sustainable, investment has to contribute to environmental and social objectives, invest in human capital or the like, and "*not significantly harm any of those objectives*". This constitutes a separate classification system based on all three ESG factors, which with its positive and negative criteria resembles the EU taxonomy.

Furthermore, the European long-term investment funds (*ELTIF*) and European social entrepreneurship funds (*EuSEF*)—so-called *special purpose vehicles* for sustainable investments—can be understood as limited versions of a taxonomy.[77] The EuSEF is a social fund label or a *designation*[78] that is based on *uniform quality criteria*.[79] Within the EU, the EuSEF Regulation[80] requires the respective host state to report to the home state any breach of the EuSEF criteria.[81] Art. 3(1)(d)(V) EuSEF Regulation provides that also third country funds, given a bilateral agreement with the host state, can be designated a EuSEF. Eligible investments involve both debt and equity instruments[82] and eligible funds must use 30% of their capital for eligible assets.[83]

Similar to other EU funding labels such as the EuSEF, the ELTIF Regulation[84] requires the identification of categories of eligible *long-term* assets. This

---

[75] EIOPA (2019c), pp. 12 et seq.

[76] JRC (2019c), p. 32.

[77] Bueren (2019), p. 851.

[78] Regulation (EU) No 346/2013 of the European Parliament and of the Council of 17 April 2013 on European social entrepreneurship funds [2013] OJ L 115/18, Recitals 30 and 35.

[79] Recital 26 Regulation (EU) No 346/2013.

[80] Regulation (EU) No 346/2013.

[81] Recitals 41 et seq. Regulation (EU) No 346/2013.

[82] Art. 3(1)(e) Regulation (EU) No 346/2013.

[83] Art. 5(1) Regulation (EU) No 346/2013; For the EuSEF funding scheme, cf. Sect. 2.2.

[84] Regulation (EU) 2015/760 of the European Parliament and of the Council of 29 April 2015 on European long-term investment funds [2015] OJ L 123/98; The Regulation (EU) No 2015/760 was amended by Regulation (EU) 2023/606 of the European Parliament and of the Council of 15 March 2023 amending Regulation (EU) 2015/760 as regards the requirements pertaining to the investment policies and operating conditions of European long-term investment funds and the scope of eligible investment assets, the portfolio composition and diversification requirements and the borrowing of cash and other fund rules (Text with EEA relevance) [2023] OJ L 80/1.

demonstrates a categorization similar to a taxonomy.[85] Based on this categorization ELTIFs aim at channeling retail investor's funds into long-term projects.[86]

2.1.2 Labeling

One of the most common strategies of rechanneling private capital is influencing the investor's decision with an increase in the amount and accessibility of information. This information particularly entails the sustainability-related performance of the company invested into, a fund or an investment intermediate like a financial service supplier. One such information tool are labels. Labels are granted either by a public or private authority based on a set of criteria. They enable particularly retail clients to take investment decision consistent with their respective ESG preferences. This is relevant, taking into account that an estimated 40% of EU-wide total financial assets are household funds.[87]

Eco-labeling in commercial products in the EU dates back to 1992, with the European Community (*EC*) Ecolabel Regulation 1992.[88] It constituted a voluntary eco-labeling scheme with the goal of informing the customers of a product's reduced environmental impact.[89] The 2010 update of the Ecolabel Regulation[90] expanded the EU Ecolabel's scope to services.[91]

Based on the respective environmental performance, EU Ecolabel criteria must be developed for each product or service group according to Art. 7(1) and Annex 1 Ecolabel Regulation.[92] For financial services such criteria have not been developed so far. As part of the second action outlined in the Sustainable Finance Action Plan, however, the Commission sees merit in using the Ecolabel Regulation's framework for voluntary labeling of financial products based on the EU taxonomy.[93] Building upon this view, the JRC published three technical reports on the development of EU Ecolabel criteria for retail financial products under the Ecolabel Regulation.[94]

---

[85] Cf. Art. 9 et seqq. and Recitals 14, 17 et seq., and 24 Regulation (EU) 2015/760.

[86] Recital 31 Regulation (EU) 2015/760; For the ELTIF funding scheme, cf. Sect. 2.2.

[87] HLEG (2018a), p. 27.

[88] Council Regulation (EEC) No. 880/92 on a Community eco-label award scheme [1992] OJ L 99/1.

[89] Recital 4 Council Regulation (EEC) No. 880/92 on a Community eco-label award scheme [1992] OJ L 99/1.

[90] Regulation (EC) No 66/2010 of the European Parliament and of the Council of 25 November 2009 on the EU Ecolabel [2009] OJ L 27/1.

[91] Art. 1, Art. 2(1), Art. 3(3), and Art. 6(1) Regulation (EC) No 66/2010 of the European Parliament and of the Council of 25 November 2009 on the EU Ecolabel [2009] OJ L 27/1; JRC (2019c), p. 1.

[92] Cf. JRC (2019c), p. 2.

[93] European Commission (2018a), p. 5; JRC (2019c), p. 2.

[94] JRC (2019b); JRC (2019c); JRC (2020).

The JRC, however, does not recommend the introduction of an optional, point-based criteria system as already in use for other product groups, holding that this would result in a mandatory system with each criterion having to be fulfilled.[95] Instead, the JRC proposes six mandatory criteria for an EU Ecolabel for financial products.[96] First and foremost, environmentally sustainable economic activity as defined by the EU taxonomy would be eligible for the EU Ecolabel.[97] Such link between the EU Ecolabel and the EU taxonomy had already been embraced in the HLEG Final Report and the second action set out in the Sustainable Finance Action Plan.[98] Furthermore, the JRC addressed environment-related exclusions,[99] social- and governance-related exclusions,[100] engagement with companies,[101] disclosure of information to retail investors,[102] and information appearing on the EU Ecolabel for financial products.[103] The TEG Green Bond Standard Report published in June 2019 recommends the prioritization of the EU GBS in the technical screening criteria of the EU Ecolabel.[104]

Apart from the introduction of an EU Ecolabel for financial products based on the already existing Ecolabel Regulation, labeling as a broad policy instrument is the second action outlined in the Sustainable Finance Action Plan.[105] Such labeling is based on the EU taxonomy described above and is considered a core instrument in bringing together companies acting in a sustainable manner on the one hand, and investors seeking to make a sustainable investment on the other. For instance, integrating labeling into comparison websites may facilitate the inclusion of sustainability considerations into retail investors' decision-making processes.[106] Such labeling could be applied to a group of financial services and products such as packaged retail and insurance-based investment products (*PRIIPs*) or SRI funds.[107]

Originally, apart from this development, the HLEG Final Report proposed a *Green Label* within the framework of the Ecolabel Regulation. This would

---

[95] JRC (2019c), pp. 8 et seq.

[96] JRC (2019c), p. 27.

[97] JRC (2019c), p. 32.

[98] European Commission (2018a), p. 5; JRC (2019c), p. 3.

[99] JRC (2019c), p. 49.

[100] JRC (2019c), p. 73.

[101] JRC (2019c), p. 80.

[102] JRC (2019c), p. 83.

[103] JRC (2019c), p. 86.

[104] TEG (2019b), p. 12; The EU Ecolabel in this case will be awarded to the financial product manufacturer, cf. JRC (2019c), p. 3.

[105] European Commission (2018a), p. 5.

[106] European Commission (2018a), p. 5.

[107] Regulation (EU) No 1286/2014 of the European Parliament and of the Council of 26 November 2014 on key information documents for packaged retail and insurance-based investment products (PRIIPs) [2014] OJ L 352/1; Cf. European Commission (2018a), p. 5.

denominate investment funds and at a later stage also PRIIPs[108] and other financial services and products that include a large share of assets related to climate-sustainable economic activities.[109] However, the HLEG Final Report's proposal for a Green Label was translated into the Sustainable Finance Action Plan.[110] It proposed the introduction of the EU Ecolabel criteria for financial products under the Ecolabel Regulation.[111]

The HLEG Final Report also recommended the introduction of universal minimum standards. These would be based on the financial product manufacturer's claims for all financial services and products, similar to the Climate BMR in respect of general requirements for indices claiming to promote sustainable development.[112] Concerning trade in goods, in its European Green Deal, the Commission stated that it would introduce a standard methodology. This methodology would allow for an assessment on whether a product, that is claimed to be *green*, is sustainable by Commission criteria.[113] For the time being, such methodology would only apply to physical products and production methods. In the future, it will have similarities to the EU taxonomy and labeling requirements for financial services.

Apart from these recommendations, sustainability-focused fund *designations* like EuSEFs and EFTIFs can be seen as a label themselves.[114] However, instead of requiring a "*substantial contribution*" to ESG factors like the EU Ecolabel referencing Art. 6 Taxonomy Regulation, EU fund designations such as the EuSEF or the ELTIF only require the relevant fund to invest a certain percentage of its capital into eligible assets.[115] For instance, Art. 1(2) ELTIF Regulation focuses on economic sustainability by aiming at rechanneling private capital into the real economy and to thus foster the EU's goal of "*smart, sustainable and inclusive growth*".

---

[108] For PRIIPs, a label for environmental and social investments was proposed regarding the Commission's 2018 revision of Regulation (EU) No 1286/2014, cf. Recital 36, Art. 33-(1) Regulation (EU) No 1286/2014; Such label has not yet been introduced since in February 2019 the ESAs recommended no amendments to the Regulation (EU) No 1286/2014 at this stage, cf. https://www.eiopa.europa.eu/sites/default/files/publications/reports/2019-02-08_final_report_priips_kid_targeted_amendments_jc_2019_6.2_0.pdf. Accessed 19 December 2021.

[109] HLEG (2018a), p. 29.

[110] European Commission (2018a), p. 5.

[111] European Commission (2018a), p. 5; JRC (2019c), p. 3; JRC (2019a).

[112] HLEG (2018a), p. 29.

[113] European Commission (2019c), p. 8.

[114] Cf. e.g. Art. 15(1) Regulation (EU) No 346/2013 of the European Parliament and of the Council of 17 April 2013 on European social entrepreneurship funds [2013] OJ L 115/18; Cf. Sect. 2.1.1.

[115] E.g. 70% in case of ELTIF (Recital 14, Art. 13(1) Regulation (EU) 2015/760 of the European Parliament and of the Council of 29 April 2015 on European long-term investment funds [2015] OJ L 123/98) and 30% in case of EuSEF (Art. 5(1) Regulation (EU) No 346/2013 of the European Parliament and of the Council of 17 April 2013 on European social entrepreneurship funds [2013] OJ L 115/18).

Similarly, the label of a *Pan-European personal pension product* (*PEPP*) is only awarded to such pension products that sufficiently take into account the sustainability of their investments.[116] PEPP providers are "*encouraged to allocate a sufficient part of their asset portfolio to sustainable investments in the real economy with long-term economic benefits*".[117] By pointing out this long-term nature of their investments, the PEPP Regulation links PEPP providers' interest in long-term risk reduction and the inclusion of ESG factors into the allocation process.[118] The PEPP Regulation requires PEPP providers to both consider risks arising from ESG factors and thus *de facto sustainability risks*, and the long-term impact on ESG factors by the investment.[119] The PEPP Regulation defines ESG factors as matters described in the Paris Agreement and the SDGs.[120]

2.1.3 Green Bond Standard

Resembling a sustainability label but usually addressed separately, is the instrument of *green bonds*. Green bonds are fixed-income debt instruments that aim at supporting climate change mitigation and sustainability-related projects and assets. This is achieved by spreading the long-term costs of climate change adaption and the shift towards sustainability onto the issuance of bonds.[121] As of 2019, there had been various green bond frameworks developed, for example by the EIB's 2007 *Awareness Bond*.[122]

Standards for green bonds so far have mostly been elaborated as industry-led and voluntary self-governing measures. Most notably, the Green Bond Principles published by the ICMA and a group of financial institutions led to increased standardization in the green bond market.[123] The Green Bond Principles were published in their most recent update in June 2018 as *Voluntary Process Guidelines for Issuing Green Bonds*.[124] They constitute a voluntary, collaborative, however, industry input-based guideline.[125] Under the Green Bond Principles, a *green bond* is

---

[116] Recital 11 Regulation (EU) 2019/1238 of the European Parliament and of the Council of 20 June 2019 on a pan-European Personal Pension Product (PEPP) [2019] OJ L 198/1.

[117] Recital 49 Regulation (EU) 2019/1238.

[118] Cf. Recital 51 Regulation (EU) 2019/1238.

[119] Art. 41(1)(b) Regulation (EU) 2019/1238.

[120] Art. 2(33) Regulation (EU) 2019/1238; Cf. Recital 51 Regulation (EU) 2019/1238; Cf. HLEG (2018a), p. 21.

[121] Jakubik and Uguz (2019), p. 66; For empiric research on the effectiveness of green bonds in the insurance sector, cf. *ibid.*

[122] Jakubik and Uguz (2019), p. 67; TEG (2019b), p. 16.

[123] TEG (2019b), p. 16.

[124] ICMA (2018); ICMA also offers Social Bond Principles, cf. ICMA (2020); ICMA published the latest version of the Social Bond Principles in June 2023, c.f. ICMA (2023).

[125] ICMA (2018), p. 3.

a bond whose proceeds are invested in eligible *green projects*. These, in turn, meet the requirements regarding the use of proceeds, evaluation, management, and reporting.[126] As the name suggests, the Green Bond Principles focus on environmental impact through said green projects. This is notwithstanding certain correlations with social impact. However, environmental impact is not limited to climate change mitigation but also entails *inter alia* biodiversity conservation and pollution prevention.[127] The Green Bond Principles encompass reporting requirements on eligibility criteria and transparency towards investors on the applied measurement methods.[128]

A unified standard for defining the conditions under which an issued bond may be denominated as an *EU Green Bond* has long been debated at EU level. The EU GBS[129] was suggested in the HLEG Final Report as a first step towards developing official EU-wide sustainability labels and standards.[130] In June 2020, the Commission launched a consultation and an inception impact assessment.[131] According to the HLEG's recommendations, the EU GBS would only apply if a bond explicitly describes itself as abiding by the EU GBS rules or calls itself an *EU Green Bond*. A positive or negative statement would have to be provided either way.[132] Although the scope of the EU GBS would be limited to bonds that explicitly claim to abide by the EU GBS rules, the HLEG expects the remaining bond market to be strongly influenced by peer pressure and the need for transition.[133]

The EU GBS was intended to differ in its restrictiveness from the already existing Green Bond Principles.[134] Under the HLEG's proposal, the EU Green Bond was to be defined by three criteria: Use of proceeds in part or entirely for *green* projects as defined by the Taxonomy Regulation,[135] the claim of alignment with the four components of the EU GBS[136] within the issuance document, and the external

---

[126] ICMA (2018), p. 3.

[127] ICMA (2018), p. 3 et seq.

[128] ICMA (2018), p. 4 et seq.; Adding to this, there are further industry-led standards such as the Global Real Estate Sustainability Benchmark (*GRESB*) and Global Infrastructure Sustainability Benchmark (*GISB*), cf. Bueren (2019), p. 842; The absence of a uniform definition of a green investment has been deemed to have lead to confusion and uncertainty in the market, cf. HLEG (2018a), p. 31.

[129] Cf. Sect. 2.1.2.

[130] HLEG (2018a), p. 30.

[131] European Commission (2020f); European Commission (2020g).

[132] HLEG (2018a), pp. 31 et seq., HLEG (2018c), pp. 1 et seqq.

[133] HLEG (2018a), p. 32.

[134] Cf. table in HLEG (2018a), p. 32; ICMA (2018).

[135] Until such taxonomy would be available, the HLEG proposed the use of the Green Bond Principles Project Categories and the Climate Bonds Initiative's Climate Bonds Taxonomy, cf. HLEG (2018c), p. 2.

[136] Namely, the use of proceeds, project evaluation and selection, management of proceeds and reporting.

verification of this alignment.[137] The issuer of an EU Green Bond must disclose the information on the process for the management of proceeds from the bond and on the process for project evaluation and selection.[138]

The HLEG's proposals were incorporated into the Commission's Sustainable Finance Action Plan according to which the EU GBS was to be developed.[139] The Commission tasked the TEG with developing the EU GBS and specifying the content of the prospectus.[140] The TEG was set up in June 2018 and published its TEG Green Bond Standard Report in June 2019.[141] The TEG's recommendations for an EU GBS were based both, on the HLEG Green Bond Supplement[142] and the Green Bond Principles.[143]

The EU GBS, in the form proposed by the TEG, was intended to be voluntary. It would apply both inside and outside the EU, and aim at increasing capital flow towards sustainable investments through transparency and comparability.[144] The TEG's proposal largely equals the HLEG's recommendations. It defines an EU Green Bond using three criteria: The confirmation of the alignment with the EU GBS, the use of proceeds for green projects, and the verification of the alignment with the EU GBS by an accredited verifier.[145] *Green projects* for this instance are defined using the Taxonomy Regulation's environmental objectives and technical screening criteria. To qualify as a green project, the relevant project must meet three criteria. First, the project needs to contribute substantially to one of the environmental objectives. Second, the project needs to not significantly harm any other objective, and third, the project must comply with the ILO minimum social safeguards.[146] Hence, these criteria significantly resemble those set out in the Taxonomy Regulation and the Sustainability Disclosures Regulation.

Additionally, the TEG outlined regulation on the content of so-called *green bond frameworks*. They prospectively need to entail *inter alia* references to the Taxonomy Regulation and are already in voluntary use by green bond issuers in the market. In the future, these green bond frameworks shall be obligatory if an issuer wishes a bond to qualify as an EU Green Bond.[147] Furthermore, the TEG's suggestion for an EU GBS involves two types of reporting obligations. First, an allocation report to be conducted annually and upon full allocation. Second, an impact report, comprising a

---

[137] HLEG (2018c), p. 1.

[138] HLEG (2018c), pp. 2 et seq.

[139] European Commission (2018a), p. 5.

[140] European Commission (2018a), p. 5; TEG (2019b), p. 14.

[141] TEG (2019b); Cf. European Commission (2020c), p. 14.

[142] HLEG (2018c).

[143] Cf. TEG (2019b), pp. 26, 57.

[144] TEG (2019b), p. 57.

[145] TEG (2019b), pp. 26, 57.

[146] TEG (2019b), pp. 57 et seq., 25.

[147] TEG (2019b), pp. 28 et seq., 59; Cf. the green bond framework template proposed in the TEG (2019b), p. 62.

description of the green projects, objectives, detailed information on the investment, environmental impacts of the investment, and the methodology used for the evaluation.[148] Finally, the proposal provides for a mandatory verification process.[149]

Based on the HLEG's recommendations, in November 2023, the Green Bond Standard was published in the EU GBS Regulation.[150]

In the future, the EU GBS could be complemented by an *EU Green Bond Label*. This would be issued by a dedicated agency or recognized market association. This approach would contrast the EU GBS, whose requirements are automatically applied if referenced by the issuer.[151] Adding to the EU GBS, the HLEG developed and recommended the subsequent introduction of other sustainability-related standards, like an *EU Social Bond Standard* and *EU Sustainability Guidelines*.[152]

2.1.4 Benchmarks

Many financial instruments refer to financial benchmarks to define their overall value, their yield, or points at which a certain event occurs.[153] Benchmarks are indices that are designed to track status quo developments or values of an underlying. Changes in the methodology, under which benchmark values are calculated or published, therefore potentially impact a financial instrument's value and market participants' behavior.

Traditional benchmarks are not suitable for representing the sustainability performance of the underlying. Sustainable development is inherently a concept of long-term value building and not necessarily reflecting the *status quo* value of the underlying by traditional measurement.[154] Plus, although a variety of benchmark administrators offer sustainability-related benchmarks, their calculation methodologies are usually not sufficiently transparent.[155] Following the Libor and Euribor manipulations in 2011, the EU Benchmarks Regulation (*BMR*)[156] was introduced as the central legislative norm. It governs benchmarks that can be used to determine the

---

[148]TEG (2019b), pp. 27, 29 et seqq., 59 et seq.

[149]TEG (2019b), pp. 31, 32 et seqq., 61.

[150]Regulation (EU) 2023/2631 of the European Parliament and of the Council of 22 November 2023 on European Green Bonds and optional disclosures for bonds marketed as environmentally sustainable and for sustainability-linked bonds [2023] OJ L 2023/2631.

[151]HLEG (2018a), p. 34.

[152]HLEG (2018a), p. 34.

[153]E.g. a *knock-out* event.

[154]European Commission (2018a), p. 7.

[155]European Commission (2018a), p. 7.

[156]Regulation (EU) 2016/1011 of the European Parliament and of the Council of 8 June 2016 on indices used as benchmarks in financial instruments and financial contracts or to measure the performance of investment funds and amending Directives 2008/48/EC and 2014/17/EU and Regulation (EU) No 596/2014 [2016] OJ L 171/1.

reference price for financial contracts and the value development of investment funds.

Necessary legislative changes in the form of delegated acts to the BMR were described in the Sustainable Finance Action Plan.[157] They were intended to allow benchmarks under the BMR to reflect the sustainability of an underlying more accurately and thus, allow for financial instruments to reference such benchmark to determine their values. Furthermore, the Sustainable Finance Action Plan proposed to harmonize low-carbon benchmarks across providers.[158] Based on the Commission's May 2018 initial Proposal on a Climate BMR,[159] the TEG finalized its Climate Benchmarks Report in September 2019,[160] a technical advice on the methodology of low-carbon or *climate benchmarks* and general ESG disclosure requirements. In accordance with the Report, a climate benchmark is to be understood as an index allowing the selection and evaluation of the underlying portfolio, not only based on economic considerations but also carbon emission reduction targets.[161]

The TEG Climate Benchmarks Report points out that its recommendation of constructing an underlying methodology for the new climate benchmarks relied on already existing methodologies. The intention was to link it as close as possible to the goals set out in the Paris Agreement.[162] Furthermore, the TEG saw its task in addressing the "*lack of harmonisation of the methodologies*" and the "*lack of clarity on the objectives*".[163]

First, it suggested a remediation procedure. This would oblige the benchmark administrator to explain, why its benchmark missed the relevant investment targets under the EU Paris-aligned Benchmark (*EU PAB*) and the EU Carbon Transition Benchmark (*EU CTB*) as set out in the Climate BMR. It would further need to explain which measures are taken to ensure future compliance. Incompliance would otherwise ultimately lead to a withdrawal of the EU PAB or EU CTB labels.[164] If a methodology is currently not used in consensus in the market, such as the green/ brown activity factor, the TEG advises that the Climate BMR should not introduce it as mandatory.[165] Second, the TEG suggested disclosure requirements concerning the methodology of calculating the input data of the respective EU PAB or EU CTB.[166] Third, regarding this calculation methodology, a benchmark marked as EU PAB shall reduce its carbon intensity by 50% in comparison to the investment

---

[157] European Commission (2018a), p. 7.

[158] European Commission (2018a), p. 7.

[159] European Commission (2018c); TEG (2019d), p. 12.

[160] TEG (2019d); Cf. TEG (2019d), p. 12.

[161] TEG (2019d), p. 8.

[162] TEG (2019d), p. 8.

[163] TEG (2019d), p. 11.

[164] TEG (2019d), pp. 48 and 60.

[165] TEG (2019d), pp. 52 and 61 et seq.

[166] TEG (2019d), pp. 58 et seq.

universe. In the case of an EU CTB the reduction shall amount to 30%.[167] Both
benchmark labels would be calculated using the Intergovernmental Panel on Climate
Change (*IPCC*) decarbonization trajectory.[168] Additionally, the TEG also
recommended that the Commission encourage companies to increase the share of
investment into companies adhering to greenhouse gas reporting requirements.[169]
However, concerning the calculation methods used, the TEG did not recommend
any measure on greenhouse gas *double counting*.[170]

It is also worth noting that the TEG understands that the difference between
already existing climate benchmarks and the newly created EU CTB and EU PAB
lies in the objective pursued by investors. Traditionally, investing into a product
referencing a climate benchmark, the investor aims at hedging against climate
transition risks.[171] The TEG understands an investor in the new EU climate benchmarks to additionally be interested in opportunities arising from the energy
transition.[172]

Finally, the TEG proposed that EU PAB and EU CTB disclose information on a
decarbonization trajectory and climate risks in general.[173] These requirements shall
further be aligned with the obligations set out in the Sustainability Disclosures
Regulation.[174] Regarding general ESG disclosure by benchmark administrators,
administrator's ESG information, a statement on its use to enhance the benchmark's
ESG performance, and the corresponding index portfolio share in the methodology
and the benchmark statement would be outlined.[175]

Ultimately, a political agreement on the amendments to the BMR was reached in
February 2019.[176] The Climate BMR,[177] indeed, as recommended by the TEG,
introduced four new tools: An EU CTB, an EU PAB, a *decarbonization trajectory*,
and the definition of *sustainability disclosure requirements*.[178]

Turning to the first tool, the label of EU CTB[179] is granted in cases where the
underlying is on a decarbonization trajectory and fulfills the minimum requirements

---

[167] TEG (2019d), p. 59.

[168] TEG (2019d), pp. 59 et seq.

[169] TEG (2019d), p. 61.

[170] TEG (2019d), pp. 42 et seq.

[171] Namely, policy, legal, technological, market reputation, and physical risk.

[172] TEG (2019d), pp. 8 et seq., 38 et seq.

[173] TEG (2019d), p. 61.

[174] TEG (2019d), p. 63.

[175] TEG (2019d), p. 32.

[176] TEG (2019d), pp. 12; Bueren (2019), p. 862.

[177] Regulation (EU) 2019/2089 of the European Parliament and of the Council of 27 November
2019 amending Regulation (EU) 2016/1011 as regards EU Climate Transition Benchmarks, EU
Paris-aligned Benchmarks and sustainability-related disclosures for benchmarks [2019] OJ L
317/17.

[178] Cf. TEG (2019d), pp. 8 and 12.

[179] Called *low-carbon benchmark* in European Commission (2018d), p. 17.

set out in the delegated regulation, yet to be published by the Commission.[180] Art. 1(3) Climate BMR[181] motivates significant benchmarks administrators to provide at least one EU CTB by January 2022.

Second, the label of EU PAB[182] is generally awarded for benchmarks whose underlying portfolio is aligned with the objectives of the Paris Agreement.[183] This means that the relevant benchmark must be calculated following the minimum requirements laid down in the Climate BMR delegated acts according to Art. 1(3) Climate BMR.[184] Plus, the underlying activities shall *not significantly harm* ESG objectives under Art. 1(1) Climate BMR.[185] The relevant methodologies for the calculation of the EU CTB and the EU PAB are outlined in the newly introduced BMR Annex 3. Overall, the EU PAB is comparatively more restrictive in its minimum standards and choice of portfolio than the EU CTB. This refers to both carbon intensity reduction compared to its investment universe and excluded activities.[186] The latter allows for a higher degree of diversification of the underlying portfolio.[187] Originally, also the TEG had suggested these climate-related activity exclusions for the EU PAB.[188]

Third, apart from these two benchmark labels, the Climate BMR introduces a *decarbonization trajectory* that represents a trajectory *"towards alignment with the objectives of the Paris Agreement"* pursuant to Art. 1(1) Climate BMR.[189] Art. 1(2) Climate BMR[190] also amends the BMR's publication requirements by adding information on the inclusion of ESG factors into the administrator's methodology.

Furthermore, Art. 1(6) subpara. 1 Climate BMR[191] introduces an information requirement regarding how ESG factors are reflected in each benchmark. In case the

---

[180] Pursuant to Art. 1(3), (1) and (8)(2) Regulation (EU) 2019/2089, corresponding to Art. 19a, Art. 49(2), and Art. 3(1)(23a) Regulation (EU) 2016/1011 of the European Parliament and of the Council of 8 June 2016 on indices used as benchmarks in financial instruments and financial contracts or to measure the performance of investment funds and amending Directives 2008/48/EC and 2014/17/EU and Regulation (EU) No 596/2014 [2016] OJ L 171/1; Cf. TEG (2019d), p. 37.

[181] Corresponding to Art. 19d Regulation (EU) 2016/1011.

[182] Called *low-carbon benchmark* in European Commission (2018d), p. 18.

[183] Namely, companies in the underlying have to disclose measurable carbon emission reduction disaggregated for each subsidy (Art. 1(3) Regulation (EU) 2019/2089, corresponding to Art. 19b (i) and (ii) Regulation (EU) 2016/1011) with annual report on progress regarding carbon emission reduction (Art. 1(3) Regulation (EU) 2019/2089, corresponding to Art. 19b(iii) Regulation (EU) 2016/1011). Certain sectors may be excluded by Commission delegated regulation pursuant to Art. 1(3) and (8)2 Regulation (EU) 2019/2089, corresponding to Art. 19c and Art. 49-(2) Regulation (EU) 2016/1011).

[184] Corresponding to Art. 19a Regulation (EU) 2016/1011.

[185] Corresponding to Art. 3(1)(23b) Regulation (EU) 2016/1011; Cf. TEG (2019d), p. 37.

[186] Cf. TEG (2019d), pp. 9 et seq.

[187] TEG (2019d), p. 9.

[188] TEG (2019d), pp. 54, 60.

[189] Corresponding to Art. 3(1)(23c) Regulation (EU) 2016/1011.

[190] Corresponding to Art. 13(1)(d) Regulation (EU) 2016/1011.

[191] Corresponding to Art. 27(2a) subpara. 1 Regulation (EU) 2016/1011.

administrator does not offer EU CTBs or EU PABs, a *negative statement* to this effect must be included into the benchmark statement of each of the benchmarks. Administrators of significant equity and bond benchmarks and EU CTBs and EU PABs according to Art. 1(6) subpara. 2 Climate BMR[192] are required to disclose certain information. This includes information on whether and how the overall aim of carbon emission reduction and the targets of the Paris Agreement are incorporated into their policies. These requirements are in accordance with the disclosure under Art. 9(3) Sustainability Disclosures Regulation.[193] The Climate BMR empowers the Commission to detail the information requirements in the benchmark statement in a delegated regulation according to Art. 1(6) subpara. 5 and (8)(2) Climate BMR.[194] Furthermore, the Climate BMR introduces an ESG minimum standard under which actions by the underlying entities may not significantly harm ESG goals[195]—a requirement resembling those of the subsequent Taxonomy Regulation.

Summing up, the newly introduced EU CTBs and PABs can be understood to be requirements for the labeling of already existing or future benchmarks.[196] The changes introduced by the Climate BMR were outlined in the HLEG Final Report.[197] However, in addition to the introduction of the Climate BMR, the HLEG recommended influencing the International Organization of Securities Commissions (*IOSCO*) to introduce ESG factors into the IOSCO Benchmark Principles.[198] This also entailed the introduction of reporting requirements of significant benchmark administrators concerning the kind and weighting of the underlying assets and disclosure requirements for funds, dedicated supervisory standards for ESG-related benchmarks.[199]

The disclosure of information on the benchmark's characteristics, together with information on the calculation of the respective index, is also required under Art. 8(1)(b) and (2) Sustainability Disclosures Regulation. Similarly, concerning benchmarks that promote sustainable investments, benchmark administrators must provide information on the alignment with sustainability factors, how the index differs from a broad market index, and how the index is calculated.[200] Benchmarks that promote carbon emission reduction while not constituting EU CTBs or EU PABs must publish an explanation on how the relevant benchmark contributes to the overall

---

[192] Corresponding to Art. 27(2a) subpara. 2 Regulation (EU) 2016/1011.

[193] Regulation (EU) 2019/2088 of the European Parliament and of the Council of 27 November 2019 on sustainability-related disclosures in the financial services sector [2019] OJ L 317/1; For more information on Regulation (EU) 2019/2088, cf. Sect. 2.1.6.

[194] Corresponding to Art. 27(2b) and Art. 49(2) Regulation (EU) 2016/1011; Cf. Bueren (2019), p. 863.

[195] Bueren (2019), p. 863.

[196] Cf. e.g. TEG (2019d), p. 48.

[197] HLEG (2018a), pp. 53 et seqq.

[198] IOSCO (2013).

[199] HLEG (2018a), p. 55.

[200] Cf. Art. 9(1)(a), (b), and (4) Regulation (EU) 2019/2088.

goal of limiting global warming as set out on the Paris Agreement and how the index is calculated.[201]

With a view to benchmark administrators located in third countries, the BMR already comprises requirements for their inclusion into the ESMA register.[202] According to Art. 30(1) BMR these additional requirements consist *inter alia* of an equivalence decision by the Commission, a registration of the administrator as such by the home state, and a cooperation arrangement. For an equivalence decision to be taken by the Commission, the third country regulatory framework and supervision practice needs to be equivalent to the BMR's requirements and consistent with the IOSCO Benchmark Principles.[203] If at any stage these criteria cease to be met, the registration of a third country benchmark administrator may be withdrawn.[204] EU benchmark users may, however, use a benchmark prior to such equivalence decision if the administrator is operating under the IOSCO Benchmark Principles and meets the legal representation criteria laid down in Art. 32(2) and (3) BMR.[205] A feasible alternative for the inclusion of a third country benchmark is for EU benchmark administrators to endorse it which would result in it being regarded as the *de jure* benchmark administrator under Art. 33(4) BMR. For this instance, Art. 1(9)(b) Climate BMR[206] introduces an exception for third country benchmarks already in use in the EU, even if they have not yet received an equivalence decision, have been endorsed or recognized.

2.1.5 Credit Rating

Labeling in a broader sense can be understood to also encompass credit rating agencies (*CRAs*). This is due to the representative nature of a rating score issued by a CRA. A rating represents on a continuous scale for instance the creditworthiness of a financial institution.

HLEG differentiates between two types of CRAs. First, traditional CRAs, which focus on financial aspects of, for example, the debtor/issuer and lender/investor. Those are usually paid by the lender/investor.[207] Second, sustainability rating agencies (*SRAs*), which focus on sustainability-related aspects of the loan/credit

---

[201] Cf. Art. 9(3) and (4) Regulation (EU) 2019/2088; Cf. Sect. 2.1.6.

[202] For the ESMA register of benchmark administrators, cf. https://registers.esma.europa.eu/publication/searchRegister?core=esma_registers_bench_entities.

[203] Cf. Art. 30(2) Regulation (EU) 2016/1011 of the European Parliament and of the Council of 8 June 2016 on indices used as benchmarks in financial instruments and financial contracts or to measure the performance of investment funds and amending Directives 2008/48/EC and 2014/17/EU and Regulation (EU) No 596/2014 [2016] OJ L 171/1.

[204] Cf. Art. 31 Regulation (EU) 2016/1011.

[205] Cf. Art. 32 Regulation (EU) 2016/1011.

[206] Corresponding to Art. 51(5) Regulation (EU) 2016/1011.

[207] HLEG (2018a), p. 75.

and the debtor/issuer and which are generally paid by the lender/investor.[208] They were first created in the mid-1990s.[209] HLEG recommends that the Commission shall promote the work of SRAs.[210]

Whether established CRAs or novel SRAs, most of these rating agencies operate under methodologies rarely transparent and usually lacking in coherence, which results in incomparability between said agencies.[211] Originally, the HLEG Final Report set out the recommendation that CRAs should increase transparency and ensure the inclusion of long-term sustainability and ESG factors in their ratings. It encouraged ESMA to issue and enforce guidelines on the inclusion of ESG factors into rating methodologies.[212]

As the sixth action outlined in the Sustainable Finance Action Plan, the Commission calls on ESMA to provide information and solutions for the integration of sustainability criteria into the CRAs' methodologies. With this proposal, the Commission's goal was a potential inclusion of these measures into the CRA Regulation.[213] Sustainability credit ratings and sustainability credit rating agencies have so far not been within the scope of the CRA Regulation.[214] Currently neither the original CRA Regulation 2009[215] nor its 2013 revision cover provisions or guidelines on the use of sustainability as a criterion for the calculation and provision of credit or sustainability ratings. Therefore, CRAs are not obligated to incorporate ESG factors into their calculation methods.[216]

In comparison to the Taxonomy Regulation, the Climate BMR or the transparency instruments outlined below (2.1.6), the Commission's proposal on amendments to the CRA Regulation is at a far earlier stage. From April 2024, ESMA consulted on an amendment to the CRA Regulation 2009 *"to ensure that relevant ESG risks are systematically captured in credit ratings and to improve transparency on the inclusion of ESG risks by credit rating agencies in credit ratings and rating outlooks."*[217]

---

[208] HLEG (2018a), p. 75.

[209] HLEG (2018a), p. 77.

[210] HLEG (2018a), p. 78.

[211] European Commission (2018a), pp. 7 et seq.

[212] HLEG (2018a), p. 78; Similarly, EIOPA recommends transparency on the use of ESG ratings in the insurance sector, cf. EIOPA (2019c), p. 11; However, Regulation (EU) No 462/2013 of the European Parliament and of the Council of 21 May 2013 amending Regulation (EC) No 1060/2009 on credit rating agencies [2013] OJ L 146/1 already includes certain disclosure requirements for CRAs, cf. ESMA (2019c), p. 6.

[213] Regulation (EU) No 462/2013, pp. 7 et seq.

[214] Bueren (2019), p. 870.

[215] Regulation (EC) No 1060/2009 of the European Parliament and of the Council of 16 September 2009 on credit rating agencies [2009] OJ L 302/1.

[216] However, ESMA called for such requirements in an upcoming CRA Regulation update, cf. Bueren (2019), p. 870.

[217] ESMA (2024).

As requested in the Sustainable Finance Action Plan, in July 2019 ESMA published its Technical Advice on CRA[218] on the inclusion of ESG considerations into ESMA's Guidelines on Disclosure[219] and current CRA practice on ESG factors.[220] ESMA points out that the CRA Regulation's definition of credit ratings only encompasses the assessment of creditworthiness and not of other criteria like sustainability. As by then, ESG factors were only incorporated in CRA methodologies in respect of their relevance to the creditworthiness of the rated entity.[221] The main challenge with regulating the inclusion of sustainability criteria into the CRA Regulation is Art. 23 CRA Regulation. It prohibits any interference in the methodology of credit ratings by regulatory authorities.[222] Thus, instead of recommending to require CRA methodologies to comprise ESG factors, ESMA would prefer to keep the CRA's focus on creditworthiness and advised against amending the CRA Regulation.[223] Instead and due to the over-reliance on credit ratings in the dawn of the 2007–2008 financial crisis, it encouraged sustainability assessments.[224] This said additional regulation governing sustainability assessments might however be necessary.[225]

2.1.6 Transparency

The data required to provide prudential Sustainable Finance instruments like labeling standards or an underlying taxonomy must be made available through regulation on transparency, reporting, disclosure, or accounting standards. The underlying rationale for the sourcing of sustainability-related data is twofold.

First, the calculations under the Taxonomy Regulation's technical screening criteria require data on the sustainability performance of the respective financial service supplier. Plus, instruments like sustainability labels, the EU GBS, sustainability benchmarks, or sustainability ratings require either such data or rely on the taxonomy's classification system to calculate their values.

Second, information on the sustainability performance of a financial product or service is necessary to improve the client's or the broader public's understanding of this performance. This can significantly influence the company's public image and ultimately a retail client's investment decision. Parallelly, sustainability disclosures ensure transparency—fostering discussion between a stock company's board and

---

[218] ESMA (2019c).

[219] ESMA (2019d).

[220] ESMA (2019c), pp. 3, 5.

[221] ESMA (2019c), pp. 6, 31.

[222] Cf. ESMA (2019c), p. 6.

[223] ESMA (2019c), pp. 32 et seqq.

[224] ESMA (2019c), p. 33.

[225] ESMA (2019c), p. 34.

shareholders to include the investor's ESG preferences into corporate business practices.[226]

Transparency, reporting and disclosure requirements, and accounting standards in EU Sustainable Finance regulation are intertwined and thus cannot be strictly separated. However, such separation is not necessary since the aim is ultimately the same—to ensure enhanced customer information on sustainability performance. Usually, reporting and disclosure requirements on information not directly within the realm of economic assertions are referred to as nonfinancial reporting (*NFR*).

Lack of transparency and insufficient rules on reporting and disclosure of sustainability-related information are two areas requiring the most urgent development in EU Sustainable Finance. Disclosures are seen as an important prerequisite to the functioning of the EU taxonomy.[227] Furthermore, EIOPA recommends disclosure requirements on information concerning the use of alternative sustainability considerations in the evaluation of assets.[228] Data scarcity is also mentioned as a major obstacle to the implementation of Sustainable Finance in general.[229]

2.1.6.1 Non-financial Reporting

Sustainability disclosure requirements like the previously mentioned instruments, are for large part integrated into already existing prudential regulation. This regulatory framework consists mainly of the NFR Directive,[230] the Sustainability Disclosures Regulation,[231] and the International Financial Reporting Standards (*IFRS*).[232] It is complemented by certain requirements introduced in regulations like MiFID

---

[226]HLEG (2018a), p. 24.

[227]TEG (2019c), p. 10.

[228]EIOPA (2019c), p. 11.

[229]NGFS (2019a), p. 30.

[230]Directive 2014/95/EU of the European Parliament and of the Council of 22 October 2014 amending Directive 2013/34/EU as regards disclosure of non-financial and diversity information by certain large undertakings and groups [2014] OJ L 330/1.

[231]Regulation (EU) 2019/2088 of the European Parliament and of the Council of 27 November 2019 on sustainability-related disclosures in the financial services sector [2019] OJ L 317/1.

[232]IASB (2024).

II,[233] the Investment Firm Regulation (*IFR*),[234] the Investment Firm Directive (*IFD*),[235] or the Taxonomy Regulation.[236]

Under the 2014 NFR Directive, which amended the 2013 Accounting Directive,[237] large undertakings and groups with more than five hundred employees are obliged to conduct a disclosure on ESG factors and risks rooted in them.[238] The NFR Directive aims at increased consistency and comparability of NFI reporting. NFI reporting should cover current and prospective environmental impacts.[239] Companies required to report are free in choosing the respective reporting standard.[240] And those with more than five hundred employees must disclose a description of the business model. This is complemented by a description of the policies in respect of environmental, social and employee aspects, human rights, corruption and bribery prevention measures. This description also comprises the actual result stemming these policies, and the respective risks stemming from these matters.[241] Furthermore, they must disclose which framework they do rely on. Thereby, the presentation of the information is up to the companies. The report can be published separately or as part of the management report.[242] The Commission is required to draft nonbinding guidelines on NFI reporting, these were published in 2017 and supplemented in 2019.[243]

---

[233] Directive 2014/65/EU of the European Parliament and of the Council of 15 May 2014 on markets in financial instruments and amending Directive 2002/92/EC and Directive 2011/61/EU [2014] OJ L 173/349.

[234] Regulation (EU) 2019/2033 of the European Parliament and of the Council of 27 November 2019 on the prudential requirements of investment firms and amending Regulations (EU) No 1093/2010, (EU) No 575/2013, (EU) No 600/2014 and (EU) No 806/2014 [2019] OJ L 314/1.

[235] Directive (EU) 2019/2034 of the European Parliament and of the Council of 27 November 2019 on the prudential supervision of investment firms and amending Directives 2002/87/EC, 2009/65/EC, 2011/61/EU, 2013/36/EU, 2014/59/EU and 2014/65/EU [2019] OJ L 314/64.

[236] Regulation (EU) 2020/852 of the European Parliament and of the Council of 18 June 2020 on the establishment of a framework to facilitate sustainable investment, and amending Regulation (EU) 2019/2088 [2020] OJ L 198/13.

[237] Directive 2013/34/EU of the European Parliament and of the Council of 26 June 2013 on the annual financial statements, consolidated financial statements and related reports of certain types of undertakings, amending Directive 2006/43/EC of the European Parliament and of the Council and repealing Council Directives 78/660/EEC and 83/349/EEC [2013] OJ L 182/19.

[238] European Commission (2018a), pp. 9 et seq.

[239] Cf. Recitals 6 and 7 Directive 2014/95/EU of the European Parliament and of the Council of 22 October 2014 amending Directive 2013/34/EU as regards disclosure of non-financial and diversity information by certain large undertakings and groups [2014] OJ L 330/1.

[240] Pursuant to Recital 9 Directive 2014/95/EU these include *inter alia*: United Nations (2011), OECD (2011), ISO (2017), ILO (2017), ILO (2022), GRI (2024).

[241] Cf. Art. 1(1) subpara. 1 and 4 Directive 2014/95/EU; In case of consolidated NFI statements, cf. Art. 1(3) Directive 2014/95/EU; TEG (2019a), p. 6.

[242] In case of consolidated NFI statements, cf. Art. 1(3)(4) Directive 2014/95/EU; Cf. ESMA (2019e), p. 24.

[243] Cf. Art. 2 Directive 2014/95/EU; European Commission (2017b); European Commission (2019b).

More recently, Art. 8 Taxonomy Regulation[244] introduced an obligation for companies under Art. 19a and Art. 29a NFR Directive to publish information on environmentally sustainable economic activities in their NFI statements. As stated above, this transparency as an informational base is key to the functioning of the EU taxonomy.

2.1.6.2 Recommendations and Guidelines

There are various further suggestions on the inclusion of ESG factors into the NFR Directive. For instance, the HLEG Final Report named disclosure requirements as one of two key components of integrating investor duties into the regulatory framework. It closely linked them to fiduciary duties on the inclusion of ESG preferences into investment decision-making.[245] It also proposed the amendment of the NFR Directive and Implementing Regulation (EU) 543/2011[246] concerning the disclosure of sustainable agriculture-related information.[247] Previously, the 2017 revision of the Commission's NFR Guidelines had already taken into account the HLEG's work on NFR even before the HLEG Interim Report.[248] Correspondingly, in its Report on Undue Short-Term Pressure, ESMA recommended the compulsory inclusion of NFI statements into the annual financial report. It further called for coherence between the NFR Directive and Transparency Directive[249] and the amendment of the NFR Directive regarding specific disclosure requirements.[250]

Adding to this, the HLEG Final Report mentions the Financial Stability Board (*FSB*) Task Force on Climate-related Financial Disclosures' (*TCFD*)[251] role as an international initiative. It recommends the inclusion of its Final Report[252] in EU legislation, for instance by aligning the NFR Directive with the recommendations of

---

[244] European Council (2019), Art. 4delta.

[245] HLEG (2018a), pp. 13, 20 et seq.

[246] Commission Implementing Regulation (EU) No 543/2011 of 7 June 2011 laying down detailed rules for the application of Council Regulation (EC) No 1234/2007 in respect of the fruit and vegetables and processed fruit and vegetables sectors [2011] OJ L 157/1.

[247] HLEG (2018a), p. 91.

[248] HLEG (2018a); Cf. HLEG (2018a), p. 7.

[249] Directive 2013/50/EU of the European Parliament and of the Council of 22 October 2013 amending Directive 2004/109/EC of the European Parliament and of the Council on the harmonisation of transparency requirements in relation to information about issuers whose securities are admitted to trading on a regulated market, Directive 2003/71/EC of the European Parliament and of the Council on the prospectus to be published when securities are offered to the public or admitted to trading and Commission Directive 2007/14/EC laying down detailed rules for the implementation of certain provisions of Directive 2004/109/EC [2013] OJ L 294/13.

[250] ESMA (2019e), pp. 10, 38 et seq.

[251] For further detail regarding the TCFD, cf. Sect. 4.1.2 and the TVFD website, c.f. https://www.fsb-tcfd.org/. Accessed 26 May 2024.

[252] TCFD (2017).

the TCFD Final Report.[253] In line with the HLEG's recommendation, in its Sustainable Finance Action Plan the Commission states that it will revise the NFR Directive and its NFR Guidelines based on the TEG metrics and the TCFD Final Report.[254] Indeed, the 2019 NFR Guidelines Supplement[255] incorporated the TCFD Final Report's findings into its climate-related information reporting framework.[256]

Furthermore, also as part of the ninth action, the Commission announced the introduction of a European Corporate Reporting Lab as part of the European Financial Reporting Advisory Group (*EFRAG*). It would share best practice information on corporate reporting, in particular climate-related reporting. This is coherent with the TCFD Final Report's recommendations.[257]

Another significant policy input was the TEG Climate-related Disclosures Report. The TEG published the report in January 2019.[258] The Report draws on the TCFD Final Report's recommendations with a view to the interlinkage between climate impact and climate risks.[259] Thereby, a set of guidelines on climate-related disclosures, based on the NFR Directive elements,[260] constitutes the TEG Climate-related Disclosures Report's core policy recommendation. The guidelines elaborate on three factors for each of the NFR Directive elements: Rationale and context, references to relevant TCFD recommendations, and specific proposals for disclosures, including climate-related Key Performance Indicators (*KPIs*).[261] Based on this, the TEG Report introduces three types of disclosure obligations depending on the climate-related risk exposure of the company: Information that companies *should* disclose (*Type 1*), *should consider* disclosing (*Type 2*), and *may consider* disclosing (*Type 3*).[262] On each of the KPIs, the TEG Climate-related Disclosures Report outlines specific disclosure requirements.[263] For instance, as a Type 2 KPI, the Report covers information on green financing including green bonds.[264]

---

[253]For a comparison between Directive 2014/95/EU of the European Parliament and of the Council of 22 October 2014 amending Directive 2013/34/EU as regards disclosure of non-financial and diversity information by certain large undertakings and groups [2014] OJ L 330/1 and the TCFD Final Report's recommendations, cf. TEG (2019a), table 2, pp. 12 et seq., figure 2, p. 14; HLEG (2018a), pp. 24 et seq.

[254]European Commission (2018a), p. 9; TEG (2019a), p. 3.

[255]European Commission (2019b).

[256]Cf. e.g. European Commission (2019b), pp. 4, 35; HLEG also recommended the encouragement of ESG reports with regard to stock exchanges, cf. HLEG (2018a), p. 80.

[257]European Commission (2018a), p. 9; Cf. Sect. 2.3.

[258]TEG (2019a), p. 3.

[259]TEG (2019a), pp. 6 et seq., 9.

[260]Description of the business model, policies and due diligence processes, outcomes, principal risks, and their management and KPIs.

[261]TEG (2019a), p. 15.

[262]TEG (2019a), pp. 7, 15.

[263]TEG (2019a), pp.19 et seqq., 25 et seqq., tables 9 and 10, pp. 27 et seqq.

[264]TEG (2019a), p. 32.

At the beginning of 2019, the Commission issued proposals amending the delegated regulations to the PRIIPs Regulation and MiFID II[265] to increase transparency for customers.[266] These proposals also included transparency requirements on ESG performance. Noteworthy, the definition of *sustainable investment* changed between the proposal and the final consensus—from covering all three ESG factors to only covering environmental and social aspects. Aspects of good governance were left out.[267] Plus, the proposed delegated regulations limit their scope of application to financial products that are already labeled as *sustainable*, following either an official or a voluntary self-labeling process.[268] The PRIIPs Regulation[269] further adds transparency requirements for the Key Information Documents (*KIDs*), which must state the product's potential ecologic and social goals.[270] It further requires PRIIPs manufacturers to incorporate into the KID, if applicable, "*specific environmental or social objectives targeted by the product*" as defined by the PRIIPs DelReg.[271]

2.1.6.3 Sustainability Disclosures Regulation

The Sustainability Disclosures Regulation[272] governs ESG disclosures at the corporate level. The Regulation was adopted in April 2019. In the negotiations, particularly the scope of application was controversial. The Commission and EU Member States wanted the Sustainability Disclosures Regulation to apply only to institutional investors. The European Parliament preferred to broaden its scope towards banks, financial institutions, and stock exchange-listed corporations. The former proposal materialized in the compromise that was ultimately adopted.[273]

---

[265] Commission Delegated Regulation (EU) 2017/653 of 8 March 2017 supplementing Regulation (EU) No 1286/2014 of the European Parliament and of the Council on key information documents for packaged retail and insurance-based investment products (PRIIPs) by laying down regulatory technical standards with regard to the presentation, content, review and revision of key information documents and the conditions for fulfilling the requirement to provide such documents [2017] OJ L 100/1; Commission Delegated Regulation (EU) 2017/565 of 25 April 2016 supplementing Directive 2014/65/EU of the European Parliament and of the Council as regards organisational requirements and operating conditions for investment firms and defined terms for the purposes of that Directive, C/2016/2398 [2016] OJ L 87/1.

[266] Bueren (2019), p. 867.

[267] Bueren (2019), p. 865.

[268] Bueren (2019), p. 858.

[269] Regulation (EU) No 1286/2014 of the European Parliament and of the Council of 26 November 2014 on key information documents for packaged retail and insurance-based investment products (PRIIPs) [2014] OJ L 352/1.

[270] Bueren (2019), p. 850.

[271] Cf. Art. 8(3)(c)(ii) Regulation (EU) No 1286/2014.

[272] Regulation (EU) 2019/2088 of the European Parliament and of the Council of 27 November 2019 on sustainability-related disclosures in the financial services sector [2019] OJ L 317/1.

[273] Bueren (2019), p. 864.

Additionally, whilst the NFR Directive only focuses on large undertakings and groups, though throughout all sectors, the Sustainability Disclosures Regulation covers transparency rules on the integration of sustainability risks and sustainability-related information. Such information must be provided by financial market participants. Under Art. 1 and Art. 2(1) Sustainability Disclosures Regulation, these comprise *inter alia* investment firms, different types of funds, and insurance providers. The Sustainability Disclosures Regulation also requires all financial market participants and investment advisors to publish information on the inclusion of sustainability risks into their investment decision-making on their website.[274]

It is worth noting that the Sustainability Disclosures Regulation introduces three new terms. Art. 1(17) Sustainability Disclosures Regulation defines the term *sustainable investment* as an investment into economic activity contributing to environmental or social objectives, while not harming any one of these objectives and subject to the recipient of the funds meeting good governance standards. Hitherto, the Art. 1(22) Sustainability Disclosures Regulation defines *sustainability risk* as "*an environmental, social or governance event or condition that, if it occurs, could cause an actual or a potential material negative impact on the value of the investment*". In this regard, *sustainability factors* do encompass not only environmental and social criteria but also employee, human rights, anti-corruption, and anti-bribery matters according to Art. 1(24) Sustainability Disclosures Regulation and explicitly comprising the governance factor.

Art. 25 Taxonomy Regulation[275] amends the Sustainability Disclosures Regulation by adding the pre-contractual disclosure requirements of Art. 5 and Art. 6 Taxonomy Regulation[276] to the information on financial products pursuant to Art. 6(1) and (3) Sustainability Disclosures Regulation. The Commission's initial proposal in May 2018 did not set out these references to the Sustainability Disclosures Regulation.

Financial market participants are also required to publish information on their due diligence policies based on internationally recognized standards. Alternatively, they must publish an explanation of such policy's absence. This also includes their investment decisions' impact on ESG factors—so-called *principal adverse impacts of investment decisions.*[277] This disclosure must consider the size, nature, and scale of these investments and how this influences the kind of financial products the relevant entity offers. These specific requirements do also apply to market participants exceeding five hundred employees on their balance sheet date.[278] Likewise, Art. 4(5) Sustainability Disclosures Regulation requires financial advisers to publish information on the abovementioned principal adverse impacts of their investment

---

[274] Cf. Art. 3(1) and (2) Regulation (EU) 2019/2088.

[275] Corresponding to European Council (2019), Art. 16c.

[276] Cf. European Council (2019), Art. 4α and Art. 4β.

[277] Cf. Art. 4(1)(a), (b) and (2) Regulation (EU) 2019/2088.

[278] Cf. Art. 4(3) and (4) Regulation (EU) 2019/2088.

advice on ESG factors and their relevant due diligence policies. Such *comply or explain* mechanisms had already been set out in the HLEG Final Report.[279]

Furthermore, financial market participants are required to draft statements on the consistency of their remuneration policies with the integration of the abovementioned sustainability risks.[280] They and financial advisers alike[281]—pre-contractually and at the issuer level—must disclose the manner of integrating sustainability risks into the relevant investment decision or advice. The same applies to the impact of sustainability risks on the return of the investment under Art. 6(1) Sustainability Disclosures Regulation. Equally at the product level, the relevant financial market participant must provide information on the inclusion of principal adverse impacts on ESG factors.[282]

While these requirements apply to all financial products under the Sustainability Disclosures Regulation, stricter rules are set out under Art. 8 and Art. 9 Sustainability Disclosures Regulation. These provisions apply to financial products that either promote environmental or social characteristics, or that have a sustainable investment as their objective.[283]

Disclosures under Art. 8 Sustainability Disclosures Regulation must encompass information on how environmental and social characteristics are met and whether a potentially used index is consistent with those characteristics.[284] Similarly, offerors of Art. 9 Sustainability Disclosures Regulation financial products must disclose information on their alignment with sustainability factors, how the underlying index differs from a broad market index, and how it is calculated. This particularly applies to benchmarks that promote sustainable investments while not constituting EU CTBs or EU PABs.[285] The same obligation exists for financial products promoting sustainable investments in general. They must be accompanied by an explanation of how sustainability objectives are to be achieved through the promoted investments.[286] Likewise, information on financial products promoting carbon emission reduction must entail an explanation of how the specific financial product contributes to the overall goal of limiting global warming as set out in the Paris Agreement.[287]

---

[279] HLEG (2018a), p. 26.

[280] Cf. Art. 5(1) Regulation (EU) 2019/2088.

[281] Cf. Art. 6(2) Regulation (EU) 2019/2088.

[282] Cf. Art. 7(1) Regulation (EU) 2019/2088.

[283] Environmental objectives pursuant to Art. 9 Regulation (EU) 2019/2088 include climate change mitigation, climate change adoption, the sustainable use and protection of water and marine resources, the transition to a circular economy, pollution prevention and control, and the protection and restoration of biodiversity and ecosystems.

[284] Art. 8(1)(a) and (b) Regulation (EU) 2019/2088; The same requirement applies to the provision of reference benchmarks together with information on the calculation of the relevant index, cf. Art. 8(2) Regulation (EU) 2019/2088.

[285] Cf. Art. 9(1)(a), (b) and (4) Regulation (EU) 2019/2088.

[286] Cf. Art. 9(2) Regulation (EU) 2019/2088.

[287] Cf. Art. 9(3) Regulation (EU) 2019/2088.

Concerning the implementation of these disclosure requirements, their aim is that the information provided on sustainability must be *"accurate, fair, clear, not misleading, simple and concise"*.[288] To this end, information on the objective, the impact, and measurement procedures of the above-mentioned financial products and benchmarks promoting sustainability must be disclosed on the financial market participant's website and in the relevant periodic reports.[289] Art. 13(1) Sustainability Disclosures Regulation further requires marketing communications to reflect and not contradict the sustainability information provided under the Sustainability Disclosures Regulation.

Art. 5 Taxonomy Regulation[290] adds to this by requiring financial products under Art. 9(1), (2), and (3) Sustainability Disclosures Regulation to disclose information on the kind and extent of the contribution to the environmental objective of the underlying economic activity. The same applies to financial products under Art. 8(1) Sustainability Disclosures Regulation according to Art. 6 Taxonomy Regulation.[291] Although, these financial products must additionally disclose a statement of *no significant harm*. All other financial products are required to pre-contractually disclose a statement that they do not take into account the taxonomy criteria.[292]

In February 2021, the Sustainability Disclosures Regulation was complemented with respective Technical Standards.[293]

2.1.6.4   Accounting Standards

Sustainability criteria may also be introduced into the accounting standards, namely the IFRS. Although IFRS are a private standard issued by the IFRS Advisory Council to the International Accounting Standards Board (*IASB*), they are incorporated into EU legislation by the IAS Regulation.[294] They therefore are relevant for sustainability-related accounting rules within the EU. This said, as part of the ninth action outlined in the Sustainable Finance Action Plan, the Commission recognizes possible inconsistencies between the aim of endorsing long-term sustainable investments and the current state of the IFRS 9[295] accounting standards. It also mentioned

---

[288] Art. 9(5) subpara. 2 and Art. 10(1) subpara. 2 Regulation (EU) 2019/2088.

[289] Cf. Art. 10(1) and 11(1) Regulation (EU) 2019/2088; Cf. Bueren (2019), p. 865.

[290] Corresponding to European Council (2019), Art. 4α.

[291] Corresponding to Art. European Council (2019), 4β.

[292] Art. 7 Regulation (EU) 2020/852 of the European Parliament and of the Council of 18 June 2020 on the establishment of a framework to facilitate sustainable investment, and amending Regulation (EU) 2019/2088 [2020] OJ L 198/13, corresponding to European Council (2019), Art. 4γ.

[293] ESMA (2021).

[294] Regulation (EC) No 1606/2002 of the European Parliament and of the Council of 19 July 2002 on the application of international accounting standards [2002] OJ L 243/1.

[295] The IFRS 9 are the IFRS' applicable set of accounting standards for financial products, cf. IASB (2024).

the potential effects a revision of the IFRS might have on Sustainable Finance in the EU.[296]

Adding to this, HLEG highlights that IFRS 9 accounting standards are partly claimed to have adverse impacts on accounting on long-term investments due to the *mark-to-market* accounting rules, implying more income statement volatility than occurred. This, HLEG claims, is counter-conducive to a company's ambition to long-termism in investment decision-making.[297] HLEG, therefore, advises the Commission to revise the IAS Regulation to the effect that international accounting standards shall only be adopted, if they are *"conducive to [...] sustainability and long-term investment objectives"* or conducting IFRS 9 adjustments by the EU itself. Also, the HLEG suggested amending the Accounting Directive to cover NFR.[298] In turn, with an eye on insurance providers, the HLEG recommends a combined approach between the different IFRS accounting standards applicable to an insurance provider on the liabilities and the assets sides.[299]

2.1.6.5 Investement Firms and Sustainability-Related Funds

Apart from accounting standards, the investment firm framework plays a significant role in the sustainability reporting of financial market participants. Based on the realization of the increasing inadequacy of the CRR[300] and CRD[301] regime towards investment firms, in November 2019, the IFR[302] and the IFD[303] were introduced. The new framework is specifically designed around the business model of investment firms in contrast to CRR institutes. This is noteworthy because the introduction of the new IFR and IFD regime comes at the height of the EU Sustainable Finance

---

[296] European Commission (2018a), pp. 9 et seq.

[297] HLEG (2018a), pp. 57 et seq.

[298] HLEG (2018a), p. 58; This recommendation was adopted through Commission Delegated Regulation (EU) 2023/2772 of 31 July 2023 supplementing Directive 2013/34/EU of the European Parliament and of the Council as regards sustainability reporting standards [2023] OJ L 2023/2772.

[299] HLEG (2018a), p. 73.

[300] Regulation (EU) No 575/2013 of the European Parliament and of the Council of 26 June 2013 on prudential requirements for credit institutions and investment firms and amending Regulation (EU) No 648/2012 [2013] OJ L 176/1.

[301] Directive (EU) 2019/878 of the European Parliament and of the Council of 20 May 2019 amending Directive 2013/36/EU as regards exempted entities, financial holding companies, mixed financial holding companies, remuneration, supervisory measures and powers and capital conservation measures [2019] OJ L 150/253.

[302] Regulation (EU) 2019/2033 of the European Parliament and of the Council of 27 November 2019 on the prudential requirements of investment firms and amending Regulations (EU) No 1093/2010, (EU) No 575/2013, (EU) No 600/2014 and (EU) No 806/2014 [2019] OJ L 314/1.

[303] Directive (EU) 2019/2034 of the European Parliament and of the Council of 27 November 2019 on the prudential supervision of investment firms and amending Directives 2002/87/EC, 2009/65/EC, 2011/61/EU, 2013/36/EU, 2014/59/EU and 2014/65/EU [2019] OJ L 314/64.

agenda.[304] It thus sheds a light on how the EU intends to integrate Sustainable Finance objectives into major regulatory reforms.

Art. 30(1)(d) IFD refers to aspects of sustainability concerning the consideration of long-term effects of the investment decisions within the relevant investment firm's remuneration policy. Art. 35 IFD calls on EBA to develop an ESG risks report by December 2021. Further consideration of ESG risks, however, are only determined to be assessed and possibly incorporated following a review of the IFD in 2024.[305] Such a review of the IFD would take into account the EU taxonomy technical screening criteria and the EBA report.[306] Art. 53 IFR, in turn, requires investment firms to disclose information on ESG risks, including physical and transition risks as defined in the Art. 35 IFD EBA report.

Apart from such considerations in the IFR and IFD framework, several EU regulations concerning sustainability-related funds and products are to be considered under EU Sustainable Finance. For instance, the EuSEF Regulation[307] includes reporting and disclosure requirements for qualifying so-called *sustainable entrepreneurship funds*.[308] Adding to this, it sets out disclosure duties in respect of *inter alia* the investment strategy pursued under the label of *social entrepreneurship fund* and a description of the portfolio's compliance with the EUSEF Regulation.[309]

Furthermore, Art. 3 g(1)(a) SRD II[310] requires reports on CSR criteria[311] and for fiduciaries and institutional investors to publish information on their social and ecological investment scheme.[312] In accordance with Art. 449a CRR[313] large institutions must disclose information on *"ESG risks, including physical risks and transition risks"*. A technical standard for this Pillar 3 reporting is to be developed by EBA.[314] Plus, the TEG Green Bond Standard Report outlined a recommendation

---

[304] Disregarding the 2019 major changes in the Prospectus Regulation.

[305] Cf. Art. 66(c) Directive (EU) 2019/2034.

[306] Cf. Art. 66(c) Directive (EU) 2019/2034.

[307] Regulation (EU) No 346/2013 of the European Parliament and of the Council of 17 April 2013 on European social entrepreneurship funds [2013] OJ L 115/18.

[308] Cf. Art. 13(1) Regulation (EU) No 346/2013.

[309] Cf. Art. 14(1) Regulation (EU) No 346/2013.

[310] Directive (EU) 2017/828 of the European Parliament and of the Council of 17 May 2017 amending Directive 2007/36/EC as regards the encouragement of long-term shareholder engagement [2017] OJ L 132/1.

[311] Bueren (2019), p. 845; Art. 6a(3) 2 Directive 2007/36/EC of the European Parliament and of the Council of 11 July 2007 on the exercise of certain rights of shareholders in listed companies [2007] OJ L 184/17.

[312] Bueren (2019), p. 846.

[313] Corresponding to Art. 1(119) Regulation (EU) 2019/876 of the European Parliament and of the Council of 20 May 2019 amending Regulation (EU) No 575/2013 as regards the leverage ratio, the net stable funding ratio, requirements for own funds and eligible liabilities, counterparty credit risk, market risk, exposures to central counterparties, exposures to collective investment undertakings, large exposures, reporting and disclosure requirements, and Regulation (EU) No 648/2012 [2019] OJ L 150/1.

[314] Cf. Art. 434a CRR, corresponding to Art. 1(119); EBA (2019a), pp. 7, 11 et seq., 16.

to the Commission to adopt disclosure rules on green bond holdings for institutional investors.[315] As the report states, the positive experience with far-reaching disclosure obligations and the subsequent transparency in the green bond market led to increased demand for green bonds.[316]

2.1.6.6 Insurance and Pension Products

The PEPP Regulation requires the inclusion of ESG-related information into the benefit statement is required.[317] The *PEPP Benefit Statement* must cover summarized information on the ESG-related investment policy. PEPP providers are further required to publish pre-offer information on the product in the form of a PEPP KID.[318] Within this PEPP KID, the PEPP provider must disclose ESG-related performance information.[319]

As regards the insurance sector, in September 2019 EIOPA published its Opinion on Sustainability within Solvency II. It is divided into seven insurance-specific sections.[320] While Solvency II[321] relies on market prices to reflect the risks of a financial product, including sustainability risks, if the financial product is ESG-rated, transparency on the rating methodology is necessary.[322] Information on "*the use of alternative valuation methods*" must be disclosed.[323] EIOPA further recommends that information on sustainability considerations in these valuation methods should be disclosed, too.[324] Further mandatory disclosure requirements for insurance undertakings in relation to Pillar 3 should be developed both on the asset and liability side.[325]

As a joint action throughout the financial institutions and insurance sectors, in April 2020 ESAs published a consultation form on ESG disclosures, including draft regulatory technical standards for ESG disclosures (*Draft RTS*).[326] They set out an

---

[315]TEG (2019b), p. 44.

[316]TEG (2019b), p. 44.

[317]Cf. Recital 43 Regulation (EU) 2019/1238.

[318]Cf. Art. 26(1) and Art. 36(1)(l) Regulation (EU) 2019/1238.

[319]Cf. Art. 28(3)(c)(xii) Regulation (EU) 2019/1238; Cf. Bueren (2019), p. 851.

[320]Cf. EIOPA (2019c), pp. 11 et seqq.

[321]Directive 2009/138/EC of the European Parliament and of the Council of 25 November 2009 on the taking-up and pursuit of the business of Insurance and Reinsurance (Solvency II) [2009] OJ L 335/1.

[322]EIOPA (2019c), p. 11.

[323]Cf. Art. 263 and 296(4) Commission Delegated Regulation (EU) 2015/35 of 10 October 2014 supplementing Directive 2009/138/EC of the European Parliament and of the Council on the taking-up and pursuit of the business of Insurance and Reinsurance (Solvency II) [2015] OJ L 12/1.

[324]EIOPA (2019c), p. 11.

[325]EIOPA (2019c), p. 17.

[326]C.f. ESMA, Joint ESA consultation on ESG disclosures, cf. https://www.esma.europa.eu/press-news/consultations/joint-esa-consultation-esg-disclosures. Accessed 26 May 2024.

obligation for the publication of an *adverse sustainability impacts statement* by financial market participants and financial advisers.[327] The Draft RTS set out a template on the *principal adverse impacts statement* in Annex 1 Draft RTS. They further comprised the pre-contractual information requirements for financial products referred to in Art. 8(1) Sustainability Disclosures Regulation, including information in the case of reference benchmarks.[328] Respectively, Art. 23 Draft RTS sets out pre-contractual information requirements for financial products referred to in Art. 9 Sustainability Disclosures Regulation. Furthermore, the Draft RTS outline website product disclosure rules and product disclosure in periodic reports, respectively.[329]

Summing up these findings, particularly the climate-related information is seen by the EU as of core importance towards the rechanneling of private capital into sustainable investments.[330] Particularly corporate NFR on sustainability criteria plays a significant role in recently adopted Sustainable Finance regulation and has also been recognized in para. 47 Rio + 20 Outcome document.[331] However, the multiple reporting standards on Sustainable Finance were deemed confusing. The current legislative undertakings in Sustainable Finance described above are therefore a step towards not only mainstreaming Sustainable Finance into all areas of financial reporting but also consolidating the NFR standards.[332]

2.1.7 Capital Requirements

A significant tool in capital markets prudential regulation in general terms is the introduction of capital requirements for financial institutions set by the financial regulator and supervisory institutions. Such regulation covers both, the amount of own funds required for conducting a specific financial activity and the applicable transparency and reporting requirements. Since the latter have already been discussed above, this chapter will focus on the policy space used by the EU regulator and the ESAs concerning the amount of own funds.

Similar, at least in this regard, to the methodologies developed and applied by CRAs and benchmark administrators, capital requirements within the EU have traditionally been calculated and applied using the specific risk of a financial

---

[327] Cf. Art. 4(1) and Art. 12 Draft RTS.

[328] Cf. Art. 14(g) and Art. 21 Draft RTS.

[329] Cf. Art. 33 et seqq. and Art. 36 et seqq. Draft RTS.

[330] TEG (2019a), p. 4.

[331] Cf. Recital 11 Directive 2014/95/EU of the European Parliament and of the Council of 22 October 2014 amending Directive 2013/34/EU as regards disclosure of non-financial and diversity information by certain large undertakings and groups [2014] OJ L 330/1.

[332] Cf. Bueren (2019), p. 838.

instrument or a financial service supplier.[333] Such calculation methods are based on a merely economic perspective. Using capital requirements to foster Sustainable Finance means broadening the underlying data from merely economic to including aspects of sustainability. *Vice versa*, however, taking such prudential action has also been reasoned with the increased economic risk unsustainable investments or short-termism in general, pose to financial service suppliers. This is due to the environmental impact for instance of climate change, natural catastrophes, or a shift in regulation.[334]

So far, the EU capital requirements regime, in its core consisting of the Capital Requirements Regulation (*CRR*), has taken sustainability into account only with regard to economic sustainability. This is achieved by discouraging "*unsustainable financial speculation without real added value*" with a focus on significant institutions (*SIs*).[335] For example, risk-based capital requirements are aimed at limiting financial institutions' exposure and contribute to a more sustainable form of banking.[336] In an international context, this translated to the additional capital requirements under Basel II and III.[337]

As part of the revision of the CRR framework, HLEG had recommended the Commission to analyze whether a *green supporting factor* is justified given a risk-differential.[338] It further suggested to use the proportionality given within the Basel III[339] framework in favor of banks that conduct business consistent with ESG targets.[340] Accordingly, with the 2019 revision of the CRR, the CRR II,[341] the EU introduced sustainability criteria into the CRR regime. Most notably, a new Art. 501a CRR was introduced, which specifies relief in own funds requirements by a multiplication factor of 0.75. This would apply in case of an entity with exposure to essential public service providers and which meets *inter alia* assessment requirements on sustainability criteria.[342] Through Recital 135 CRR II, even the prospect of a dedicated prudential treatment of ESG-related exposures was introduced resembling a green supporting factor.[343] In respect of this green supporting factor in the

---

[333] These risks include *inter alia* liability risks, regulatory risks, and legal risks.

[334] Cf. European Commission (2018a), p. 9; It is estimated that at least half of all investments by banks in the Euro area are exposed to risks rooted in climate change, cf. *ibid.*

[335] Cf. Recital 32 CRR.

[336] Cf. Recital 91 CRR.

[337] BCBS (2006); BCBS (2010); Cf. Recital 92 CRR.

[338] HLEG (2018a), p. 69.

[339] BCBS (2010).

[340] HLEG (2018a), p. 70.

[341] Regulation (EU) 2019/876 of the European Parliament and of the Council of 20 May 2019 amending Regulation (EU) No 575/2013 as regards the leverage ratio, the net stable funding ratio, requirements for own funds and eligible liabilities, counterparty credit risk, market risk, exposures to central counterparties, exposures to collective investment undertakings, large exposures, reporting and disclosure requirements, and Regulation (EU) No 648/2012 [2019] OJ L 150/1.

[342] Cf. Art. 501a(1)(o) CRR; Cf. Recital 134 Regulation (EU) 2019/876.

[343] Cf. Art. 501c CRR.

calculation of capital requirements, Art. 501c CRR II requires EBA to assess the development of a regulation on a separate treatment for activities closely related to environmental or social objectives within the framework of Pillar 1 requirements.[344] EBA in turn stated that the report will be built upon the EU taxonomy.[345]

Regarding Pillar 2 requirements, the NGFS First Comprehensive Report's recommendation 1.2 outlined a proposal in this regard to reflect a company's sustainability-related criteria into its risk assessment.[346] Equally, Art. 34(1) and (2) IFR calls on EBA to report by December 2021 on the potential dedicated prudential treatment of activities *"associated substantially with environmental or social objectives"*. Such dedicated treatment could lead both to a *de facto* green supporting factor but also to increased consideration of regulatory and other sustainability risks when determining an asset's risk profile.[347] Thus, depending on the respective exposure, dedicated prudential treatment might lead to a positive or to an adverse change in an asset's value.[348]

These recommendations were already stated as part of the eighth action outlined in the Sustainable Finance Action Plan. Therein, the Commission explained that it would work towards the inclusion of risk factors relating to climate change into the CRR and CRD based on the EU taxonomy.[349] Furthermore, the Commission requested EIOPA to submit an opinion on the inclusion of sustainability in the prudential framework under Solvency II[350] for insurance companies.[351] The report was published in September 2019.[352]

In April 2024, the European Parliament approved the amendments to the CRR II and CRD IV (*CRR III*[353] and *CRD VI*,[354] respectively). These amendments include a reporting requirement on ESG exposures to the competent authority, the inclusion of

---

[344] EBA (2019a), pp. 7, 13.

[345] EBA (2019a), p. 13.

[346] NGFS (2019a), p. 28.

[347] Cf. Art. 34 (1)(b) and (c) IFR.

[348] Cf. Art.34 (1)(d) IFR.

[349] European Commission (2018a), p. 9.

[350] Directive 2009/138/EC of the European Parliament and of the Council of 25 November 2009 on the taking-up and pursuit of the business of Insurance and Reinsurance (Solvency II) [2009] OJ L 335/1.

[351] European Commission (2018a), p. 9.

[352] EIOPA (2019c).

[353] European Parliament (2024b) European Parliament legislative resolution of 24 April 2024 on the proposal for a regulation of the European Parliament and of the Council amending Regulation (EU) No 575/2013 as regards requirements for credit risk, credit valuation adjustment risk, operational risk, market risk and the output floor (COM(2021)0664 – C9–0397/2021–2021/0342 (COD)). 24 April 2024. P9_TA(2024)0363. https://www.europarl.europa.eu/doceo/document/TA-9-2024-0363_EN.pdf. Accessed 27 May 2024, Art. 4(52d–52 h, 152a), Art. 177(2a).

[354] European Parliament (2024a) European Parliament legislative resolution of 24 April 2024 on the proposal for a directive of the European Parliament and of the Council amending Directive 2013/36/EU as regards supervisory powers, sanctions, third-country branches, and environmental, social and governance risks, and amending Directive 2014/59/EU (COM(2021)0663 – C9–0395/2021–2021/

ESG risks into regular stress tests, supervisory powers regarding ESG risks, the inclusion of ESG risks into the Supervisory Review and Evaluation Process (*SREP*) and the Internal Capital Adequacy Assessment Process (*ICAAP*). Exposures to fossil fuel sector entities could be subject to additional capital charges. The amendments will also introduce definitions of ESG risk, including physical risk, transition risk, social risk, governance risk.

Concerning the insurance sector, similar recommendations have been voiced with a view to a solvency relief clause, equally referred to as a *green supporting factor*, consistent with the ESG factors.[355] Such considerations were also mentioned in the Sustainable Finance Action Plan.[356] HLEG in turn, not only called for the revision of the Solvency II framework[357] but also for the revision of ESAs' mandates as regards the inclusion of ESG factors in supervisory standards. Amendments to the supervisory standards would focus on procyclical effects and assessment of ESG risks.[358]

Finally, EIOPA is also working on standard risk parameters for natural catastrophes.[359] It recommends further work on capital requirements in respect of market risks and natural catastrophe risks about which data still needs to be generated.[360] EIOPA suggests that internal model users that rely on the external provision of models should require the external provider to give information on the inclusion of sustainability-related criteria.[361] Instead of introducing revised capital requirements, EIOPA recommended focusing on scenario analysis and stress testing.[362] This recommendation also refered to "*that undertakings should assess their exposure to sustainability risks*" such as transition risks, resulting in the revaluation of assets.[363] While EIOPA states that the current Solvency II framework does not prohibit sustainability valuation, insurance undertakings should adjust their valuation methods to increase resilience and preparedness.[364]

0341(COD)). 24 April 2024. P9_TA(2024)0362. https://www.europarl.europa.eu/doceo/document/ TA-9-2024-0362_EN.pdf. Accessed 27 May 2024.

[355] Bueren (2019), p. 872.

[356] Bueren (2019), p. 872; However, this proposal has been criticized for not sufficiently taking into account the capital requirements' *raison d'être* as a tool for fostering the financial market's resilience rather than climate change mitigation, cf. *ibid*. Additionally, it is argued that such supporting factors would have few, if any, influence on the actual investment decision, which will keep being under the much stronger influences of risk and profit maximization, cf. *ibid*. Finally, it is argued that it is not necessary to introduce a *green supporting factor* as financial service suppliers as of now already may conduct internal risk management weighted *inter alia* by ESG factors, cf. *ibid*.

[357] HLEG (2018a), p. 72.

[358] HLEG (2018a), p. 43.

[359] EIOPA (2024); EIOPA (2019c), p. 9.

[360] EIOPA (2019c), pp. 14 et seq.

[361] EIOPA (2019c), p. 16.

[362] EIOPA (2019c), pp. 16 et seq.

[363] EIOPA (2019c), p. 16.

[364] EIOPA (2019c), p. 12.

2.1.8 Fiduciary and Advisory Duties

Another long-standing debate closely related to Sustainable Finance involves fiduciary and advisory duties concerning sustainable financial services and products. It gives rise to two questions. First, whether a portfolio or fund manager can take into consideration ESG factors in his or her investment decision, without the client having explicitly voiced such preference.[365] And second, whether an investment advisor needs to consider the client's sustainability preferences in selecting suitable financial services and products for the client.

Current EU legislation requires fiduciaries to act in their clients' *best interest*. In cases, where the client expresses enthusiasm for sustainable financial services and products, it is not sufficiently clear as to how these requirements address ESG factors and which disclosure requirements the fiduciary has to follow in his or her assessment of these criteria.[366] As the seventh action outlined in the Sustainable Finance Action Plan, the Commission stated that it would bring forward a proposal to clarify fiduciary duties with regard to the inclusion of sustainability in the investment process and transparency in this regard.[367]

One example of such fiduciary duties considering certain aspects of ESG factors is Art. 41(1)(b) PEPP Regulation[368] which introduces a fiduciary duty as part of the *prudent person rule*. Thereby, the financial services provider not only considers the risks and benefits of its financial service but also long-term effects on ESG factors.[369]

Through the provision of investment advice to investors, investment firms and insurance distributors are key in the rechanneling of private capital towards more sustainable investments. Advisory duties, like the fiduciary duties discussed above, are centered on risk assessment in a traditional, economic understanding and economic preferences.[370] However, considering MiFID II and IDD[371] provisions on

---

[365] Bueren (2019), p. 847.

[366] These include e.g. Directive 2009/138/EC of the European Parliament and of the Council of 25 November 2009 on the taking-up and pursuit of the business of Insurance and Reinsurance (Solvency II) [2009] OJ L 335/1, Directive 2014/91/EU of the European Parliament and of the Council of 23 July 2014 amending Directive 2009/65/EC on the coordination of laws, regulations and administrative provisions relating to undertakings for collective investment in transferable securities (UCITS) as regards depositary functions, remuneration policies and sanctions [2014] OJ L 257/186, and Directive 2011/61/EU of the European Parliament and of the Council of 8 June 2011 on Alternative Investment Fund Managers and amending Directives 2003/41/EC and 2009/65/EC and Regulations (EC) No 1060/2009 and (EU) No 1095/2010 [2011] OJ L 174/1; Cf. European Commission (2018a), p. 8.

[367] European Commission (2018a), pp. 8 et seq.

[368] Regulation (EU) 2019/1238 of the European Parliament and of the Council of 20 June 2019 on a pan-European Personal Pension Product (PEPP) [2019] OJ L 198/1.

[369] Bueren (2019), p. 851; Cf. Recitals 46 and 47 Regulation (EU) 2019/1238.

[370] European Commission (2018a), p. 6.

[371] Directive (EU) 2016/97 of the European Parliament and of the Council of 20 January 2016 on insurance distribution (recast) [2016] OJ L 26/19.

advisory duties, these service suppliers are required to consider *suitable* products for the investor. However, this suitability test is conducted based on the client's preferences encompassing preferences concerning ESG factors. Therefore, investment firms and insurance distributors would need to enquire into the client's ESG preferences.[372] This, too, was covered as the fourth action of the Sustainable Finance Action Plan and in the HLEG Final Report's recommendations.[373]

MiFID II, however, previously had not set out explicit advisory duties concerning the inclusion of ESG preferences. A study found that these advisory duties were systematically left out of the provision of investment advice.[374] Two 2018 draft Delegated Regulations[375] amending MiFID II DelReg[376] and IDD DelReg[377] proposed the introduction of additional duties for investment firms and insurance distributors respectively that provide investment advice to retail clients. These draft rules covered the inclusion of the client's ESG preferences in the process of assessment, selection, and advice. In August 2021, the final MiFID II DelReg[378] and IDD DelReg[379] were adopted.

The investment firm must provide an *ex ante* description of the financial instrument's nature and risk, in particular taking into account the client's ESG preferences.[380] Under Art. 1(2) MiFID II DelReg[381] these investment firms are obliged to describe *inter alia* the ESG factors taken into consideration in the selection process. Art. 1(6)(b) MiFID II DelReg[382] thereby sets out that the information about the

---

[372] European Commission (2018a), pp. 6 et seq.

[373] European Commission (2018a), p. 7; HLEG (2018a), p. 11.

[374] HLEG (2018a), p. 27; Cf. Two Degrees Investing Initiative (2017), p. 29.

[375] European Commission (2018b); European Commission (2018d).

[376] Commission Delegated Regulation (EU) 2017/565 of 25 April 2016 supplementing Directive 2014/65/EU of the European Parliament and of the Council as regards organisational requirements and operating conditions for investment firms and defined terms for the purposes of that Directive, C/2016/2398 [2016] OJ L 87/1.

[377] Commission Delegated Regulation (EU) 2017/2359 of 21 September 2017 supplementing Directive (EU) 2016/97 of the European Parliament and of the Council with regard to information requirements and conduct of business rules applicable to the distribution of insurance-based investment products, C/2017/6229 [2017] OJ L 341/8.

[378] Commission Delegated Regulation (EU) 2021/1253 of 21 April 2021 amending Delegated Regulation (EU) 2017/565 as regards the integration of sustainability factors, risks and preferences into certain organisational requirements and operating conditions for investment firms (Text with EEA relevance) [2021] OJ L 277/1; The Commission Delegated Regulation (EU) 2021/1253 was further specified by respective ESMA Guidelines, c.f. ESMA (2023).

[379] Commission Delegated Regulation (EU) 2021/1257 of 21 April 2021 amending Delegated Regulations (EU) 2017/2358 and (EU) 2017/2359 as regards the integration of sustainability factors, risks and preferences into the product oversight and governance requirements for insurance undertakings and insurance distributors and into the rules on conduct of business and investment advice for insurance-based investment products (Text with EEA relevance) [2021] OJ L 277/18.

[380] Art. 1(5) MiFID II DelReg; Cf. European Commission (2018b), Art. 1(3).

[381] European Commission (2018b).

[382] Art. 1(2)(b) draft IDD Delegated Regulation, respectively; European Commission (2018b).

client's investment objectives must cover *inter alia* his or her ESG preferences. Likewise, investment firms must have in place policies that ensure the understanding of *inter alia* the ESG considerations with a view to the investments or financial instruments that they select. This also requires a report on how this selection reflects and takes into account *inter alia* the client's ESG preferences.[383]

The fiduciary duties described above had already been outlined in the HLEG Final Report in January 2018. It had also addressed such duties for asset managers, pension funds, investment consultants, and investment banks as sell-side market analysts.[384] This, in turn, was based on the HLEG Interim Report.[385] It had advised the Commission to introduce ESG factors into the regulatory framework on fiduciary duties of institutional investors and asset managers.[386] Subsequently, in November 2017, the Commission had launched a public consultation on ESG-related fiduciary duties.[387]

However, the inclusion of ESG-related fiduciary and advisory duties has also been suggested regarding other regulatory frameworks. For instance, EIOPA recommended the introduction of sustainability risks into the prudent person principle within the Solvency II DelReg[388] when assessing the security of an insurance portfolio.[389] Additionally, EIOPA recommends the integration of the customer's ESG profile into the insurance advice under the IDD.[390] It highlights the importance of considering sustainability factors when conducting underwriting activities.[391]

Just like Solvency II, the PEPP Regulation is based on the prudent person rule.[392] It requires fiduciaries such as retirement funds, to only invest into assets whose risk profile they deem appropriate. This is particularly relevant in the light of a retirement fund's long-term nature.[393] Within this prudent person rule, the PEPP provider is encouraged to take into account ESG factors in order to prevent stranded assets.[394] Equally, under the Sustainability Disclosures Regulation, financial advisers are obliged to publish information on the aforementioned adverse impacts of their

---

[383] Art. 1(6)(c) and (d) MiFID II DelReg; Cf. European Commission (2018b), Art. 1(5)(c) and (d).

[384] HLEG (2018a), pp. 23, 28, 74 et seq., 82 et seq.

[385] HLEG (2018a).

[386] HLEG (2018a), pp. 22 et seqq.; HLEG (2018a), p. 7.

[387] European Commission (2017d); HLEG (2018a), p. 7.

[388] Commission Delegated Regulation (EU) 2015/35 of 10 October 2014 supplementing Directive 2009/138/EC of the European Parliament and of the Council on the taking-up and pursuit of the business of Insurance and Reinsurance (Solvency II) [2015] OJ L 12/1.

[389] EIOPA (2019b), pp. 24 et seq.

[390] EIOPA (2019b), pp. 37 et seqq.

[391] EIOPA (2019c), pp. 13 et seq.

[392] To which the Regulation (EU) 2019/1238 of the European Parliament and of the Council of 20 June 2019 on a pan-European Personal Pension Product (PEPP) [2019] OJ L 198/1refers to as an *underlying principle*, Recital 47 Regulation (EU) 2019/1238.

[393] Cf. Recital 47 Regulation (EU) 2019/1238.

[394] Cf. Recitals 47 and 50 et seq. Regulation (EU) 2019/1238; With regard to stranded assets cf. Sect. 1.1.

advice on ESG factors and their relevant due diligence policies.[395] Financial market participants and financial advisers alike,[396] pre-contractually and on an issuer level must disclose the manner of integrating sustainability risks in the relevant investment decision or advice, and the impact of sustainability risks on the return of the investment.[397]

In addition, prospective EU Sustainable Finance regulation thus might allow fiduciaries to consider ESG factors independent from or not exclusively relying on shareholders' or investors' decisions and preferences.[398]

2.1.9 Corporate Governance

Another policy field in which Sustainable Finance has been introduced and can thus be understood as an instrument of such, is the regulation of corporate governance of financial institutes and service suppliers. Sustainable Finance within corporate governance regulation has so far mostly addressed the issue of short-termism in corporate decision-making processes.[399]

Addressing corporate governance was prominently mentioned as one of eight key recommendations in the HLEG Final Report. The aim was to ensure long-termism through the translation of sustainability risks into corporate action.[400] Additionally, the HLEG suggested minimum standards on stewardship responsibilities and rights, so-called *Stewardship Principles*. This was to be achieved, in particular, by ensuring the exercise of corporate voting rights.[401] These Stewardship Principles could be included in a revision of the SRD, too.[402] This minimum standard would be complemented by sustainability-related corporate director duties.[403]

---

[395] Cf. Art. 4(5) Regulation (EU) 2019/2088 of the European Parliament and of the Council of 27 November 2019 on sustainability-related disclosures in the financial services sector [2019] OJ L 317/1.

[396] Cf. Art. 6(2) Regulation (EU) 2019/2088.

[397] Cf. Art. 6(1) Regulation (EU) 2019/2088; Cf. Sect. 2.1.6.

[398] A question still to be answered, however, is whether and which indemnity claims investors would have at their disposal against fiduciaries that invest into unauthorized unsustainable investments. In such case, the fiduciary might be liable for violating duties laid down in public law but might not be accountable in relation to his or her client, cf. Bueren (2019), p. 853. Furthermore, the concern has been raised, what the damages enforced are constituted of in case the investment's profits were not narrowed by the fiduciary's decision. In this case, immaterial damages were discussed, cf. Bueren (2019), p. 853.

[399] For a more detailed description of short-termism and long-termism, cf. Sect. 1.1.

[400] HLEG (2018a), p. 38.

[401] HLEG (2018a), pp. 38 et seq.

[402] Cf. HLEG (2018a), p. 40.

[403] HLEG (2018a), pp. 40 et seq.

Besides, the tenth action outlined in the Commission's Sustainable Finance Action Plan sets out several measures to counter the issue of undue short-term pressure. The aim of these measures, too, was to encourage companies and managers to take long-term and sustainable investment decisions.[404] These measures comprise a corporate reporting requirement with a view to a board's sustainability strategy and targets. Furthermore, the Commission considers an obligation of clarifying each company's policy towards its directors' responsibility of including long-term goals into the decision-making process.

To this end, the Commission also called onto the ESAs to report on evidence of undue short-term pressure.[405] In December 2019, EBA published its report on this issue.[406] It concluded that there is limited evidence of such undue short-termism taking place.[407] However, EBA recommended explicit legal provisions on sustainability. These include adding ESG factors to the CRD's general principles of institutions' processes, revising governance requirements, or amending the CRD risk management requirements.[408] Previously, Art. 98(8) CRD had already tasked EBA with including ESG factors into its supervisory mechanisms, particularly by assessing institutions' ESG risks' impact on their stability and processes.[409] This provision is mirrored in Art. 35 IFD for investment firms. Adding to this, EBA suggested increased sustainability risks and opportunities disclosure obligations by including more companies into the NFR Directive framework.[410] This could be accompanied by increased awareness through data access and information flows, for instance by providing a dedicated information platform.[411]

In December 2019, ESMA, too, published its report on undue short-term pressure.[412] Adding to the suggestions already set out by EBA, as regards to the remuneration of corporate directors, ESMA did not consider any action necessary. However, ESMA recommended including ESG factors into the Art. 9a and Art. 9b SRD II remuneration reports.[413] A similar proposal has been brought forward by EIOPA's December 2019 respective report on undue short-term pressure. Therein, EIOPA stated that concerning the insurance sector, it understands insurance company remuneration as a tool to introduce sustainability into decision-making processes.[414]

---

[404] European Commission (2018a), p. 11.

[405] European Commission (2018a), p. 11.

[406] EBA (2019b).

[407] EBA (2019b), p. 5.

[408] Cf. Art. 74 et seq., 76–96 CRD, respectively; EBA (2019b), pp. 5, 65 et seq.

[409] EBA (2019a), p. 6.

[410] EBA (2019b), pp. 5, 67 et seqq.

[411] EBA (2019b), pp. 5, 70 et seqq.

[412] ESMA (2019e).

[413] ESMA (2019e), pp. 11, 88.

[414] EIOPA (2019b), pp. 18 et seq., 23.

Complementary measures recommended by ESMA encompass the integration of sustainability risks into the operation of management companies through an amendment to Commission Directive 2010/43/EU.[415] The same was suggested for the integration of sustainability risks into the management of Alternative Investment Funds (*AIFs*) under the AIFM Directive through an amendment to Commission Delegated Regulation (EU) No 231/2013.[416] ESMA further outlined the inclusion of ESG risks into the MiFID II DelReg's organizational requirements, risk management requirements, and the provisions on the prevention of conflicts of interest of investment firms.[417] Such reduction of sell-side conflicts of interest concerning short-termism in the market analysis provided by investment banks had also been addressed by the HLEG Final Report.[418]

2.1.10 Shareholder Engagement

Due to the shareholders' supervision and information rights, their long-term engagement is an effective instrument for introducing Sustainable Finance into corporate decision-making processes.

The rules governing the long-term engagement of institutional investors and shareholders are laid down in SRD II. Shareholder engagement is partially based on the idea that long-term shareholders decrease short-term pressure on investors and thus influence towards more sustainability in the relevant company.[419] The rules set out in the SRD II are aimed at ensuring an effective engagement of shareholders. For instance, intermediaries must facilitate the exercise of rights of a shareholder. This is complemented by corresponding transparency duties for asset owners and asset managers regarding their engagement policy towards ESG factors in Art. 3 g

---

[415] Commission Directive 2010/43/EU of 1 July 2010 implementing Directive 2009/65/EC of the European Parliament and of the Council as regards organisational requirements, conflicts of interest, conduct of business, risk management and content of the agreement between a depositary and a management company [2009] OJ L 176/42; Cf. ESMA (2019b), pp. 12 et seqq.

[416] Commission Delegated Regulation (EU) No 231/2013 of 19 December 2012 supplementing Directive 2011/61/EU of the European Parliament and of the Council with regard to exemptions, general operating conditions, depositaries, leverage, transparency and supervision [2011] OJ L 83/1; Cf. ESMA (2019b), p. 14 et seqq.

[417] Cf. Art. 21(1), Art. 23(a), and Recital 59(bis) Commission Delegated Regulation (EU) 2017/565 of 25 April 2016 supplementing Directive 2014/65/EU of the European Parliament and of the Council as regards organisational requirements and operating conditions for investment firms and defined terms for the purposes of that Directive, C/2016/2398 [2016] OJ L 87/1; ESMA (2019a), pp. 15 et seq.

[418] HLEG (2018a), pp. 82 et seq.

[419] ESMA (2019e), pp. 53 et seq.

SRD II.[420] Adding to this, companies must disclose remuneration policies, with shareholders being able to vote on them.[421]

Recital 14 SRD II understands active shareholder engagement as being of core importance to the ESG performance of a company. Thus, companies are encouraged to allow shareholders to vote on the remuneration policy. This allows ESG factors to be represented in the company's remuneration policy and ensures long-termism in the relevant company's decision-making processes.[422] Adding to this, ESMA suggested a vote on the NFI statement by shareholders.[423]

However, shareholder engagement also plays a certain role in other regulatory fields. For instance, the concept of a taxonomy relies heavily on the engagement of shareholders and their influence on the company's decision-making process—a so-called *chain of influence*.[424]

2.1.11 Awareness

Another instrument of Sustainable Finance used by the EU to be mentioned is the raising of awareness among not only private investors already active in the financial market but also the general public to rechannel private capital into sustainable financial services.

Enhancing the financial education of citizens, in general, can lead to increased investments in sustainable economic activities. The HLEG Final Report further underlined the support of national strategies on the financial education of citizens. This would be complemented by increased accessibility of information on Sustainable Finance and the facilitation of engagement in the financial market for citizens.[425] To this end, HLEG called upon the Commission to raise awareness of the importance of the use of sustainability-related indices.[426] A separate approach was taken by the NGFS's recommendation for training for central bank employees on sustainability-related risks and knowledge-sharing throughout the financial system.[427]

Finally, it is to be noted that raising awareness, particularly with a view to private investors, is closely linked to the efficient and transparent provision and

---

[420]Cf. Art. 3c Directive (EU) 2017/828 of the European Parliament and of the Council of 17 May 2017 amending Directive 2007/36/EC as regards the encouragement of long-term shareholder engagement [2017] OJ L 132/1.

[421]Cf. Art. 9a and Art. 9b Directive (EU) 2017/828; ESMA (2019e), pp. 53 et seq.

[422]Cf. Recital 29 Directive (EU) 2017/828.

[423]ESMA (2019e), p. 70.

[424]TEG (2019c), p. 10.

[425]HLEG (2018a), p. 50.

[426]HLEG (2018a), p. 55.

[427]NGFS (2019a), p. 30.

comprehensiveness of ESG information. An investor aware of the provision of ESG information and able to contextualize it, is more likely to consider it when eventually taking the investment decision.[428]

2.2   Fiscal Instruments

This chapter examines Sustainable Finance instruments that pursue a fiscal approach. This means the EU using its financial resources to create investment incentives to private market participants towards more sustainable economic activities. In contrast to the instruments described in Sect. 2.1, fiscal instruments do not primarily aim to rechannel private capital into more sustainable economic activity through increased information or relevant rights and duties. Instead, such fiscal instruments use the EU's fiscal resources to increase the share of sustainable economic activity and, intermediately, private investments in such.

To this end, financial resources conducive to or in support of Sustainable Finance are typically mobilized using the EU's funding mechanisms. All of these funding mechanisms have adopted some sort of sustainability scheme as regards the selection of their investment universe. In some cases, however, the EU may use its financial resources to directly fund sustainable economic activity. Such support can, for example, be conducted by targeted funding or by the consideration of ESG factors in public-private partnerships. Inversely, the EU can create incentives for sustainable economic activities and investment into such by divesting from unsustainable activities or take respective action in public procurement.

Finally, the EU may also use its trade policy and screening criteria to influence the type and number of financial services and products investing into sustainable or unsustainable economic activities from abroad.

If the EU uses its financial resources for funding through designated funds and investment schemes, this is usually conducted as *leveraged* or *blended finance*. Leverage means the issuance of guarantees that lower the respective investor's risk of default and that thus encourage investments into sustainable economic activities.[429] As a general concept, it had also been named in the 2030 Agenda.[430]

The 2030 Agenda furthermore outlined the idea of international public and sustainable investment funds. These public funds offer greater security for investors than direct investment into sustainable economic activities as the risk is effectively being transferred to the fund.[431] Thus, through leveraging, investors are more likely

---

[428] Cf. Sect. 2.1.6.
[429] UN PAGE (2018), p. 4.
[430] UN PAGE (2018), p. 4.
[431] UN PAGE (2018), p. 4.

to make sustainable investments. This scheme compares to the issuance of traditional guarantees. The 2030 Agenda refers to this process as leveraging, too.[432]

An example of such a scheme at the EU level is the EU External Investment Plan (*EIP*).[433] It facilitates investments in partner countries through a pool of public and private capital under the auspices of the European Fund for Sustainable Development (*EFSD*).[434] Similarly, the European Fund for Strategic Investments (*EFSI*) leverages private investments of about €265 billion.[435] As part of the Investment Plan for Europe,[436] the EFSI is a strategic investment fund under the auspices of the EIB. It leverages private investments through a shared guarantee scheme between the EIB and the Commission.[437] The EFSI was created in July 2015 and prolonged in December 2017 aiming at leveraging up to €500 billion of private investments.[438]

Another form of leveraging sustainable private investments into small- and medium-sized enterprises and large-scale infrastructure projects is through the use of private ELTIFs. Through these, the EIB can channel private investments into large infrastructure projects.[439] Building onto the Commission's Investment Plan for Europe, the HLEG Final Report recommended strengthening project development expertise, found to be a bottleneck in the allocation of sustainable investments through the EFSI, through a new entity called the *Sustainable Infrastructure Europe*.[440] Through the leveraged funding schemes, the EU also aims at advising investors on sustainability considerations in their investment decisions. An example of this is the *European Investment Advisory Hub* as an integral part of the *Investment Plan for Europe*.[441] Improving such advisory mechanisms is named as the third action outlined in the Sustainable Finance Action Plan.[442]

Another term commonly used in sustainability-focused funding and development assistance is *blending* or *blended finance*.[443] Although not universally defined, it encompasses combined funding by public sources, such as official development assistance (*ODA*), and private capital. The aim is to incentivize private investments by reducing risks for the investors while increasing impact through larger investment volume.[444] Thus, there are significant similarities and overlapping with the concept

---

[432] UN PAGE (2018), p. 4.

[433] Cf. European Commission (2016a).

[434] European Commission (2018a), p. 6.

[435] Cf. HLEG (2018a), p. 2; European Commission (2018a), p. 6.

[436] Cf. European Council (2015).

[437] Guaranteeing €7.5 billion and €26 billion, respectively.

[438] Cf. EIB (2024).

[439] Cf. Recital 31 Regulation (EU) 2015/760 of the European Parliament and of the Council of 29 April 2015 on European long-term investment funds [2015] OJ L 123/98.

[440] HLEG (2018a), pp. 35 et seqq.

[441] European Commission (2018a), p. 6; Cf. EIB (2023).

[442] European Commission (2018a), p. 6.

[443] Cf. e.g. European Commission (2019c), p. 22.

[444] For more information cf. Pereira (2017).

of leveraging. The Commission supports such third country measures through its development assistance using leveraging and blending.[445]

More recently, through the *Sustainable Europe Investment Plan*, the Commission provided an enabling framework and advice on *green projects* to facilitate private investments.[446]

Another form of Sustainable Finance through fiscal instruments is the provision of *public-private partnerships*. In such partnerships, a public entity enters into a contract with a private entity to lower investment costs for one side and create a business incentive for the other, while simultaneously creating an increase in sustainability.

Examples of such a scheme are so-called *energy performance contracts*. Such contracts provide for a private energy provider to conduct energy-saving measures on a public entity's premises, for instance, insulation. The public entity subsequently pays the guaranteed difference in savings for the duration of the contract to the private entity. After the duration of the contract, the public entity experiences much lower energy costs. It reduces its carbon footprint, while not having to bear the investment costs associated with the energy-saving measures.[447] For the private entity, an energy performance contract creates an incentive to take a sustainable investment. In this regard, it is to be noted that the HLEG Interim Report[448] recommended the revision of accounting standards for energy efficiency investments. It subsequently was implemented by Eurostat in September 2017.[449]

Sustainable Finance can, however, also take form of targeted funding of sustainable economic activities through public resources. This may materialize as a direct investment or as an acquisition of sustainability-related bonds and other financial services and products. For instance, the second recommendation outlined in the NGFS First Comprehensive Report was to integrate sustainability criteria into central banks' portfolio management.[450] The TEG added that it recommends central banks express a preference for EU Green Bonds when buying green bonds.[451]

Another fiscal instrument in Sustainable Finance is the use of public procurement as a tool for funding sustainable economic activities.[452] By deciding how public funds in procurement are invested, the EU can significantly influence the amount and type of products and services offered to public entities in the market. The

---

[445] European Commission (2019c), p. 22.

[446] European Commission (2019c), p. 15.

[447] For further information, cf. EIB (2018); Cf. Ministry of Finance of the Slovak Republic (2014); Cf. European Commission (2024a).

[448] HLEG (2018a).

[449] Eurostat (2017); HLEG (2018a), p. 7.

[450] NGFS (2019a), p. 28; Cf. NGFS (2019c).

[451] TEG (2019b), p. 12.

[452] For an overview of how public procurement is *"greening national budgets"*, cf. European Commission (2019c), pp. 17 et seq.

Commission also intends to use this instrument in its international relations by influencing third countries' public procurement towards the purchase of sustainable products and services through its international trade policy and trade agreements.[453] Likewise to incentivize sustainable investment, the EU may withdraw funds from investments it considers unsustainable, practice referred to as *divestment*.[454]

Sustainability considerations are also taken into account when negotiating trade agreements and defining the precondition for cross-border trade in financial services concerning sustainability considerations. This can be viewed as another instrument to introduce Sustainable Finance as a concept into the EU's fiscal policies. Regarding Sustainable Finance in trade policy, this chapter only examines measures that aim at influencing the type of financial services offered within the EU through trade agreements. The propagation of Sustainable Finance through trade negotiations and international relations will be examined in Chap. 4 and Sect. 5.4.

The Commission uses the EU external trade policy as a platform to support the green transition and to incorporate the implementation of the goals set at the international level, such as in the Paris Agreement, into bilateral relations.[455] The Commission's action is twofold. On the one hand, it comprises sustainable development, climate action, and the implementation and ratification of the Paris Agreement into its more recent trade agreements. On the other hand, it focuses on enforcement of sustainability commitments in trade agreements.[456] For upcoming comprehensive trade agreements, the Commission states that it will center its efforts around the respect of the Paris Agreement and thus, implementation rather than merely ratification.[457] The Commission claims that through its trade policy, it facilitates investment and trade in sustainable or green products and services.[458]

Trade policy is also used to promote EU regulatory standards on products and services and remove non-tariff barriers, particularly in green energy.[459] Through its trade policy, the Commission also tries to influence partner countries to adopt similar regulatory standards.[460] It expressed that the EU should use *"its economic weight to shape international standards that are in line with EU environmental and climate ambitions"* and *"to facilitate trade in environmental goods and services, in bilateral and multilateral forums"* in particular by using its influence on global value chains as the largest international single market.[461]

---

[453] European Commission (2019c), p. 21.

[454] In EU legislation the term *divestment*, however, so far only refers to the aim of rechanneling capital flows—private investors divesting from certain economic activities deemed unsustainable in favor of sustainable activities, cf. e.g. Art. 39(2)(e) Directive (EU) 2019/2034.

[455] European Commission (2019c), p. 21.

[456] European Commission (2019c), p. 21.

[457] European Commission (2019c), p. 21.

[458] European Commission (2019c), p. 21.

[459] European Commission (2019c), p. 21.

[460] European Commission (2019c), p. 21; Cf. European Commission (2019d), p. 4.

[461] European Commission (2019c), p. 22.

Another measure in the broader sense of Sustainable Finance policy could be the inclusion of Sustainable Finance objectives into the EU's FDI screening framework. In 2019, a comprehensive EU FDI screening framework was introduced, centered around the FDI Screening Regulation.[462] Recital 3 FDI Screening Regulation states that FDI screening is conducted on grounds of security and public order considering and in line with WTO, OECD, and bilateral trade commitments. However, the FDI Screening Regulation does not cover portfolio investments and thus neither applies to financial services.[463]

Alternatively, portfolio investments and different types of financial services may be incorporated in a comprehensive sustainability screening scheme. However, such investment screening applicable to financial services, for various reasons, does not yet exist. Proposals as to the introduction of such sustainability screenings in the form of carbon border measures for trade in services, together with other prospective measures will be discussed in Sect. 3.3.3.

2.3 Current EU Sustainable Finance Regulatory Processes and Proposals

The policy recommendations and reports, particularly, by the HLEG, the TEG, and the ESAs have only in part been translated into legislation. The same applies to the more recent further proposals by Commission policy frameworks, such as the renewed Sustainable Finance strategy or the European Green Deal. Measured by the number of specific policy goals set, the need for legislative action as claimed by the Commission, and the further targets set in these more recent policy frameworks, it can be argued that EU Sustainable Finance legislation is only in its early stages. In other areas of sustainable development policy, later stages of legislation often led to stricter, more limiting rules. Examples of such stricter rules are carbon emission and other pollution norms. This can be understood as the result of the short timeframe envisaged for the implementation of the EU's 2030 Agenda commitments.

If regulation in these areas in fact further intensifies—thereby potentially limiting cross-border trade in financial services—would this change the regulation's potential inconsistency under GATS and the EU FTAs? Certainly, these future EU Sustainable Finance measures, once they are adopted, will be highly relevant for the assessment of the concept of EU Sustainable Finance under GATS and the EU FTAs. As EU Sustainable Finance is a policy field shaped by major policy agendas

---

[462] Regulation (EU) 2019/452 of the European Parliament and of the Council of 19 March 2019 establishing a framework for the screening of foreign direct investments into the Union [2019] OJ L 79I/1.

[463] With a view to the applicability of the Agreement on Technical Barriers to Trade, Marrakesh Agreement Establishing the World Trade Organization, Annex 1A. 15 April 1994. U.N.T.S. 1867 (1994) or the EU FTAs to sustainability provisions in FDI regulation, cf. Sects. 4.2.3 and 5.1, respectively.

such as the Sustainable Finance Action Plan, several upcoming and current measures can be identified. This chapter will give a brief overview of such regulatory processes and proposals currently underway.

There are several large-scale policy frameworks scheduled to be introduced or reviewed. These revisions may have a significant influence on all upcoming EU Sustainable Finance regulations. For instance, the Commission published a proposal for a *European Climate Law* in March 2020.[464] Such European Climate Law had already been envisaged as part of the European Green Deal.[465] The European Climate Law was introduced in June 2021.[466]

The Commission initiated consultation on a *renewed Sustainable Finance strategy* in April 2020.[467] According to the Commission, this renewed strategy as a successor of the Sustainable Finance Action Plan, aims to support the implementation of the European Green Deal, "*to manage and integrate climate and environmental risks into our financial system*" and to create "*additional enabling frameworks for the European Green Deal Investment Plan.*"[468] On the one hand, the Commission's statement on the renewed Sustainable Finance strategy reflects the aim of rechanneling of private capital as described in Sect. 2.1. On the other hand, the statement also refers to using public financial resources to incentivize private market participants to invest or to engage in sustainable economic activities as described in Sect. 2.2.[469] Based on the Commission's statement, the renewed Sustainable Finance strategy was adopted in July 2021.[470]

However, there are more detailed proposals and legislative processes for Sustainable Finance amendments to prudential regulation, too. For instance, Art.

---

[464] European Parliament (2020).

[465] European Commission (2019c), p. 4; European Commission (2019d), p. 2; European Commission (2020c), p. 4.

[466] Regulation (EU) 2021/1119 of the European Parliament and of the Council of 30 June 2021 establishing the framework for achieving climate neutrality and amending Regulations (EC) No 401/2009 and (EU) 2018/1999 ('European Climate Law') [2021] OJ L 243/1.

[467] European Commission (2019c), p. 17.

[468] Cf. the consultation website, https://ec.europa.eu/info/consultations/finance-2020-sustainable-finance-strategy_en; European Commission (2020a).

[469] Pursuant to the European Green Deal, the reviewed Sustainable Finance strategy is expected to focus on three aspects, namely strengthening the regulatory foundations of Sustainable Finance (the taxonomy, sustainable corporate governance, or long-termism in general), disclosure requirements (in particular a revision of the Directive 2014/95/EU of the European Parliament and of the Council of 22 October 2014 amending Directive 2013/34/EU as regards disclosure of non-financial and diversity information by certain large undertakings and groups [2014] OJ L 330/1) and support, also internationally, work on natural capital accounting standards, cf. European Commission (2019d), p. 4.

[470] European Commission (2021) Communication from the Commission to the European Parliament, the Council, the European Economic and Social Committee and the Committee of the Regions, Strategy for Financing the Transition to a Sustainable Economy. 6 July 2021. COM/2021/390 final. https://eur-lex.europa.eu/legal-content/EN/TXT/?uri=CELEX:52021DC0390. Accessed 26 May 2024.

1(6) subpara. 5 and (8)(2) Climate BMR[471] empowers the Commission to detail the information requirements of the benchmark statement in a delegated regulation.[472] A delegated regulation to the Climate BMR was published in July 2020 and sets out further details on the calculation and transparency of the EU PABs and EU CTBs.[473] It remains to be seen how, for instance, the phase-in mechanism for greenhouse gas emissions in Art. 5(1) Delegated Regulation evolves and affects the actual calculation of the EU PAB and EU CTB.

Concerning the application of the EU Ecolabel to financial products, according to the JRC, the "*Delegated Act on activities substantially contributing to the climate objectives will be adopted by 31 December 2020, and, in the first instance, the EU Ecolabel criteria will refer to it.*" Neither the Ecolabel Regulation[474] has been amended nor have relevant delegated acts been adopted further specifying an EU Ecolabel's requirements applicable for financial products.[475]

Further legislation to be expected on capital requirements comprises the technical standard for this Pillar 3 reporting to be developed by EBA under Art. 434a CRR,[476] the final draft of which was published in January 2022.[477] This technical standard complements the requirement set out in Art. 449a CRR[478] pursuant to which large companies must disclose information on "*ESG risks, including physical risks and transition risks*".[479] Further, Art. 501c CRR II requires EBA to assess the development of a regulation that would set out a separate treatment towards activities closely

---

[471] Corresponding to Art. 27(2b) and Art. 49(2) Regulation (EU) 2016/1011 of the European Parliament and of the Council of 8 June 2016 on indices used as benchmarks in financial instruments and financial contracts or to measure the performance of investment funds and amending Directives 2008/48/EC and 2014/17/EU and Regulation (EU) No 596/2014 [2016] OJ L 171/1.

[472] Commission Delegated Regulation (EU) 2018/1643 of 13 July 2018 supplementing Regulation (EU) 2016/1011 of the European Parliament and of the Council with regard to regulatory technical standards specifying further the contents of, and cases where updates are required to, the benchmark statement to be published by the administrator of a benchmark (Text with EEA relevance.) [2018] OJ L 274/29.

[473] Commission Delegated Regulation (EU) 2020/1818 of 17 July 2020 supplementing Regulation (EU) 2016/1011 of the European Parliament and of the Council as regards minimum standards for EU Climate Transition Benchmarks and EU Paris-aligned Benchmarks, C/2020/4757 [2020] OJ L 406/17.

[474] Regulation (EC) No 66/2010 of the European Parliament and of the Council of 25 November 2009 on the EU Ecolabel [2009] OJ L 27/1.

[475] JRC (2019c), p. 89.

[476] Corresponding to Art. 1 (119) Regulation (EU) 2019/876 of the European Parliament and of the Council of 20 May 2019 amending Regulation (EU) No 575/2013 as regards the leverage ratio, the net stable funding ratio, requirements for own funds and eligible liabilities, counterparty credit risk, market risk, exposures to central counterparties, exposures to collective investment undertakings, large exposures, reporting and disclosure requirements, and Regulation (EU) No 648/2012 [2019] OJ L 150/1.

[477] C.f. EBA (2022).

[478] Corresponding to Art. 1(119) Regulation (EU) 2019/876.

[479] EBA (2019a), pp. 7, 11 et seq., 16.

related to environmental or social objectives within the framework of Pillar 1, as already stated above (2.1.7).[480] Likewise, regarding the prudential treatment of investment firms, Art. 34(1) and (2) IFR called on EBA to report on the possible dedicated prudential treatment of activities *"associated substantially with environmental or social objectives"*, as already stated above (2.1.7). This report was published in October 2023.[481]

Finally, in the European Green Deal, the Commission stated that it will generally focus on the inclusion of climate and environmental risks into the prudential framework and reviewing the prudential requirements on green assets.[482] The first steps towards the inclusion of such green assets were set out in CRR III[483] and CRD VI[484] as described in Sect. 2.1.7.

Such ESG risks are also to be further incorporated into the IFR and IFD framework. The obligation for investment firms to take into account sustainability risks in their risk management has already been included in Art. 21(1) and Art. 23(1) MiFID II DelReg.[485] Adding to this, EBA published an ESG risks report in June 2021.[486] Further consideration of ESG risks is to be assessed and potentially integrated following a review of the IFD in 2024.[487] Furthermore, a review in particular with a view to the inclusion of ESG factors and risks in remuneration policy, internal governance, and treatment of risks will be conducted by June 2024.[488]

In relation to the Sustainable Finance prudential treatment of insurance providers, Solvency II[489] itself does not entail sustainability-related regulatory measures. However, Art. 29 and Recital 13 Solvency II DelReg do mention the inclusion of

---

[480] EBA (2019a), pp. 7, 13.

[481] C.f. EBA (2023).

[482] European Commission (2019c), p. 17; European Commission (2019d), p. 4.

[483] European Parliament (2024b) European Parliament legislative resolution of 24 April 2024 on the proposal for a regulation of the European Parliament and of the Council amending Regulation (EU) No 575/2013 as regards requirements for credit risk, credit valuation adjustment risk, operational risk, market risk and the output floor (COM(2021)0664 – C9 0397/2021 – 2021/0342 (COD)). 24 April 2024. P9_TA(2024)0363. https://www.europarl.europa.eu/doceo/document/TA-9-2024-0363_EN.pdf. Accessed 27 May 2024, Art. 4(52d–52h, 152a), Art. 177(2a).

[484] European Parliament (2024a) European Parliament legislative resolution of 24 April 2024 on the proposal for a directive of the European Parliament and of the Council amending Directive 2013/36/EU as regards supervisory powers, sanctions, third-country branches, and environmental, social and governance risks, and amending Directive 2014/59/EU (COM(2021)0663 – C9-0395/2021 – 2021/0341(COD)). 24 April 2024. P9_TA(2024)0362. https://www.europarl.europa.eu/doceo/document/TA-9-2024-0362_EN.pdf. Accessed 27 May 2024.

[485] Cf. Art. 1(2) MiFID II Draft RTS; Cf. Sect. 3.3.2.

[486] Cf. EBA (2021); Cf. Art. 35 Directive (EU) 2019/2034.

[487] Cf. Art. 66(c) Directive (EU) 2019/2034.

[488] Cf. Art. 66 Directive (EU) 2019/2034.

[489] Directive 2009/138/EC of the European Parliament and of the Council of 25 November 2009 on the taking-up and pursuit of the business of Insurance and Reinsurance (Solvency II) [2009] OJ L 335/1.

inter alia prospective social, environmental, and economic developments into value definition methodologies. Further legislative proposals are thus yet to be expected. Adding to this, EIOPA consults on *standard risk parameters* for natural catastrophes.[490]

Supplementing these proposals, upcoming legislation EU Sustainable Finance instruments may further comprise fiscal measures like those outlined in Sect. 2.2. For instance, although most of the fiscal measures outlined in the European Green Deal have already been implemented, like the *Sustainable Europe Investment Plan,*[491] in January 2020, the Commission published its proposal for the introduction of a *Just Transition Fund,* as envisaged in the European Green Deal.[492] The Just Transition Fund was launched in 2021.[493] The Commission also plans to revise the EU Emission Trading System (*EU ETS*) and several energy efficiency and taxation regulations as provided for in the European Green Deal.[494] Furthermore, experience from the EU financial markets given the entry into force of the FDI Screening Regulation from October 2020 onwards might hint towards the need for a future complementary framework for portfolio investments or cross-border trade in financial services.

Finally, there are several institutional suggestions with a view to Sustainable Finance policy yet to be implemented by the Commission. These involve HLEG's outline on an *Observatory on Sustainable Finance* under the auspices of the European Environment Agency to ensure that Sustainable Finance regulation is in line with scientific evidence.[495] This observatory has not been established yet.[496] Apart from this, as part of the ninth action outlined in its Sustainable Finance Action Plan, the Commission requested the EFRAG to share best practice information on corporate reporting, in particular climate-related reporting, coherent with the TCFD recommendations.[497] A summary report was published in February 2020.[498] A further advisory group was envisaged in the TEG Green Bond Standard Report denominated the *EU Platform on Sustainable Finance* and set up as a Commission Expert Group.[499] It was established through Art. 20 Taxonomy Regulation and held its inaugural meeting in October 2020.[500]

---

[490] Cf. EIOPA (2024).

[491] European Commission (2019d), p. 4.

[492] European Commission (2019d), p. 4; European Commission (2020h).

[493] Cf. European Commission (2019e); Regulation (EU) 2021/1056 of the European Parliament and of the Council of 24 June 2021 establishing the Just Transition Fund [2021] OJ L 231/1.

[494] European Commission (2019c), p. 4; European Commission (2019d), p. 2; An agreement on the revision of the EU ETS has been reached on 25 April 2023, c.f. European Council (2023).

[495] HLEG (2018a), pp. 51 et seqq.

[496] A similar, industry-led project, however, has been initiated in October 2020 and co-funded by the EU, cf. Observatoire de la finance durable (2024).

[497] European Commission (2018a), p. 9.

[498] EFRAG (2020).

[499] TEG (2019b), p. 28.

[500] Cf. European Commission (2020i).

2.4 Conclusion: The Current Scope of EU Sustainable Finance Policy

The foregoing overview and explanation of EU Sustainable Finance regulation leads to conclusions that will be relevant for its assessment under international trade law in the upcoming Chaps. 3 and 5.

First, it can be concluded that EU Sustainable Finance regulation is dispersed over many regulatory fields and subfields. Its policy is based on Commission plans and guidance issued by the ESAs, while its implementation can take various forms. Sustainable Finance regulation can be introduced through dedicated legislation solely for that purpose such as the Sustainability Disclosures Regulation, the NFR Directive, or the Taxonomy Regulation. Alternatively, it can be introduced by amending existing financial services regulations such as MiFID II, the BMR, the CRR, or the CRD. Or, it can also be introduced as part of large-scale revisions of a regulatory field such as the adoption of the IFR and IFD framework.

Second, the more recent prudential instruments of EU Sustainable Finance regulation exhibit a two-stage regulatory structure. At stage one, the Taxonomy Regulation defines sustainable economic activities. At stage two, the respective substantive regulation bases its measures on this definition. The reference point for the assessment under international trade law can be either the Taxonomy Regulation's categorization system or the substantive provisions in the respective regulation.

Third, EU Sustainable Finance regulation, on the one hand, is heavily influenced by international policy frameworks, particularly on environmental protection, climate action, and labor rights. On the other hand, dedicated international panel reports and guidelines on Sustainable Finance are systematically referenced and incorporated into EU Sustainable Finance regulation adding a comprehensive international aspect related regulation. Likewise, EU Sustainable Finance regulation is based not only on the furtherance of the ESG factors, particularly environmental protection and labor rights, but also on furthering the long-term stability of the financial system. This is particularly visible in the regular assessment of sustainability risks *to* investments rather than *by* investments in EU Sustainable Finance policy publications.

Fourth, EU Sustainable Finance regulation can roughly be subdivided into prudential and fiscal instruments, with their respective policy approach already described above.[501] Although fiscal instruments such as ODA, public procurement, and targeted funding are more traditional tools of the EU furthering sustainable development, due to the lack of public financial resources to meet the SDGs, the introduction of Sustainable Finance prudential instruments will likely accelerate in the upcoming years. Plus, in contrast to the fiscal instruments, the prudential instruments aim at altering the financial service supplier's or the customer's

---

[501] Cf. Sects. 2.1 and 2.2.

decision-making process. It is for this reason that the assessment in Sect. 3.2 will focus on prudential instruments. For the same reason, the assessment of prospective EU Sustainable Finance legislation conducted in Sect. 3.3 can be deemed particularly relevant.

Legislation

Agreement on Technical Barriers to Trade, Marrakesh Agreement Establishing the World Trade Organization, Annex 1A. 15 April 1994. U.N.T.S. 1867 (1994)

General Agreement on Trade in Services, Marrakesh Agreement Establishing the World Trade Organization, Annex 1B. 15 April 1994. U.N.T.S. 1867 (1994)

Council Regulation (EEC) No. 880/92 on a Community eco-label award scheme [1992] OJ L 99/1

Regulation (EC) No 1606/2002 of the European Parliament and of the Council of 19 July 2002 on the application of international accounting standards [2002] OJ L 243/1

Directive 2007/36/EC of the European Parliament and of the Council of 11 July 2007 on the exercise of certain rights of shareholders in listed companies [2007] OJ L 184/17

Regulation (EC) No 1060/2009 of the European Parliament and of the Council of 16 September 2009 on credit rating agencies [2009] OJ L 302/1

Directive 2009/138/EC of the European Parliament and of the Council of 25 November 2009 on the taking-up and pursuit of the business of Insurance and Reinsurance (Solvency II) [2009] OJ L 335/1

Regulation (EC) No 66/2010 of the European Parliament and of the Council of 25 November 2009 on the EU Ecolabel [2009] OJ L 27/1

Commission Directive 2010/43/EU of 1 July 2010 implementing Directive 2009/65/EC of the European Parliament and of the Council as regards organisational requirements, conflicts of interest, conduct of business, risk management and content of the agreement between a depositary and a management company [2009] OJ L 176/42

Commission Implementing Regulation (EU) No 543/2011 of 7 June 2011 laying down detailed rules for the application of Council Regulation (EC) No 1234/2007 in respect of the fruit and vegetables and processed fruit and vegetables sectors [2011] OJ L 157/1

Directive 2011/61/EU of the European Parliament and of the Council of 8 June 2011 on Alternative Investment Fund Managers and amending Directives 2003/41/EC and 2009/65/EC and Regulations (EC) No 1060/2009 and (EU) No 1095/2010 [2011] OJ L 174/1

Commission Delegated Regulation (EU) No 231/2013 of 19 December 2012 supplementing Directive 2011/61/EU of the European Parliament and of the Council with regard to exemptions, general operating conditions, depositaries, leverage, transparency and supervision [2011] OJ L 83/1

Regulation (EU) No 346/2013 of the European Parliament and of the Council of 17 April 2013 on European social entrepreneurship funds [2013] OJ L 115/18

Regulation (EU) No 462/2013 of the European Parliament and of the Council of 21 May 2013 amending Regulation (EC) No 1060/2009 on credit rating agencies [2013] OJ L 146/1

Regulation (EU) No 575/2013 of the European Parliament and of the Council of 26 June 2013 on prudential requirements for credit institutions and investment firms and amending Regulation (EU) No 648/2012 [2013] OJ L 176/1

Directive 2013/34/EU of the European Parliament and of the Council of 26 June 2013 on the annual financial statements, consolidated financial statements and related reports of certain types of undertakings, amending Directive 2006/43/EC of the European Parliament and of the Council and repealing Council Directives 78/660/EEC and 83/349/EEC [2013] OJ L 182/19

Directive 2013/50/EU of the European Parliament and of the Council of 22 October 2013 amending Directive 2004/109/EC of the European Parliament and of the Council on the harmonisation of transparency requirements in relation to information about issuers whose securities are admitted to trading on a regulated market, Directive 2003/71/EC of the European Parliament and of the Council on the prospectus to be published when securities are offered to the public or admitted to trading and Commission Directive 2007/14/EC laying down detailed rules for the implementation of certain provisions of Directive 2004/109/EC [2013] OJ L 294/13

Directive 2014/65/EU of the European Parliament and of the Council of 15 May 2014 on markets in financial instruments and amending Directive 2002/92/EC and Directive 2011/61/EU [2014] OJ L 173/349

Directive 2014/91/EU of the European Parliament and of the Council of 23 July 2014 amending Directive 2009/65/EC on the coordination of laws, regulations and administrative provisions relating to undertakings for collective investment in transferable securities (UCITS) as regards depositary functions, remuneration policies and sanctions [2014] OJ L 257/186

Directive 2014/95/EU of the European Parliament and of the Council of 22 October 2014 amending Directive 2013/34/EU as regards disclosure of non-financial and diversity information by certain large undertakings and groups [2014] OJ L 330/1

Regulation (EU) No 1286/2014 of the European Parliament and of the Council of 26 November 2014 on key information documents for packaged retail and insurance-based investment products (PRIIPs) [2014] OJ L 352/1

Commission Delegated Regulation (EU) 2015/35 of 10 October 2014 supplementing Directive 2009/138/EC of the European Parliament and of the Council on the taking-up and pursuit of the business of Insurance and Reinsurance (Solvency II) [2015] OJ L 12/1

Regulation (EU) 2015/760 of the European Parliament and of the Council of 29 April 2015 on European long-term investment funds [2015] OJ L 123/98

General Assembly Resolution 70/1, Transforming our World: The 2030 Agenda for Sustainable Development. 25 September 2015. A/RES/70/1

Directive (EU) 2016/97 of the European Parliament and of the Council of 20 January 2016 on insurance distribution (recast) [2016] OJ L 26/19

Commission Delegated Regulation (EU) 2017/565 of 25 April 2016 supplementing Directive 2014/65/EU of the European Parliament and of the Council as regards organisational requirements and operating conditions for investment firms and defined terms for the purposes of that Directive, C/2016/2398 [2016] OJ L 87/1

Regulation (EU) 2016/1011 of the European Parliament and of the Council of 8 June 2016 on indices used as benchmarks in financial instruments and financial contracts or to measure the performance of investment funds and amending Directives 2008/48/EC and 2014/17/EU and Regulation (EU) No 596/2014 [2016] OJ L 171/1

Commission Delegated Regulation (EU) 2017/653 of 8 March 2017 supplementing Regulation (EU) No 1286/2014 of the European Parliament and of the Council on key information documents for packaged retail and insurance-based investment products (PRIIPs) by laying down regulatory technical standards with regard to the presentation, content, review and revision of key information documents and the conditions for fulfilling the requirement to provide such documents [2017] OJ L 100/1

Directive (EU) 2017/828 of the European Parliament and of the Council of 17 May 2017 amending Directive 2007/36/EC as regards the encouragement of long-term shareholder engagement [2017] OJ L 132/1

Commission Delegated Regulation (EU) 2017/2359 of 21 September 2017 supplementing Directive (EU) 2016/97 of the European Parliament and of the Council with regard to information requirements and conduct of business rules applicable to the distribution of insurance-based investment products, C/2017/6229 [2017] OJ L 341/8

Commission Delegated Regulation (EU) 2018/1643 of 13 July 2018 supplementing Regulation (EU) 2016/1011 of the European Parliament and of the Council with regard to regulatory technical standards specifying further the contents of, and cases where updates are required to, the benchmark statement to be published by the administrator of a benchmark (Text with EEA relevance.) [2018] OJ L 274/29

Regulation (EU) 2019/452 of the European Parliament and of the Council of 19 March 2019 establishing a framework for the screening of foreign direct investments into the Union [2019] OJ L 79I/1

Regulation (EU) 2019/876 of the European Parliament and of the Council of 20 May 2019 amending Regulation (EU) No 575/2013 as regards the leverage ratio, the net stable funding ratio, requirements for own funds and eligible liabilities, counterparty credit risk, market risk, exposures to central counterparties, exposures to collective investment undertakings, large exposures, reporting and disclosure requirements, and Regulation (EU) No 648/2012 [2019] OJ L 150/1

Directive (EU) 2019/878 of the European Parliament and of the Council of 20 May 2019 amending Directive 2013/36/EU as regards exempted entities, financial holding companies, mixed financial holding companies, remuneration, supervisory measures and powers and capital conservation measures [2019] OJ L 150/253

Regulation (EU) 2019/1238 of the European Parliament and of the Council of 20 June 2019 on a pan-European Personal Pension Product (PEPP) [2019] OJ L 198/1

Regulation (EU) 2019/2033 of the European Parliament and of the Council of 27 November 2019 on the prudential requirements of investment firms and amending Regulations (EU) No 1093/2010, (EU) No 575/2013, (EU) No 600/2014 and (EU) No 806/2014 [2019] OJ L 314/1

Directive (EU) 2019/2034 of the European Parliament and of the Council of 27 November 2019 on the prudential supervision of investment firms and amending Directives 2002/87/EC, 2009/65/EC, 2011/61/EU, 2013/36/EU, 2014/59/EU and 2014/65/EU [2019] OJ L 314/64

Regulation (EU) 2019/2088 of the European Parliament and of the Council of 27 November 2019 on sustainability-related disclosures in the financial services sector [2019] OJ L 317/1

Regulation (EU) 2019/2089 of the European Parliament and of the Council of 27 November 2019 amending Regulation (EU) 2016/1011 as regards EU Climate Transition Benchmarks, EU Paris-aligned Benchmarks and sustainability-related disclosures for benchmarks [2019] OJ L 317/17

Regulation (EU) 2020/852 of the European Parliament and of the Council of 18 June 2020 on the establishment of a framework to facilitate sustainable investment, and amending Regulation (EU) 2019/2088 [2020] OJ L 198/13

Commission Delegated Regulation (EU) 2020/1818 of 17 July 2020 supplementing Regulation (EU) 2016/1011 of the European Parliament and of the Council as regards minimum standards for EU Climate Transition Benchmarks and EU Paris-aligned Benchmarks, C/2020/4757 [2020] OJ L 406/17

Commission Delegated Regulation (EU) 2021/1253 of 21 April 2021 amending Delegated Regulation (EU) 2017/565 as regards the integration of sustainability factors, risks and preferences into certain organisational requirements and operating conditions for investment firms (Text with EEA relevance) [2021] OJ L 277/1

Commission Delegated Regulation (EU) 2021/1257 of 21 April 2021 amending Delegated Regulations (EU) 2017/2358 and (EU) 2017/2359 as regards the integration of sustainability factors, risks and preferences into the product oversight and governance requirements for insurance undertakings and insurance distributors and into the rules on conduct of business and investment advice for insurance-based investment products (Text with EEA relevance) [2021] OJ L 277/18

Commission Delegated Regulation (EU) 2021/2139 of 4 June 2021 supplementing Regulation (EU) 2020/852 of the European Parliament and of the Council by establishing the technical screening criteria for determining the conditions under which an economic activity qualifies as contributing substantially to climate change mitigation or climate change adaptation and for determining whether that economic activity causes no significant harm to any of the other environmental objectives (Text with EEA relevance) [2021] OJ L 44271

Regulation (EU) 2021/1056 of the European Parliament and of the Council of 24 June 2021 establishing the Just Transition Fund [2021] OJ L 231/1

Commission Delegated Regulation (EU) 2021/2178 of 6 July 2021 supplementing Regulation (EU) 2020/852 of the European Parliament and of the Council by specifying the content and presentation of information to be disclosed by undertakings subject to Articles 19a or 29a of Directive 2013/34/EU concerning environmentally sustainable economic activities, and specifying the methodology to comply with that disclosure obligation (Text with EEA relevance) [2021] OJ L 443/9

Regulation (EU) 2021/1119 of the European Parliament and of the Council of 30 June 2021 establishing the framework for achieving climate neutrality and amending Regulations (EC) No 401/2009 and (EU) 2018/1999 ('European Climate Law') [2021] OJ L 243/1

Commission Delegated Regulation (EU) 2022/1214 of 9 March 2022 amending Delegated Regulation (EU) 2021/2139 as regards economic activities in certain energy sectors and Delegated Regulation (EU) 2021/2178 as regards specific public disclosures for those economic activities (Text with EEA relevance) [2022] OJ L 188/1

Regulation (EU) 2023/606 of the European Parliament and of the Council of 15 March 2023 amending Regulation (EU) 2015/760 as regards the requirements pertaining to the investment policies and operating conditions of European long-term investment funds and the scope of eligible investment assets, the portfolio composition and diversification requirements and the borrowing of cash and other fund rules (Text with EEA relevance) [2023] OJ L 80/1

Commission Delegated Regulation (EU) 2023/2485 of 27 June 2023 amending Delegated Regulation (EU) 2021/2139 establishing additional technical screening criteria for determining the conditions under which certain economic activities qualify as contributing substantially to climate change mitigation or climate change adaptation and for determining whether those activities cause no significant harm to any of the other environmental objectives [2023] OJ L 2023/2485

Commission Delegated Regulation (EU) 2023/2486 of 27 June 2023 supplementing Regulation (EU) 2020/852 of the European Parliament and of the Council by establishing the technical screening criteria for determining the conditions under which an economic activity qualifies as contributing substantially to the sustainable use and protection of water and marine resources, to the transition to a circular economy, to pollution prevention and control, or to the protection and restoration of biodiversity and ecosystems and for determining whether that economic activity causes no significant harm to any of the other environmental objectives and amending Commission Delegated Regulation (EU) 2021/2178 as regards specific public disclosures for those economic activities, OJ L 2023/2486

Commission Delegated Regulation (EU) 2023/2772 of 31 July 2023 supplementing Directive 2013/34/EU of the European Parliament and of the Council as regards sustainability reporting standards [2023] OJ L 2023/2772

Regulation (EU) 2023/2631 of the European Parliament and of the Council of 22 November 2023 on European Green Bonds and optional disclosures for bonds marketed as environmentally sustainable and for sustainability-linked bonds [2023] OJ L 2023/2631

European Parliament (2024a) European Parliament legislative resolution of 24 April 2024 on the proposal for a directive of the European Parliament and of the Council amending Directive 2013/36/EU as regards supervisory powers, sanctions, third-country branches, and environmental, social and governance risks, and amending Directive 2014/59/EU (COM(2021)0663 – C9-0395/2021 – 2021/0341(COD)). 24 April 2024. P9_TA(2024)0362. https://www.europarl.europa.eu/doceo/document/TA-9-2024-0362_EN.pdf. Accessed 27 May 2024

European Parliament (2024b) European Parliament legislative resolution of 24 April 2024 on the proposal for a regulation of the European Parliament and of the Council amending Regulation (EU) No 575/2013 as regards requirements for credit risk, credit valuation adjustment risk, operational risk, market risk and the output floor (COM(2021)0664 – C9-0397/2021 – 2021/0342(COD)). 24 April 2024. P9_TA(2024)0363. https://www.europarl.europa.eu/doceo/document/TA-9-2024-0363_EN.pdf. Accessed 27 May 2024

References

Bibliography

Bueren E (2019) Sustainable Finance. Zeitschrift für Unternehmens- und Gesellschaftsrecht 48(5): 813–875. https://doi.org/10.1515/zgr-2019-0022. Accessed 19 Dec 2021

Busch D et al (2018) The European Commission's sustainable finance action plan. Social Science Research Network. https://doi.org/10.2139/ssrn.3263690. Accessed 19 Dec 2021

Jakubik P, Uguz S (2019) Impact of green bond policies on insurers: evidence from the European Equity Market. In: EIOPA, Financial Stability Report, 1 July 2019, pp 66–75. https://www.eiopa.europa.eu/sites/default/files/publications/reports/thematic_article_fsr_june2019.pdf. Accessed 19 Dec 2021

Pereira J (2017) European Network on Debt and Development, Research Report, Blended Finance, What it is, how it works and how it is used. https://eurodad.org/files/pdf/58a1e294657ab.pdf. Accessed 19 Dec 2021

Documents

BCBS (2006) International convergence of capital measurement and capital standards, A revised framework comprehensive version. https://www.bis.org/publ/bcbs128.pdf. Accessed 8 May 2024

BCBS (2010) A global regulatory framework for more resilient banks and banking systems. https://www.bis.org/publ/bcbs189.pdf. Accessed 8 May 2024

EBA (2019a) EBA Action Plan on sustainable finance. https://eba.europa.eu/sites/default/documents/files/document_library//EBA%20Action%20plan%20on%20sustainable%20finance.pdf. Accessed 8 May 2024

EBA (2019b) EBA Report on undue short-term pressure from the financial sector on corporations, 18 December 2019. https://eba.europa.eu/file/461440/download?token=gM-ur7b2. Accessed 8 May 2024

EBA (2021) EBA Report on management and supervision of ESG risks for credit institutions and investment firms. 23 June 2021. https://www.eba.europa.eu/sites/default/files/document_library/Publications/Reports/2021/1015656/EBA%20Report%20on%20ESG%20risks%20management%20and%20supervision.pdf. Accessed 25 May 2024

EBA (2022) Final Report, Final draft implementing technical standards on prudential disclosures on ESG risks in accordance with Article 449a CRR. 24 January 2022. EBA/ITS/2022/01. https://www.eba.europa.eu/sites/default/files/document_library/Publications/Draft%20Technical%20Standards/2022/1026171/EBA%20draft%20ITS%20on%20Pillar%203%20disclosures%20on%20ESG%20risks.pdf. Accessed 28 May 2024

EBA (2023) EBA report on the role of environmental and social risks in the prudential framework. 12 October 2023. EBA/REP/2023/34. https://www.eba.europa.eu/sites/default/files/document_library/Publications/Reports/2023/1062711/Report%20on%20the%20role%20of%20environmental%20and%20social%20risks%20in%20the%20prudential%20framework.pdf. Accessed 25 May 2024

EFRAG (2020) How to improve climate-related reporting, A summary of good practices from Europe and beyond. February 2020. http://www.efrag.org/Lab1?AspxAutoDetectCookieSupport=1. Accessed 19 Dec 2021

EIB (2016) Restoring EU competitiveness. January 2016. https://www.eib.org/attachments/efs/restoring_eu_competitiveness_en.pdf. Accessed 19 Dec 2021

EIB (2018) A guide to the statistical treatment of energy performance contracts. May 2018. https://www.eib.org/attachments/pj/guide_to_statistical_treatment_of_epcs_en.pdf. Accessed 19 Dec 2021

EIB (2023) Website on the European Investment Advisory Hub. https://eiah.eib.org/. Accessed 19 Dec 2021

EIB (2024) Website on the EFSI. https://www.eib.org/en/efsi/index.htm. Accessed 19 Dec 2021

EIOPA (2019b) Technical advice on the integration of sustainability risks and factors in Solvency II and the Insurance Distribution Directive. 30 April 2019. https://www.eiopa.europa.eu/sites/default/files/publications/advice/technical_advice_for_the_integration_of_sustainability_risks_and_factors.pdf. Accessed 19 Dec 2021

EIOPA (2019c) Opinion on Sustainability within Solvency II. 30 September 2019. EIOPA-BoS-19/241. https://www.eiopa.europa.eu/sites/default/files/publications/opinions/2019-09-30_opinionsustainabilitywithinsolvency ii.pdf. Accessed 19 Dec 2021

EIOPA (2024) 2023/2024 (Re)Assessment of the Nat Cat Standard Formula. EIOPA-BoS-24/080. 3 April 2024. https://www.eiopa.europa.eu/document/download/57d2637d-049e-4019-bb2a-9afb386b113b_en?filename=EIOPA-BoS-24-080_2023%202024%20Reassessment%20exercise%20of%20the%20nat%20cat%20standard%20formula.pdf. Accessed 27 May 2024

ESMA (2019a) Final report on integrating sustainability risks and factors in the MIFID II. 3 May 2019. https://www.esma.europa.eu/file/51276/download?token=6b4Tp3Bu. Accessed 19 Dec 2021

ESMA (2019b) Final report on integrating sustainability risks and factors in the UCITS Directive and the AIFMD. 3 May 2019. https://www.esma.europa.eu/file/51275/download?token=laoFYfvk. Accessed 19 Dec 2021

ESMA (2019c) Technical advice to the European Commission on Sustainability Considerations in the credit rating market. 18 July 2019. https://www.esma.europa.eu/sites/default/files/library/esma33-9-321_technical_advice_on_sustainability_considerations_in_the_credit_rating_market.pdf. Accessed 19 Dec 2021

ESMA (2019d) Final report guidelines on disclosure requirements applicable to credit ratings. 18 July 2019. https://www.esma.europa.eu/sites/default/files/library/esma33-9-320_final_report_guidelines_on_disclosure_requirements_applicable_to_credit_rating_agencies.pdf. Accessed 19 Dec 2021

ESMA (2019e) Report on undue short-term pressure on corporations from the financial sector. 18 December 2019. https://www.esma.europa.eu/sites/default/files/library/esma30-22-762_report_on_undue_short-term_pressure_on_corporations_from_the_financial_sector.pdf. Accessed 19 Dec 2021

ESMA (2020) Joint Consultation Paper concerning ESG disclosures, Draft regulatory technical standards with regard to the content, methodologies and presentation of disclosures pursuant to Article 2a, Article 4(6) and (7), Article 8(3), Article 9(5), Article 10(2) and Article 11(4) of Regulation (EU) 2019/2088. 23 April 2020. JC 2020 16. https://www.esma.europa.eu/sites/default/files/jc_2020_16_-_joint_consultation_paper_on_esg_disclosures.pdf. Accessed 19 Dec 2021

ESMA (2021) Final Report on draft Regulatory, Technical Standards with regard to the content, methodologies and presentation of disclosures pursuant to Article 2a(3), Article 4(6) and (7), Article 8(3), Article 9(5), Article 10(2) and Article 11(4) of Regulation (EU) 2019/2088. 2 February 2021. https://www.esma.europa.eu/sites/default/files/library/jc_2021_03_joint_esas_final_report_on_rts_under_sfdr.pdf. Accessed 25 May 2024

ESMA (2023) Guidelines on certain aspects of the MiFID II suitability requirements. 3 April 2023. https://www.esma.europa.eu/sites/default/files/2023-04/ESMA35-43-3172_Guidelines_on_certain_aspects_of_the_MiFID_II_suitability_requirements.pdf. Accessed 25 May 2024

ESMA (2024) Consultation Paper, Proposed Revisions to Commission Delegated Regulation (EU) 447/2012 and Annex I of CRA Regulation. 2 April 2024. https://www.esma.europa.eu/sites/default/files/2024-04/ESMA84-2037069784-2112_Consultation_Paper_on_Changes_to_Delegated_Reg_447-2012_and_Annex_I_of_CRAR.pdf. Accessed 26 May 2024

European Commission (2016a) Communication from the Commission to the European Parliament, the Council, the European Central Bank, the European Economic and Social Committee, the Committee of the Regions and the European Investment Bank, Strengthening European Investments for jobs and growth: Towards a second phase of the European Fund for Strategic Investments and a new European External Investment Plan. 15 September 2016. COM/2016/0581 final. https://eur-lex.europa.eu/legal-content/EN/TXT/PDF/?uri=CELEX:52016DC0581&from=EN. Accessed 19 Dec 2021

European Commission (2016b) Commission decision on the creation of a High-Level Expert Group on Sustainable Finance in the context of the Capital Markets Union. 28 October 2016. C(2016) 6912 final. https://ec.europa.eu/transparency/regdoc/index.cfm?fuseaction=list&n=10&adv=0&coteId=&year=2016&number=6912&dateFrom=&dateTo=&serviceId=&documentType=&title=&titleLanguage=&titleSearch=EXACT&sortBy=NUMBER&sortOrder=DESC. Accessed 19 Dec 2021

European Commission (2017a) Communication from the Commission to the European Parliament, the Council, the European Economic and Social Committee and the Committee of the Regions on the Mid-Term Review of the Capital Markets Union Action Plan. 8 June 2017. COM(2017) 292 final. https://ec.europa.eu/transparency/regdoc/rep/1/2017/EN/COM-2017-292-F1-EN-MAIN-PART-1.PDF. Accessed 19 Dec 2021

European Commission (2017b) Communication from the Commission, Guidelines on non-financial reporting (methodology for reporting non-financial information) [2017] OJ C 215/1. https://eur-lex.europa.eu/legal-content/EN/TXT/PDF/?uri=CELEX:52017XC0705(01)&from=EN. Accessed 19 Dec 2021

European Commission (2017d) Public consultation on institutional investors and asset managers' duties regarding sustainability. 13 November 2017. https://ec.europa.eu/info/consultations/finance-2017-investors-duties-sustainability_en. Accessed 19 Dec 2021

European Commission (2018a) Communication from the Commission, Action Plan: Financing Sustainable Growth. 8 March 2018. COM(2018) 97 final. https://eur-lex.europa.eu/legal-content/EN/TXT/PDF/?uri=CELEX:52018DC0097&from=EN. Accessed 19 Dec 2021

European Commission (2018b) Commission Draft Delegated Regulation (EU) .../... amending Regulation (EU) 2017/565 supplementing Directive 2014/65/EU of the European Parliament and of the Council as regards organisational requirements and operating conditions for investment firms and defined terms for the purposes of that Directive. 24 May 2018. Ares(2018) 2681500. https://eur-lex.europa.eu/legal-content/NL/ALL/?uri=PI_COM:Ares(2018)2681500. Accessed 19 Dec 2021

European Commission (2018c) Proposal for a regulation amending Regulation (EU) 2016/1011 on low carbon benchmarks and positive carbon impact benchmarks. 24 May 2018. https://ec. europa.eu/info/law/better-regulation/initiatives/ares-2017-5524115_en#pe-2018-3335. Accessed 19 Dec 2021

European Commission (2018d) Commission Draft Delegated Regulation amending Delegated Regulation (EU) 2017/2359 with regard to environmental, social and governance preferences in the distribution of insurance-based investment products. 24 May 2018. Ares(2018)2681527. https://ec.europa.eu/info/law/better-regulation/initiatives/ares-2017-5524115_en#isc-201 8-03038. Accessed 19 Dec 2021

European Commission (2018e) Proposal for a Regulation of the European Parliament and of the Council on the establishment of a framework to facilitate sustainable investment. 24 May 2018. COM(2018) 353 final. https://ec.europa.eu/transparency/regdoc/rep/1/2018/EN/COM-2018-3 53-F1-EN-MAIN-PART-1.PDF. Accessed 19 Dec 2021

European Commission (2019a) Communication from the Commission to the European Parliament, the Council, the European Economic and Social Committee and the Committee of the Regions, United in delivering the Energy Union and Climate Action – Setting the foundations for a successful clean energy transition. 18 June 2019. COM(2019) 285 final. https://ec.europa.eu/ transparency/regdoc/rep/1/2019/EN/COM-2019-285-F1-EN-MAIN-PART-1.PDF. Accessed 19 Dec 2021

European Commission (2019b) Communication from the Commission, Guidelines on non-financial reporting: Supplement on reporting climate-related information [2019] OJ C 209/1. https://eur-lex.europa.eu/legal-content/EN/TXT/PDF/?uri=CELEX:	52019XC0620(01)&from=EN. Accessed 19 Dec 2021

European Commission (2019c) Communication on The European Green Deal: COM(2019) 640 final, Communication from the Commission to the European Parliament, the European Council, the Council, the European Economic and Social Committee and the Committee of the Regions, The European Green Deal. 11 December 2019. https://ec.europa.eu/info/sites/info/ files/european-green-deal-communication_en.pdf. Accessed 19 Dec 2021

European Commission (2019d) Annex to the Communication from the Commission to the European Parliament, the European Council, the Council, the European Economic and Social Committee and the Committee of the Regions, The European Green Deal, Annex, Roadmap and key actions. 11 December 2019. COM(2019) 640 final. https://ec.europa.eu/info/sites/info/files/ european-green-deal-communication-annex-roadmap_en.pdf. Accessed 19 Dec 2021

European Commission (2019e) Website on the Just Transition Fund. https://ec.europa.eu/info/ strategy/priorities-2019-2024/european-green-deal/actions-being-taken-eu/just-transition-mech anism/just-transition-funding-sources_en. Accessed 19 Dec 2021

European Commission (2020a) The European Green Deal Investment Plan and Just Transition Mechanism. 14 January 2020. https://ec.europa.eu/info/publications/200114-european-green-deal-investment-plan_en. Accessed 19 Dec 2021

European Commission (2020c) Consultation on the Renewed Sustainable Finance Strategy. 8 April 2020. https://ec.europa.eu/info/sites/info/files/business_economy_euro/banking_and_finance/ documents/2020-sustainable-finance-strategy-consultation-document_en.pdf.	Accessed 19 Dec 2021

European Commission (2020f) Targeted consultation on the establishment of an EU Green Bond Standard. 12 June 2020. https://ec.europa.eu/eusurvey/runner/eu-green-bond-standard-2020? surveylanguage=en. Accessed 19 Dec 2021

European Commission (2020g) Commission, Inception Impact Assessment, Establishment of an EU Green Bond Standard. 12 June 2020. https://ec.europa.eu/info/law/better-regulation/have-your-say/initiatives/12447-EU-Standard-for-Green-Bond-. Accessed 19 Dec 2021

European Commission (2020h) Proposal for a Regulation of the European Parliament and of the Council establishing the Just Transition Fund. 14 January 2020. COM(2020) 22 final. https://ec.europa.eu/info/law/better-regulation/have-your-say/initiatives/12113-Fast-track-interservice-consultation-on-the-SEIP-including-a-JTM-and-the-JTF-. Accessed 19 Dec 2021

European Commission (2020i) Website on the Platform on Sustainable Finance. https://ec.europa.eu/info/business-economy-euro/banking-and-finance/sustainable-finance/overview-sustainable-finance/platform-sustainable-finance_en. Accessed 19 Dec 2021

European Commission (2021) Communication from the Commission to the European Parliament, the Council, the European Economic and Social Committee and the Committee of the Regions, Strategy for Financing the Transition to a Sustainable Economy. 6 July 2021. COM/2021/390 final. https://eur-lex.europa.eu/legal-content/EN/TXT/?uri=CELEX:52021DC0390. Accessed 26 May 2024

European Commission (2024) Website on energy performance contracts. https://ec.europa.eu/energy/content/energy-performance-contracting_en?redir=1. Accessed 19 Dec 2021

European Council (2015) Website on the European investment Plan. https://www.consilium.europa.eu/en/policies/investment-plan/. Accessed 19 Dec 2021

European Council (2019) Proposal for a Regulation of the European Parliament and of the Council on the establishment of a framework to facilitate sustainable investment, approval of the final compromise text. 17 December 2019. COM (2018) 353 final. https://data.consilium.europa.eu/doc/document/ST-14970-2019-ADD-1/en/pdf. Accessed 19 Dec 2021

European Council (2023) Press Release. 'Fit for 55': Council adopts key pieces of legislation delivering on 2030 climate targets. 25 April 2023. https://www.consilium.europa.eu/en/press/press-releases/2023/04/25/fit-for-55-council-adopts-key-pieces-of-legislation-delivering-on-2030-climate-targets/. Accessed 27 May 2024

European Parliament (2019) Legislative resolution on the proposal for a regulation of the European Parliament and of the Council on establishing a framework to facilitate sustainable investment. 28 March 2019. 2018/0178 (COD). https://oeil.secure.europarl.europa.eu/oeil/popups/printsummary.pdf?id=1580252&l=en&t=E. Accessed 19 Dec 2021

European Parliament (2020) Proposal for a Regulation of the European Parliament and of the Council establishing the framework for achieving climate neutrality and amending Regulation (EU) 2018/1999 (European Climate Law). 4 March 2020. COM (2020) 80 final. https://eur-lex.europa.eu/legal-content/EN/TXT/PDF/?uri=CELEX:52020PC0080&from=EN. Accessed 19 Dec 2021

Eurostat (2017) Eurostat Guidance Note, The Recording of Energy Performance Contracts in Government Accounts. 19 September 2017. https://ec.europa.eu/eurostat/documents/1015035/7959867/Eurostat-Guidance-Note-Recording-Energy-Perform-Contracts-Gov-Accounts.pdf/. Accessed 19 Dec 2021

GRI (2024) Global Reporting Initiative Standards, cf. https://www.globalreporting.org/how-to-use-the-gri-standards/gri-standards-english-language/. Accessed 19 Dec 2021

HLEG (2017) High-Level Expert Group on Sustainable Finance interim report to advice on developing a comprehensive EU strategy on sustainable finance. 12 July 2017. https://ec.europa.eu/info/sites/info/files/170713-sustainable-finance-report_en.pdf. Accessed 19 Dec 2021

HLEG (2018a) Final report of the High-Level Expert Group on Sustainable Finance. 31 January 2018. https://ec.europa.eu/info/publications/180131-sustainable-finance-report_en. Accessed 19 Dec 2021

HLEG (2018c) Informal Supplementary Document on Green Bonds. 31 January 2018. https://ec.europa.eu/info/publications/180131-sustainable-finance-report_en. Accessed 19 Dec 2021

IASB (2024) International Financial Reporting Standards, https://www.ifrs.org/issued-standards/. Accessed 19 Dec 2021

ICMA (2018) Green bond principles, voluntary process guidelines for issuing green bonds. 14 June 2018. https://www.icmagroup.org/assets/documents/Regulatory/Green-Bonds/June-2018/Green-Bond-Principles%2D%2D-June-2018-140618-WEB.pdf. Accessed 19 Dec 2021

ICMA (2020) Social bond principles, voluntary process guidelines for issuing social bonds. 9 June 2020. https://www.icmagroup.org/assets/documents/Regulatory/Green-Bonds/June-2020/Social-Bond-PrinciplesJune-2020-090620.pdf. Accessed 26 May 2024

ICMA (2023) Social bond principles, voluntary process guidelines for issuing social bonds. 22 June 2023. https://www.icmagroup.org/assets/documents/Sustainable-finance/2023-updates/Social-Bond-Principles-SBP-June-2023-220623.pdf. Accessed 26 May 2024

ILO (2017) Tripartite declaration of principles concerning multinational enterprises and social policy (MNE Declaration). 5th edn. March 2017. https://www.ilo.org/wcmsp5/groups/public/%2D%2D-ed_emp/%2D%2D-emp_ent/%2D%2D-multi/documents/publication/wcms_0943 86.pdf. Accessed 19 Dec 2021

ILO (2022) Tripartite declaration of principles concerning multinational enterprises and social policy (MNE Declaration). 6th edn. 2022. https://www.ilo.org/publications/tripartite-declaration-principles-concerning-multinational-enterprises-and-3. Accessed 26 May 2024

IOSCO (2013) Principles for Financial Benchmarks Final Report. July 2013. FR07/13. https://www.iosco.org/library/pubdocs/pdf/IOSCOPD415.pdf. Accessed 19 Dec 2021

ISO (2017) Guidance on social responsibility. 2017. 26000:2010. https://www.iso.org/standard/42 546.htm. Accessed 19 Dec 2021

JRC (2019a) EU Ecolabel criteria for Financial Products, Preliminary Report, First draft. 15 March 2019. https://susproc.jrc.ec.europa.eu/Financial_products/docs/20190315%20PR%201.0%20 EU%20Ecolabel%20Financial%20Products_Final%20consultation.pdf. Accessed 19 Dec 2021

JRC (2019b) Development of EU Ecolabel criteria for Retail Financial Products, (Draft) Technical Report v1.0, Draft criteria proposal for the product scope and ecological criteria 15 March 2019. https://susproc.jrc.ec.europa.eu/Financial_products/docs/20190315%20TR%201.0%20EU%20 EL%20Financial%20Products_Final%20consultation.pdf. Accessed 19 Dec 2021

JRC (2019c) Development of EU Ecolabel criteria for Retail Financial Products, Technical Report 2.0, Draft proposal for the product scope and criteria. 20 December 2019. https://susproc.jrc.ec. europa.eu/Financial_products/docs/20191220_EU_Ecolabel_FP_Draft_Technical_Report_2-0. pdf. Accessed 19 Dec 2021

JRC (2020) Development of EU Ecolabel criteria for Retail Financial Products, Technical Report 3.0, Draft proposal for the product scope and criteria, October 2020. https://susproc.jrc.ec. europa.eu/product-bureau/sites/default/files/2020-10/Draft%20Technical%20Report%203% 20-%20Retail%20financial%20products.pdf. Accessed 19 Dec 2021

Ministry of Finance of the Slovak Republic (2014) Website on energy performance contracts. https://www.mfsr.sk/en/finance/public-private-partnership-ppp/energy-performance-contracts/. Accessed 19 Dec 2021

NGFS (2019a) First comprehensive report, A call for action – Climate change as a source of financial risk. 17 April 2019. https://www.ngfs.net/en/first-comprehensive-report-call-action. Accessed 19 Dec 2021

NGFS (2019b) First comprehensive report A call for action – Climate change as a source of financial risk, Technical Supplement. 23 July 2019. https://www.ngfs.net/en/technical-supplement-first-ngfs-comprehensive-report. Accessed 19 Dec 2021

NGFS (2019c) Technical document, A sustainable and responsible investment guide for central banks' portfolio management. 17 October 2019. https://www.ngfs.net/sites/default/files/medias/documents/ngfs-a-sustainable-and-responsible-investment-guide.pdf. Accessed 19 Dec 2021

Observatoire de la finance durable (2024) Website. https://observatoiredelafinancedurable.com/en/. Accessed 19 Dec 2021

OECD (2011) Guidelines for Multinational Enterprises. http://www.oecd.org/daf/inv/mne/4 8004323.pdf. Accessed 19 Dec 2021

TCFD (2017) Final Report, Recommendations of the Task Force on Climate-related Financial Disclosures. 15 June 2017. https://www.fsb-tcfd.org/wp-content/uploads/2017/06/FINAL-201 7-TCFD-Report-11052018.pdf. Accessed 19 Dec 2021

TEG (2019a) Report on Climate-related Disclosures. 10 January 2019. https://ec.europa.eu/info/sites/info/files/business_economy_ euro/banking_and_finance/documents/190110-sustainable-finance-teg-report-climate-related-disclosures_en.pdf. Accessed 19 Dec 2021

TEG (2019b) Report on EU Green Bond Standard. 18 June 2019. https://ec.europa.eu/info/sites/info/files/business_economy_ euro/banking_and_finance/documents/190618-sustainable-finance-teg-report-green-bond-standard_en.pdf. Accessed 19 Dec 2021

TEG (2019c) Taxonomy Technical Report. 18 June 2019. https://ec.europa.eu/info/sites/info/files/business_economy_ euro/banking_and_finance/documents/190618-sustainable-finance-teg-report-taxonomy_en.pdf. Accessed 19 Dec 2021

TEG (2019d) Final Report on Climate Benchmarks and Benchmarks' ESG Disclosures. 30 September 2019. https://ec.europa.eu/info/sites/info/files/business_economy_euro/banking_and_finance/documents/190930-sustainable-finance-teg-final-report-climate-benchmarks-and-disclosures_en.pdf. Accessed 19 Dec 2021

Two Degrees Investing Initiative (2017) Two degrees investing initiative report, Non-financial message in a bottle, 2017, A contribution to the EC High-Level Expert Group on Sustainable Finance. https://2degrees-investing.org/wp-content/uploads/2017/10/Retail-savings-report.pdf. Accessed 19 Dec 2021

UN PAGE (2018) International Investment Agreements and Sustainable Development: Safeguarding Policy Space and Mobilizing Investment for a Green Economy. https://www.greengrowthknowledge.org/sites/default/files/downloads/resource/international_investment_agreements_sustainable_development_1.pdf. Accessed 8 May 2024

United Nations (2011) UN Guiding Principles on Business and Human Rights, Implementing the United Nations Protect, Respect and Remedy Framework, 2011, https://www.ohchr.org/Documents/Publications/GuidingPrinciplesBusinessHR_EN.pdf. Accessed 19 December 2021

Chapter 3
Legality of Current and Prospective EU Sustainable Finance Measures under GATS

Following this overview of EU Sustainable Finance regulation, the question arises of how this regulation is to be assessed under the EU's bilateral and multilateral obligations.

In the realm of trade in financial services, the EU is bound by several multilateral agreements, especially GATS and the General Agreement on Tariffs and Trade (*GATT*).[1] Both were drafted in the context of the 1994 revision of the GATT 1947,[2] as part of the Marrakesh Agreement founding the WTO.[3] As a signatory to the Marrakesh Agreement and as a WTO Member, the EU is bound by these agreements. With a view to the EU's domestic legislation affecting trade, obligations (*disciplines*) and rights (*policy space*) derive from them.

GATT as a matter of denomination is only applicable to tariffs and trade in physical goods. The provision of financial services does not, at least immediately, concern the vending and purchase of physical goods and is not subject to tariff regulation. Trade in goods and trade in services are inherently different. This is particularly evident in trade in financial services, where a service may commonly be provided over an extended period, whereas trade in goods is usually understood as a single transaction.[4] Hence, GATT does not apply to the Sustainable Finance measures described in Chap. 2.[5]

GATS, in contrast, is the core WTO agreement on trade in services. Under GATS, each WTO Member makes concessions, so-called *commitments*. Each WTO

---

[1]General Agreement on Tariffs and Trade 1994, Marrakesh Agreement Establishing the World Trade Organization, Annex 1A. 15 April 1994. U.N.T.S. 1867 (1994).

[2]General Agreement on Tariffs and Trade. 30 October 1947. U.N.T.S. 55 (1950).

[3]Marrakesh Agreement establishing the World Trade Organization. 15 April 1994. U.N.T.S. 1867 (1994); General Agreement on Tariffs and Trade. 30 October 1947. U.N.T.S. 55 (1950).

[4]Trachtman (1996), p. 46.

[5]However, several aspects and interpretative opinions found in jurisprudence under GATT may be applicable to financial services under GATS.

© The Author(s), under exclusive license to Springer Nature Switzerland AG 2024
S. N. Pauls, *EU Sustainable Finance and International Trade Law*, EYIEL Monographs - Studies in European and International Economic Law 37, https://doi.org/10.1007/978-3-031-73853-1_3

Member publishes a Schedule of Specific Commitments outlining its commitments in market access, national treatment, and additional commitments. Pursuant to Art. XX(1) GATS, the substantive GATS provisions apply only to sectors inscribed therein.

The EU made commitments *inter alia* in the financial services sector, effectively obliging itself to abide by the substantive disciplines set by GATS. The EU's commitments are specified in the May 2019 EU Schedule of Specific Commitments.[6] It was originally published in the aftermath of the Uruguay Round in April 1994 as the EC Schedule of Specific Commitments.[7] These commitments comprise the sub-sectors *Insurance and Insurance-Related Services*[8] and *Banking and Other Financial Services (excluding insurance).*[9]

GATS uses four *modes* to categorize the way a service is supplied. GATS applies if the supply of a service through one of these modes is affected by domestic legislation (usually referred to as a *measure*[10]). First, a service may be supplied *"from the territory of one [WTO] Member into the territory of any other [WTO] Member"* (Mode 1 or *cross-border trade*). This mode applies when a financial service, such as fiduciary or advisory services or the provision of benchmarks or credit ratings, is provided outside the EU to customers inside the EU. Second, GATS covers services supplied *"in the territory of one [WTO] Member to the service consumer of any other [WTO] Member"* (Mode 2 or *consumption abroad*). Such consumption abroad is conceivable with regard to EU citizens receiving a financial service, like advisory or fiduciary services, a loan, or other baking services in a country outside the EU. Third, a service may be provided *"by a service supplier of one [WTO] Member, through commercial presence in the territory of any other [WTO] Member"* (Mode 3 or *commercial presence*). This usually encompasses cases of international corporate banks and financial institutions headquartered outside the EU and providing financial services through commercial presence in the EU. Fourth, a service can be provided *"by a service supplier of one [WTO] Member, through presence of natural persons of a [WTO] Member in the territory of any other [WTO] Member"* (Mode 4 or *presence of natural persons*). Such cases are conceivable with a view to cross-border in-person financial advisory and fiduciary services.

The necessity of defining modes of supply under GATS challenges the assessment of the cross-border supply of financial services. In contrast to cross-border trade in goods under the GATT, financial services by nature do not physically cross borders. Likewise, a complex international financial system results in cross-border

---

[6]European Union, Schedule of Specific Commitments. 7 May 2019. GATS/SC/157.

[7]European Communities and their Member States, Schedule of Specific Commitments. 15 April 1994. GATS/SC/31.

[8]European Union, Schedule of Specific Commitments. 7 May 2019. GATS/SC/157, pp. 118 et seqq., 142 et seqq.

[9]European Union, Schedule of Specific Commitments. 7 May 2019. GATS/SC/157, pp. 127 et seqq., 149 et seqq.

[10]Cf. Sect. 1.2.

supply of services being the rule rather than the exception. Hence, the long-standing discussion under GATS about the point at which a service *crosses* the border is intensified in financial services.

For EU Sustainable Finance measures to conflict with the EU's commitments under GATS, financial services regulated by EU Sustainable Finance instruments would need to meet the GATS definition of financial services. To this end, Sect. 3.1 examines the scope of the definitions of *financial services* and *financial service suppliers* used in EU Sustainable Finance and the equivalent scope of the respective terms under GATS.

Following this, Sect. 3.2 assesses the consistency of the existing EU Sustainable Finance measures, described in the previous chapter, with GATS. Section 3.3 extends this analysis to three types of potential prospective EU Sustainable Finance measures concerning the GATS disciplines:

> compulsory sustainability labeling requirements for financial services and products,
> additional amendments to the fiduciary, advisory, and product governance duties,
> sustainability-related border measures.

3.1 Scope of Application of GATS

When considering EU Sustainable Finance measures under GATS, the initial point is to determine whether the legislation concerned falls into the scope of application of GATS. As a multilateral agreement, GATS is limited to the regulatory fields enumerated therein. EU Sustainable Finance, in turn, is a comparatively vague concept. It may, first, encompass financial services not covered by GATS. Second, it primarily aims to regulate financial services within the EU, not necessarily the cross-border trade in such services.

Therefore, as precondition for analyzing the interrelation between Sustainable Finance and international trade in financial services, the common ground between GATS and EU Sustainable Finance must be identified. This refers to their respective scope—regarding *financial services* and *financial service suppliers*.

First and foremost, EU Sustainable Finance intends to, and indeed does, address virtually all regulatory fields of financial regulation in the EU. It thus has a very broad scope of application. However, the addressees of the current EU Sustainable Finance measures are nearly exclusively on the supply side, rather than on the demand or retail client side.[11] Therefore, current Sustainable Finance measures, although lacking a clear definition, address financial service suppliers in the broad sense—whether such service consists of the provision of loans, financial instruments, bonds, advice, fiduciary services, benchmarks, or credit ratings.

---

[11] This is with few exceptions such as shareholder rights.

GATS applies to all measures affecting trade in services and service suppliers. Its *prima facie* scope covers all fields of services regulation and thus also those EU Sustainable Finance measures regulating financial services.

In addition to the substantive GATS provisions, the GATS Annex on Financial Services sets out further provisions on trade in financial services. It therefore complements the more general GATS disciplines and sets out financial services-related exceptions. Para. 5 GATS Annex on Financial Services defines a financial service as "*any service of a financial nature offered by a financial service supplier of a [WTO] Member.*"[12] It thus needs to be assessed which parts of EU prudential regulation in general and which EU Sustainable Finance measures in particular are covered by this definition and the subsequently enumerated examples. However, this definition of a "*financial service*" under the GATS Annex on Financial Services does not exactly correspond to the respective terms used in EU prudential regulation.

For this comparison to the terms in use under GATS, five categories in EU prudential regulation can be identified, which may fall under the GATS definition of financial services. In general terms, EU prudential regulation refers to the offer of "*investment services*", "*ancillary services*", "*financial instruments*", and "*retail financial products*" and the entity-level term of "*financial institution*".[13] Each of these terms is used by one or more of the EU Sustainable Finance measures described in Chap. 2 and may constitute a financial service under the GATS Annex on Financial Services.

First, investment services and activities according to Annex I Section A MiFID II[14] comprise *inter alia* the "*[r]eception and transmission of orders in relation to one or more financial instruments*", "*[d]ealing on own account*", "*[p]ortfolio management*", and "*[i]nvestment advice*". EU Sustainable Finance measures falling under this definition are the fiduciary and advisory services governed by the provisions described in Sect. 2.1.8. These measures also constitute "*[a]dvisory, inter-mediation and other auxiliary financial services*" under para. 5(a)(xvi) GATS Annex on Financial Services. They are therefore financial services under GATS.

Second, ancillary services pursuant to Annex I Section B MiFID II encompass *inter alia* the "*[s]afekeeping and administration of financial instruments for the*

---

[12] Para. 5 GATS Annex on Financial Services continues to define more precisely that "*[f]inancial services include all insurance and insurance-related services, and all banking and other financial services (excluding insurance). [. . .].*" This equals the regulatory split in EU financial regulation between the regulation of insurance providers and financial service suppliers, cf. Trachtman (1996), p. 49.

[13] Cf. Annex I Directive 2014/65/EU of the European Parliament and of the Council of 15 May 2014 on markets in financial instruments and amending Directive 2002/92/EC and Directive 2011/61/EU [2014] OJ L 173/349; EU prudential regulation further addresses "*data reporting services*" pursuant to Annex I Section D Directive 2014/65/EU of the European Parliament and of the Council of 15 May 2014 on markets in financial instruments and amending Directive 2002/92/EC and Directive 2011/61/EU [2014] OJ L 173/349, which will be neglected hereinafter.

[14] Directive 2014/65/EU of the European Parliament and of the Council of 15 May 2014 on markets in financial instruments and amending Directive 2002/92/EC and Directive 2011/61/EU [2014] OJ L 173/349.

account of clients", *"Investment research and financial analysis"* and underwriting services. Although such ancillary services are indirectly affected by EU Sustainable Finance measures, they are not explicitly addressed by them. Therefore, these ancillary services are not of high relevance to this assessment. In any case, they would constitute financial services under para. 5(a)(xvi) GATS Annex on Financial Services.

Third, financial instruments according to Annex I Section C MiFID II include *inter alia "[t]ransferable securities"*, *"[m]oney-market instruments"*, units in UCITS, *"derivative contracts"* and *"emission allowances"*. Such financial instruments are addressed for instance through the MiFID II DelReg[15] as an EU Sustainable Finance measure as described in Sect. 2.1.6. The trading with them thus constitutes a financial service under para. 5(a)(x) GATS Annex on Financial Services. The provision of benchmarks and credit ratings such financial instruments refer to is auxiliary financial services under para. 5(a)(xvi) GATS Annex on Financial Services. EU Sustainable Finance measures regulating sustainability in such benchmarks and credit ratings thus address financial services under GATS.[16]

Fourth, the term of financial products is used in relation to certain retail financial instruments and set out in the PRIIPs Regulation[17] already mentioned above (2.1.2, 2.1.6). Packaged retail investment products (*PRIPs*) according to Art. 4(1) PRIIPs Regulation are defined *inter alia* as investments *"where, regardless of the legal form of the investment, the amount repayable to the retail investor is subject to fluctuations because of exposure to reference values or to the performance of one or more assets which are not directly purchased by the retail investor"*. This term is used for instance by the EU Ecolabel for financial products (2.1.2), which will likely refer to the PRIIPs Regulation for defining its scope of application, and by the proposed PRIIPs DelReg (2.1.6).[18] These EU Sustainable Finance measures also fall under the definition of trading of *derivative products* or *exchange rate and interest rate instruments* in para. 5(a)(x)(C) and (D) GATS Annex on Financial Services. They, therefore, constitute *financial services* under GATS.

---

[15] Commission Delegated Regulation (EU) 2017/565 of 25 April 2016 supplementing Directive 2014/65/EU of the European Parliament and of the Council as regards organisational requirements and operating conditions for investment firms and defined terms for the purposes of that Directive, C/2016/2398 [2016] OJ L 87/1.

[16] Cf. Sects. 2.1.4 and 2.1.5.

[17] Regulation (EU) No 1286/2014 of the European Parliament and of the Council of 26 November 2014 on key information documents for packaged retail and insurance-based investment products (PRIIPs) [2014] OJ L 352/1.

[18] Cf. Art. 8(3)(c)(ii) Regulation (EU) No 1286/2014; Commission Delegated Regulation (EU) 2017/653 of 8 March 2017 supplementing Regulation (EU) No 1286/2014 of the European Parliament and of the Council on key information documents for packaged retail and insurance-based investment products (PRIIPs) by laying down regulatory technical standards with regard to the presentation, content, review and revision of key information documents and the conditions for fulfilling the requirement to provide such documents [2017] OJ L 100/1.

In Art. 2(12) Sustainability Disclosures Regulation, constituting an EU Sustainable Finance measure,[19] offers a broader definition of *financial products* encompassing *inter alia* managed portfolios, alternative investment funds, UCITS, and PEPPs. The management of such portfolios or funds is a financial service according to para. 5(a)(xiii) GATS Annex on Financial Services.

Finally, the entity-level definitions of a credit institution and an investment firm. A credit institution according to Art. 4(1)(1) CRR[20] is *"an undertaking the business of which is to take deposits or other repayable funds from the public and to grant credits for its own account"*. EU Sustainable Finance measures addressing credit institutions are the proposed capital requirements described in Sect. 2.1.7. Thereby, the CRR definition closely resembles the example for a financial service given in para. 5(a)(v) GATS Annex on Financial Services stating *"[a]cceptance of deposits and other repayable funds from the public"*. Such financial institutions thus regularly conduct financial services under GATS.

The closely connected term of an investment firm has been defined in Art. 4(22) IFR[21] with reference to Art. 4(1)(1) MiFID I as *"any legal person whose regular occupation or business is the provision of one or more investment services"*. As this definition is based on investment services under Annex I Section A MiFID II, all entities conducting such investment services as described above do *prima facie* fall under the IFR and IFD[22] framework. The transparency and capital requirements provisions and proposals described above (2.1.6, 2.1.7) are thus made in relation to financial services under GATS.

Furthermore, the issuance of EU Green Bonds, as regulated by the EU GBS,[23] constitutes a *"[p]articipation in issues of all kinds of securities"* according to para. 5 (a)(xi) GATS Annex on Financial Services. It is thus a financial service under GATS. Therefore, service suppliers under the EU Sustainable Finance measures are to be considered service suppliers under Art. XXVIII(b) and (g) GATS and under para. 5(b) GATS Annex on Financial Services, too.

Para. 5(a) GATS Annex on Financial Services further covers *direct insurance* and *reinsurance* under *insurance and insurance-related services*. Although sustainable investments do play a significant role in the insurance sector, Sustainable Finance as a regulatory concept did so far only develop in some insurance-specific regulations, as described above (2.1). Therefore, despite for instance the PEPP Regulation having

---

[19] Cf. Sect. 2.1.6.

[20] Regulation (EU) No 575/2013 of the European Parliament and of the Council of 26 June 2013 on prudential requirements for credit institutions and investment firms and amending Regulation (EU) No 648/2012 [2013] OJ L 176/1.

[21] Regulation (EU) 2019/2033 of the European Parliament and of the Council of 27 November 2019 on the prudential requirements of investment firms and amending Regulations (EU) No 1093/2010, (EU) No 575/2013, (EU) No 600/2014 and (EU) No 806/2014 [2019] OJ L 314/1.

[22] Directive (EU) 2019/2034 of the European Parliament and of the Council of 27 November 2019 on the prudential supervision of investment firms and amending Directives 2002/87/EC, 2009/65/EC, 2011/61/EU, 2013/36/EU, 2014/59/EU and 2014/65/EU [2019] OJ L 314/64.

[23] Cf. Sect. 2.1.3.

been the first EU regulation, which introduced a significantly more detailed definition of ESG factors than previous EU legislation,[24] as stated above, the focus will not be put on insurance-related regulation but rather, on prudential regulation of financial service suppliers.[25]

Adding to these substantive requirements set out in the GATS Annex on Financial Services, the mode of supply of the respective financial service must fall within the scope of GATS. This will be assessed in the introduction to the subsequent Sect. 3.2.

Under the GATS regulatory framework, there are several other potentially applicable agreements related to the provision of financial services, which could also affect the scope of application. Apart from the substantive articles of the GATS and the GATS Annex on Financial Services, under the auspices of the Marrakesh Agreement, the Understanding on Commitments in Financial Services was agreed.[26] The Understanding on Commitments in Financial Services constitutes a voluntary multilateral, unenforceable declaration of intent that exceeds the obligations outlined in the GATS. A particularly relevant discipline concerning Sustainable Finance measures is no. B.10 Understanding on Commitments in Financial Services, which governs regulatory barriers to trade in financial services and will be discussed in Sect. 3.2.1.2. The Understanding on Commitments in Financial Services, too, will be described in more detail therein. As part of the Marrakesh Agreement, the Understanding on Commitments in Financial Services relies on the definitions set in the GATS Annex on Financial Services.[27]

Furthermore, the commitments and applicable schedules submitted by the EU are not only of high relevance to the understanding of the consistency of Sustainable Finance measures under GATS but also with a view to the scope of application of the GATS disciplines themselves. However, as they do not contain a definition of financial services, they will be assessed in more detail in Sect. 3.2.1.

Hence, it can be concluded that the financial instruments, investment services *et cetera* regulated by EU Sustainable Finance measures do fall under the GATS definition of financial services. Therefore, given an applicable mode of supply of

---

[24] Cf. Chap. 2; Bueren (2019), p. 851.

[25] Further, another observation can be made in relation to the scope of application of GATS. Subsidies are governed by Art. XV GATS and thus constitute an integral part of its regulatory regime. As the position in one of the substantive articles of GATS already indicates, rules on subsidies are applicable to all areas of trade and not restricted to financial services as described in the GATS Annex on Financial Services. In terms of financial services, subsidies pursuant to Art. XV GATS could be understood to encompass the fiscal instruments described in Sect. 2.2, in particular with regard to targeted funding. However, as described above, focus will be laid on prudential instruments aiming at rechanneling private capital.

[26] Understanding on Commitments in Financial Services, Marrakesh Agreement Establishing the World Trade Organization. 15 April 1994.

[27] The definitions made in para. D Understanding on Commitments in Financial Services are merely defining the newly introduced terms of the Understanding on Commitments in Financial Services such as *non-resident supplier of financial services, commercial presence* or *new financial service.*

the respective financial service, EU Sustainable Finance measures may be assessed under the GATS substantive disciplines.[28]

3.2 Legality of Current EU Sustainable Finance under GATS

The EU Sustainable Finance measures described in Chap. 2 span over virtually all parts of EU financial and prudential legislation.[29] This is to be attributed to the long-term purpose of Sustainable Finance—to rechannel private capital into sustainable investment alternatives. This is exemplified in the Commission's 2017 CMU Mid-Term Review,[30] which states that a "*deep re-engineering of the financial system*" was necessary to achieve this rechanneling and thus ultimately ensure that the EU's 2030 Agenda commitments are met.[31]

Such *deep re-engineering* of the financial system certainly may come at the cost of financial market participants' commercial freedoms. For instance, the regulator could *de facto* and indirectly steer a potential client's investment decision-making process by introducing labeling and reporting requirements, or fiduciary duties. These requirements might be perceived as additional regulatory obstacles to the provision of financial services or the distribution of financial products.

Due to the cross-border nature of the EU financial market and its interconnection with the global financial system, such *deep re-engineering* also affects third country financial service suppliers. This is intensified, because the EU is arguably the most advanced international actor when it comes not only to the drafting of sustainable development regulation but also specifically in respect of Sustainable Finance measures. Adding to this, Sustainable Finance, like sustainable development itself, is a highly internationalized policy field—owing to the global nature of the problems it addresses.

This chapter conducts an examination based on the GATS disciplines. Section 3.2.1 assesses the market access disciplines in respect of Sustainable Finance measures that are *de jure* or *de facto* limiting market access to foreign financial service suppliers. Section 3.2.2 examines possible breaches of the most-favored-nation (*MFN*) standard and national treatment (*NT*) standard. Both GATS disciplines are jointly assessed and referred to as *nondiscrimination standards*. Section 3.2.3

---

[28] For this reason, hereinafter financial services and financial products or financial instruments will be used interchangeably for the purposes of the assessment of EU Sustainable Finance measures under international trade law.

[29] Adding to this, financial services regulation contains references and interdependencies into multiple other fields of the economy, cf. Trachtman (1996), p. 53; Cf. Sect. 5.4.

[30] European Commission (2017).

[31] European Commission (2017), p. 9; Cf. Chap. 2.

assesses the GATS disciplines on domestic regulation, and is followed by Sect. 3.2.4 on the GATS general exceptions clauses.

To better comprehend the interconnection between Sustainable Finance and the WTO jurisprudence on sustainable development, the interrelation between Sustainable Finance and sustainable development must be closely examined. As stated in Sect. 1.2, Sustainable Finance in this book will be understood as an implementation tool to the sustainable development objectives and goals adopted at the international level since the Rio Declaration in 1992.[32] Furthermore, Recital 1 Marrakesh Agreement saw sustainable development as one of the newly founded WTO's core objectives.[33] This is further exemplified and intensified by the 2030 Agenda's SDG 17 (*Revitalize the global partnership for sustainable development*) explicitly addressing finance and trade.

3.2.1 Market Access

In order to offer and provide a service in a country different from its home state, a service supplier needs to access the host state's market. For WTO Members it can, however, be tempting to limit or hinder market access to their territory as to not expose their domestic service suppliers to foreign competition. Market access provisions in WTO law aim to prevent such undue limitation to market access. Certain EU Sustainable Finance measures *de jure* or *de facto* limiting market access for third-country services or services suppliers, may fall short of these provisions. Thereby, an EU Sustainable Finance measure inconsistent with WTO market access requirements would violate the EU's external commitments as a WTO Member.

Therefore, this chapter will conduct a test of consistency under Art. XVI (1) GATS of the Sustainable Finance measures reviewed in Chap. 2. Art. XVI (1) GATS outlines the WTO Member's market access obligations with a view to trade in service. It requires that concerning such market access "*each [WTO] Member shall accord services and service suppliers of any other [WTO] Member treatment no less favourable than that provided for under the terms, limitations and conditions agreed and specified in its Schedule.*"

Thus the market access obligations outlined in Art. XVI GATS are subject to the commitments specified in the May 2019 EU Schedule of Specific Commitments, originally published in the aftermath of the Uruguay Round in April 1994 as the EC Schedule of Specific Commitments.[34] The financial services sector is one of the

---

[32] Report of the United Nations Conference on Environment and Development, Rio de Janeiro, 3 to 14 June 1992, Annex I, Rio Declaration on Environment and Development. 12 August 1992.

[33] Hush (2018), p. 100.

[34] European Union, Schedule of Specific Commitments. 7 May 2019. GATS/SC/157; European Communities and their Member States, Schedule of Specific Commitments. 15 April 1994. GATS/SC/31.

sectors in which the EU undertook such specific commitments on market access under Art. XVI(1) GATS in the EU Schedule of Specific Commitments.[35] These comprise namely of the sub-sectors *Insurance and Insurance-Related Services*[36] and *Banking and Other Financial Services (excluding insurance).*[37] However, the EU Schedule on Specific Commitments does contain various limitations on market access as well, either described in the financial services section or the *"all sectors"* section.

The commitments in market access described above are further subject to the requirements set forth in Art. XVI(2) GATS (3.2.1.1) and no. B.10 Understanding on Commitments in Financial Services (3.2.1.2).

3.2.1.1 Numerical limitations: Art. XVI(2) GATS

Concerning the commitments made in the EU Schedule on Specific Commitments, Art. XVI(2) GATS requires the EU to refrain from maintaining or adopting measures that meet any of the six numerical limitations or restrictions enumerated therein.[38] Thus, the chapeau of Art. XVI(2) GATS is limited to *"sectors where market-access commitments are undertaken"* and hence to those sectors stated in the WTO Member's Schedule of Specific Commitments.[39] For trade in financial service, the EU Schedule of Specific Commitments contains such commitments.[40]

The six subparagraphs of Art. XVI(2) GATS thereby constitute an exhaustive enumeration of limitations to market access pursuant to Art. XVI(1) GATS. When interpreting them, it is not only impossible to add further limitations than those stated therein in order not to *"unduly broaden the scope of Article XVI".*[41] Also, *"any interpretation of Article XVI:2 of the GATS must give effect to each of the six subparagraphs of the provision".*[42]

The first of *"the measures which a [WTO] Member shall not maintain or adopt"* and potentially applicable to EU Sustainable Finance measures, is any measure limiting *"the number of service suppliers whether in the form of numerical quotas,*

---

[35] Cf. European Union, Schedule of Specific Commitments. 7 May 2019. GATS/SC/157, pp. 118 et seqq.

[36] European Union, Schedule of Specific Commitments. 7 May 2019. GATS/SC/157, pp. 118 et seqq., 142 et seqq.

[37] European Union, Schedule of Specific Commitments. 7 May 2019. GATS/SC/157, pp. 127 et seqq., 149 et seqq.

[38] Cf. Trachtman (1996), p. 77.

[39] Cf. WTO DSB (2005) United States – Measures Affecting the Cross-Border Supply of Gambling and Betting Services, Appellate Body report, para. 233.

[40] Cf. Sect. 3.2.1.

[41] WTO DSB (2015) Argentina – Measures Relating to Trade in Goods and Services, Panel report, para. 7.419; WTO (2020e), p. 4.

[42] WTO DSB (2015) Argentina – Measures Relating to Trade in Goods and Services, Panel report, para. 7.420; WTO (2020e), p. 4.

monopolies, exclusive service suppliers or the requirements of an economic needs test" according to Art. XVI(2)(a) GATS.[43] It is first to be stated that EU Sustainable Finance measures do not yet entail explicit limitations on the number of service suppliers in the EU. However, through the maintenance or adoption of EU Sustainable Finance measures, such as labeling provisions, the EU GBS, or sustainability-related benchmark labels, a *de facto* limitation on the number of service suppliers could take place. This could first be the case due to such labels and standards *de jure* only allowing market access to the respective market segment to financial service suppliers that meet the relevant criteria or disclosure requirements. Therefore, a limitation on the number of service suppliers occurs, which could be interpreted as a zero quota for those financial service suppliers not being able to access what is likely to be a more favorable market segment.

To assess whether such a *de facto* limitation may be deemed a numerical one, reference can be made to the Appellate Body's reasoning in *US–Gambling*. It found that the *"fact that the word 'numerical' encompasses things which 'have the characteristics of a number' suggests that limitations 'in the form of a numerical quota' would encompass limitations which, even if not in themselves a number, have the characteristics of a number."*[44] Transferred to the assessment of the EU Sustainable Finance measures described above, it can thus be reasoned that although there are no numerical limitations on the number of service suppliers, these measures constitute limitations under Art. XVI(2)(a) GATS as long as they *have the characteristics of a number.*[45]

In the case of EU Sustainable Finance measures, however, the *de facto* limitations amount to merely a qualitative limitation. They will be discussed in further detail particularly in Sects. 3.2.2.2 and 3.2.4.1. A limitation on the quality of a service, in this case, its sustainability, does not have the characteristics of a number, despite potentially being calculated based on a numerical taxonomy. This can be exemplified by the prospective EU GBS. Despite being a voluntary standard, it would include or exclude financial products from the *official* EU green bond market segment based on their respective sustainability. However, this limitation is not based on a maximum number of financial services or financial service suppliers allowed within that segment but is based on qualitative criteria. This indicates the contrast to quantitative criteria as required for the application of Art. XVI(2)(a) GATS. Thus, a numerical restriction on service suppliers is not given.

---

[43] Trachtman (1996), p. 56.

[44] WTO DSB (2005) United States – Measures Affecting the Cross-Border Supply of Gambling and Betting Services, Appellate Body report, para. 227; Cf. WTO DSB (2004a) United States – Measures Affecting the Cross-Border Supply of Gambling and Betting Services, Panel report, para. 6.331; WTO (2020e), pp. 7 et seq.

[45] WTO DSB (2005) United States – Measures Affecting the Cross-Border Supply of Gambling and Betting Services, Appellate Body report, para. 227; Cf. WTO DSB (2004a) United States – Measures Affecting the Cross-Border Supply of Gambling and Betting Services, Panel report, 10 November 2004, WT/DS285/R, para. 6.331; WTO (2020e), pp. 7 et seq.

Furthermore, it should be noted that when the Appellate Body in *US–Gasoline* determined that a measure only suffices the requirement of a *numerical limitation* if it has *"the characteristics of a number"*,[46] this determination was made regarding the application of Art. XVI(2)(a) GATS to a zero quota. As stated above, the EU Sustainable Finance measures in the form of labels or standards and the disclosure requirements for sustainability-related benchmarks, could constitute a zero quota for all noncomplying financial services and financial service suppliers. This, however, is contrasted by the fact that the Appellate Body found, disagreeing with the Panel, that a zero quota does have the characteristics of a number and thus is to be deemed *numerical*.[47] In turn, this means that a qualitative limitation, such as the application of a label or the admittance to a standard is not *numerical* and thus in any case does not fall under Art. XVI(2)(a) GATS.

Finally, the Taxonomy Regulation and its underlying regulatory technical standards, too, could be deemed a *numerical limitation* under Art. XVI(2)(a) GATS. As described above (2.1.1), the Taxonomy Regulation serves as a central source of reference for determining the sustainability of an economic activity. The subsequent legal consequences then are set out in the applicable, field-specific regulations such as the EU GBS, in the SFDR, or the Climate BMR. In itself, the Taxonomy Regulation does not define legal obligations to a financial service supplier[48] and thus rather serves as a categorization tool for other measures. This in itself can be seen as an argument against defining the Taxonomy Regulation as a *measure* under Art. XVI(2)(a) GATS.

Adding to this, the Taxonomy Regulation, while potentially using a set of numerical indicators in its technical screening criteria according to Art. 10-(3) Taxonomy Regulation, does exclusively use nonnumerical or qualitative criteria to define sustainable economic activity. Apart from the *positive list* set out in Art. 9 Taxonomy Regulation, the requirement of *no significant harm* or the so-called *black list* is not, in itself, a numerical criterion. This is also true for the Art. 18 Taxonomy Regulation criteria that the economic activity respects the ILO minimum safeguards. The taxonomy thus only provides for a partly numerical approach, depending on the exact design of the technical screening criteria. Therefore, it can be concluded that as regards the Taxonomy Regulation it does not qualify as a *measure* under Art. XVI(2)(a) GATS and neither constitutes a wholly *numerical* limitation.

---

[46] WTO DSB (2005) United States – Measures Affecting the Cross-Border Supply of Gambling and Betting Services, Appellate Body report, para. 227; Cf. WTO DSB (2004a) United States – Measures Affecting the Cross-Border Supply of Gambling and Betting Services, Panel report, 10 November 2004, WT/DS285/R, para. 6.331; WTO (2020e), pp. 7 et seq.

[47] WTO DSB (2005) United States – Measures Affecting the Cross-Border Supply of Gambling and Betting Services, Appellate Body report, para. 238; Analytical Index GATS – Article XVI (Jurisprudence), p. 8.

[48] Except for the disclosure requirements set out in Art. 5 to 8 Regulation (EU) 2020/852 as described in Sect. 2.1.6.

Arguendo, similar to the issue of a zero quota, EU Sustainable Finance measures could be understood to provide for *"exclusive service suppliers"* pursuant to Art. XVI(2)(a) GATS with a view to those financial service suppliers deemed sustainable under the Taxonomy Regulation. This could be particularly relevant given the Appellate Body's findings in *US–Gambling*, in that focus should be put on whether a measure *"in form or in effect"*[49] provides for exclusive service suppliers. Thus, EU Sustainable Finance measures would equally only need to have the effect of providing for exclusive service suppliers. However, even though the current or prospectively much stricter—as will be discussed in Sect. 3.3—EU Sustainable Finance labels and standards could lead to and thus have the *effect* of providing for an exclusive financial service supplier, the prohibition of such under Art. XVI(2)(a) GATS needs to be read in conjunction with the requirement of a numerical limitation. This lead the Appellate Body in *US–Gambling* to the conclusion that in respect of exclusive service suppliers *"the thrust of sub-paragraph (a) is not on the form of limitations, but on their numerical, or quantitative, nature."*[50] Therefore, even if a current or prospective EU Sustainable Finance measure would have the *effect* of *de facto* providing for an exclusive service supplier, its lack of being numerical leads to the conclusion that such measure would not breach this aspect of Art. XVI(2)(a) GATS.

Another question to be raised in particular in relation to Art. XVI(2)(a) GATS is how the prohibition of an economic needs test is to be interpreted with a view to the EU Sustainable Finance measures. Deriving from its explicit wording, an economic needs test only encompasses a measure of prior examination of a given service based on the economic needs or benefits of the relevant sector or geographical region. EU Sustainable Finance measures do not comprise such examination of financial services or products based on the economic needs of or the benefits to the EU financial market.

This conclusion could, however, be different if an economic needs test would encompass tests based on sustainability or ESG considerations. This would for instance apply to Sustainable Finance measures that restrict access to the EU market in cases where the relevant service or service supplier is not found to be sustainable. In favor of this understanding speaks that the main underlying objective of Sustainable Finance is fostering sustainable development. Sustainable development in turn, encompasses sustainable economic growth and in particular, a social sphere, which both may fall within the scope of an economic needs test under Art. XVI(2)(a) GATS. Plus, financial stability considerations as the second policy objective of Sustainable Finance do have an economic aspect. Thus an examination that focuses on whether a financial service contributes to financial stability under an EU Sustainable Finance measure could be deemed an economic needs test. On the other hand,

---

[49] WTO DSB (2005) United States – Measures Affecting the Cross-Border Supply of Gambling and Betting Services, Appellate Body report, para. 230; WTO (2020e), p. 7.

[50] WTO DSB (2005) United States – Measures Affecting the Cross-Border Supply of Gambling and Betting Services, Appellate Body report, para. 232; WTO (2020e), pp. 7 et seq.

the social sphere and respective economic considerations are just one sphere of sustainable development, and financial stability is just one policy objective of Sustainable Finance. Plus, ESG-related EU Sustainable Finance measures as of now focus nearly exclusively on environmental and labor rights considerations and hence do not fall in the scope of an economic needs test under Art. XVI(2) (a) GATS.

Finally, as of now, there are no sustainability tests in EU Sustainable Finance measures that correspond to an economic needs test.[51] For the feasibility of prospective EU border measures, including a CBA or sustainability screening see Sect. 3.3.3. This is also true if such market access measures are not only understood to encompass *de facto* border measures but also EU Sustainable Finance measures that closely resemble a restriction to market access on basis of sustainability considerations. An example of such a measure is the *comply or explain* provision for financial market participants in Art. 4(1)(a) and (b) and Art. 4(2) Sustainability Disclosures Regulation, requiring them to publish information on their due diligence policies based on internationally recognized standards—or an explanation of such policy's absence—towards their investment decisions' principal adverse impacts. They require a benchmark provider to disclose how the relevant benchmark contributes to ESG factors but do not prohibit the provision of a certain benchmark service if it does not contribute sufficiently to ESG factors, despite what it may claim. Thus, such requirements although potentially *de facto* hindering, are not legally prohibiting market access as required to constitute a limitation under Art. XVI(2)(a) GATS.[52]

In conclusion, the EU Sustainable Finance measures granting exclusive market (segment) access to a labeled service such as the provision of EU Green Bonds or EU PABs and EU CTBs could be seen as *de facto* limitations of the provision of the service in question to only the number of those service suppliers able meet the requirements. However, as discussed above, they do not constitute limitations on the number of service suppliers in terms of Art. XVI(2)(a) GATS. This is also true for the leveraging and blending tools under the EU's fiscal instruments described in Sect. 2.2. These measures do not constitute market access restrictions for service suppliers as they merely limit the access to EU-backed guarantees (e.g., for the supply of a financial service in developing countries) but do not in themselves constitute a limitation on the service suppliers' ability to offer such services without such guarantees.

The second of the measures a WTO Member must not adopt under Art. XVI(2) (b) GATS is limiting *"the total value of service transactions or assets in the form of numerical quotas or the requirement of an economic needs test"*. Given such limitation to the total value of financial service transactions, similar reasoning to the one adopted above with a view to Art. XVI(2)(a) GATS can be applied. Thereby,

---

[51] Regarding a potential future sustainability screening cf. Sect. 3.3.3.

[52] However, it is questionable whether such post-entry treatment of third country financial service suppliers is actually governed by the GATS market access provisions or merely the national treatment, most-favored-nation, and domestic regulation standards, cf. Trachtman (1996), p. 64.

certain EU Sustainable Finance measures discussed above can hinder market access and *de facto* limit the number of service transactions. They, however, do not *de jure* impose a numerical limitation on the value of service transactions. This is for two reasons. First, a comparison to other international treaty-based sustainability-related numerical restrictions such as the EU ETS,[53] does in itself *de facto* limit the total number of possible service transactions by a given service supplier. However, these restrictions are only applicable to unsustainable economic activity and it does not restrict based on the value of the economic activity but rather on its impact on ESG factors. Second, as argued above, the EU taxonomy provides only for the analytical basis to assess the sustainability of a certain financial service or financial service supplier. It does not, however, provide for a sufficient restriction on the provision of a certain service to be considered a numerical quota as a form of limitation pursuant to Art. XVI(1)(b) GATS. Finally, with regard to the economic needs test as a restriction on the total value of service transactions, reference is made to the above considerations in light of Art. XVI(2)(a) GATS.

The same considerations apply to the third type of measure not to be adopted pursuant to Art. XVI(2)(c) GATS. It prohibits measures limiting *"the total number of service operations or on the total quantity of service output expressed in terms of designated numerical units in the form of quotas or the requirement of an economic needs test"*. Again, similar to the considerations detailed regarding Art. XVI(2) (a) GATS, certain EU Sustainable Finance measures can *de facto* limit the total number of service operations taking place pursuant to Art. XVI(2)(c) GATS by limiting or hindering the provision of services that the relevant regulation defines as unsustainable. The two subsequent categories of Art. XVI(2) GATS measures do not encompass the current regulatory design of EU Sustainable Finance. Namely, these measures would have to constitute *"limitations on the participation of foreign capital [. . .]"* under Art. XVI(2)(f) GATS and *"limitations on the total number of natural persons that may be employed in a particular service sector [. . .]"* under Art. XVI(2)(d) GATS.

Finally, EU Sustainable Finance measures may not *"restrict or require specific types of legal entity or joint venture through which a service supplier may supply a service"* according to Art. XVI(2)(e) GATS. However, *"restrict or require"* does not mean that the measure restricts or requires an action from the entity. In other words, the Panel in *EU–Energy Package* found that such *"measures do not generally restrict legal entities from doing something, nor do they require legal entities to do something."*[54] EU Sustainable Finance in contrast requires such action from financial service suppliers but does not require a certain type of legal entity. Therefore, EU Sustainable Finance measures do not fall under Art. XVI(2) (e) GATS.

---

[53] Cf. European Parliament (2020), p. 7.

[54] WTO DSB (2018) European Union and its Member States – Certain Measures Relating to the Energy Sector, Panel report, para. 7.627, 7.632, and 7.642; Analytical Index GATS – Article XVI (Jurisprudence), p. 11.

Summing up, in respect of the EU Sustainable Finance measures described in Chap. 2, the only limitations on market access in terms of Art. XVI(2) GATS that can be deemed relevant are limitations on the number of service suppliers under Art. XVI(2)(a) GATS, limitations on the total number of service transactions pursuant to Art. XVI(2)(b) GATS, and limitations on the total number of service operations pursuant to Art. XVI(2)(c) GATS. However, as of now, the EU Sustainable Finance measures are not designed in such a way that would amount to a violation of these provisions.

3.2.1.2 Regulatory barriers: No. B.10 Understanding on Commitments in Financial Services

The financial services commitments made in the EU Schedule of Specific Commitments under Art. XVI(1) GATS are partly set following the Understanding on Commitments in Financial Services.[55] The Understanding on Commitments in Financial Services is a voluntary multilateral, unenforceable declaration of intent that exceeds the obligations set forth in the GATS.[56]

In part, the financial services commitments set out in the EU Schedule on Specific Commitments were not made under the Understanding on Commitments in Financial Services and are thus not subject to its provisions. In turn, commitments that were made in accordance with the Understanding on Commitments in Financial Services are subject to its limitations. The EU Member States undertaking commitments in the first part of the EU Schedule of Specific Commitments undertake these commitments under the Understanding on Commitments in Financial Services.[57] The EU Member States undertaking commitments in the second part of the EU Schedule of Specific Commitments, however, did not do so in accordance with the Understanding.[58] As regards market access, this particularly encompasses the requirements outlined in no. B.10 Understanding on Commitments in Financial Services, which instructs that each WTO Member "*shall endeavour to remove or to limit any significant adverse effects on financial service suppliers of any other [WTO] Member*" of the types of measures enumerated subsequently therein.[59]

---

[55]Cf. European Union, Schedule of Specific Commitments. 7 May 2019. GATS/SC/157, pp. 118 et seqq.

[56]The Understanding on Commitments in Financial Services is optional since during negotiations it became clear that it could not be included into the GATS Annex on Financial Services due to many WTO Members not being expected to follow it, cf. Trachtman (1996), p. 70.

[57]Cf. European Union, Schedule of Specific Commitments. 7 May 2019. GATS/SC/157, p. 118; Cf. European Communities and their Member States, Schedule of Specific Commitments. 15 April 1994. GATS/SC/31, p. 61.

[58]Cf. European Union, Schedule of Specific Commitments. 7 May 2019. GATS/SC/157, pp. 141 et seqq.

[59]Cf. Trachtman (1996), p. 78.

The measures set to be limited or removed according to no. B.10(a) and (b) Understanding on Commitments in Financial Services are nondiscriminatory measures, either preventing permitted *"financial service suppliers from offering in the [WTO] Member's territory"* or preventing *"the expansion of the activities of financial service suppliers into the entire territory of the [WTO] Member"*. As discussed above, EU Sustainable Finance measures that limit or hinder market access to certain market segments such as the EU green bond segment, may be deemed preventive measures. However, it is questionable whether such limitations exhibit a sufficiently restrictive impact to be considered as such under the market access disciplines of GATS and thus the Understanding on Commitments in Sustainable Finance.

More relevant, in turn, is the alternative under which no. B.10(d) Understanding on Commitments in Financial Services applies if measures *"although respecting the provisions of the [GATS], affect adversely the ability of financial service suppliers of any other [WTO] Member to operate, compete or enter the [WTO] Member's market"*. This is certainly the case with the EU Sustainable Finance labeling regulations, the EU GBS and even the Climate BMR and the transparency provisions discussed above (2.1.6). These provisions adversely affect a financial service supplier's ability to compete in the market if this supplier is found to be unsustainable.

However, the removal or limitation of *"any significant adverse effects on financial service suppliers"* in no. B.10 Understanding on Commitments in Financial Services is only an *"endeavor"* and not an enforceable obligation. Plus, these limitations are subject to the counter-exception set out at the end of no. B.10, which states that the endeavor described above is only to be pursued if it *"would not unfairly discriminate against financial service suppliers of the [WTO] Member taking such action"*. It thus anticipates any unfair repercussion on domestic financial service suppliers due to an action taken under no. B.10 Understanding on Commitments in Financial Services and therefore favoring third country competition. As *Trachtman* concludes, practically every such measure of limitation discriminates against the host state's financial service suppliers due to its very nature as a so-called *"better than national"* treatment measure.[60] Thus, the question must state under which circumstances such action constitutes unfair discrimination against the host state's financial service suppliers. *Trachtman* explains this with the concept of equivalence. If a third country financial service supplier is subject to similar costs or protection due to Sustainable Finance measures in its home state, a limitation with regard to no. B.10 Understanding on Commitments in Financial Services might not be seen as unfair discrimination by the host state against its domestic financial service suppliers.[61]

In other words, just granting national treatment to third country service suppliers is insufficient if a host state's regulations are *de facto* prohibiting market access. Thus, the host state might be required to adopt policies of *negative harmonization* to

---

[60] Trachtman (1996), p. 79.
[61] Trachtman (1996), p. 79.

ensure market access. This is an example of the better than national treatment. However, interpreting market access as a requirement for better than national treatment would implicate the discrimination of domestic financial service suppliers, thus also incentivizing the host state to lower regulatory burdens on both, domestic and foreign financial service suppliers.[62] So far, however, as discussed above, the EU Sustainable Finance measures do not *de facto* prohibit market access to a degree of restrictive impact that would trigger a need for negative harmonization.

It can thus be concluded that EU Sustainable Finance measures might constitute nondiscriminatory barriers to third country financial service suppliers under no. B.10 Understanding on Commitments in Financial Services. However, if the EU decided to unilaterally lower standards for foreign financial service suppliers, this would unfairly discriminate against its domestic financial service suppliers, unless the respective foreign suppliers are subject to equally strict Sustainable Finance measures in their respective home states.

3.2.1.3   New Financial Services: No. B.7 Understanding on Commitments in Financial Services

Finally, the provisions on new financial services set out in no. B.7 Understanding on Commitments in Financial Services could apply to EU Sustainable Finance measures addressing financial services that are new to the EU financial market. It requires that a *"[WTO] Member shall permit financial service suppliers of any other [WTO] Member established in its territory to offer in its territory any new financial service."*

The Understanding on Commitments in Financial Services does not set out a definition of new financial services. However, taking into account the wording of no. B.7 Understanding on Commitments in Financial Services such services most likely are to be found to cover services that have not yet been offered in the respective WTO Member's territory. As most sustainability-related financial services have only been introduced in recent years, EU Sustainable Finance measures covering these services and their market access have been drafted simultaneously. Plus, EU Sustainable Finance measures themselves may be understood to have introduced new financial services by creating product categories such as EU Green Bonds or other types of labels.

In addition to no. B.7 Understanding on Commitments in Financial Services also only being a provision of endeavor, these EU Sustainable Finance measures do not restrict new financial services that are found to be sustainable but encourage them in one way or another. Plus, no. B.7 Understanding on Commitments in Financial Services only states that WTO Members shall *"permit"* such services. This is the case with EU Sustainable Finance measures, which potentially have a certain *de*

---

[62]Trachtman (1996), p. 76; *Trachtman* also finds that financial service suppliers are particularly affected by differences between host state and home state regulation, cf. *ibid.*, p. 77.

facto impact on market access but do not reject permittance to such new financial services.[63] The latter argument is particularly relevant in view of new *unsustainable* financial services.

The EU Sustainable Finance measures thus do not constitute a violation of no. B.7 Understanding on Commitments in Financial Services.

3.2.2 Nondiscrimination Standards

One of the distinctive characteristics of the WTO agreements are strong nondiscrimination standards. Their intention is to prevent an undue discrimination between products and services from different WTO Members. For instance, if a WTO Member introduces a measure facilitating the supply of a service from another Member, under GATS this facilitation must be granted to all other WTO Members (*most-favored-nation treatment*). Likewise, domestic service suppliers ought not to be privileged above service suppliers of other WTO Members (*national treatment*). With the set of criteria laid down in GATS, these nondiscrimination standards aim at "*securing an overall balance of rights and obligations*"[64] in trade in services.

This chapter will assess the most-favored-nation and national treatment standards under Art. II(1) GATS and Art. XVII GATS, respectively.

The most-favored-nation standard in Art. II(1) GATS requires that "*each [WTO] Member shall accord immediately and unconditionally to services and service suppliers of any other [WTO] Member treatment no less favourable than that it accords to like services and service suppliers of any other country.*" The national treatment standard in Art. XVII GATS states that "*each [WTO] Member shall accord to services and service suppliers of any other [WTO] Member [. . .] treatment no less favourable than that it accords to its own like services and service suppliers.*" This is subject to the sectors inscribed in the WTO Member's Schedule.

Hence, both standards inhere two preconditions under which the assessment of the legality of EU Sustainable Finance measures must be conducted. First, the disadvantaged WTO Member's financial service suppliers would need to be *alike* to those of the respective comparison group.[65] Second, the treatment of financial service suppliers from the disadvantaged WTO Member would have to be less favorable than the treatment accorded to the respective comparison group.[66] For their similarities in nature, both the most-favored-nation and national treatment standards will be jointly referred to as *nondiscrimination standards*.

---

[63] Cf. Sect. 3.2.1.

[64] Recital 3 GATS; Cf. Sect. 3.2.2.1.

[65] Cf. Sect. 3.2.2.1.

[66] Cf. Sect. 3.2.2.2.

3.2.2.1   Like Services and Service Suppliers: Art. II and XVII GATS

The first requirement, which the GATS nondiscrimination standards of Art. II and Art. XVII GATS equally require, is that the services and service suppliers that are subject to a treatment potentially less favorable constitute *"like services and service suppliers"*.[67] In other words, this chapter tries to assess whether unsustainable financial services and service suppliers and their sustainable counterparts are *alike* under the most-favored-nation and national treatment standards.

The most-favored-nation standard as a core principle of GATS constitutes that concessions made by a host state favoring another WTO Member shall be granted to all other WTO Members on a multilateral basis.[68] This, as stated above, is subject to the condition that this treatment concerns like services and service suppliers.

Whether the difference in treatment between a service supplier providing sustainable financial services and its counterpart that is providing unsustainable financial services is relevant under the most-favored-nation standard, in essence, depends on the interpretation of the likeness criterion under Art. II(1) GATS.

In fact, there is extensive jurisprudence on the likeness criterion of the most-favored-nation and national treatment standards both under GATS and GATT. First and foremost, it needs to be stated that *like* does not necessarily mean that the two services or service suppliers are virtually the same but rather *"sharing a number of identical or similar characteristics or qualities"*, as indicated by the French and Spanish versions of Art. II(1) GATS.[69] The mere fact that both, sustainable and unsustainable financial services are *financial* services should not immediately lead to the conclusion that they are alike. These similarities only take into account the service's financial aspects and not the hereby critical sustainability aspects.

Adding to this, the likeness criterion in Art. II(1) GATS implies a competitive relationship between the two services or service suppliers in question.[70] This competitive relationship is analyzed by using the criteria developed in GATT jurisprudence.

The WTO jurisprudence on GATT does not immediately apply to trade in services under GATS, much less to the evaluation of Sustainable Finance measures. As described above (3.1), GATT only applies to trade in services. There are, however, two reasons why to apply GATT jurisprudence to assessments of measures under GATS. The GATT was preceded by GATT 1947.[71] As a result there is significantly more jurisprudence on GATT than on GATS. Plus, the substantive

---

[67] Cf. Sect. 3.2.2.2.

[68] Trachtman (1996), p. 98.

[69] WTO DSB (2016) Argentina – Measures Relating to Trade in Goods and Services, Appellate Body report, para. 6.21; Cf. WTO (2020b), p. 3.

[70] WTO DSB (2016) Argentina – Measures Relating to Trade in Goods and Services, Appellate Body report, para. 6.24; Cf. WTO (2020b), p. 3; Regarding the competitive relationship under Art. XVII(1) GATS, cf. WTO DSB (2012) China – Certain Measures Affecting Electronic Payment Services, Panel report, para. 7.700; Cf. WTO (2020f), p. 3.

[71] General Agreement on Tariffs and Trade. 30 October 1947. U.N.T.S. 55 (1950).

provisions of GATS—particularly those assessed in this chapter—strongly resemble those of GATT. Therefore, interpretations and arguments within GATT jurisprudence are regularly adapted to GATS.[72]

This also applies to the competitive relationship requirement of the likeness criterion in Art. II(1) GATS. Since there is a *"spectrum of degrees of 'competitiveness' or 'substitutability' of products in the marketplace"*,[73] the assessment needs essentially to be conducted on a case-by-case basis, *"taking into account the specific circumstances of the particular case."*[74]

Based on GATT trade in goods, the criteria for assessing the spectrum of competitiveness developed by the Appellate Body are namely the product's *"properties, nature, and quality"* and its *"end-uses"*.[75] This is complemented by considerations on *"consumers' tastes and habits or consumers' perceptions and behaviour in respect of the products"* and their *"tariff classification"*.[76] These criteria could be applied to trade in services. Although these criteria can be useful in determining whether a sustainable financial service is alike an unsustainable financial service, *"the intangible nature of services, their supply through four different modes, and possible differences in how trade in services is conducted and regulated"*[77] need to be considered.

The first criterion of *"properties, nature, and quality of the products"*[78] may also be applied to the assessment of trade in services under Art. II(1) GATS.[79] The sustainability of the respective service can usually be deemed one of its core properties. This is also the case when it comes to sustainable financial services. Adding to this understanding is the fact that the grade of sustainability is often a significant aspect of a service's overall quality. Therefore, financial services despite their respective sustainability would be alike under Art. II(1) GATS.

---

[72]Cf. e.g. WTO DSB (2005) United States – Measures Affecting the Cross-Border Supply of Gambling and Betting Services, Appellate Body report, para. 291; WTO DSB (2016) Argentina – Measures Relating to Trade in Goods and Services, Appellate Body report, para. 6.127; Cf. Van den Bossche and Zdouc (2017), pp. 535, 606; Cf. Sects. 3.2.2.2 and 3.2.4.1.

[73]WTO DSB (2016) Argentina – Measures Relating to Trade in Goods and Services, Appellate Body report, para. 6.25 et seq.; Cf. WTO (2020b), p. 3.

[74]WTO DSB (2016) Argentina – Measures Relating to Trade in Goods and Services, Appellate Body report, para. 6.25 et seq.; Cf. WTO (2020b), p. 3; Regarding the assessment of competitive relationship under Art. XVII(1) GATS; Cf. WTO DSB (2012) China – Certain Measures Affecting Electronic Payment Services, Panel report, para. 7.701 et seq; Cf. WTO (2020f), pp. 3 et seq.

[75]WTO DSB (2016) Argentina – Measures Relating to Trade in Goods and Services, Appellate Body report, para. 6.30; Cf. WTO (2020b), p. 4.

[76]WTO DSB (2016) Argentina – Measures Relating to Trade in Goods and Services, Appellate Body report, para. 6.30; Cf. WTO (2020b), p. 4.

[77]WTO DSB (2012) China – Certain Measures Affecting Electronic Payment Services, Panel report, para. 7.698; Cf. WTO (2020f), p. 3.

[78]WTO DSB (2016) Argentina – Measures Relating to Trade in Goods and Services, Appellate Body report, para. 6.30; Cf. WTO (2020b), p. 4.

[79]WTO DSB (2016) Argentina – Measures Relating to Trade in Goods and Services, Appellate Body report, para. 6.32; Cf. WTO (2020b), p. 4.

This assessment might, however, be different regarding the criteria of *"the end-uses of the products"*[80] and *"consumers' tastes and habits or consumers' perceptions and behaviour in respect of the products"*[81] under which the Panel in *China–Electronic Payment Services* also considered *"the evidence that the service suppliers at issue 'describe[d] their business scope in very similar terms', and that this suggested that 'these suppliers compete[d] with each other in the same business sector'."*[82] First, it needs to be stated that sustainable financial services eventually have the same end-use as unsustainable financial services. For instance, a green bond is still a bond and as such primarily an investment product. This argument may, however, not apply to sustainability ratings in which CRAs take into account exclusively sustainability criteria.[83] Hence, in this regard sustainability ratings are not *alike* traditional credit ratings based exclusively on economic criteria.

With a view to sustainable financial services under the EU Sustainable Finance measures, however, the aspect of the *same business sector* might be decisive. There are sustainable financial services under the EU Sustainable Finance measures, that do not compete with their unsustainable counterparts in the same business (sub-)sector. For example, EU Green Bonds and financial services and products falling under other labeling standards, such as benchmarks under the Climate BMR, may be understood as a separate market segment under which they are not *like* traditional bonds or benchmarks.[84]

Finally, the criterion of *"the tariff classification of the products"*,[85] although not *verbatim* applicable to trade in services, might be relevant in respect of *"the classification and description of services under, for instance, the UN Central Product Classification (UN CPC)".*[86] The UN CPC lists financial services in section seven (*Financial and related services, real estate services, and rental and leasing services*).[87] However, it does not contain a dedicated class or subclass on sustainable financial services. Congruously, sustainable and unsustainable financial services would be *alike* under Art. II(1) GATS. This deduction is also supported with a view to the Panel Report's findings in *EC–Bananas*. It can be argued that the sustainable and unsustainable financial services with a view to the classification of financial services in the UN CPC, are *"virtually the same and can only be*

---

[80]WTO DSB (2016) Argentina – Measures Relating to Trade in Goods and Services, Appellate Body report, para. 6.30; Cf. WTO (2020b), p. 4.

[81]WTO DSB (2016) Argentina – Measures Relating to Trade in Goods and Services, Appellate Body report, para. 6.30; Cf. WTO (2020b), p. 4.

[82]WTO DSB (2012) China – Certain Measures Affecting Electronic Payment Services, Panel report, para. 7.706; Cf. WTO DSB (2016) Argentina – Measures Relating to Trade in Goods and Services, Appellate Body report, para. 6.32; Cf. WTO (2020b), p. 4.

[83]Cf. Sect. 2.1.5.

[84]Cf. already on market access in Sect. 3.2.1.

[85]WTO DSB (2016) Argentina – Measures Relating to Trade in Goods and Services, Appellate Body report, para. 6.30; Cf. WTO (2020b), p. 4.

[86]United Nations (2015).

[87]United Nations (2015), pp. 114 et seqq.

distinguished by referring to the"[88] sustainability of the respective underlying economic activity. Insofar, it can thus be concluded that sustainable and unstainable financial services are alike under Art. II(1) GATS.

Finally, similar to EU Sustainable Finance measures, Art. II(1) GATS established the likeness both of service suppliers and the services themselves. As sustainable financial services under EU Sustainable Finance measures can be expected to be provided by financial market participants who simultaneously undertake unsustainable financial services, the question arises how the *likeness* of the respective service supplier relates to the *likeness* of the service it provides. On one hand, it has been argued that if services are like, the service suppliers are like, too. This is, however, only the case *"to the extent that entities provide these like services"*.[89] On the other hand, it has also been argued that this is only a presumption and *"that, in the specific circumstances of other cases, a separate inquiry into the 'likeness' of the suppliers may be called for."*[90] It further has been argued that both, the likeness of services and service suppliers interdepend and are relevant to each other.[91] Finally, the Appellate Body in *Argentina–Financial Services* concluded that *"a holistic analysis"* of services and service suppliers needs to be conducted *"in the light of its context and the object and purpose of the agreement in which the relevant provision appears."*[92]

It can be concluded that two financial service suppliers providing sustainable and unsustainable financial services, respectively, are not necessarily alike just by the fact of their services being alike. This is especially the case since the above findings on the likeness of sustainable financial services to unsustainable financial services are also based on the UN CPC. However, taking into account the objective and purpose of GATS, which according to Recital 3 GATS *inter alia* lies in *"securing an overall balance of rights and obligations, while giving due respect to national policy objectives"*, the conclusion must be drawn that if and insofar financial service suppliers are providing sustainable financial services, they are like to each other.

Likewise, the criteria for a distinction between such services or service suppliers, namely sustainability, is defined by each WTO Member. The nondiscrimination standards, in turn, are rooted in GATS, at the international level. Each WTO Member could individually define the scope of the likeness criterion under Art. II(1) GATS. This would impede a fair application of the most-favored-nation standard and annul the intended protection from discrimination. Plus, construing the likeness of such

---

[88] WTO DSB (1997a) European Communities – Regime for the Importation, Sale and Distribution of Bananas, Panel report, para. 7.322; Cf. WTO (2020b), p. 2.

[89] WTO DSB (1997a) European Communities – Regime for the Importation, Sale and Distribution of Bananas, Panel report, para. 7.322; Cf. WTO (2020b), p. 2.

[90] WTO DSB (2012) China – Certain Measures Affecting Electronic Payment Services, Panel report, para. 7.705; Cf. WTO (2020f), p. 4.

[91] WTO DSB (2016) Argentina – Measures Relating to Trade in Goods and Services, Appellate Body report, para. 6.29; Cf. WTO (2020b), p. 4.

[92] WTO DSB (2016) Argentina – Measures Relating to Trade in Goods and Services, Appellate Body report, para. 6.31; Cf. WTO (2020b), p. 4.

services and service suppliers in such a way does not endanger the WTO Member's policy space. To this end, WTO Members may invoke general exceptions like Art. XIV GATS.

This leads to the conclusion that a distinction between a financial service, that is found to be sustainable, and a financial service, that is found to be unsustainable, differs between *like services* under Art. II(1) GATS. As to the supply of these services, the respective financial service suppliers are to be deemed *alike* pursuant to Art. II(1) GATS, too. However, as shown above, the margin of interpretation is considerable and it is not assured that a Panel would adhere to the interpretation conducted above. The question that arises, however, is whether the same conclusion can be drawn from an assessment of the likeness criterion under the national treatment standard of Art. XVII(1) GATS.

First and foremost, a WTO Member is obligated to apply national treatment in all sectors it includes in its Schedule of Specific Commitments.[93] Hence, national treatment under GATS Art. XVII(1) is subject to the enumeration of sectors inscribed in the schedule and to the respective restrictions.[94] As demonstrated above (3.2.1), in the case of the EU, the EU Schedule on Specific Commitments does cover various limitations on national treatment, either described in the "*financial services*" section or the "*all sectors*" section.[95] Art. XVII(1) GATS, therefore, *prima facie* is applicable.

Concerning the assessment of the likeness criterion, the findings of the respective assessment under Art. II(1) GATS are indeed transferrable to Art. XVII(1) GATS despite the differences in wording.[96]

3.2.2.2   Treatment No Less Favorable: Art. II(1) GATS

As already stated above, the treatment of financial service suppliers from one WTO Member would have to be less favorable than the treatment accorded to the respective comparison group. Subsequently, first the Art. II(1) GATS most-favored-nation standard will be examined as regards the consistency of the EU Sustainable Finance measures, followed by the respective examination under the Art. XVII(1) GATS national treatment standard in Sect. 3.2.2.3.

Art. II(1) GATS obliges "*each [WTO] Member [to] accord immediately and unconditionally to services and service suppliers of any other [WTO] Member treatment no less favourable than that it accords to [. . .] services and service*

---

[93] Trachtman (1996), p. 56.

[94] Trachtman (1996), pp. 68 et seq.

[95] European Union, Schedule of Specific Commitments. 7 May 2019. GATS/SC/157, pp. 127 et seqq., 149 et seqq.

[96] WTO DSB (2016) Argentina – Measures Relating to Trade in Goods and Services, Appellate Body report, para. 6.22, 6.24; Cf. WTO DSB (2018) European Union and its Member States – Certain Measures Relating to the Energy Sector, Panel report, para. 7.419; Cf. WTO (2020b), pp. 3 et seq.

suppliers of any other country." Thus, the most-favored-nation standard aims to prevent discrimination between service suppliers of different third countries. For the EU Sustainable Finance measures to breach the most-favored-nation standard, it is thus necessary that one or more of the instruments described in Chap. 2 constitute a measure, which under Art. II(1) GATS can be considered not only treatment *not favorable* but indeed *less favorable* when compared to a hypothetical service supplier of a third country.

With regard to the structure of the assessment of the less favorable treatment criterion under Art. II(1) GATS, the Appellate Body in *Argentina–Financial Services* referred to the respective assessment under GATT and found that it "*'must begin with careful scrutiny of the measure, including consideration of the design, structure, and expected operation of the measure at issue'*".[97] This first step has already been undertaken in the assessment of the design and regulatory structure of EU Sustainable Finance measures in Chap. 2. The subsequent question to be discussed is whether formal discrimination occurs through the implementation of these regulations. In general, as has already been mentioned in the previous Sect. 3.2.1 on market access, EU Sustainable Finance measures in multiple provisions indeed can have a detrimental effect on the provision of a financial service if the sustainability requirements set out therein are not met. Under Art. II(1) GATS, however, an additional comparison between service suppliers of differing origin needs to be undertaken through which the detrimental effect emerges.

The EU Sustainable Finance measures described in Chap. 2 do not explicitly enumerate specific WTO Members whom to favor or disadvantage for instance based on their respective Sustainable Finance legislation. It further does not discriminate based on nationality or origin of the financial service or product. A *de jure* discrimination is therefore evidently not on hand.

There are, however, several references to a service supplier's origin in EU Sustainable Finance measures, for instance concerning third country benchmarks as discussed in Sect. 2.1.4. However, such provisions do not restrict the supply of a service *per se* but require such benchmark providers to have an EU legal entity acting as a representative. Plus, references to a service supplier's origin are not an issue specific to Sustainable Finance but are found throughout existing EU prudential legislation. Besides, regulation governing financial services and not specifically discriminating based on the origin of the service supplier is difficult to assess regarding the GATS nondiscrimination standards.[98] Such is the case with EU Sustainable Finance measures, as shown above. Therefore, the EU Sustainable Finance measures may pose a *de facto* discrimination against other WTO Members'

---

[97] WTO DSB (2016) Argentina – Measures Relating to Trade in Goods and Services, Appellate Body report, para. 6.127; Cf. WTO (2020b), p. 11; However, the Appellate Body, EC-Bananas III, "*rejected the application of the so-called 'aims-and-effects' test which had been previously adopted by several GATT panels*", cf. WTO (2020b), p. 11; Therein: WTO DSB (1997b) European Communities – Regime for the Importation, Sale and Distribution of Bananas, Appellate Body report, para. 241.

[98] Trachtman (1996), p. 46.

financial service suppliers. To this end, *de facto* discrimination would need to be admissible under Art. II(1) GATS.

Art. XVII(3) GATS defines for the national treatment standard, *"that 'treatment shall be considered to be less favourable if it modifies the conditions of competition in favour of services or service suppliers of [one WTO] Member compared to like services or service suppliers of any other [WTO] Member.*"[99] The national treatment standard therefore not only covers *de jure* discrimination but also *de facto* discrimination. The question arises whether such broad interpretation would also apply to the most-favored-nation standard despite the wording in Art. II(1) GATS lacking a clause similar to Art. XVII(1) GATS.

In rejection of the EC's argument, the Panel in *EC–Bananas III* ruled that concerning treatment no less favorable, Art. II(1) and Art. XVII(1) GATS have the same ordinary meaning under Art.31(1) Vienna Convention on the Law of Treaties.[100] This was despite the *"absence of similar language in Article II".*[101] It added that a different interpretation would frustrate *"the objective behind Article II which is to prohibit discrimination between like services and service suppliers of other [WTO] Members".*[102] The Appellate Body in *EC–Bananas III* did not incorporate the wording of Art. XVII(3) GATS into Art. II(1) GATS but also concluded *"that 'treatment no less favourable' in Article II:1 of the GATS should be interpreted to include de facto, as well as de jure, discrimination."*[103] In *Argentina–Financial Services*, however, the Appellate Body referred to these earlier findings and concluded that the definition of Art. XVII(3) GATS *"should also be pertinent context to the meaning of the same term in Article II:1."*[104] Therefore, the application of the Art. II(1) GATS requirement of *treatment no less favorable* will be guided by the Art. XVII(3) GATS definition of a *modification of the conditions of competition* comparatively in favor of one WTO Member's services or service suppliers.[105]

---

[99] WTO DSB (2016) Argentina – Measures Relating to Trade in Goods and Services, Appellate Body report, para. 6.22; Panel Report, Cf. China-Electronic Payment Services, para. 7.687; Cf. WTO (2020f), pp. 3, 5.

[100] Vienna Convention on the Law of Treaties. 23 May 1969. U.N.T.S. 1155 (1969).

[101] WTO DSB (1997a) European Communities – Regime for the Importation, Sale and Distribution of Bananas, Panel report, para. 7.301; Cf. WTO (2020b), p. 7.

[102] WTO DSB (1997a) European Communities – Regime for the Importation, Sale and Distribution of Bananas, Panel report, para. 7.303; Cf. WTO (2020b), p. 7.

[103] WTO DSB (1997b) European Communities – Regime for the Importation, Sale and Distribution of Bananas, Appellate Body report, paras. 233–234; Cf. WTO (2020b), p. 8.

[104] WTO DSB (2016) Argentina – Measures Relating to Trade in Goods and Services, Appellate Body report, para. 6.105; Cf. WTO DSB (2018) European Union and its Member States – Certain Measures Relating to the Energy Sector, Panel report, para. 7.489; Cf. WTO DSB (1997b) European Communities – Regime for the Importation, Sale and Distribution of Bananas, Appellate Body report, para. 233; Cf. WTO (2020b), pp. 8 et seq.

[105] Cf. WTO DSB (2016) Argentina – Measures Relating to Trade in Goods and Services, Appellate Body report, para. 6.106; Cf. WTO DSB (2018) European Union and its Member States – Certain Measures Relating to the Energy Sector, Panel report, para. 7.489; WTO DSB (1997b) European

Thereby the question is whether an EU Sustainable Finance measure that differentiates between two service suppliers, which may happen to originate in two different WTO Members, based on sustainability, constitutes a treatment less favorable. EU Sustainable Finance measures link legal consequences to the identification or nonidentification of a financial service (or its underlying economic activity, respectively) or financial service supplier as *sustainable, green,* or taxonomy compliant. This would constitute a treatment less favorable if it would modify *"the conditions of competition in favour of services or service suppliers of [one WTO] Member compared to like services or service suppliers of any other [WTO] Member."*[106] Referring to the Appellate Body's findings under the GATT national treatment standard, the Panel in *China–Publications and Audiovisual Products* stated that the *"examination of whether a measure involves 'less favourable treatment' [. . .] must be grounded in close scrutiny of the 'fundamental thrust and effect of the measure itself'".*[107]

The prudential instruments of EU Sustainable Finance legislation as described in Sect. 2.1 aim at rechanneling private capital towards more sustainable investments. As described in Chap. 2, this has been clearly stated by the Commission in its Sustainable Finance Action Plan[108] and is undertaken in furtherance of large-scale sustainability and climate action targets such as the SDGs and the Paris Agreement.[109] Therefore, the *fundamental thrust and effect* of prudential EU Sustainable Finance measures can be described as altering market participant's decision-making processes in favor of more sustainable investments. This is intended to be primarily achieved by increased transparency via the introduction of legislation on *inter alia* disclosure, reporting, labeling, and benchmarks as described in Sect. 2.1. Insofar, as these requirements apply to all market (segment) participants, they do not alter the conditions of competition by themselves, for instance through hindering market access.[110] Certain EU Sustainable Finance measures, however, may through their transparency requirements create such economic pressure onto market participants that they *de facto* modify the conditions of competition.

One such example is the differentiation between comparative labels and endorsement labels.[111] Whereas comparative labels are usually mandatory, offer information to customers, and thus enable them to do a comparison, voluntary endorsement

---

Communities – Regime for the Importation, Sale and Distribution of Bananas, Appellate Body report, paras. 240–248; Cf. WTO (2020b), p. 9.

[106] WTO DSB (2016) Argentina – Measures Relating to Trade in Goods and Services, Appellate Body report, para. 6.22; Cf. WTO (2020b), p. 3.

[107] WTO DSB (2009a) Panel Report, China – Measures Affecting Trading Rights and Distribution Services for Certain Publications and Audiovisual Entertainment Products, Panel report, para. 7.1131; Cf. WTO (2020f), p. 5.

[108] European Commission (2018).

[109] European Commission (2018), p. 2.

[110] Cf. Sect. 3.2.1.

[111] WTO (2009), pp. 121 et seq.

labels usually represent that the service meets a certain non-mandatory standard.[112] Mandatory comparative labels, therefore, can modify the conditions of competition to a higher degree than voluntary endorsement labels. Comparative labels for financial services are thus more likely to constitute a treatment less favorable under Art. II(1) GATS than endorsement labels. The EU Ecolabel for financial products will likely take the form of an endorsement label and thus be voluntary and only stating that a certain sustainability threshold is met. The same can be said about the more advanced EU GBS and the already implemented Climate BMR's EU PAB and EU CTB, which all have in common that an authoritative label is granted if a certain sustainability threshold is met.

It could further be argued that through the introduction of transparency requirements, financial market participants are at increased risk of potential claims for damages if they do not meet the stated sustainability thresholds. The same applies to fiduciary duties as described in Sect. 2.1.8. However, such damages to investments are difficult to prove. For instance, the ESG-based information requirements laid down in the PEPP Regulation do not establish an indemnity claim against the offeror unless damage is proven.[113] Yet, obstacles are significant in order to prove such damage caused by the lack of provision of ESG-related information.[114]

Apart from these observations on the effect of EU Sustainable Finance measures, the fact that there is a potential modification of competition in detriment of a service or service supplier of a different WTO Member is sufficient and there is no requirement for the assessment of for instance the underlying policy objective.[115] Consequentially, these are instead only relevant at the level of GATS exceptions as discussed in Sect. 3.2.4.[116]

Adding to the requirement that there needs to be a treatment less favorable in comparison to that of another financial service supplier, this comparison needs to be conducted between financial service suppliers of different WTO Members and thus an actual discrimination based on origin needs to be on hand. In other words, the Appellate Body in *Argentina–Financial Services* in reference to footnote 10 to Art. XVII(1) GATS (and thus also relevant to the interpretation of Art. II(1) GATS) found that as "*its text indicates, the 'inherent competitive disadvantages' referred to in footnote 10 result from the 'foreign character' of the relevant services or service*

---

[112] WTO (2009), pp. 121 et seq.

[113] Bueren (2019), p. 853; Cf. Art. 31(2) Regulation (EU) 2019/1238 of the European Parliament and of the Council of 20 June 2019 on a pan-European Personal Pension Product (PEPP) [2019] OJ L 198/1.

[114] Bueren (2019), p. 853.

[115] WTO DSB (2016) Argentina – Measures Relating to Trade in Goods and Services, Appellate Body report, para. 6.106, 6.109 et seqq.; Cf. WTO DSB (2018) European Union and its Member States – Certain Measures Relating to the Energy Sector, Panel report, para. 7.489; WTO DSB (1997b) European Communities – Regime for the Importation, Sale and Distribution of Bananas, Appellate Body report, paras. 240–248; Cf. WTO (2020b), pp. 9 et seq.

[116] WTO DSB (2016) Argentina – Measures Relating to Trade in Goods and Services, Appellate Body report, para. 6.115; Cf. WTO (2020b), p. 10.

suppliers, rather than from the contested measure adopted by the importing [WTO] Member."[117]

As stated above, however, EU Sustainable Finance measures establish legal consequences based on sustainability and not, neither *de jure* nor with a sufficiently restrictive impact *de facto*, based on origin. There can, however, exist adverse effects on third country financial service suppliers in the EU in the form of an accumulation of host state and home state Sustainable Finance measures.[118] However, first, such adverse effects are not sufficiently consistent and severe to count as a *de facto* discrimination against financial service suppliers of one WTO Member. Plus, with the possibility of recognition and prudential equivalence decisions, there is sufficient regulatory policy space for the EU to counter such effects.

It can thus be concluded that the EU Sustainable Finance measures described in Chap. 2 although having the potential for modifying the conditions of competition between different financial services and service suppliers, do not modify either *de jure* or *de facto* these conditions between financial services or financial service suppliers of two different states. Therefore, EU Sustainable Finance measures do not constitute a treatment less favorable according to Art. II(1) GATS.

3.2.2.3 Treatment No Less Favorable: Art. XVII(1) GATS

The national treatment standard laid down in Art. XVII(1) GATS requires each WTO Member to treat "*services and service suppliers of any other [WTO] Member [. . .] no less favourable*" in comparison to "*its own like services and service suppliers.*" Thereby, the respective WTO Member may satisfy this national treatment standard by treating the other WTO Member's similar services or service suppliers formally identically, and different services or service suppliers formally differently compared to its own services and service suppliers, respectively.[119]

Similar to the considerations made under the criterion of "*like services and service suppliers*", the question arises whether the findings made with regard to the most-favored-nation standard in the previous chapter also apply to the national treatment standard under Art. XVII(1) GATS.

As described in the previous chapter, national treatment requires that a treatment no less favorable ought to be applied to third country entities in comparison to that applied to domestic entities.[120] Thereby, the national treatment standard equals the wording of Art. II(1) GATS insofar as it, too, refers to "*treatment no less favorable*".

---

[117] WTO DSB (2016) Argentina – Measures Relating to Trade in Goods and Services, Appellate Body report, para. 6.103 et seq.; Cf. WTO (2020f), pp. 5 et seq.; Cf. WTO DSB (2018) European Union and its Member States – Certain Measures Relating to the Energy Sector, Panel report, para. 7.744.

[118] Trachtman (1996), p. 46.

[119] Cf. Art. XVII(2) GATS.

[120] Trachtman (1996), pp. 63, 68.

In this regard, the jurisprudence taken into consideration above on treatment no less favorable also applies to Art. XVII(1) GATS.[121] This is particularly because congruously to the argumentation thereunder due to the similarity in wording between Art. XVII(1) and Art. II(1) GATS there is no need for a differing interpretation of a *"treatment no less favorable"* under the most-favored-nation and national treatment standards. Plus, most of the jurisprudence discussed above evolved around the Art. XVII(3) GATS interpretation of treatment no less favorable and then projected onto Art. II(1) GATS. Therefore, also the deductions made from the interpretation and jurisprudence on *"treatment no less favorable"* under the most-favored-nation standard must remain the same under the national treatment standard. This applies both to the findings on *de jure* and *de facto* discrimination by EU Sustainable Finance measures. Therefore, EU Sustainable Finance measures do not constitute a violation of Art. XVII(1) GATS.

3.2.3   Domestic Regulation

Barriers to the trade in services can either consist of measures which restrict market access (3.2.1) or discriminate against foreign service suppliers under the most-favored-nation and national treatment standards (3.2.2). However, trade in services regularly faces impediments by domestic regulation, called *other barriers to trade in services*.[122] GATS presents a set of rules concerning domestic regulation posing a barrier to trade in services. These rules can be subdivided into provisions generally applicable to all WTO Members (e.g., Art. III and Art. VI(2)(a) GATS) and provisions only applicable given a respective market access commitment (e.g. Art. VI (1) GATS).[123]

Such disciplines only applicable given a respective market access commitment encompass the reasonable, objective, and impartial application of a measure (Art. VI (1) GATS) and the prohibition of licensing and qualification requirements and technical standards impairing the relevant commitment made (Art. VI(5) GATS). The same applies to government procurement (Art. XIII(1) GATS), the maintenance of judicial, arbitral, and administrative tribunals (Art. VI(2)(a) GATS), and the possibility of recognizing education, licenses, or certifications (Art. VII(1) GATS) and WTO Members' obligations in relation to monopoly suppliers (Art. VIII (1) GATS).[124]

However, only certain GATS disciplines governing domestic regulation can be objectively and reasonably deemed relevant to the assessment of the EU Sustainable Finance measures described in Chap. 2. The two most relevant GATS domestic

---

[121] Cf. WTO (2020f), p. 6.

[122] Cf. e.g. Van den Bossche and Zdouc (2017), p. 534.

[123] Van den Bossche and Zdouc (2017), p. 534.

[124] Van den Bossche and Zdouc (2017), pp. 534–540.

regulation disciplines are subsequently illustrated and constitute the basis on which a test of consistency will be conducted. These standards are set out in Art. VI(1) GATS regarding reasonable, objective, and impartial administration of the measures (3.2.3.1) and in Art. VI(5) GATS regarding the licensing and qualification requirements and technical standards (3.2.3.2).

3.2.3.1 Reasonable, Objective, and Impartial Administration: Art. VI(1) GATS

One of the domestic regulation standards relevant for the assessment of EU Sustainable Finance under GATS is Art. VI(1) GATS. It requires that in *"sectors where specific commitments are undertaken, each [WTO] Member shall ensure that all measures of general application affecting trade in services are administered in a reasonable, objective and impartial manner."* Art. VI(1) GATS requirements thus are subject to certain conditions. First, the discipline set out in Art. VI(1) GATS only applies to WTO Members who made respective sectoral commitments. As highlighted in Sect. 3.2.1 the EU made far-reaching commitments in the EU Schedule of Specific Commitments towards the financial services sector and thus meets this criterion. Second, Art. VI(1) GATS obligates WTO Members to ensure that the administration of the measures affecting trade in services is conducted in a reasonable, objective, and impartial manner. Thus, the requirements set out in Art. VI(1) GATS have a scope of application limited to the specific legal instrument being challenged under the discipline. Art. VI(1) GATS does not apply to the legal instruments themselves but to the manner these measures are administered.[125]

On the one hand, there is no evidence that might suggest that parts of EU Sustainable Finance measures are administered structurally or commonly in an unreasonable, subjective, and partial manner. On the other hand, Sustainable Finance as a nascent overall guiding principle in EU financial regulation is a rather recent concept (Chap. 2) with many regulations and directives still being developed or not yet being in force and thus lacking the required implementation.

The requirements of Art. VI(1) GATS, however, are also applicable to legal instruments regulating the *"application or implementation of that instrument"* as ruled by the Appellate Body in *EC–Selected Customs Matters* regarding Art. X(3) (a) GATT.[126] Thereby, Art. VI(1) GATS is substantially based on Art. X(3) (a) GATT, which requires each WTO Member to *"administer in a uniform, impartial*

---

[125] Van den Bossche and Zdouc (2017), p. 505; Therein: WTO DSB (1997b) European Communities – Regime for the Importation, Sale and Distribution of Bananas, Appellate Body report, para. 200.

[126] Van den Bossche and Zdouc (2017), p. 505; Therein: WTO DSB (2006) European Communities – Selected Customs Matters, Appellate Body report, para. 200; WTO DSB (2000c) Argentina – Measures Affecting the Export of Bovine Hides and the Import of Finished Leather, Panel report, para. 11.71 et seq.

and reasonable manner all its laws, regulations, decisions and rulings [...]".[127] EU Sustainable Finance is substantially comprised of level 2 and level 3 measures (jointly the *delegated acts*) such as delegated regulations, delegated directives, regulatory technical standards (*RTS*), and implementation guidelines. These delegated acts constitute such legal instruments that regulate the application of the relevant Sustainable Finance measures laid down in the referring primary legislation according to the above understanding of Art. VI(1) GATS.[128]

Again, it is to be noted that a significant portion of the delegated acts on the major advances in EU Sustainable Finance legislation throughout recent years is still in the drafting process, particularly level 3 guidance is still to be elaborated for instance by the ESAs. Those delegated acts already in place, however, whether already applicable or about to enter applicability, will subsequently be assessed under the Art. VI (1) GATS domestic regulation standard.

Similarly, given the requirements of Art. X(3)(a) GATT, the Panel in US–COOL found "*that the act of providing guidance on the meaning of specific requirements of a measure amounts to an act of administering such measure within the meaning of Article X:3(a)*".[129] Transferred to the issue at hand with Art. VI(1) GATS, this means that EU delegated acts that provide guidance on the interpretation of the Sustainable Finance measure in question, are to be deemed part of the administration of measures in the meaning thereof, too. Aforementioned delegated acts that define certain terms and thus provide guidance on their understanding are thus to be deemed an administration of the relevant Sustainable Finance measures to which they refer.

A question, however, with much more profound implications, is whether the Taxonomy Regulation can be subsumed under the Panel's understanding in *US–COOL* of the administration of measures under the domestic regulation standard. The Taxonomy Regulation, as described in further detail in Sect. 2.1.1, sets out universal criteria on the definition of sustainability in respect of financial services and financial service suppliers.[130] It thus serves as the central tool of interpretation and categorization as to all financial market regulations that differentiate based on sustainability. The assessment of sustainability within the Taxonomy Regulation is conducted under Art. 4 Taxonomy Regulation. Thereby, the core definition of the Taxonomy Regulation is the definition of the term "*environmentally sustainable investment*".[131]

Thus, the central aim of the Taxonomy Regulation is guiding the interpretation and thereby offering a set of categorization instruments to subsequent Sustainable Finance measures. One such (future) regulation is the JRC's recommendation for an

---

[127] Van den Bossche and Zdouc (2017), pp. 535, 505.

[128] In case of a regulatory process governed by the *Lamfalussy* procedure, this would translate into level 2 and level 3 measures and guidance.

[129] WTO DSB (2011) United States – Certain country of origin labelling (COOL) requirements, Panel reports, para. 7.833; Cf. Van den Bossche and Zdouc (2017), p. 505.

[130] Cf. Art. 1(1) Regulation (EU) 2020/852.

[131] Cf. Art. 2(1) Regulation (EU) 2020/852.

EU Ecolabel for financial products, which refers to the Taxonomy Regulation for the definition of a green economic activity.[132] Therefore, the Taxonomy Regulation can be understood as *"providing guidance on the meaning of specific requirements of a measure"* according to the Panel in *US–COOL*.[133] Thus, the Taxonomy Regulation's interpretation and categorization standards can be subsumed under the term 'administration' in Art. VI(1) GATS.

Similarly, the introduction of the EU GBS could be subsumed under the definition of an administration of a measure according to Art. VI(1) GATS. This is because the EU GBS, too, provides a measure for categorizing financial action, in this case, bonds. This categorization can be used subsequently to introduce measures aimed at e.g. incentivizing the use or regulating the marketing and distribution of such green bonds. In this case, the differentiation between the legislative act counting as the measure under Art VI(1) GATS and the implementing regulation is not as clear as with the Taxonomy Regulation. It can be argued that the subsequent regulation on EU green bonds referring to the EU GBS would be considered implementing regulation. However, the Panel in *US–COOL* concluded that an implementing act was an *"act of providing guidance on the meaning of specific requirements"*.[134] The interpretation under Art. VI(1) GATS thus must be conducted to the effect that the EU GBS itself is the *implementing regulation* and that any subsequent legislation based on the EU GBS is the *measure* itself. This interpretation is supported by the fact that the TEG's proposal, as already detailed above (2.1.3), defines an EU Green Bond using three criteria: The confirmation of the alignment with the EU GBS, the use of proceeds for green projects, and the verification of the alignment with the EU GBS by an accredited verifier.[135] The central *green projects* component of this assessment in turn refers to the Taxonomy Regulation and its technical screening criteria.

Thus, the Taxonomy Regulation and the EU GBS alongside those EU Sustainable Finance delegated acts that already materialized will subsequently be assessed under the requirement of Art. VI(1) GATS. The material requirement of Art. VI(1) GATS domestic regulation standard is the reasonable, objective, and impartial administration of measures. This requirement consists of three *"legally independent"* criteria, as ruled by the Panel in *Thailand–Cigarettes (Philippines)* in relation to Art. X(3) (a) GATT.[136] These criteria, however, are cumulative requirements in the way that

---

[132] Cf. JRC (2019), p. 32.

[133] WTO DSB (2011) United States – Certain country of origin labelling (COOL) requirements, Panel reports, para. 7.833; Cf. Van den Bossche and Zdouc (2017), p. 505.

[134] WTO DSB (2011) United States – Certain country of origin labelling (COOL) requirements, Panel reports, para. 7.833.

[135] TEG (2019b), pp. 26, 57.

[136] WTO DSB (2010) Thailand – Customs and Fiscal Measures on Cigarettes from the Philippines, Panel report, para. 7.866 et seq.; Van den Bossche and Zdouc (2017), p. 505.

all three criteria must be met.[137] Therefore, subsequently, all three criteria will be assessed separately.

The first material requirement of the Art. VI(1) GATS domestic regulation standard applicable to the EU Sustainable Finance delegated acts the Taxonomy Regulation, and the EU GBS is the requirement of a reasonable administration of measures. Implementation of a measure in a *reasonable* manner according to the Panel in *Dominican Republic–Import and Sale of Cigarettes* can be understood as referring "*to notions such as 'in accordance with reason', 'not irrational or absurd', 'proportionate', 'having sound judgement', 'sensible', 'not asking for too much', 'within the limits of reason, not greatly less or more than might be thought likely or appropriate', 'articulate '*".[138] With a view to the Taxonomy Regulation and the EU GBS, the EU Sustainable Finance delegated acts, the notions of "*proportionate*" and "*not greatly less or more than might be thought likely or appropriate*" are to be understood as the requirement of a proportionality. It mandates an analysis between the goal that the relevant delegated acts aim to achieve and the appropriateness of the means they use to do so.

Both, the EU GBS and the Taxonomy Regulation aim to offer a categorization instrument to other primary and secondary EU legislation by defining economic activity as sustainable or unsustainable. The goal, therefore, is not immediately to incentivize increased investment into sustainable economic activity or the rechanneling of private capital, as is the case with EU Sustainable Finance measures in general but simply providing an administration and implementation tool.

The means used to achieve this aim would have to be not only necessary but also neither less nor more than what might be deemed appropriate. Now, the argument that a numerical taxonomy for sustainable and unsustainable economic activities, in general, is essential for drafting effective legislation, is not new. The increased use of not only ambitious but numerical targets in the 2030 Agenda, the Paris Agreement succeeding the Kyoto Protocol as part of the UN Framework Convention on Climate Change (*UNFCCC*)[139] with its 2 °C goal and the AAAA, demonstrate that the use of numerical targets is indeed a regulatory reality.[140] The subsequent domestic regulatory interpretation of such numerical targets is effectively a taxonomy. Not only the Taxonomy Regulation but also the EU GBS constitute such taxonomies. Considering the developments at the UN level, they are therefore necessary for the administration of the relevant EU Sustainable Finance measures. Without proper categorization, these regulations are *blind* to the actual issues they aim to address.

The question of whether such taxonomies administer the underlying regulations in a manner deemed appropriate is closely related to the question of necessity.

---

[137] Van den Bossche and Zdouc (2017), p. 505.

[138] WTO DSB (2004b) Dominican Republic – Measures Affecting the Importation and Internal Sale of Cigarettes, Panel report, para. 7.385; Cf. Van den Bossche and Zdouc (2017), p. 508.

[139] United Nations Framework Convention on Climate Change. 9 May 1992. U.N.T.S. 1771 (1992).

[140] For further detail on the EU's role in the drafting of the 2030 Agenda, the Paris Agreement and the AAAA, cf. Sect. 4.1.1.

Thereby, the report of the Panel in *Argentina–Hides and Leather* can be considered as a guiding interpretation. It *"conclude[d] that a process aimed at assuring the proper classification of products, but which inherently contains the possibility of revealing confidential business information, is an unreasonable manner of administering the laws, regulations and rules identified in Article X:1 and therefore is inconsistent with Article X:3(a)."* Different from, for example, the transparency, reporting, disclosure, and accounting requirements described above (2.1.6), the Taxonomy Regulation's and the EU GBS' aim is not the disclosure of information *per se* and as a means of publication and information. Instead, they solely require information to enable said classification. Furthermore, the Taxonomy Regulation's and the EU GBS' disclosure requirements exhibit a far lower potential for inconsistency with GATS regarding the disclosure of confidential business information than the transparency, reporting, disclosure, and accounting requirements described in Sect. 2.1.6.

The second of the requirements of Art. VI(1) GATS is that the administration of the measure needs to be in an objective manner. The underlying *raison d'être* of this rule is that the *"unfair and arbitrary"*[141] administration of domestic regulation concerning both trade in goods and trade in services is likely to pose an impediment to trade due to subsequent uncertainty.[142] Keeping in mind this rationale of preventing unfairness and arbitrariness in the administration of domestic regulation, it is necessary to interpret the objectivity standard to that effect. Objectivity in juxtaposition with subjectivity would require the relevant domestic authority that conducts the administration of the delegated acts not to act on subjective or arbitrary interpretations or based on criteria not laid down therein. The relevant delegated acts would need to specify criteria that can be administered by the relevant authority in an objective manner. The Taxonomy Regulation introduces such objectivity to a sufficient extend by using numerical criteria in its technical screening criteria to define a sustainable or unsustainable economic activity, as already mentioned above. The same accounts for the EU GBS, which according to the TEG uses the Taxonomy Regulation's technical screening criteria to define green projects.[143] Therefore, both taxonomies can be deemed an objective administration under Art. VI(1) GATS.

The third and final requirement stated in Art. VI(1) GATS is that the relevant measure needs to be administered impartially. The Panel in *Thailand–Cigarettes (Philippines)* concluded that with a view to Art. X(3)(a) GATT such impartial administration of a measure comprises *"the application or implementation [. . .] in a fair, unbiased and unprejudiced manner"*.[144] As already described above with regard to the objective administration of the measures under Art. VI(1) GATS, it is not apparent that the EU Sustainable Finance delegated acts, and in particular, the

---

[141] Van den Bossche and Zdouc (2017), p. 504.

[142] Van den Bossche and Zdouc (2017), pp. 504, 534.

[143] Cf. Sect. 2.1.3; TEG (2019b), pp. 57 et seq., 25.

[144] Van den Bossche and Zdouc (2017), p. 507; Therein: WTO DSB (2010) Thailand – Customs and Fiscal Measures on Cigarettes from the Philippines, Panel report, para. 7.899.

Taxonomy Regulation or the EU GBS are to be considered to be based on a subjective or arbitrary decision. Equally, an administration in an unfair, biased, or prejudiced manner is to be negated. The EU Sustainable Finance delegated acts thus do not provide sufficient inconsistency to amount to a breach of the criteria of impartiality under Art. VI(1) GATS.

Finally, according to the Panel in *Argentina–Hides and Leather* determining a breach of Art. X(3)(a) GATT may require *"an examination of the real effect that a measure might have on traders operating in the commercial world."*[145] Translated into GATS terms, this would mean that the unreasonable, subjective or partial manner of implementing the relevant regulation has *"a possible impact on the competitive situation"*.[146] For instance, sustainability labels for financial services and products might constitute a distortion of competition. In the case of the Taxonomy Regulation and the EU GBS, the implementing act—or the *administration* of the underlying Sustainable Finance regulation—and that regulation itself are to be differentiated. The Taxonomy Regulation defines certain terms used in several Sustainable Finance measures and thus, as described above, constitutes an implementing act or administration of a measure under Art. VI(1) GATS. It is not apparent that the Taxonomy Regulation itself, nor the actual Sustainable Finance measure referring to it, constitute a distortion of the competition in favor of sustainable financial services or products. The same applies to the taxonomy part of the EU GBS, which merely defines green projects and thereby does not constitute a distortion in the market.

It can thus be concluded that the Taxonomy Regulation, the EU GBS, and the delegated acts constitute a reasonable, objective, and impartial administration of EU Sustainable Finance measures and thus do not breach the provisions of Art. VI (1) GATS.

3.2.3.2   Licensing and Qualification Requirements and Technical Standards: Art. VI(5) GATS

Another of the domestic regulation standards relevant for the assessment of EU Sustainable Finance under GATS is Art. VI(5) GATS. It constitutes an obligation for WTO Members to respect their specific commitments and to not impose *"licensing and qualification requirements and technical standards that nullify or impair such specific commitments"* inconsistent with the requirements of Art. VI(4)(a) to (c) GATS.[147]

---

[145] Van den Bossche and Zdouc (2017), p. 505; Therein: WTO DSB (2000c) Argentina – Measures Affecting the Export of Bovine Hides and the Import of Finished Leather, Panel report, para. 11.77.

[146] Van den Bossche and Zdouc (2017), p. 505; Therein: WTO DSB (2000c) Argentina – Measures Affecting the Export of Bovine Hides and the Import of Finished Leather, Panel report, para. 11.77.

[147] Trachtman (1996), p. 88.

Therefore, the scope of application of Art. VI(5)(a) GATS is limited threefold. First, it is limited to *"sectors in which a [WTO] Member has undertaken specific commitments"*. This refers to market access commitments made under Art. XVI (1) GATS in the relevant Schedule on Specific Commitments. As described above (3.2.1), the EU made far-reaching market access commitments in the field of financial services.[148] Thus, the requirement of a given market access commitment under Art. VI(5)(a) GATS is fulfilled. As regards this commitment, if a domestic regulation does not constitute a market access barrier under Art. XVI(2) GATS, it still might nullify or impair the market access commitment under Art. VI(5) (a) GATS. While both provisions are seen as *"mutually exclusive"*,[149] domestic regulation is much more likely to pose a *de facto* market access barrier to trade in services than market access barriers according to Art. XVI(2) GATS.[150]

Second, the scope of application of Art. VI(5)(a) GATS is limited to the time *"pending the entry into force of disciplines developed in these sectors pursuant to"* Art. VI(4) GATS. Art. VI(4) GATS comprises a mandate to the Council for Trade in Services to develop any necessary disciplines addressing domestic regulation such as licensing and qualification requirements and technical standards constituting unnecessary barriers to trade.[151] Following its mandate in Art. VI(4) GATS, the Council for Trade in Services created the Working Party on Domestic Regulation in April 1999.[152] The Working Party on Domestic Regulation is yet to produce the intended disciplines on domestic regulation.[153] The same applies to the parallel Joint Initiative on Services Domestic Regulation founded by fifty-nine WTO Member at the 11th Ministerial Conference (*MC11*) in Buenos Aires in December 2017.[154] Hence, the requirement of the entry into force of disciplines to be developed by the Council for Trade in Services under Art. IV(4) GATS is fulfilled.

Third, the scope of application of Art. VI(5)(a) GATS is limited to the application of *"licensing and qualification requirements and technical standards"*. In contrast, Art. VI(1) to (3) GATS apply to measures of general application and administrative and implementing decisions and thus have a much broader scope of application.[155] There are several EU Sustainable Finance measures described in Chap. 2 that could fall under *licensing and qualification requirements and technical standards*

---

[148] European Union, Schedule of Specific Commitments. 7 May 2019. GATS/SC/157, pp. 127 et seqq., 149 et seqq.; Cf. Sect. 3.2.1.

[149] Van den Bossche and Zdouc (2017), p. 536, fn. 337; Therein: WTO DSB (2004a) United States – Measures Affecting the Cross-Border Supply of Gambling and Betting Services, Panel report, para. 6.305.

[150] Van den Bossche and Zdouc (2017), p. 536.

[151] Trachtman (1996), p. 56.

[152] Decision on Domestic Regulation. 28 April 1999. S/L/70, para. 1 et seq.

[153] Except for the *Disciplines on Domestic Regulation in the Accountancy Sector*, 17 December 1998, S/L/64; Cf. Van den Bossche and Zdouc (2017), p. 537, fn. 340.

[154] Cf. however the Joint Initiative's *Joint Statement on Services Domestic Regulation* discussed in Sect. 4.2.1.

[155] Cf. Van den Bossche and Zdouc (2017), p. 536, fn. 338.

according to Art. VI(5)(a) GATS. On the one hand, the Taxonomy Regulation and the EU GBS described above and particularly their relevant technical screening criteria as partly numerical classification systems or taxonomies are to be considered a technical standard under Art. VI(5)(a) GATS. The EU Sustainable Finance measures referring to these taxonomies, like the labeling standards (2.1.2), the labeling-related part of the EU GBS (2.1.3) but also the sustainability-based benchmarks and credit rating regulations (2.1.4, 2.1.5), in turn, are to be considered licensing requirements.

Art. VI(5)(a) GATS thereby constitutes that "*the [WTO] Member shall not apply licensing and qualification requirements and technical standards that nullify or impair such specific commitments*". An application of licensing and qualification requirements and technical standards is considered nullifying if it either "*does not comply with the criteria outlined in subparagraphs 4(a), (b) or (c)*" according to Art. V(5)(a)(i) GATS, or "*could not reasonably have been expected of that [WTO] Member at the time the specific commitments in those sectors were made*" under Art. V(5)(a)(ii) GATS. As a third requirement, Art. VI(5)(b) GATS adds that with a view to the assessment of the legality under above disciplines, "*account shall be taken of international standards of relevant international organizations applied by that [WTO] Member.*" The licensing and qualification requirements and technical standards set out in EU Sustainable Finance measures will subsequently be assessed concerning these three requirements of Art. VI(5)(a) and (b) GATS.[156] It is to be noted that although the use of international standards pursuant to Art. VI(5) (b) GATS shall function as an interpretation instrument concerning the first two requirements set out in Art. VI(5)(a) GATS. However, due to the relevance of international standards with regard to Sustainable Finance's roots in the internationally developed sustainable development agenda, they will be described and assessed separately in Sect. 3.2.3.2.3.

It is further to be noted that Art. VII GATS comprises the facility of recognition by the host state of the entirety or parts of the regulatory regime of the home state through unilateral application or harmonization. Para. 3 GATS Annex on Financial Services specifies this for financial services prudential measures. However, neither Art. VII GATS nor the GATS Annex on Financial Services constitute an obligation for recognition of other WTO Members' regulatory measures.[157] For this feasibility of such recognition regarding Sustainable Finance, see also in Sect. 4.2.2.

3.2.3.2.1   Substantive Requirements

As described above, Art.VI(5) GATS refers to Art. VI(4)(a) to (c) GATS to determine a measure's nullification or impairment of a market access commitment. Thereby, noncompliance with any of these subpara. (a) to (c) is sufficient to fulfill

---

[156]Cf. Sects. 3.2.3.2.1–3.2.3.2.3.

[157]Trachtman (1996), p. 96.

the requirement of Art. VI(5)(a)(i) GATS.[158] Art. VI(4)(a) to (c) GATS, in turn, provides that "*qualification requirements and procedures, technical standards and licensing requirements*" shall "*not constitute unnecessary barriers to trade in services*". The term of *qualification requirements and procedures, technical standards and licensing requirements*, although including the addition of qualification procedures, is effectively to be interpreted in coherence with the term of "*licensing and qualification requirements and technical standards*" of Art. VI(5)(a) GATS. Therefore, Art. VI(5)(a) can be understood to make merely a reference to the material requirements of Art. VI(4) described below rather than requiring yet another examination of its scope of application.

The relevant technical screening criteria of the Taxonomy Regulation and the EU GBS constitute such licensing requirements and technical standards as described in the introduction to this chapter. Furthermore, the EU Sustainable Finance measures referring to these taxonomies, such as labeling standards (2.1.2), the labeling-related part of the EU GBS (2.1.3) but also sustainability-based benchmarks and credit rating regulations described (2.1.4, 2.1.5), can be considered licensing requirements under Art. VI(4) GATS.[159]

These licensing standards first need to be based on "*objective and transparent criteria, such as competence and the ability to supply the service*" as set out in Art. VI(4)(a) GATS. As already discussed in Sect. 3.2.3.1 concerning the administration of the EU Sustainable Finance measures and in particular, the Taxonomy Regulation and the EU GBS, objective criteria may be defined by contrasting them to subjective criteria. Furthermore, Art. VI(4)(a) GATS gives two examples of such objective criteria as "*competence and the ability to supply the service*". Thereby, the conclusions made in Sect. 3.2.3.1 can also be applied to EU Sustainable Finance licensing provisions. Although Art. VI(1) GATS focuses on the administration of the measure and less so on the measure itself, the EU Sustainable Finance licensing provisions referred to above themselves can be deemed sufficiently objective and transparent due to the predetermination of the administrative decision in the form of the NFR Directive's KPIs[160] and the EU taxonomy's technical screening criteria as set out in Art. 14(1) Taxonomy Regulation.[161] Further examples of such objective criteria in licensing provisions is Art. 5(1) EuSEF Regulation,[162] which defines eligible funds

---

[158] Cf. the wording of Art. VI(5)(a)(i), which refers to "*subparagraphs 4(a), (b) or (c)*".

[159] Cyprus explicitly noted "*that non-discriminatory qualitative measures pertaining to technical standards, public health and environmental considerations, licensing, prudential consideration, professional qualifications and competency requirements have not been listed as conditions or limitations to market access and national treatment*", cf. EU Schedule on Specific Commitments, p. 141.

[160] Cf. TEG (2019a), p. 15; Directive 2014/95/EU of the European Parliament and of the Council of 22 October 2014 amending Directive 2013/34/EU as regards disclosure of non-financial and diversity information by certain large undertakings and groups [2014] OJ L 330/1.

[161] Cf. the considerations made regarding numerical limitations in Sect. 3.2.1.1.

[162] Regulation (EU) No 346/2013 of the European Parliament and of the Council of 17 April 2013 on European social entrepreneurship funds [2013] OJ L 115/18.

as such that have 30% of their capital invested into eligible assets. Similarly, Art. 13(1) and Recital 14 ELTIF Regulation[163] require the relevant fund to invest 70% of its capital into eligible assets.

A recurring regulatory scheme in drafting EU Sustainable Finance measures that may conflict with the requirement of objectivity, however, is a *no significant harm* clause integrated for instance into the definition of a *sustainable investment* under Art. 1(17) Sustainability Disclosures Regulation or Art. 3(b) and Art. 1(1) Climate BMR,[164] and Art. 9 Taxonomy Regulation. This, however, would disregard the fact that in EU financial legislation unprecise legal terms, such as the no significant harm clause, are common. They are usually defined more precisely in an implementing legislative act. Thus, the use of broad legal terms in EU Sustainable Finance measures is proof of the further necessity of specifying these terms and not a violation of Art. VI(4)(a) GATS. Adding to this, for the reasons for which the EU Sustainable Finance licensing provisions meet the objectivity requirements of Art. VI(4)(a) GATS, they also satisfy the *transparency* requirement.

Finally, the licensing and qualification requirements and technical standards implemented according to Art. VI(5)(a)(i) GATS may not be "*more burdensome than necessary to ensure the quality of the service*".[165] Disregarding the proportionality of the actual substantive EU Sustainable Finance measure, the relevant technical screening criteria, the EU GBS, and the Taxonomy Regulation would be necessary if no other equally effective measure with a lower restrictive impact would be feasibly available. Thereby, it is first to be noted that a form of numerical classification system was long nonexistent throughout EU sustainability legislation. It was, however, a precondition for fair administration and predictability—and ultimately for objective and transparent criteria as set out in Art. VI(4)(a) GATS. Thus, an equally effective measure with (even) lower impact is not feasibly available, and the licensing and qualification requirements or technical standards implemented pursuant to Art. VI(5)(a)(i) GATS are not more burdensome than necessary according to Art. VI(4)(a) GATS.

3.2.3.2.2 Not Reasonably Expectable

Furthermore, Art. VI(5) GATS requires that the relevant measure must not have been reasonably expectable—or *foreseeable*—"*of that [WTO] Member at the time the specific commitments in those sectors were made*". In the case at hand, the EU published its Schedule of Specific Commitments according to Art. XX(1) GATS first

---

[163] Regulation (EU) 2015/760 of the European Parliament and of the Council of 29 April 2015 on European long-term investment funds [2015] OJ L 123/98.

[164] Corresponding to Art. 3(1)(23b) Regulation (EU) 2016/1011 of the European Parliament and of the Council of 8 June 2016 on indices used as benchmarks in financial instruments and financial contracts or to measure the performance of investment funds and amending Directives 2008/48/EC and 2014/17/EU and Regulation (EU) No 596/2014 [2016] OJ L 171/1; Cf. TEG (2019d), p. 37.

[165] Cf. Art. VI(4)(a) GATS.

in April 1994,[166] with an updated version published in May 2019. Specific commitments in financial services were already undertaken by the European Communities and their Member States in the 1994 Schedule.[167]

The question arises whether the EU Sustainable Finance measures taken in recent years and expected to be increasing in their restrictive impact, were foreseeable in 1994 or 2019 when the specific commitments under Art. XX(1) GATS were made. This is not only due to the significant internal developments in membership and changes in competences of the EU but also due to the evolution of the deployment of external policy resources on the international stage. The answer to this question primarily depends on the perspective taken based on Art. VI(5)(a)(ii) GATS, which requires the foreseeability of a measure based on the time the specific commitments it impairs were undertaken.

Several arguments speak in favor of referring to the earliest point in time—when a GATS commitment is made—as the basis of the examination under Art. VI(5)(a) (ii) GATS. First, the very rationale of this norm of providing objectivity, transparency, and a form of proportionality in the drafting of such licensing and qualification requirements and technical standards as referred to therein. Second, foreseeability is based on the rationale of allowing the respective market participant to prepare and adapt to the measure in question. Third, foreseeability derives from the GATS principle of *"progressively higher level of liberalization"* of Art. XIX(1) GATS, which means that once a specific commitment is included in a Schedule on Specific Commitments, subsequent changes ought to be more liberal and less restrictive.

If the 1994 Schedule of Specific Commitments is taken as the reference point for determining whether EU Sustainable Finance measures were *reasonably expectable*, there are certain observations to be made. First, the EC back in 1994 already heavily engaged in the negotiation and drafting of international climate action, environmental protection, and large-scale sustainable development agreements and simultaneously worked on an internal strategy and its implementation.[168] Second, although Sustainable Finance as a policy base for an entire re-engineering of the financial system was not yet existent, certain approaches like financing for development conferences and bilateral development measures like the European Development Fund's *(EDF)* agreements were.[169] Taking into account these developments, a policy concept aimed at sustainability like EU Sustainable Finance was conceivable and forseeable already in 1994.

In contrast, however, aforementioned development in the institutional structure of the EU suggests the EU's 2019 Schedule of Specific Commitments as the relevant point in time for the examination under Art. VI(5)(a)(ii) GATS. Foreseeability

---

[166]European Communities and their Member States, Schedule of Specific Commitments. 15 April 1994. GATS/SC/31, pp. 94–1029.

[167]European Communities and their Member States, Schedule of Specific Commitments. 15 April 1994. GATS/SC/31, p. 61.

[168]Cf. Pauls (2020), pp. 9 et seqq.; Cf. Sect. 4.1.1.

[169]Pauls (2020), pp. 5 et seq.; Cf. Sect. 4.1.1.

referring to commitments made in financial services under the GATS is not subject to internal structural or policy changes of the WTO Member undertaking them. Instead, Foreseeability inherently refers to the WTO Member as an institution and such institutions are subject to significant changes, particularly in its composition of Member States. Plus, updated Schedules of Commitments result out of multilateral negotiations[170] and thus in themselves do not constitute a breach of Art. VI(5)(a) (ii) GATS but rather are supportive a measure's foreseeability.

If the 2019 Schedule on Specific Commitments is taken as the reference point for the examination under Art. VI(5)(a)(ii) GATS, similar observations as those made in respect of foreseeability in 1994 can be done. First, the EU's commitment to sustainable development policy drafting at the international level, has strongly increased in the past decade with the EU ultimately claiming a "*leadership*" role in the drafting of international climate action agreements.[171] Second, regulation in EU Sustainable Finance under that specific term and the correlating policy concept, as described in Chap. 2, has significantly increased since the March 2018 introduction of the Sustainable Finance Action Plan.[172] Latter in turn, outlined the subsequent and most of the currently planned EU Sustainable Finance measures. Indeed, it was issued by the Commission as the main policy-directing organ, and thus it and the measures under it are to be deemed reasonably and highly expectable under Art. VI (5)(a)(ii) GATS.

3.2.3.2.3 International Standards

The final criterion of Art. VI(5)(b) GATS is that there are "*international standards of relevant international organizations applied by that [WTO] Member.*" This, however, is not a criterion for determining the inconsistency of EU Sustainable Finance *per se* but an indicator that shall be considered in "*determining whether a [WTO] Member is in conformity with the obligation under paragraph 5(a)*".[173]

The EU frequently and systematically adopts and applies international standards of relevant international organizations and bodies into its Sustainable Finance regulatory framework. This chapter thereby refers to international standards by international organizations referred to in the EU Sustainable Finance measures whereas the inverse influence of the EU on the setting of these standards is addressed in Sect. 4.1.2. Due to the wording of Art. VI(5)(b) GATS, which refers to international standards *applied* by the WTO Member, due differentiation will be conducted between mere referencing of such international standards in the preambles of EU Sustainable Finance measures and the incorporation into the prerequisites or implementation of such measure.

---

[170] Cf. Art. XIX GATS.

[171] Pauls (2020), pp. 9 et seqq.; Cf. Sect. 4.1.1.

[172] European Commission (2018).

[173] Cf. Van den Bossche and Zdouc (2017), p. 537, fn. 339.

First, many of the EU Sustainable Finance measures contain references to international agreements on environmental protection or climate action to which the EU is a party. They incorporate the policy goals set at an international level into their domestic policy-setting. An example of this is Recitals 3 and 4 Climate BMR referring to the Paris Agreement and the IPCC Special Report on Global Warming of 1.5 °C, respectively.[174] Similarly, Recital 51 PEPP Regulation refers to the EU's sustainability targets under the Paris Agreement and the 2030 Agenda and Art. 2(33) PEPP Regulation defines ESG factors referencing the Paris Agreement and the SDGs.

Second, on a structural policy level, international standards in the narrower sense, too, are incorporated into the substantive parts of EU Sustainable Finance legislation. One example of this is the incorporation of the ILO minimum safeguards as defined in Art. 18 Taxonomy Regulation into the determination of an ecologically sustainable economic activity in Art. 3 Taxonomy Regulation. Furthermore, the 2019 NFR Guidelines Supplement[175] incorporated the TCFD Final Report's findings into its climate-related information reporting framework.[176] Adding to this, the EU CTB and EU PAB are being calculated using the IPCC decarbonization trajectory.[177] Recital 9 NFR Directive refers to various international reporting standards and initiatives.[178] Similarly, the Sustainable Finance Action Plan refers to the IFRS 9, which in turn are incorporated into EU legislation through the IAS Regulation.[179] Finally, proposals such as the HLEG Final Report's recommendation of an EU GBS referred to market-led best practice standards such as the ICMA GBPs.[180]

Therefore, it can be summarized that EU Sustainable Finance measures not only regularly but systematically reference international standards set by international organizations leading negotiations and multilateral policy-setting in the respective fields and which thus can be deemed *relevant* as of Art. VI(5)(b) GATS.

Thus, since Art. VI(5)(b) GATS sets out these international standards as criteria to be taken into account in *"determining whether a [WTO] Member is in conformity with the obligation under paragraph 5(a)"* as regards Sustainable Finance measures, the assessment or determination in this respect must be undertaken not only taking

---

[174] IPCC (2019).

[175] European Commission (2019b).

[176] Cf. e.g. European Commission (2019b), pp. 4, 35; This had been proposed by the HLEG Final Report, cf. HLEG (2018a), pp. 24 et seq.; Cf. European Commission (2018), p. 9; Cf. TEG (2019a), p. 3.

[177] TEG (2019d), pp. 59 et seq.

[178] In turn, corporate NFR on sustainability criteria is recognized in para. 47 'The future we want' Outcome Document; Cf. Recital 11 Directive 2014/95/EU of the European Parliament and of the Council of 22 October 2014 amending Directive 2013/34/EU as regards disclosure of non-financial and diversity information by certain large undertakings and groups [2014] OJ L 330/1.

[179] European Commission (2018), pp. 9 et seq.; Regulation (EC) No 1606/2002 of the European Parliament and of the Council of 19 July 2002 on the application of international accounting standards [2002] OJ L 243/1.

[180] HLEG (2018a), p. 31.

into account large-scale policies such as the Paris Agreement but also the more detailed international guidelines and standards incorporated into EU Sustainable Finance measures.[181] However, the mostly dynamic references made in EU Sustainable Finance legislation to these guidelines and standards and thereby their incorporation and transposition into EU legislation is a self-fulfilling prophecy under the *international standards* requirement of Art. VI(5)(b) GATS. By this incorporation by reference, the EU assures that an interpretation based *inter alia* on these international standards applied by the EU will likely conclude that the respective legislation is in line with these standards. This conclusion will evenly apply to EU Sustainable Finance legislation not dynamically referencing these standards but being substantially based on them.

3.2.4 Exceptions

GATS further sets out general exceptions. If these general exceptions are met, WTO Members may undertake measures otherwise inconsistent with the obligations and commitments.[182] Regarding EU Sustainable Finance provisions, this would mean that in case any current or prospective Sustainable Finance measure would be found to breach a specific GATS commitment or discipline, if a general exception applies to it, this would establish the Sustainable Finance measure in question as GATS-consistent.

GATS comprises several exception clauses, the most prominent of which is Art. XIV GATS. It provides for a set of regulatory subjects that constitute a justification for an otherwise inconsistent measure.

Furthermore, Recital 4 GATS recognizes *"the right of [WTO] Members to regulate, and to introduce new regulations, on the supply of services within their territories in order to meet national policy objectives"*. Whether this right of WTO Members to regulate to meet national policy objectives, provides for additional regulatory policy space with a view to Sustainable Finance measures, will be discussed below.

Finally, para. 2(a) GATS Annex on Financial Services indicates that *"a [WTO] Member shall not be prevented from taking measures for prudential reasons"*. This particularly concerns measures taken *"for the protection of investors, depositors, policyholders or persons to whom a fiduciary duty is owed by a financial service supplier, or to ensure the integrity and stability of the financial system."*

---

[181] Cf. Van den Bossche and Zdouc (2017), p. 537, fn. 339.

[182] Van den Bossche and Zdouc (2017), p. 605.

3.2.4.1 General Exceptions: Art. XIV GATS

As mentioned above, Art. XIV GATS provides for a set of regulatory subjects that constitute a justification for an otherwise GATS-inconsistent measure. It stipulates that *"nothing in [the GATS] shall be construed to prevent the adoption or enforcement by any [WTO] Member of"* one of these regulatory subjects. To EU Sustainable Finance provisions, only Art. XIV(a) and (b) GATS providing for general exceptions for measures *"necessary to protect public morals or to maintain public order"* and for measures *"necessary to protect human, animal or plant life or health"* are potentially relevant.

Thereby, the wording of Art. XIV GATS resembles that of Art. XX GATT. Despite the substantial similarities, both provisions vary on matters like the protection of safety and privacy and the collection of taxes. However, due to the similarities concerning the protection of public order and human, animal, and plant life, jurisprudence on Art. XX GATT can be referenced in the interpretation of Art. XIV GATS obligations.[183] The same was concluded by the Appellate Body in *US–Gambling*, which found that Art. XIV GATS *"sets out the general exceptions from obligations under that Agreement in the same manner as does Article XX of the GATT 1994."*[184] It further stated that *"[b]oth of these provisions affirm the right of [WTO] Members to pursue objectives identified in the paragraphs of these provisions even if, in doing so, [WTO] Members act inconsistently with obligations set out in other provisions of the respective agreements, provided that all of the conditions set out therein are satisfied."*[185] The Appellate Body rendered *"previous decisions under Article XX of the GATT 1994 relevant for [its] analysis under Article XIV of the GATS."*[186]

It further found that both Art. XIV GATS and Art. XX GATT require *"a 'two-tier analysis' of a measure that a [WTO] Member seeks to justify under that*

---

[183] Van den Bossche and Zdouc (2017), p. 606; Therein: WTO DSB (2005) United States – Measures Affecting the Cross-Border Supply of Gambling and Betting Services, Appellate Body report, para. 291.

[184] WTO DSB (2005) United States – Measures Affecting the Cross-Border Supply of Gambling and Betting Services, Appellate Body report, para. 291; WTO (2020d), pp. 2 et seq., 6; Cf. WTO DSB (2015) Argentina – Measures Relating to Trade in Goods and Services, Panel report, para. 7.586.

[185] Most notably, the Appellate Body found that *"[s]imilar language is used in both provisions, notably the term 'necessary' and the requirements set out in their respective chapeaux.",* cf. WTO DSB (2005) United States – Measures Affecting the Cross-Border Supply of Gambling and Betting Services, Appellate Body report, para. 291; Cf. WTO (2020d), pp. 2 et seq., 6; Cf. WTO DSB (2015) Argentina – Measures Relating to Trade in Goods and Services, Panel report, para. 7.586.

[186] WTO DSB (2005) United States – Measures Affecting the Cross-Border Supply of Gambling and Betting Services, Appellate Body report, para. 291; Cf. WTO (2020d), pp. 2 et seq., 6; Cf. WTO DSB (2015) Argentina – Measures Relating to Trade in Goods and Services, Panel report, para. 7.586.

provision."[187] As a first step, it is to be determined "*whether the challenged measure falls within the scope of one of the paragraphs of Article XIV.*" To this end, the measures need to address the particular interest of the respective paragraph. Furthermore, a sufficient nexus must be present. There are five types of measures that, according to Art. XIV GATS, are not to be prevented by the construction of the GATS articles, only the first two of which are relevant and potentially applicable to EU Sustainable Finance. First, measures not to be prevented by the GATS articles pursuant to Art. XIV(a) GATS, are those "*necessary to protect public morals or to maintain public order*" examined above (3.2.4.1.1, 3.2.4.1.2). The second exception set out in Art. XIV(b) GATS and examined above (3.2.4.1.3) encompasses measures "*necessary to protect human, animal or plant life or health*". The other exceptions under Art. XIV GATS refer to compliance with laws or regulations such as those relating to fraud prevention, privacy protection, and (physical) safety (Art. XIV(c) (i) to (iii) GATS), the imposition or collection of direct taxes (Art. XIV(d) GATS), and the avoidance of double taxation (Art. XIV(e) GATS). These latter exceptions are not as relevant to this assessment of EU Sustainable Finance measures and will not be discussed further.

Subsequently the requirements of the chapeau of Art. XIV GATS are to be applied.[188] This second step is conducted in Sect. 3.2.4.1.4. Pursuant to the chapeau of Art. XIV GATS, the exceptions set out in Art. XIV(a) to (e) GATS are subject to a restriction resembling Art. VI(1) GATS. This restriction states that "*such measures are not applied in a manner which would constitute a means of arbitrary or unjustifiable discrimination between countries where like conditions prevail, or a disguised restriction on trade in services*". This restriction thus only applies to the administration of the relevant measure and not the measure itself.

As regards the aspects of the measure under assessment to be taken into considerations the Appellate Body in *Argentina–Financial Services* found that "*with respect to each individual measure, the aspects of the measure addressed are the same as those that gave rise to its earlier finding of inconsistency.*"[189] Thereby, when analyzing a measure under Art. XIV GATS, focus shall be put on the measure itself, rather than its consequences for competition in the market, and on the aspects of the measure that led to the inconsistency in the first place.[190] Therefore, following the Appellate Body's interpretation, only those EU Sustainable Finance measures found to be GATS-inconsistent in Sects. 3.2.1–3.2.3 can be assessed under Art. XIV

---

[187] WTO DSB (2005) United States – Measures Affecting the Cross-Border Supply of Gambling and Betting Services, Appellate Body report, para. 292; Cf. WTO (2020d), p. 3; Cf. WTO DSB (2015) Argentina – Measures Relating to Trade in Goods and Services, Panel report, para. 7.586.

[188] WTO DSB (2005) United States – Measures Affecting the Cross-Border Supply of Gambling and Betting Services, Appellate Body report, para. 292; Cf. WTO (2020d), p. 3; Cf. WTO DSB (2015) Argentina – Measures Relating to Trade in Goods and Services, Panel report, para. 7.586.

[189] WTO DSB (2016) Argentina – Measures Relating to Trade in Goods and Services, Appellate Body report, para. 6.169; Cf. WTO (2020d), p. 4.

[190] WTO DSB (2016) Argentina – Measures Relating to Trade in Goods and Services, Appellate Body report, para. 6.168; Cf. WTO (2020d), p. 3.

GATS. However, to gain a broader understanding of a possible inconsistency of Sustainable Finance measures and the potentially applicable general exceptions, all measures described in Chap. 2 will be assessed.[191]

Furthermore, for Sustainable Finance this means that the analysis under Art. XIV GATS must be based on the very aspect of the relevant Sustainable Finance measure that would be found to be inconsistent with a GATS discipline. This would usually be the aspect of the measure that defines the treatment of the service supplier or service. Thus, for instance, an inconsistent disclosure or capital requirements measure cannot be justified by referring to other aspects covered in the same regulation. This in turn means that each of Sustainable Finance measures and the aspects that govern the service suppliers' treatment would need to have a sufficiently close nexus (*ergo* no absence of relationship between the measure and the objective) to the relevant underlying rationale, such as the furthering of sustainable development or financial stability.

3.2.4.1.1 Necessary to protect public morals

Introducing EU Sustainable Finance measures affecting trade in financial service could be provisionally justified under Art. XIV(a) GATS. It instructs that nothing in the GATS "*shall be construed to prevent the adoption or enforcement by any [WTO] Member of measures [. . .] necessary to protect public morals or to maintain public order [. . .]*".

Applying Art. XIV(a) GATS, the Panel in *US–Gambling* found that "*in determining whether a challenged measure is provisionally justified under that Article, the [WTO] Member invoking that provision must demonstrate two elements*".[192] First, the measure must be "*designed to 'protect public morals' or to 'maintain public order'*" and, second, it must be "*necessary*" to do so.[193] Therefore, this chapter inspects public morals and its necessity, the subsequent chapter public order and its necessity.

Examining the "*public morals*" aspect, the Appellate Body in *Colombia–Textiles* added that the term "*'to protect public morals' calls for an initial, threshold examination in order to determine whether there is a relationship between an*

---

[191] In fact, the Panel in *EC-Asbestos* made findings on Art. XX(b) GATT despite not having found these measures to be consistent with substantive GATT provisions, cf. Van den Bossche and Zdouc (2017), p. 560.

[192] WTO DSB (2004a) United States – Measures Affecting the Cross-Border Supply of Gambling and Betting Services, Panel report, para. 6.455; WTO DSB (2018) European Union and its Member States – Certain Measures Relating to the Energy Sector, Panel report, para. 7.229 et seqq.; Cf. WTO (2020d), p. 6.

[193] WTO DSB (2004a) United States – Measures Affecting the Cross-Border Supply of Gambling and Betting Services, Panel report, para. 6.455; WTO DSB (2018) European Union and its Member States – Certain Measures Relating to the Energy Sector, Panel report, para. 7.229 et seqq.; Cf. WTO (2020d), p. 6.

otherwise GATT-inconsistent measure and the protection of public morals."[194] If there is no such relationship, the second element, "*necessity*", would not have to be examined. If, however, the examination of the "*public morals*" element results in the potential existence of such a relationship, a further examination of the "*necessity*" is required.[195] These findings were made based on Art. XX(a) GATT. However, as reasoned above, they are usually applied accordingly to the respective GATS provision, namely Art. XIV(a) GATS.

The assessment of the relationship between the measure and the protection of public morals is conducted in three steps. First, the policy objective pursued by the measure needs to be identified. Second, an initial test of design of the measure concerning its capability of such protection needs to be conducted. Third, the necessity of such measure to protect public morals is inspected.[196] For the initial threshold examination and whether the EU Sustainable Finance measures are *capable* of protecting public morals, the measure's policy objective needs to first be identified.[197]

The definition of a single policy objective pursued by all of the EU Sustainable Finance measures described in Chap. 2, however, proves to be challenging. This is due to these EU Sustainable Finance measures being integrated into and set in a variety of different regulatory fields and environments, as concluded in Sect. 2.4. Furthermore, as described in Sect. 1.1, rechanneling private capital is the immediate aim of these measures.

This, however, must not be confused with policy objectives protected under Art. XIV GATS. The policy objective is defined by the WTO Member's claim and articulation of what constitutes the policy objective pursued by a measure. In the case of EU Sustainable Finance measures, the numerous references to the Paris Agreement, the IPCC, and the SDGs[198] indicate that the underlying policy objective is to implement these agreements. These political targets are namely: sustainable development and climate change mitigation. This connection was also explicitly drawn by the Sustainable Finance Action Plan's statement that it "*will be instrumental to help deliver on the Paris Climate Agreement and the Sustainable Development Goals*".[199]

---

[194] WTO DSB (2016b) Colombia – Measures Relating to the Importation of Textiles, Apparel and Footwear, Appellate Body report, para. 5.68; Cf. Van den Bossche and Zdouc (2017), p. 579.

[195] WTO DSB (2016b) Colombia – Measures Relating to the Importation of Textiles, Apparel and Footwear, Appellate Body report, para. 5.68; Cf. Van den Bossche and Zdouc (2017), p. 579.

[196] WTO DSB (2016b) Colombia – Measures Relating to the Importation of Textiles, Apparel and Footwear, Appellate Body report, para. 5.67; Cf. Van den Bossche and Zdouc (2017), p. 579; Cf. the regulatory impact assessment process described in Sheargold and Mitchell (2016), p. 603.

[197] Although the Appellate Body conducted its assessment with a view to Art. 2.2 TBT Agreement, cf. WTO DSB (2014) European Communities – Measures Prohibiting the Importation and Marketing of Seal Products, Appellate Body reports, para. 5.144; Van den Bossche and Zdouc (2017), pp. 581 et seq.; Cf. Sheargold and Mitchell (2016), p. 603.

[198] As discussed in Sect. 3.2.3.2.3.

[199] European Commission (2018), p. 12.

Likewise, many of the EU Sustainable Finance measures are incorporated into already existing EU legislation protecting financial stability. This is particularly visible with provisions on sustainability and transition risks aimed at preventing stranded assets.[200] Examples of this are Art. 1(22), Art. 5(1), and Art. 6-(1) Sustainability Disclosures Regulation,[201] Art. 41(1)(b) PEPP Regulation[202] and Art. 1(2) MiFID II Draft RTS.[203]

Thus, according to the EU's claims, the main policy objective of EU Sustainable Finance can be identified as fostering sustainable development. In particular, this comprises environmental protection and fostering financial stability, for instance by supporting long-termism.

Investor protection as feasible policy objective is addressed in some EU Sustainable Finance measures. In some cases, it had been the original goal of introducing the regulations these new Sustainable Finance measures are inserted into. It has also a close thematical relation to these Sustainable Finance measures.[204] However, investor protection is not *per se* an aspect of Sustainable Finance. If anything, it could constitute an aspect of the social or governance factors of sustainable development. However, as described above, sustainable development as such is already one of the two core policy objectives of Sustainable Finance. Naming the social ESG factor separately would diverge too far from the original meaning of Art. XIV(a) GATS, *"to protect public morals"*.

Apart from the EU's claims, however, other evidence on Sustainable Finance's policy objectives is to be considered. The Appellate Body in *EC–Seal Products* assumed that the *"[WTO] Member's characterizations of such objective(s)"* are not binding to the process of assessing this evidence. This evidence comprises *"'the texts of statutes, legislative history, and other evidence regarding the structure and operation' of the measure [. . .]."*[205] In respect of EU Sustainable Finance measures and in lack of an actual case and defense by the EU in this regard, the text of statutes is what has been used above as an indication for the EU's articulation of policy objective. Therefore, at this stage in particular the legislative history and structure are relevant for the further determination of the policy objective pursued by EU Sustainable Finance measures.

The legislative history of Sustainable Finance legislation in general and EU Sustainable Finance measures in particular has been described above (1.1, 2). Therefore, at the EU level, first sustainable development developed, interdependently with international developments on the field and paralleled by

---

[200] Regarding stranded assets cf. Sect. 1.1.

[201] Cf. Sects. 1.1 and 2.1.6.

[202] Cf. Sect. 2.1.2.

[203] Cf. Sect. 3.3.2.

[204] Cf. Sects. 2.1.6 and 2.1.11.

[205] WTO DSB (2014) European Communities – Measures Prohibiting the Importation and Marketing of Seal Products, Appellate Body reports, para. 5.144; Cf. Van den Bossche and Zdouc (2017), p. 582; Cf. Sheargold and Mitchell (2016), p. 605.

agreements on financial stability. In the late 2000s, following the 2007–2008 financial crisis, an even stronger focus on financial stability, investor protection, and accountability was set in financial regulation. Around the same time, the first considerations of domestic Sustainable Finance measures were developed. As described in Sect. 1.1, all three policy fields and approaches influenced each other strongly.

This is supported by the legislative structure of EU Sustainable Finance measures. This sees, as discussed in Chap. 2 and above, the integration of EU Sustainable Finance measures into an existing regulatory environment of financial market legislation, both on investor protection and financial stability. Also, the expected operation of EU Sustainable Finance measures involves RTS, technical screening criteria, or another classification system based on the Taxonomy Regulation, which in turn are based on ESG factors or consider sustainability risks. These examples show that EU Sustainable Finance is heavily intertwined with its regulatory environment addressing financial stability and investor protection. Therefore, the regulatory environment and the significance and change EU Sustainable Finance measures pose to it are to be considered when assessing its policy objective under Art. XIV GATS. Hence, the legislative history and legislative structure of EU Sustainable Finance measures does not lead to a differing conclusion on the underlying policy objectives. These can thus be summarized as fostering sustainable development, particularly environmental protection, and fostering financial stability.

Taking these policy objectives into account, it must be examined *"whether there is a relationship between an otherwise GATT-inconsistent measure and the protection of public morals"*[206] and thus whether there this measure is capable of protecting public morals. To determine whether the EU Sustainable Finance measures do pass such initial threshold of at least being capable of protecting public morals and thus constituting a certain relationship between Sustainable Finance and public morals, yet another reference can be made to the Appellate Body in *Colombia–Textiles*. It found that for this determination, *"evidence regarding the design of the measure at issue, including its content, structure, and expected operation"* must be examined.[207]

The definition of the public morals term in GATT and GATS has a history in its own right. The Panel in *US–Gambling* used the Shorter Oxford English Dictionary's definition of public *"as: 'Of or pertaining to the people as a whole; belonging to, affecting, or concerning the community or nation. '"*[208] In relation to both, public morals and public order, the Panel found *"that a measure that is sought to be justified under Article XIV(a) must be aimed at protecting the interests of the people within a*

---

[206] WTO DSB (2016b) Colombia – Measures Relating to the Importation of Textiles, Apparel and Footwear, Appellate Body report, para. 5.68; Cf. Van den Bossche and Zdouc (2017), p. 579.

[207] WTO DSB (2016b) Colombia – Measures Relating to the Importation of Textiles, Apparel and Footwear, Appellate Body report, para. 5.69.

[208] WTO DSB (2004a) United States – Measures Affecting the Cross-Border Supply of Gambling and Betting Services, Panel report, para. 6.463; Cf. WTO (2020d), p. 6; Van den Bossche and Zdouc (2017), p. 608.

community or a nation as a whole."[209] A Sustainable Finance measure would thus be deemed to have a sufficiently close relationship to the protection of public morals if the policy objectives described above can be understood to be aimed at the protection of a WTO Member's or its community's moral interest. *Morals* thereby were defined by the very Panel in *US–Gambling* again with reference to the Shorter Oxford English Dictionary "*as: '[...] habits of life with regard to right and wrong conduct.*"[210] The Panel, therefore, concludes that "*the term 'public morals' denotes standards of right and wrong conduct maintained by or on behalf of a community or nation.*"[211] The policy objectives of EU Sustainable Finance, above found to be the fostering of sustainable development and financial stability, are based on *standards of right and wrong* insofar as that both concepts of sustainable development and financial stability immediately relate to ongoing debates around significant social safeguards, corporate responsibility, and generational duties.

Jurisprudence on this determination can so far only be drawn from the Panel Report in *EC–Seal Products*, which determined that in the case of animal welfare the requirement of public morals was met.[212] In contrast to the wider concept of sustainable development, animal welfare indeed exhibits a rather direct connection to the ordinary understanding of *morals*. Sustainable development, however, unites approaches aimed at not only climate change mitigation and environmental protection but also poverty eradication, labor rights, and good governance. Alike animal welfare these ESG factors, too, possess direct links to the ordinary meaning of morals. This, in contrast, cannot be said with a view to financial stability. First, financial stability in the first place aims to protect the financial system. At a second stage, it aims to protect the real economy from backlashes from financial instabilities and shortages of funding for economic activities. Only then, the concept of financial stability reconnects to the actual livelihoods in a society and only then its implementation could be deemed relevant to *public morals*. Second, those parts of financial regulation that do fall under the concept of financial stability and are aimed at financial crime prevention (e.g., regulations addressing money laundering or crime financing) are connected more closely to *public morals* but cannot be considered an aspect of Sustainable Finance. Hence, Sustainable Finance measures

---

[209] WTO DSB (2004a) United States – Measures Affecting the Cross-Border Supply of Gambling and Betting Services, Panel report, para. 6.463; Cf. WTO (2020d), p. 6; Van den Bossche and Zdouc (2017), p. 608.

[210] WTO DSB (2004a) United States – Measures Affecting the Cross-Border Supply of Gambling and Betting Services, Panel report, para. 6.464; Cf. WTO; Van den Bossche and Zdouc (2017), p. 608.

[211] WTO DSB (2004a) United States – Measures Affecting the Cross-Border Supply of Gambling and Betting Services, Panel report, para. 6.465; WTO DSB (2005) United States – Measures Affecting the Cross-Border Supply of Gambling and Betting Services, Appellate Body report, para. 296; Cf. WTO (2020d), pp. 6 et seq.; Van den Bossche and Zdouc (2017), pp. 581, 608 et seq.

[212] WTO DSB (2013) European Communities – Measures Prohibiting the Importation and Marketing of Seal Products, Panel reports, para. 7.410; Van den Bossche and Zdouc (2017), p. 581.

addressing financial stability do not fall under the public morals requirement of Art. XIV(a) GATS, whereas sustainable development-related provisions do.

Sustainable development as a core policy objective of Sustainable Finance furthermore fulfills the requirement set out by the Panel in *US–Gambling* of being *"aimed at protecting the interests of the people within a community or a nation as a whole"*. The intensity and timeframe in which the debate surrounding topics of sustainable development is conducted shows that this issue is a matter of cross-generational, cross-partisan, and even cross-national importance (and urgency) and, thus, can be deemed to be *"aimed at protecting the interests of the people within a community or a nation as a whole"*.

It is to be noted that the concept of public morals *"can vary in time and space, depending upon a range of factors, including prevailing social, cultural, ethical and religious values"*. Therefore, WTO Members *"have the right to determine the level of protection that they consider appropriate."*[213] This is supported by the Appellate Body in *US–Shrimp*, shifting the focus from the parties' objectives at the time of the measure's drafting, towards those objectives held at the time of the Appellate Body decision and the way Art. XX GATT had been modified through its 1994 adaptation.[214] To interpret Art. XX GATT, the Appellate Body did not only refer to its plain language or explicit WTO Member practice but also to modern science and contemporary concerns of the international community in relation to environmental protection.[215] This shows that sustainable development can be incorporated into the interpretation of Art. XX GATT and equally of Art. XIV GATS also due to the mere fact of being of core concern of the international community.

Concerning the EU, both sustainable development, particularly its environmental and social factors, and financial stability are prevailing social and ethical values in the EU. This may be exemplified by the emphasis placed on environmental protection in Art. 11, Art. 114(3), and title twenty (*Environment*) TFEU,[216] and Art. 21(2) (d) TEU[217] and its preamble. Labor standards are only mentioned in Art. 156 TFEU. Financial stability, however, is stated in Art. 127(5) and Art. 141(2) TFEU and Art.

---

[213] WTO DSB (2004a) United States – Measures Affecting the Cross-Border Supply of Gambling and Betting Services, Panel report, para. 6.461; Referring to WTO DSB (2000b) Korea – Measures Affecting Imports of Fresh, Chilled and Frozen Beef, Appellate Body reports, para. 176, and WTO DSB (2001a) European Communities – Measures Affecting Asbestos and Products Containing Asbestos, Appellate Body report, para. 168; Cf. WTO (2020d), p. 6; Van den Bossche and Zdouc (2017), p. 608; The Panel applied the Appellate Body's findings despite them being originally based on Art. XX GATT, cf. WTO DSB (2004a) United States – Measures Affecting the Cross-Border Supply of Gambling and Betting Services, Panel report, para. 6.461; Cf. WTO (2020d), p. 6; Van den Bossche and Zdouc (2017), p. 608.

[214] WTO DSB (1998) United States – Import Prohibition of Certain Shrimp and Shrimp Products, Appellate Body report, para. 129 et seq.; Cf. Hush (2018), p. 134.

[215] WTO DSB (1998) United States – Import Prohibition of Certain Shrimp and Shrimp Products, Appellate Body report, para. 128 et seq.; Hush (2018), p. 134.

[216] Consolidated version of the Treaty on the Functioning of the European Union [2012] OJ C 326/47.

[217] Consolidated version of the Treaty on European Union [2012] OJ C 326/13.

25.1 TFEU Protocol (no. 4) on the Statute of the European System of Central Banks and the European Central Bank. From this follows that the EU does define the scope of its public morals according to its prevailing social, cultural, and ethical values. Following the above considerations of the TFEU and TEU, these values can be seen as including sustainable development, or more precisely environmental protection, labor standards, and financial stability.

The EU Sustainable Finance measures under consideration must further be considered to *protect public morals*. With a view to Art. XX(a) GATT the Appellate Body in *EC–Seal Products* did not find *"that the term 'to protect', when used in relation to 'public morals' under Article XX(a), required the Panel [. . .] to identify the existence of a risk to EU public moral concerns [. . .]."*[218] Therefore, under Art. XIV(a) GATS, too, it can be considered unnecessary to identify a specific risk to public morals concerning sustainable development. Nevertheless, such risks are widely conceivable in the form of global warming and social instability created by global value chains and economic inequalities.[219]

Finally, regarding their capability of offering such protection to public morals, it needs to be stated that these measures vary in their respective restrictiveness. As described above, the EU Sustainable Finance measures are dispersed throughout EU financial market regulation and address varying issues as described in Chap. 2. However, WTO *"Members may set different levels of protection even when responding to similar interests of moral concern."*[220] Therefore, measures based on the same public moral policy objective, may differ in their restrictive impact and still be considered to protect public morals. Adding to this, the observation can be consulted that despite the varying degree of its intensity, EU Sustainable Finance legislation is comparatively far developed. There are only a few other jurisdictions with similar advances in Sustainable Finance legislation alongside members of the Association of South-East Asian Nations and some Latin American countries.[221]

To sum up, the EU Sustainable Finance measures described in Chap. 2 can be understood to protect public morals. However, the examination of the design element of Art. XIV(a) GATS, pursuant to the Appellate Body in *Colombia–Textiles*, is not to be structured in *"a way as to lead it to truncate [the] analysis prematurely and thereby foreclose consideration of crucial aspects of the*

---

[218] WTO DSB (2014) European Communities – Measures Prohibiting the Importation and Marketing of Seal Products, Appellate Body reports, para. 5.198; Cf. Van den Bossche and Zdouc (2017), p. 583.

[219] Cf. e.g. the 2030 Agenda's SDG 10 (*Reduce inequality within and among countries*) and the IPCC (2019), pp. 3 et seqq.

[220] As the Appellate Body in EC-Seal Products found in reference to the Panel in US-Gambling, cf. WTO DSB (2014) European Communities – Measures Prohibiting the Importation and Marketing of Seal Products, Appellate Body reports, para. 5.200; Cf. Van den Bossche and Zdouc (2017), p. 583.

[221] Cf. TEG (2019c), p. 12; To be noted is also China's 2015 introduction of its green bond taxonomy, cf. NGFS (2019), p. 34.

respondent's defence relating to the 'necessity' analysis."[222] Hence, the third step in the analysis of Art. XIV(a) GATS is assessing the *necessity* of the measure to protect public morals.[223] Thereby, the measure itself, and not the objective pursued, must be *necessary*.[224]

To determine whether a measure is necessary under Art. XIV(a) GATS and thus whether there is a "*sufficient nexus between the measure and the interest protected*",[225] first, "*an assessment of the 'relative importance' of the interests or values furthered by the challenged measure*" needs to be conducted. This is followed by a process in which all factors, particularly including "*the contribution of the measure to the realization of the ends pursued by it*" and "*the restrictive impact of the measure on international commerce*", are "*weighed and balanced*".[226] This process may also entail a comparison with feasible alternatives to the measure.[227] Thereby, the extensive case law on the requirement of *necessity* under Art. XX GATT is relevant and applicable to the interpretation of Art. XIV(a) GATS.[228]

Pursuant to the above process set by the Panel in *US–Gambling*, first, the *relative importance* of the interest pursued by the otherwise GATS-inconsistent measure needs to be determined, since the "*more vital or important the interests or values*

---

[222] WTO DSB (2016b) Colombia – Measures Relating to the Importation of Textiles, Apparel and Footwear, Appellate Body report, para. 5.77; Cf. Van den Bossche and Zdouc (2017), p. 580; Cf. WTO DSB (2016) Argentina – Measures Relating to Trade in Goods and Services, Appellate Body report, para. 6.203.

[223] With a view to Art. XX(a) GATT cf. WTO DSB (2016b) Colombia – Measures Relating to the Importation of Textiles, Apparel and Footwear, Appellate Body report, para. 5.67; Cf. Van den Bossche and Zdouc (2017), p. 579; Cf. Trachtman (1996), p. 89; Cf. Martin and Mercurio (2017), p. 82.

[224] WTO DSB (2009a) Panel Report, China – Measures Affecting Trading Rights and Distribution Services for Certain Publications and Audiovisual Entertainment Products, Panel report, para. 7.789; Cf. Van den Bossche and Zdouc (2017), p. 584.

[225] WTO DSB (2014) European Communities – Measures Prohibiting the Importation and Marketing of Seal Products, Appellate Body reports, para. 5.169; Van den Bossche and Zdouc (2017), pp. 584 et seq.

[226] WTO DSB (2005) United States – Measures Affecting the Cross-Border Supply of Gambling and Betting Services, Appellate Body report, para. 306; WTO DSB (2009a) Panel Report, China – Measures Affecting Trading Rights and Distribution Services for Certain Publications and Audiovisual Entertainment Products, Panel report, para. 7.788; WTO DSB (2014) European Communities – Measures Prohibiting the Importation and Marketing of Seal Products, Appellate Body reports, para. 5.169; WTO DSB (2000b) Korea – Measures Affecting Imports of Fresh, Chilled and Frozen Beef, Appellate Body reports, para. 164; WTO DSB (2001a) European Communities – Measures Affecting Asbestos and Products Containing Asbestos, Appellate Body report, para. 172; Cf. WTO (2020d), pp. 7 et seq.; Cf. Van den Bossche and Zdouc (2017), pp. 561, 584 et seq., 610.

[227] WTO DSB (2005) United States – Measures Affecting the Cross-Border Supply of Gambling and Betting Services, Appellate Body report, para. 307; Cf. WTO DSB (2014) European Communities – Measures Prohibiting the Importation and Marketing of Seal Products, Appellate Body reports, para. 5.169; Cf. WTO (2020d), p. 8; Van den Bossche and Zdouc (2017), p. 584 et seq., 610.

[228] Van den Bossche and Zdouc (2017), pp. 609 et seq.

that are reflected in the objective of the measure, the easier it would be to accept a measure as 'necessary'."[229] The importance of the first policy objective, the fostering of sustainable development, is exemplified by the rapid inclusion of the SDGs and the Paris Agreement's carbon emission reduction goals into EU legislation and mainstreaming these goals into all EU measures. Also, as discussed above, pursuant to the Appellate Body the way a WTO Member characterizes its regulatory approach with regard to the objectives and effectiveness of the measure for instance via *"texts of statutes, legislative history, and pronouncements of government agencies or officials"* guides the assessment on the necessity requirement.[230] The importance of the second policy objective of EU Sustainable Finance measures, namely financial stability, has been regarded as of high importance since the 2007–2008 financial crisis. The interest pursued would thus be of high relative importance regarding the assessment of the necessity requirement. This, however, is not relevant at this stage since the policy objective of financial stability did not pass the initial capability threshold of public morals.

In a second step, to determine the necessity of a measure, the measure itself and reasonably available alternatives are to be compared within the light of the relative importance of the interests described above. In *China-Audiovisual Products*, with a view to Art. XX(a) GATT, the Panel weighted and balanced three elements: The importance of the issue, the contribution of the measure to the policy objective, and the restrictive impact.[231] As the importance of sustainable development has already been demonstrated above, hence the *contribution of the measure* to this policy objective is to be determined. As described in Sect. 1.1, Sustainable Finance aims at rechanneling private capital towards more sustainable investment alternatives. This approach received increased attention due to the size of investments needed to transpose the SDGs and the Paris Agreement's targets. This shows the contribution Sustainable Finance may offer to the achievement of such targets. More precisely, the EU Sustainable Finance measures described in Chap. 2 and Sect. 2.1, do not only contribute to this rechanneling of private capital but as a second stream of financing for these targets, add to the conventional public funding. For this reason, these EU Sustainable Finance measures also suffice the requirement of a sufficient nexus between the measure and the Art. XIV GATS interest of public morals. The Appellate Body clarifies that this nexus *"is specified in the language of the*

---

[229] WTO DSB (2016b) Colombia – Measures Relating to the Importation of Textiles, Apparel and Footwear, Appellate Body report, para. 5.71; WTO DSB (2001a) European Communities – Measures Affecting Asbestos and Products Containing Asbestos, Appellate Body report, para. 172; Van den Bossche and Zdouc (2017), pp. 560, 585.

[230] WTO DSB (2005) United States – Measures Affecting the Cross-Border Supply of Gambling and Betting Services, Appellate Body report, para. 304.

[231] WTO DSB (2009a) Panel Report, China – Measures Affecting Trading Rights and Distribution Services for Certain Publications and Audiovisual Entertainment Products, Panel report, para. 7.817, 7.828, 7.788; Cf. WTO DSB (2007b) Brazil – Measures Affecting Imports of Retreaded Tyres, Appellate Body report, para. 145; Van den Bossche and Zdouc (2017), pp. 584, 586.

paragraphs themselves, through the use of terms such as 'relating to' and 'necessary to'."[232]

Subsequently, the restrictive impact on international trade in financial services of EU Sustainable Finance measures in view of its contribution needs to be determined. The Appellate Body in *Colombia–Textiles* found that in "*assessing this factor, 'a panel must seek to assess the degree of a measure's trade-restrictiveness, rather than merely ascertaining whether or not the measure involves some restriction on trade.*"[233] Thereby, the "*less restrictive the effects of the measure, the more likely it is to be characterized as 'necessary'.*"[234] As discussed in Sect. 3.2.2.2, EU Sustainable Finance measures do have the ability to have a detrimental effect on international trade in financial services. This restrictive impact, however, is neither intended nor the predominant effect. Rather, the respective restrictive impact depends on the design of the relevant measure. EU Sustainable Finance measures can be divided into voluntary measures, with a low restrictive impact, and compulsory measures, with a respectively higher restrictive impact.[235]

Voluntary measures include the proposed EU Ecolabel for financial products based on the Ecolabel Regulation[236] and the Taxonomy Regulation,[237] and the EU GBS.[238] Thus, voluntary measures mostly consist of labeling standards. Examples of compulsory EU Sustainable Finance measures, in contrast, are the reporting and disclosures requirements pursuant to the SRD and the SRD II,[239] the Solvency II

---

[232] WTO DSB (2005) United States – Measures Affecting the Cross-Border Supply of Gambling and Betting Services, Appellate Body report, para. 292; Cf. WTO (2020d), p. 3; Cf. WTO DSB (2015) Argentina – Measures Relating to Trade in Goods and Services, Panel report, para. 7.586.

[233] WTO DSB (2016b) Colombia – Measures Relating to the Importation of Textiles, Apparel and Footwear, Appellate Body report, para. 5.73, referring to WTO DSB (2016) Argentina – Measures Relating to Trade in Goods and Services, Appellate Body report, para. 6.234; Van den Bossche and Zdouc (2017), p. 587.

[234] WTO DSB (2009b) China – Measures Affecting Trading Rights and Distribution Services for Certain Publications and Audiovisual Entertainment Products, Appellate Body report, para. 310, referring to WTO DSB (2000b) Korea – Measures Affecting Imports of Fresh, Chilled and Frozen Beef, Appellate Body reports, para. 163 and WTO DSB (2007b) Brazil – Measures Affecting Imports of Retreaded Tyres, Appellate Body report, para. 150; Van den Bossche and Zdouc (2017), p. 584.

[235] For an overview of the restrictive impact of the respective EU Sustainable Finance measure, cf. Table 1.

[236] Cf. Art. 1 and Art. 2(1) Regulation (EC) No 66/2010 of the European Parliament and of the Council of 25 November 2009 on the EU Ecolabel [2009] OJ L 27/1.

[237] European Commission (2018), p. 5; JRC (2019), pp. 1 et seq.

[238] HLEG (2018a), p. 32.

[239] Art. 6a(3)(2) Directive 2007/36/EC of the European Parliament and of the Council of 11 July 2007 on the exercise of certain rights of shareholders in listed companies [2007] OJ L 184/17 and Art. 3 g(1)(a) Directive (EU) 2017/828 of the European Parliament and of the Council of 17 May 2017 amending Directive 2007/36/EC as regards the encouragement of long-term shareholder engagement [2017] OJ L 132/1, respectively; Cf. Bueren (2019), p. 845.

DelReg,[240] the PEPP Regulation, and the PRIIPs Regulation.[241] Further examples encompass the CRR and the CRR II,[242] the NFR Directive, the Sustainability Disclosures Regulation,[243] the Taxonomy Regulation, and the Climate BMR.[244] These reporting and disclosure provisions, however, although being compulsory, do not have a significant restrictive impact. This is primarily due to such reporting and disclosure standards being common to financial regulation and constitute established oversight mechanisms that are merely extended to sustainability information.[245]

Finally, pursuant to the Appellate Body in *US–Gambling* it is to be determined *"whether another, WTO-consistent measure is 'reasonably available'"* considering *"the interests or values at stake".*[246] Thereby, the alternative measure must not be *"merely theoretical in nature"* or imposing *"an undue burden on [the respective WTO] Member, such as prohibitive costs or substantial technical difficulties".*[247]

---

[240] Art. 263 and Art. 296(4) Commission Delegated Regulation (EU) 2015/35 of 10 October 2014 supplementing Directive 2009/138/EC of the European Parliament and of the Council on the taking-up and pursuit of the business of Insurance and Reinsurance (Solvency II) [2015] OJ L 12/1.

[241] Art. 28(3)(c)(xii), Art. 36(1), and Art. 37(1) Regulation (EU) 2019/1238 and Art. 8(3)(c) (ii) Regulation (EU) No 1286/2014 of the European Parliament and of the Council of 26 November 2014 on key information documents for packaged retail and insurance-based investment products (PRIIPs) [2014] OJ L 352/1, respectively.

[242] Art. 501a Regulation (EU) No 575/2013 of the European Parliament and of the Council of 26 June 2013 on prudential requirements for credit institutions and investment firms and amending Regulation (EU) No 648/2012 [2013] OJ L 176/1; Art. 1(119) Regulation (EU) 2019/876 of the European Parliament and of the Council of 20 May 2019 amending Regulation (EU) No 575/2013 as regards the leverage ratio, the net stable funding ratio, requirements for own funds and eligible liabilities, counterparty credit risk, market risk, exposures to central counterparties, exposures to collective investment undertakings, large exposures, reporting and disclosure requirements, and Regulation (EU) No 648/2012 [2019] OJ L 150/1.

[243] Art. 53 IFR, Art. 1(1) subpara. 1 Directive 2014/95/EU of the European Parliament and of the Council of 22 October 2014 amending Directive 2013/34/EU as regards disclosure of non-financial and diversity information by certain large undertakings and groups [2014] OJ L 330/1 and Art. 4, Art. 8, and Art. 9 Regulation (EU) 2019/2088 of the European Parliament and of the Council of 27 November 2019 on sustainability-related disclosures in the financial services sector [2019] OJ L 317/1, respectively.

[244] Art. 5 Regulation (EU) 2020/852 and Art. 1(6) subpara. 1 Regulation (EU) 2019/2089 of the European Parliament and of the Council of 27 November 2019 amending Regulation (EU) 2016/1011 as regards EU Climate Transition Benchmarks, EU Paris-aligned Benchmarks and sustainability-related disclosures for benchmarks [2019] OJ L 317/17, respectively.

[245] In turn, more effective measures would also be of a higher restrictive impact and thus are more likely to be GATS-inconsistent. This is exemplified by the prospective EU Sustainable Finance measures demonstrated in Sect. 3.3.

[246] WTO DSB (2005) United States – Measures Affecting the Cross-Border Supply of Gambling and Betting Services, Appellate Body report, para. 307; Cf. WTO (2020d), p. 8; Van den Bossche and Zdouc (2017), p. 610; Cf. Sheargold and Mitchell (2016), p. 605.

[247] WTO DSB (2005) United States – Measures Affecting the Cross-Border Supply of Gambling and Betting Services, Appellate Body report, para. 308; Van den Bossche and Zdouc (2017), pp. 610, 588; Cf. WTO DSB (2001a) European Communities – Measures Affecting Asbestos and Products Containing Asbestos, Appellate Body report, paras. 172–174; WTO DSB (2000b)

But rather, it must offer the same level of protection of public morals as the challenged measure.[248] With a view to the policy objective of fostering sustainable development, the same level of protection would only be provided by sufficient funds by conventional public sources. However, this supersedes the financial capability of EU Member States and is the very reason for the creation of Sustainable Finance policy in this regard. This is recognized by the Appellate Body in *Brazil–Retreated Tyres*, which found that "*reasonably available alternatives*" depended *inter alia* on a WTO Member's financial capacity.[249] Thus, exclusively public funding for sustainable development is not a feasible alternative.

Necessity under Art. XIV(a) GATS also requires that there is no measure of less restrictive impact equally capable of protecting public morals and thus achieving the measure's policy objective.[250] Lacking an equally effective, feasible alternative to the rechanneling of private capital into more sustainable investments, a weighting process based on the respective measure's restrictive impact is not required. However, the findings made in Sect. 3.2.3.2.1 can be reriterated. EU Sustainable Finance measures do contribute substantially to the pursued policy objective while their restrictive impact, even that of compulsory measures, is rather low. Furthermore, different provisions apply based on the respective sustainability of each financial service. These classes of provisions then have increasing restrictiveness corresponding to their effectiveness. An example of such regulatory scheme is the TEG's proposal of three types of disclosure obligations based on the climate-related risk exposure of the company.[251] Another example is the differentiation between financial products covered by Art. 8 and those covered by Art. 9 Sustainability Disclosures Regulation.[252] Concluding, EU Sustainable Finance measures aimed at fostering sustainable development are provisionally justified under the public morals exception of Art. XIV(a) GATS.

Korea – Measures Affecting Imports of Fresh, Chilled and Frozen Beef, Appellate Body reports, para. 180.

[248] WTO DSB (2005) United States – Measures Affecting the Cross-Border Supply of Gambling and Betting Services, Appellate Body report, para. 308; Van den Bossche and Zdouc (2017), pp. 610, 588; Cf. WTO DSB (2001a) European Communities – Measures Affecting Asbestos and Products Containing Asbestos, Appellate Body report, paras. 172–174; WTO DSB (2000b) Korea – Measures Affecting Imports of Fresh, Chilled and Frozen Beef, Appellate Body reports, para. 180.

[249] Sheargold and Mitchell (2016), p. 606; referring to WTO DSB (2007b) Brazil – Measures Affecting Imports of Retreaded Tyres, Appellate Body report, para. 171.

[250] Cf. Trachtman (1996), p. 85.

[251] Cf. Sect. 2.1.6; TEG (2019a), pp. 7, 15.

[252] Cf. Sect. 2.1.6.

3.2.4.1.2 Necessary to Maintain Public Order

Art. XIV(a) GATS further lists *"public order"* as a feasible cause for the acceptance of an otherwise GATS-inconsistent measure. The examination of public order follows the same structure as has been described and applied above in relation to public morals. The main policy objective of EU Sustainable Finance measures, as stated above, is the fostering of sustainable development and financial stability, whilst measure falling under Art XIV(a) GATS must be capable of maintaining public order.

The Panel in *US–Gambling* consulted the 2002 Shorter Oxford English Dictionary's[253] definition of *"order"* and found that it encompasses *"[a] condition in which the laws regulating the public conduct of members of a community are maintained and observed; the rule of law or constituted authority; absence of violence or violent crimes."*[254] This is not the case with Sustainable Finance. EU Sustainable Finance measures, as stated above, aim to introduce new rules to *inter alia* rechannel private capital. These measures, however, are not *per se* about maintaining laws. This, too, is the case for the policy objective of financial stability. As argued above, the aspect of financial stability-oriented regulations that aims at the prevention of finance-related crime does not form an immediate aspect of the Sustainable Finance concept. Thus, EU Sustainable Finance measures cannot be understood as addressing the maintenance of laws under the Panel's interpretation in *US–Gambling*.

If, however, the above definition is read in conjunction with fn. 5 to Art. XIV GATS, the Panel in *US–Gambling* considered that *"'public order' refers to the preservation of the fundamental interests of a society, as reflected in public policy and law. These fundamental interests can relate, inter alia, to standards of law, security and morality."*[255] This, on the one hand, means that there can be a certain overlap with the concept of public morals, as has been admitted by the Panel.[256] On the other hand, this means that if the policy objectives of EU Sustainable Finance fall under the definition of fundamental interests of society—namely standards of law, security, and morality—they would constitute a case where the public order exception under Art. XIV(a) GATS can be invoked.

---

[253] Trumble and Stevenson (2002).

[254] WTO DSB (2004a) United States – Measures Affecting the Cross-Border Supply of Gambling and Betting Services, Panel report, para. 6.466; WTO DSB (2005) United States – Measures Affecting the Cross-Border Supply of Gambling and Betting Services, Appellate Body report, para. 296; Cf. WTO (2020d), pp. 6 et seq.; Van den Bossche and Zdouc (2017), p. 609.

[255] WTO DSB (2004a) United States – Measures Affecting the Cross-Border Supply of Gambling and Betting Services, Panel report, para. 6.467; WTO DSB (2005) United States – Measures Affecting the Cross-Border Supply of Gambling and Betting Services, Appellate Body report, para. 298; Cf. WTO (2020d), p. 7; Van den Bossche and Zdouc (2017), p. 609; Cf. Martin and Mercurio (2017), p. 82.

[256] WTO DSB (2004a) United States – Measures Affecting the Cross-Border Supply of Gambling and Betting Services, Panel report, para. 6.468; Van den Bossche and Zdouc (2017), p. 609.

Environmental protection and climate change mitigation as aspects of sustainable development are both policy concepts rooted in society's need for (material) security and in its morality concerning environmental protection. This resembles the afore-mentioned arguments in relation to public morals. The requirement of a genuine and sufficient threat to the environment does not have to be specified any further. Climate change and the issues targeted in the SDGs can be seen as a sufficiently serious threat to the preservation of a society's fundamental interests like security and morality.

The second main policy objective of EU Sustainable Finance—financial stability excluding crime-prevention provisions—cannot be subsumed under the Panel's examples of standards of law, security, and morality. These examples constitute a non-exhaustive enumeration. To determine whether an additional, unwritten example would be applicable, EU Sustainable Finance measures would need to be aimed at preserving such fundamental interests of a society. Financial stability is certainly in the interest of a society since financial instability would likely affect other parts of the economy and the livelihoods of people participating in it. However, considering again the examples given by the Panel in *US–Gambling* of standards of law, security, and morality, such instability would need to pose a sufficient threat to security, morality, or the rule of law. It would need to reach further than economic or political struggles. The aim of fostering financial stability arguably does not initially provide for such profound threats. Thus, such measures with financial stability as their main policy objective do not fall under the public order exception of Art. XIV(a) GATS. Thus, the public order exception is only applicable to Sustainable Finance measures with sustainable development as their policy objective.

The EU Sustainable Finance measures must further be necessary to maintain public order. This includes each measure's *"relative importance"*, *"the contribution of the measure to the realization of the ends pursued by it"* and *"the restrictive impact of the measure on international commerce"*. Feasible alternatives ought to be considered through a process of weighting and balancing.[257] As described above, the policy objective of sustainable development is of high relative importance. Given the large number of investments needed to achieve the SDGs and insufficient public funds, Sustainable Finance measures also offer a key contribution to the achievement of the SDGs and climate mitigation targets. This is intended to result in the prevention or attenuation of, for instance, global warming. In this regard, the conclusion remains equal to that found concerning public morals.

More critical, however, is the assessment of whether EU Sustainable Finance measures aiming at fostering sustainable development can be deemed necessary to

---

[257] WTO DSB (2005) United States – Measures Affecting the Cross-Border Supply of Gambling and Betting Services, Appellate Body report, para. 306 et seq.; WTO DSB (2009a) Panel Report, China – Measures Affecting Trading Rights and Distribution Services for Certain Publications and Audiovisual Entertainment Products, Panel report, para. 7.788; WTO DSB (2014) European Communities – Measures Prohibiting the Importation and Marketing of Seal Products, Appellate Body reports, para. 5.169; WTO DSB (2000b) Korea – Measures Affecting Imports of Fresh, Chilled and Frozen Beef, Appellate Body reports, para. 164; Cf. WTO (2020d), pp. 7 et seq.; Cf. Van den Bossche and Zdouc (2017), pp. 584 et seq., 610.

maintain public order. Again, the measures' restrictive impact and feasible alternatives must be considered. In other words, as argued above regarding public morals, despite there being a nexus between public order and sustainable development, the question is whether this nexus is sufficiently strong to suffice the necessity requirement. Introducing some form of ESG-related legislation can be deemed without alternative considering the domestic and international sustainable development targets. Thereby, the rechanneling of private capital by introducing Sustainable Finance legislation is just one of several policy options. Some equally effective measures, namely fiscal instruments, lack the uncertainty inherent to most EU Sustainable Finance measures. This is because it is ultimately the investor's decision whether to invest in sustainable economic activity. These measures are more effective while not necessarily being more restrictive than measures aimed at rechanneling private capital. However, due to the investment sum required large-scale fiscal measures are not *feasible*. They, therefore, do not constitute a reasonably available alternative.

Likewise, the approach EU Sustainable Finance measures take is to be considered relatively mediate. This translates into a largely negligible *restrictive impact* of these measures. Under Art. XIV(a) GATS, however, their nexus with the prevention of material damage to a society—such as the mitigation of climate change—is very loose. This is supported by the Appellate Body's view in *US–Gambling* that *"substantive GATS obligations should not be deviated from lightly"*.[258] Thus, the required nexus must be sufficiently close. A sufficient nexus between EU Sustainable Finance measures aimed at fostering sustainable development, on the one hand, and the maintenance of public order, on the other, cannot be established. Therefore, EU Sustainable Finance measures aimed at fostering sustainable development would not be provisionally justified under the public order exception of Art. XIV(a) GATS.

3.2.4.1.3 Necessary to Protect Human, Animal or Plant Life or Health

The general exception specified in Art. XIV(b) GATS first requires the measure to be taken in pursuance of the protection of *"human, animal or plant life or health"*, and second, it must fulfill the *"necessity"* requirement already described above.[259] Thus, Art. XIV(b) GATS requires the same two-tier analysis as already conducted in Sect. 3.2.4.1.1 concerning Art. XIV(a) GATS.[260] So far, there has been no case brought forward regarding Art. XIV(b) GATS. However, the extensive jurisprudence both

---

[258] WTO DSB (2005) United States – Measures Affecting the Cross-Border Supply of Gambling and Betting Services, Appellate Body report, para. 308; Van den Bossche and Zdouc (2017), pp. 588, 610; Cf. WTO DSB (2001a) European Communities – Measures Affecting Asbestos and Products Containing Asbestos, Appellate Body report, paras. 172–174; WTO DSB (2000b) Korea – Measures Affecting Imports of Fresh, Chilled and Frozen Beef, Appellate Body reports, para. 180.

[259] Cf. Van den Bossche and Zdouc (2017), p. 614.

[260] Van den Bossche and Zdouc (2017), p. 557.

concerning Art. XIV(a) and (c) GATS and Art. XX(a), (b) and (d) GATT can be considered.[261] The policy objective of EU Sustainable Finance measures according to Art. XIV GATS is the fostering of sustainable development and financial stability.[262] The question is whether sustainable development and financial stability fall under the term of human, animal or plant life or health according to Art. XIV (b) GATS.

Of the three ESG factors only the environmental factor such as environmental protection and climate mitigation, and the social factor such as labor rights can be considered to be within the scope of human, animal or plant life or health. This is supported by the findings of the Appellate Body in *US–Shrimp* regarding Art. XX (g) GATT, recalling both the increased acknowledgment and action on environmental protection and the mentioning of sustainable development in the Marrakesh Agreement preamble. From this, the Appellate Body deduced that Art. XX (g) GATT, which in its wording mirrors Art. XIV(b) GATS, is not *"referring only to the conservation of exhaustible mineral or other non-living natural resources."*[263]

Supported by the same reasoning, it must be argued that the general exception set out in Art. XIV(b) GATS necessarily comprises certain aspects of sustainable development. This is at least true for the environmental ESG factor, which possesses a substantially closer nexus to human, animal or plant life or health than for instance the social or governance spheres. If Sustainable Finance is regarded as an implementation tool for sustainable development, its measures, too, must be eligible for the exception on human, animal or plant life or health—at least as far as these Sustainable Finance measures focus on environmental protection. The requirement that there is sufficient risk to the environment as one of the underlying objectives of Sustainable Finance, as set out by the Panel in *Brazil–Retreated Tyres* has already been identified and discussed in Sect. 3.2.4.1.1.[264] Financial stability in turn, despite the adverse impacts of financial and subsequent economic instability on human wellbeing, does not possess a sufficiently close nexus to human, animal or plant life or health and thus does not fall under Art. XIV(b) GATS.

The question is whether the EU Sustainable Finance measures are *capable* of protecting human, animal or plant life or health pursuant to Art. XIV(b) GATS. To assess this capability of measures aimed at fostering sustainable development, the jurisprudence of application of sustainable development measures under Art. XX (b) GATT can be considered. Art. XX(b) GATT was invoked for policy objectives such as reduction of the smoking of cigarettes, reduction of air pollution, and the protection of dolphins, which all indicate a close relationship between the issue

---

[261] Van den Bossche and Zdouc (2017), pp. 559 et seq., 614.

[262] Cf. Sect. 3.2.4.1.1.

[263] WTO DSB (1998) United States – Import Prohibition of Certain Shrimp and Shrimp Products, Appellate Body report, para. 131; Cf. Van den Bossche and Zdouc (2017), p. 599.

[264] WTO DSB (2007a) Brazil – Measures Affecting Imports of Retreaded Tyres, Panel report, para. 7.46; Van den Bossche and Zdouc (2017), p. 559.

addressed and the policy objective pursued under Art. XX(b) GATT.[265] It is questionable whether, with EU Sustainable Finance, this policy objective is sufficiently closely related to human, animal or plant life or health. In this regard, the Panel in *Brazil–Retreated Tyres* found that the "*policy of reducing exposure to the risks to human, animal or plant life or health arising from the accumulation of waste tyres falls within the range of policies covered by Article XX(b)*."[266] Thus, even policy approaches ultimately aiming at human, animal or plant life or health but not closely enough related to it may be addressed under the policy objectives stated in Art. XX(b) GATT. There is no reason, why in the case of financial services this jurisprudence would not be transferrable to assessments under Art. XIV(b) GATS.

This understanding is supported by the Uruguay Round Decision on Trade in Services and the Environment.[267] In it, the Council for Trade in Services exemplified the uncertainty of whether environmental protection measures fall under Art. XIV (b) GATS by "*[a]cknowledging that measures necessary to protect the environment may conflict with the provisions of the [GATS]*". It further noted that "*measures necessary to protect the environment typically have as their objective the protection of human, animal or plant life or health, it is not clear that there is a need to provide for more than is contained in paragraph (b) of Article XIV*". This in turn means that the Council for Trade in Services deemed environmental measures to fall under Art. XIV(b) GATS. Thus, EU Sustainable Finance measures aimed at furthering environmental protection but arguably not those aimed at fostering sustainable development, in general, are covered by the Art. XIV(b) GATS exception. Other aspects of the ESG factors may not be regarded as having a sufficiently close nexus to the protection of human, animal or plant life or health and thus would not be considered admissible policy objectives under Art. XIV(b) GATS.

The EU Sustainable Finance measures aimed at environmental protection would further need to be *necessary* to protect human, animal or plant life or health. As discussed in Sect. 3.2.4.1.1, a process of weighting and balancing is conducted, including the measure's "*relative importance*", "*the contribution of the measure to the realization of the ends pursued by it*" and "*the restrictive impact of the measure on international commerce*" along with feasible alternatives.[268] As concluded in

---

[265] Van den Bossche and Zdouc (2017), p. 558.

[266] WTO DSB (2007a) Brazil – Measures Affecting Imports of Retreaded Tyres, Panel report, para. 7.102; Van den Bossche and Zdouc (2017), p. 558.

[267] Decision on Trade in Services and the Environment, Uruguay Round ministerial decisions and declarations, Decisions adopted by the Trade Negotiations Committee on 15 December 1993 and 14 April 1994, Final Act Embodying the Results of the Uruguay Round of Multilateral Trade Negotiations. 15 April 1994. U.N.T.S. 1867 (1994).

[268] WTO DSB (2005) United States – Measures Affecting the Cross-Border Supply of Gambling and Betting Services, Appellate Body report, para. 306 et seq.; WTO DSB (2009a) Panel Report, China – Measures Affecting Trading Rights and Distribution Services for Certain Publications and Audiovisual Entertainment Products, Panel report, para. 7.788; WTO DSB (2014) European Communities – Measures Prohibiting the Importation and Marketing of Seal Products, Appellate Body reports, para. 5.169; WTO DSB (2000b) Korea – Measures Affecting Imports of Fresh,

Sect. 3.2.4.1.1, the policy objective of sustainable development is of high relative importance. As this conclusion was based on both the SDGs and climate action targets pursued by the EU through Sustainable Finance, the same deduction can be made *a maiori ad minus* for such EU Sustainable Finance measures aimed at environmental protection. Equally, the findings concerning the restrictive impact of the EU Sustainable Finance measures made in Sect. 3.2.4.1.1 can be applied to the assessment under Art. XIV(b) GATS, too.

The remaining criterion for the process of weighting and balancing is the contribution of the relevant measure to environmental protection. As described above (1.1, 3.2.4.1.1), Sustainable Finance aims at rechanneling private capital towards more sustainable investment alternatives. This was found to be a sufficient contribution concerning sustainable development under Art. XIV(a) GATS. Environmental protection is thus covered by Art. XIV(b) GATS as EU Sustainable Finance measures can be deemed to contribute to this policy objective sufficiently. This is also due to environmental protection being an inherent aspect of ESG-based sustainable development and being the policy objective most referred to within both, international sustainability agreements and EU Sustainable Finance legislation.

It can thus be concluded that EU Sustainable Finance measures based on environmental protection are indeed necessary to protect human, animal or plant life or health and thus fall under the general exception of Art. XIV(b) GATS.

3.2.4.1.4   Requirements of the Chapeau

The second step of the two-tier analysis under Art. XIV GATS is determining the consistency with the requirements of the chapeau of Art. XIV GATS.[269] The chapeau further determines that the measures under scrutiny must constitute neither *"a means of arbitrary or unjustifiable discrimination between countries where like conditions prevail"* nor *"a disguised restriction on trade in services"*.[270] The chapeau of Art. XIV GATS does have significant similarities to the chapeau of Art. XX GATT. Thus when examining the former, relevant jurisprudence on the interpretation and application of the latter may also be considered.[271]

Chilled and Frozen Beef, Appellate Body reports, para. 164; Cf. WTO (2020d), pp. 7 et seq.; Cf. Van den Bossche and Zdouc (2017), pp. 584 et seq., 610;

[269] WTO DSB (2014) European Communities – Measures Prohibiting the Importation and Marketing of Seal Products, Appellate Body reports, para. 5.169; Van den Bossche and Zdouc (2017), pp. 584 et seq.

[270] Cf. Van den Bossche and Zdouc (2017), pp. 615 et seq.; Therein: WTO DSB (2004a) United States – Measures Affecting the Cross-Border Supply of Gambling and Betting Services, Panel report, para. 6.581.

[271] Cf. Van den Bossche and Zdouc (2017), p. 616; Cf. WTO DSB (2004a) United States – Measures Affecting the Cross-Border Supply of Gambling and Betting Services, Panel report, para. 6.581.

The analysis of the two standards under the chapeau of Art. XIV GATS, which will be jointly examined hereafter, follows a three-step approach. First, there needs to be an arbitrary or unjustifiable discrimination under one of the substantive GATS disciplines. Thereby, the focus of the examination is on the application of the specific Sustainable Finance measure and less so on the measure itself, as the Panel in *US–Gambling* found in relation to the chapeau of Art. XX GATT.[272] Second, between the WTO Members subject to the discrimination, the same conditions must prevail.[273] Third, the measure must not constitute a disguised restriction on trade in services.

A Means of Arbitrary or Unjustifiable Discrimination

As argued above (3.2.2), an outright discrimination between different WTO Members by the EU Sustainable Finance measures is not apparent, but there are arguments in favor of such interpretation. Hence, hereinafter *arguendo* will be discussed whether such discrimination, in turn, would fulfill the requirements of the chapeau of Art. XIV GATS.

As discussed in Sect. 3.2.2.2, the differentiation between service suppliers, which by EU Sustainable Finance standards are considered sustainable and those who are not, may constitute a treatment less favorable. As will be further discussed in 4 and 5.4, the EU has an interest in propagating Sustainable Finance as a global concept through UN institutions and trade relations. This in turn could not only incentivize but effectively force other WTO Members to adopt similar Sustainable Finance legislation themselves and thus constitute an arbitrary discrimination against those WTO Members, which do not adopt such legislation—a *de facto* coercive effect. The Appellate Body in *US–Shrimp* assumed an arbitrary discrimination if one WTO Member's methods are "*identical to those employed*" by another WTO Member and if yet the other WTO Member's products are excluded "*solely because [. . .] have not been certified by*" former WTO Member.[274] This conclusion can be adapted to EU Sustainable Finance measures that exclusively focus on the existence of a label. These would be inconsistent with the aim of effectively enforcing the underlying policy objective of the measure, *ergo* furthering sustainable development.

The Appellate Body continued that a measure must not be "*more concerned with effectively influencing WTO Members to adopt essentially the same comprehensive regulatory regime as that applied by the [the respective WTO Member], even though*

---

[272] Cf. in the introduction to 3.2.4.1; WTO DSB (2004a) United States – Measures Affecting the Cross-Border Supply of Gambling and Betting Services, Panel report, para. 6.581; Van den Bossche and Zdouc (2017), p. 616.

[273] WTO DSB (1998) United States – Import Prohibition of Certain Shrimp and Shrimp Products, Appellate Body report, para. 150; Cf. Van den Bossche and Zdouc (2017), p. 595.

[274] WTO DSB (1998) United States – Import Prohibition of Certain Shrimp and Shrimp Products, Appellate Body report, para. 156; Cf. Van den Bossche and Zdouc (2017), p. 595.

many of those [WTO] Members may be differently situated."[275] EU Sustainable Finance measures so far do not comprise such explicit border measures as those the Appellate Body referred to in *US–Shrimp*. Nevertheless, there is no reason why the same rationale applied by the Appellate Body would not apply to domestic EU Sustainable Finance measures effectively hindering market access for third country financial services and products. Examples of such products are the EU taxonomy-based instruments described in Sect. 2.1 such as labeling requirements, the EU GBS, and the requirements for sustainability-related benchmarks and credit ratings. Thus, the question is whether these measures are *"more concerned with effectively influencing WTO Members to adopt essentially the same comprehensive regulatory regime as that applied by"*[276] the EU and therefore having a *de facto* coercive effect on these other WTO Members.

The EU's and particularly the Commission's statements imply such an interpretation, particularly when one considers their respective intended leadership roles in international climate change mitigation and sustainable development efforts.[277] Adding to this, the EU takes an active part in shaping multinational policy-setting efforts in and through various international fora.[278] Even the HLEG Final Report explicitly states the EU's efforts to propagate Sustainable Finance policy on a global level through various channels of influence.[279]

However, at least six points contrast this understanding of EU Sustainable Finance measures having a *de facto* coercive effect and thus are administered in an arbitrary or unjustifiable manner. First, EU Sustainable Finance measures do not require the underlying of the financial product to be located in a specific WTO Member's territory disregarding for instance the method of production. Instead, the EU Sustainable Finance measures, in particular those based on the EU taxonomy, are relating to the sustainability of the underlying economic activity disregarding its location. Thus, these cases are considerably different from the case in *US-Shrimp*, in which the United States did not allow for certification and thus market access, despite the possibility of the third country's product objectively meeting the United States' requirements.

Second, the Taxonomy Regulation itself gives sufficient flexibility. This is supported by it being just the underlying methodology and delegating the specification of requirements to the substantial regulations. This has already been discussed above (3.2.1.1) concerning numerical limitations to market access.

---

[275] WTO DSB (1998) United States – Import Prohibition of Certain Shrimp and Shrimp Products, Appellate Body report, para. 156; Cf. Van den Bossche and Zdouc (2017), p. 595; Hush (2018), p. 132.

[276] WTO DSB (1998) United States – Import Prohibition of Certain Shrimp and Shrimp Products, Appellate Body report, para. 156; Cf. Van den Bossche and Zdouc (2017), p. 595.

[277] Cf. Gregersen et al. (2016); Pauls (2020), pp. 17 et seq.; Cf. Sect. 4.1.1.

[278] Cf. Sect. 4.1.2.

[279] HLEG (2018a), pp. 26, 55, 63 et seq.; Cf. Sect. 4.1.1.

Third, the Panel in *US–Gambling* defined the tool for assessing whether a measure constitutes an arbitrary or unjustifiable discrimination under the chapeau of Art. XIV GATS *inter alia* to be an *"absence of consistency"*.[280] Thereby the Appellate Body in *Argentina–Financial Services* with reference to the Appellate Body in *EC–Seal Products* refers to *"the design, the architecture, and the revealing structure of a measure "*.[281] With a view to EU Sustainable Finance, the extensive legislative process, reasoning, the multiple levels of legislation and administration, the consultations prior to the adoption of a measure, and subsequent transparency strongly indicate that there is sufficient regulatory consistency to suffice the non-arbitrariness requirement in the chapeau of Art. XIV GATS. This is supported by the Appellate Body's *abus du droit* interpretative approach, which states that the chapeau of Art. XIV GATS is an *"expression of the principle of good faith"* according to which a right *"must be exercised bona fide, that is to say, reasonably"* and which *"prohibits the abusive exercise of a state's rights"*.[282] However, even if the EU effectively implements its aim of international leadership in sustainable development and climate action efforts and of propagating Sustainable Finance to other WTO Members, this would certainly not amount to an *"abusive exercise"*[283] of its rights.

Fourth, this is also highlighted by the Appellate Body in *US–Shrimp*, which for an arbitrary discrimination required *"a single, rigid and unbending requirement"* that the third country adopts *"a comprehensive regulatory program that is essentially the same"* as that of the host state.[284] On the one hand, non-EU financial service suppliers are at a disadvantage compared to EU financial service suppliers, due to potentially not being accustomed to sustainability requirements and thus experiencing a higher pressure for adopting thereof. However, EU Sustainable Finance measures with a substantial relation to third country financial service suppliers allow for recognition of a financial service supplier's characteristics even in cases where they potentially do not meet the domestic regulatory requirements. Examples of this are the possibility of recognition discussed in Sect. 4.2.2 and equivalence decisions for third country benchmarks set out in Art. 30(1) and (2) BMR.[285]

---

[280] WTO DSB (2004a) United States – Measures Affecting the Cross-Border Supply of Gambling and Betting Services, Panel report, para. 6.584; Van den Bossche and Zdouc (2017), p. 616.

[281] WTO DSB (2015) Argentina – Measures Relating to Trade in Goods and Services, Panel report, para. 7.748; WTO DSB (2014) European Communities – Measures Prohibiting the Importation and Marketing of Seal Products, Appellate Body reports, para. 5.302; Cf. WTO (2020d), p. 5.

[282] WTO DSB (1998) United States – Import Prohibition of Certain Shrimp and Shrimp Products, Appellate Body report, para. 158; Cf. Van den Bossche and Zdouc (2017), p. 594.

[283] WTO DSB (1998) United States – Import Prohibition of Certain Shrimp and Shrimp Products, Appellate Body report, para. 158; Cf. Van den Bossche and Zdouc (2017), p. 594.

[284] WTO DSB (1998) United States – Import Prohibition of Certain Shrimp and Shrimp Products, Appellate Body report, para. 177; Cf. Van den Bossche and Zdouc (2017), p. 596.

[285] As discussed in Sect. 2.1.4, the Art. 30 Regulation (EU) 2016/1011 of the European Parliament and of the Council of 8 June 2016 on indices used as benchmarks in financial instruments and

Fifth, the Art. 21.5 DSU Appellate Body in *US–Shrimp* concluded that *"there is an important difference between conditioning market access on the adoption of essentially the same programme, and conditioning market access on the adoption of a programme comparable in effectiveness."*[286] Such conditioning of a program merely comparable in effectiveness to the EU's is the case with a view to EU Sustainable Finance legislation. Neither the third country rules in the BMR nor the EU taxonomy require the same certification, labeling, or registration scheme as in the EU to grant full market access to a third country financial service supplier. Instead, they relate either to the sustainability of the underlying economic activity (as in the case of the EU taxonomy) or to the equivalence of the third country regulatory framework and supervision practice with a view to benchmarks, as is the case in Art. 30(2) BMR.

Finally, the Panel in *Argentina–Financial Services* with reference to the Appellate Body in *Brazil–Retreaded Tyres* found that *"the absence of a relationship between the measures and the objectives indicates that the measures discriminate in an 'arbitrary or unjustifiable' way."*[287] With EU Sustainable Finance, however, such absence of a relationship is not apparent. As described above, despite a possible influence on other WTO Members, both the concept and regulatory structure of EU Sustainable Finance measures are based on international sustainable development, climate mitigation, and financial stability agreements.

In other words, the Appellate Body in *US–Gasoline* stated that an arbitrary and unjustifiable discrimination *"must have been foreseen, and was not merely in advertent or unavoidable."*[288] A discrimination is in turn considered unavoidable if alternative measures were available.[289] As has been stated in Sect. 3.2.4.1.1, equally effective, alternative domestic measures were not available.[290] Such alternative measures also involve *"serious, across-the-board negotiations with the*

---

financial contracts or to measure the performance of investment funds and amending Directives 2008/48/EC and 2014/17/EU and Regulation (EU) No 596/2014 [2016] OJ L 171/1 requires a regulatory framework and supervision practice equivalent to the Regulation (EU) 2016/1011 and the IOSCO Benchmark Principles, cf. IOSCO (2013).

[286] WTO DSB (2001b) *United States – Import Prohibition of Certain Shrimp and Shrimp Products*, Appellate Body report, para. 144; Cf. Van den Bossche and Zdouc (2017), p. 596.

[287] WTO DSB (2015) Argentina – Measures Relating to Trade in Goods and Services, Panel report, para. 7.761; WTO DSB (2007b) Brazil – Measures Affecting Imports of Retreaded Tyres, Appellate Body report, para. 232; Cf. WTO (2020d), p. 5; Other Reports also refer to the criteria of a *"rational connection"*, cf. WTO DSB (2014) European Communities – Measures Prohibiting the Importation and Marketing of Seal Products, Appellate Body reports, para. 5.306; Cf. Van den Bossche and Zdouc (2017), p. 602; Cf. WTO DSB (1998) United States – Import Prohibition of Certain Shrimp and Shrimp Products, Appellate Body report, para. 165.

[288] Appellate Body Report, US-Gasoline, para. 28; Cf. Van den Bossche and Zdouc (2017), p. 597.

[289] Cf. Argentina-Hides and Leather, para. 11.324 et seqq.; Cf. Van den Bossche and Zdouc (2017), p. 597.

[290] Cf. Sects. 3.2.4.1.1 and 3.2.4.1.3.

objective of concluding bilateral or multilateral agreements [...]."[291] Thus, the EU would need to take part or initiate negotiations on the underlying objectives of its Sustainable Finance measures, namely sustainable development and financial stability. It is to be highlighted, however, that the chapeau of Art. XIV GATS only requires "*serious, good faith efforts [...] to negotiate an international agreement*" and not necessarily the conclusion of such an agreement.[292] The EU is engaged heavily in the negotiation of multilateral frameworks on sustainable development and financial stability, as will be assessed in more detail in Sect. 4.1. Furthermore, the EU engages and in various cases initiated, negotiations and research on Sustainable Finance. Therefore, the EU can be deemed to fulfill the requirement set out by the Appellate Body. If the EU would not engage in international negotiations on Sustainable Finance, it would also contradict its claims and policy objectives of conducting such negotiations, a fact that was discussed in *US–Shrimp*.[293]

Yet another method of determining an arbitrary or unjustifiable discrimination is by assessing the equilibrium between the right under Art. XIV GATS and the duties under the substantive provisions. The interpretation of this equilibrium depends on the respective circumstances. In this regard, the Panel in *Brazil–Retreated Tyres* with reference to the Appellate Body in *US–Shrimp* stated "*that the 'location of the line of equilibrium [...], as expressed in the chapeau, is not fixed and unchanging; the line moves as the kind and the shape of the measures at stake vary and as the facts making up specific cases differ'.*"[294] Concerning the EU Sustainable Finance measures described above, the measures do arguably have a considerable significant impact and scope of application throughout the financial market. However, most EU Sustainable Finance measures are not very restrictive in the way they are designed and to be applied.[295] It can thus be concluded that the EU Sustainable Finance measures described above do not constitute an arbitrary or unjustifiable discrimination under the chapeau of Art. XIV GATS.

Where Like Conditions Prevail

For an EU Sustainable Finance measure to fulfill the requirements of the first two options of the chapeau of Art. XIV GATS, it would further have to constitute a discrimination between countries *where like conditions prevail*. Thereby, − similar to the most-favored-nation and national treatment standards discussed above

---

[291] WTO DSB (1998) United States – Import Prohibition of Certain Shrimp and Shrimp Products, Appellate Body report, para. 166; Cf. Van den Bossche and Zdouc (2017), p. 598.

[292] WTO DSB (2001b) United States – Import Prohibition of Certain Shrimp and Shrimp Products, Appellate Body report, para. 134; Cf. Van den Bossche and Zdouc (2017), p. 599.

[293] WTO DSB (1998) United States – Import Prohibition of Certain Shrimp and Shrimp Products, Appellate Body report, para. 172; Cf. Van den Bossche and Zdouc (2017), p. 598.

[294] WTO DSB (2007a) Brazil – Measures Affecting Imports of Retreaded Tyres, Panel report, para. 7.262; Cf. Van den Bossche and Zdouc (2017), p. 599; Cf. WTO DSB (1998) United States – Import Prohibition of Certain Shrimp and Shrimp Products, Appellate Body report, para. 159.

[295] Cf. Sects. 3.2.2.2 and 3.2.3.

(3.2.2)—a discrimination *"could occur not only between different exporting [WTO] Members, but also between exporting [WTO] Members and the importing [WTO] Member concerned."*[296]

Concerning the definition of the conditions in the chapeau of Art. XIV GATS, the Appellate Body in *EC–Seal Products* clarified that these *"should be understood by reference to the applicable subparagraph [. . .] under which the measure was provisionally justified and the substantive obligations [. . .] with which a violation has been found."*[297] In the given case, both the subparagraphs on public morals and human, animal or plant life or health under Art. XIV(a) and (b) GATS would provisionally justify at least such EU Sustainable Finance measures that aim at fostering sustainable development. Like conditions concerning these EU Sustainable Finance measures thus would need to be assessed taking into account these public morals and human, animal or plant life or health exceptions.

WTO Members with similar conditions regarding sustainable development would thus also need to have a comparable *standard of protection* regarding Sustainable Finance. Other WTO Members that do not have domestic Sustainable Finance legislation akin to the EU would therefore not constitute jurisdictions where like conditions prevail. A potential discrimination through the adoption or implementation of EU Sustainable Finance measures would not constitute a discrimination between countries where like conditions prevail. Thereby, reference can be made to the considerations made concerning the definition of like services and service suppliers in Sect. 3.2.2.1.

Disguised Restriction on Trade in Services

The third option of a measure considered incompliant with the chapeau of Art. XIV GATS is a disguised restriction on trade in services. EU Sustainable Finance measures do not necessarily create a discrimination in respect of the national treatment and most-favored-nation standards, as discussed above (3.2.2). Therefore, the above remarks and examination under the first two options of the chapeau of Art. XIV GATS regarding arbitrary or unjustifiable discrimination are made only *arguendo* in case the EU Sustainable Finance provisions discussed therein would not stand a Panel's scrutiny on a substantive level. Thus, a disguised restriction on trade in services is not only conceivable but highly relevant since this exception is applicable without previously identifying the discriminatory nature of a measure. Hence, this last option of the chapeau of Art. XIV GATS is also applicable to measures inconsistent with other GATS disciplines. As regards EU Sustainable

---

[296] WTO DSB (1998) United States – Import Prohibition of Certain Shrimp and Shrimp Products, Appellate Body report, para. 150; Cf. Van den Bossche and Zdouc (2017), p. 603; Cf. WTO DSB (1996) United States – Standards for Reformulated and Conventional Gasoline, Appellate Body report. Para. 23.

[297] WTO DSB (2014) European Communities – Measures Prohibiting the Importation and Marketing of Seal Products, Appellate Body reports, para. 5.301; Cf. Van den Bossche and Zdouc (2017), p. 603.

Finance measures, this would entail, in particular, the remarks on domestic regulation made above (3.2.3).

Within this assessment of the disguised restrictions option, however, the arbitrary and unjustifiable discriminations discussed above may very well be considered, too. As the Appellate Body in *US–Gasoline* found, "*'arbitrary or unjustifiable discrimination', may also be taken into account in determining the presence of a 'disguised restriction' on international trade.*"[298] This means that if any of the exemptions specified in Art. XIV(a) to (e) GATS apply to an EU Sustainable Finance measure, which they, as discussed in Sects. 3.2.4.1.1 and 3.2.4.1.3, indeed do, and if this measure, in turn, breaches any of the substantial GATS provisions, the measure must not be taken as a disguised restriction on trade in services.

In identifying such disguised restriction in any of the EU Sustainable Finance measures, the understanding of the Panel in *EC–Asbestos* has to be considered. The Panel found, first "*that the key to understanding what is covered by 'disguised restriction on international trade' is not so much the word 'restriction' [. . .] but the word 'disguised'*". This is, the Panel notes, due to effectively all measures falling under Art. XX GATT constituting restrictions. Instead, the Panel found that in "*accordance with the approach defined in Article 31 of the Vienna Convention, [. . .] as ordinarily understood, the verb 'to disguise' implies an intention.*"[299] The intention to disguise thereby implies a misrepresentation of an EU Sustainable Finance measure as compliant with one of the options of Art. XIV(a) to (e) GATS while the actual aim of the measure is to restrict international trade.

Whether the administration of the EU Sustainable Finance measures discussed above (3.2.3.1), can be considered misrepresentation and thus a disguise, again depends on its "*design, the architecture, and the revealing structure*".[300] The structure and design of the EU Sustainable Finance measures show that they are increasingly based on the Taxonomy Regulation and thereby, explicitly rather than implicitly, on ESG factors. Furthermore, the intention to rechannel private capital into more sustainable investment alternatives is openly stated, particularly in Commission policy papers.[301] Thus, there is no evidence for a disguise of the EU Sustainable Finance measures' policy objectives. This finding is reinforced when taking into consideration the purpose of the chapeau of Art. XIV GATS "*of avoiding*

---

[298] WTO DSB (1996) United States – Standards for Reformulated and Conventional Gasoline, Appellate Body report. Para. 25; Cf. Van den Bossche and Zdouc (2017), p. 604.

[299] WTO DSB (2000a) *European Communities – Measures Affecting Asbestos and Products Containing Asbestos*, Panel report, para. 8.236; Cf. Van den Bossche and Zdouc (2017), p. 604.

[300] WTO DSB (2015) Argentina – Measures Relating to Trade in Goods and Services, Panel report, para. 7.748; WTO DSB (2014) European Communities – Measures Prohibiting the Importation and Marketing of Seal Products, Appellate Body reports, para. 5.302; Cf. WTO (2020d), p. 5; Cf. WTO DSB (2000a) European Communities – Measures Affecting Asbestos and Products Containing Asbestos, Panel report, para. 8.236.

[301] Cf. Chap. 2.

abuse or illegitimate use of the exceptions to substantive rules".[302] Such illegitimate use or abuse of the exceptions discussed above is not visible in EU Sustainable Finance measures.

It can thus be concluded that EU Sustainable Finance measures, if they would be found to breach one of the GATS substantive provisions, would be partially justified under Art. XIV GATS. Thereby, both EU Sustainable Finance measures with the underlying policy objectives of fostering sustainable development and of fostering financial stability would, to an extent, fall under the Art. XIV(a) GATS exception for measures necessary to protect public morals. Measures whose objective is the former, namely fostering of sustainable development, would also fall under the Art. XIV(b) GATS exception for measures necessary to protect human, animal or plant life or health.

3.2.4.2   National Policy Objectives: Recital 4 GATS

Apart from the aforementioned general exceptions, certain preambulatory provisions may effectively constitute exception clauses. If applied, the exception clause would justify EU Sustainable Finance policy violating one of the GATS substantive provisions.

The most relevant of these preambulatory clauses is Recital 4 GATS, which constitutes *"the right of [WTO] Members to regulate, and to introduce new regulations, on the supply of services within their territories in order to meet national policy objectives"*. Through this right to regulate clause, according to the Appellate Body in *Argentina–Financial Services*, *"the GATS seeks to strike a balance between a [WTO] Member's obligations assumed under the [GATS] and that [WTO] Member's right to pursue national policy objectives."* National policy objective, pursuant to the Appellate Body, may further *"cover a wide array of objectives"*. This led to the conclusion that each WTO Member retains *"various means to pursue these objectives"*.[303] These means comprise *"measures [. . .] taken outside the sectors or supply modes"* inscribed in the respective Schedule on Specific Commitment.[304] The Appellate Body further argues that even the commitments themselves may serve to further said national policy objectives. Plus, if a measure eventually violates one of the GATS substantive provisions, the Appellate Body refers to Art. XIV GATS and its underlying policy objectives.[305] Therefore, on the one hand, Recital 4 GATS does not necessarily constitute a further exception to the ones already constituted in

---

[302] WTO DSB (1996) United States – Standards for Reformulated and Conventional Gasoline, Appellate Body report. Para. 25; Cf. Van den Bossche and Zdouc (2017), p. 604.

[303] WTO DSB (2016) Argentina – Measures Relating to Trade in Goods and Services, Appellate Body report, para. 6.114.

[304] WTO DSB (2016) Argentina – Measures Relating to Trade in Goods and Services, Appellate Body report, para. 6.114.

[305] WTO DSB (2016) Argentina – Measures Relating to Trade in Goods and Services, Appellate Body report, para. 6.114.

Art. XIV GATS. On the other hand, it might cover further policy objectives not explicitly mentioned in its wording.

Based on such interpretation, the EU Sustainable Finance policy objectives described above (3.2.4.1.1) concerning Art. XIV GATS would fall under the broad understanding of the term 'national policy objectives.' The issue with such broad interpretation was also addressed by the Appellate Body in *Argentina–Financial Services*. With reference to the Panel Report, it concluded that Recital 4 GATS *"does not reflect the 'relatively few' exceptions contained in Article XIV, or [...] paragraph 2(a) of the [GATS] Annex on Financial Services."*[306] To still ensure the justification of the GATS nondiscrimination principle, the Appellate Body further restated the preceding Panel Report in the sense that national policy objectives do not equal the constellations inscribed in the scope of application of Art. XIV GATS. It concluded that Recital 4 GATS shall not be *"'confined' to the situations covered by the 'few general exceptions' under Article XIV of the GATS and other provisions of the GATS that provide for exceptions."*[307] The Appellate Body, therefore, agreed that the scope of application of Recital 4 GATS *"is broader than the objectives listed in the exceptions. As long as [WTO] Members comply with their GATS obligations and commitments, they are free to pursue national policy objectives that they consider appropriate."*[308] Hence, Recital 4 GATS, due to its broad scope of application, does not replace the GATS *commitment* and *exception* paradigm. Rather, if a WTO Member acts consistent with its GATS commitments when introducing new legislation, it does not require exceptions under GATS in the first place.[309]

When applied to EU Sustainable Finance measures, Recital 4 GATS, therefore, does not broaden the policy space set by the GATS substantive provisions for these measures. Neither does it constitute an additional exception to these substantive provisions potentially applicable to EU Sustainable Finance measures. Rather, Recital 4 GATS must be understood as a mere preambulatory clause generally introducing the GATS scheme of rule and exception expressed and further detailed through Art. XIV GATS.

---

[306] WTO DSB (2016) Argentina – Measures Relating to Trade in Goods and Services, Appellate Body report, para. 6.116.

[307] WTO DSB (2016) Argentina – Measures Relating to Trade in Goods and Services, Appellate Body report, para. 6.116; Therein: WTO DSB (2015) Argentina – Measures Relating to Trade in Goods and Services, Panel report, para. 7.216.

[308] WTO DSB (2016) Argentina – Measures Relating to Trade in Goods and Services, Appellate Body report, para. 6.117.

[309] The Appellate Body in Argentina-Financial Services further elaborated that *"the pursuit of a [WTO] Member's national policy objectives is not equivalent to violation of a [WTO] Member's GATS obligations, and can be accommodated without the need to invoke exceptions. Only when a [WTO] Member, in pursuing its objectives, imposes measures that are inconsistent with its GATS obligations – e.g. by modifying the conditions of competition to the detriment of like services or service suppliers of any other [WTO] Member – would the need to invoke exceptions arise"*, cf. WTO DSB (2016) Argentina – Measures Relating to Trade in Goods and Services, Appellate Body report, para. 6.117.

3.2.4.3   Measures for Prudential Reasons: Para. 2(a) GATS Annex on Financial Services

In addition to the exceptions in Art. XIV GATS and on national policy objectives in Recital 4 GATS, para. 2(a) GATS Annex on Financial Services further sets out a carve-out clause for prudential reasons. With a view to Sustainable Finance measures, this exception is particularly relevant. Prudential reasons comprise considerations such as investor protection and financial stability. This relates to EU Sustainable Finance, where risks from sustainability in the form of stranded assets and risks to sustainability in the form of unsustainable investments are increasingly debated and considered.

Para. 2(a) GATS Annex on Financial Services allows for a further exception from the substantive requirements discussed in Sects. 3.2.1–3.2.3. This exception is conditioned on two requirements.[310] First, the measure must have been taken for one of the prudential reasons stated in para. 2(a) GATS Annex on Financial Services, which specifies that "*[n]otwithstanding any other provisions of the [GATS], a [WTO] Member shall not be prevented from taking measures for prudential reasons, including for the protection of investors, depositors, policyholders or persons to whom a fiduciary duty is owed by a financial service supplier, or to ensure the integrity and stability of the financial system.*"[311] Second, the WTO Member must not have been used the measure as "*a means of avoiding its commitments or obligations under the GATS*".[312]

Adding to this language, the Panel in *Argentina–Financial Services* found para. 1 (a) GATS Annex on Financial Services, which "*defines the scope of the [GATS] Annex on Financial Services as being confined to 'measures affecting the supply of financial services*'", to serve "*as context for the interpretation of paragraph 2(a)*" GATS Annex on Financial Services.[313] The Sustainable Finance measures described in Chap. 2 as such aim at rechanneling private capital,[314] and to this end try to influence all participants and stages of financial market transactions—for instance by obliging the offeror of a financial product to offer or be transparent about investment alternatives and incentivize the investor to use such financial services and products. Both scenarios, either directly or through an immediate market and peer pressure, affect the supply of financial services. They, therefore, fall under the broad scope of application of para. 2(a) GATS Annex on Financial Services.

---

[310]Cf. WTO DSB (2015) Argentina – Measures Relating to Trade in Goods and Services, Panel report, para. 7.821; Van den Bossche and Zdouc (2017), p. 618.

[311]Martin and Mercurio (2017), p. 88; Trachtman (1996), p. 71.

[312]Cf. WTO DSB (2015) Argentina – Measures Relating to Trade in Goods and Services, Panel report, para. 7.821; Van den Bossche and Zdouc (2017), p. 618.

[313]WTO DSB (2015) Argentina – Measures Relating to Trade in Goods and Services, Panel report, para. 7.825; Van den Bossche and Zdouc (2017), p. 618.

[314]Cf. Sect. 1.1.

The question, however, arises whether para. 2(a) GATS Annex on Financial Services is applicable only to such EU Sustainable Finance measures relating to licensing and qualification requirements and technical standards. This is due to the title of para. 2(a) GATS Annex on Financial Services, which reads *"domestic regulation"* and thus uses the same title as para. 2(b) GATS Annex on Financial Services and Art. VI GATS, which is restricted to licensing and qualification requirements and technical standards. This argument was brought forward by Panama as the claimant in *Argentina-Financial Services*, where it further added that *"GATS does not contain any definition of the expressions 'domestic regulation' and 'regulation'."*[315] The Panel in *Argentina–Financial Services* found, however, that para. 2(a) GATS Annex on Financial Services does not only cover domestic regulation in the meaning of Art. VI GATS, or even more restrictively, only licensing and qualification requirements and technical standards. The Panel found instead that para. 2(a) GATS Annex on Financial Services encompasses all measures falling under para. 1(a) GATS Annex on Financial Services *"and not only those measures that could be characterized as 'domestic regulations' within the meaning of Article VI of the GATS"*.[316] Any interpretation of para. 2(a) GATS Annex on Financial Services that was more restrictive, as the Appellate Body in *Argentina–Financial* found, *"would not be in consonance with the balance of rights and obligations that is expressly recognized in the preamble of the GATS"*.[317] It congruously found that national policy objectives as in Recital 4 GATS, as discussed above (3.2.4.2), may also constitute measures for prudential reasons under para. 2(a) GATS Annex on Financial Services.[318]

Therefore, not only those EU Sustainable Finance measures concerning licensing and qualification requirements and technical standards such as the Taxonomy Regulation, the EU GBS, and other labeling schemes, which have been discussed above (3.2.3.2), fall within the scope of application of para. 2(a) GATS Annex on Financial Services. Instead, all EU Sustainable Finance measures described in Chap. 2 may potentially fall under the exception clause. Now, that the general scope of application of para. 2(a) GATS Annex on Financial Services is found to be applicable, it needs to be examined whether the EU Sustainable Finance measures described in Chap. 2 are being taken *for prudential reasons* according to para.

---

[315] WTO DSB (2015) Argentina – Measures Relating to Trade in Goods and Services, Panel report, para. 7.835 et seq.

[316] WTO DSB (2015) Argentina – Measures Relating to Trade in Goods and Services, Panel report, para. 7.847; Van den Bossche and Zdouc (2017), p. 618.

[317] WTO DSB (2016) Argentina – Measures Relating to Trade in Goods and Services, Appellate Body report, para. 6.260, 6.254 et seq., 6.272; WTO, Analytical Index GATS – Annex on Financial Services (Jurisprudence), pp. 5 et seq.; Van den Bossche and Zdouc (2017), p. 618; Cf. WTO (2020a), pp. 4 et seq.; Martin and Mercurio (2017), p. 88 et seq.

[318] WTO DSB (2016) Argentina – Measures Relating to Trade in Goods and Services, Appellate Body report, para. 6.260; WTO, Analytical Index GATS – Annex on Financial Services (Jurisprudence), pp. 6; Van den Bossche and Zdouc (2017), p. 618; Cf. WTO (2020a), pp. 4 et seq.

2(a) GATS Annex on Financial Services. Prudential reasons thereby embody at the minimum financial stability and investor protection.

Financial stability is one of the EU Sustainable Finance measures' two core policy objectives identified in Sect. 3.2.4.1.1 alongside the fostering of sustainable development. Several EU Sustainable Finance measures address financial stability as a sustainability-related measure. Chapter 2 thereby does only describe those financial stability-addressing regulations, which have a sufficiently close relation to ESG-based sustainability. This is to not exceed the scope of that chapter as a brief overview of EU Sustainable Finance. Such EU Sustainable Finance measures addressing financial stability as an issue related to sustainability are the sustainability-related capital requirements set out in the CRR, the CRD, and Solvency II[319] such as Art. 501a CRR as discussed in Sect. 2.1.7. Furthermore, financial stability aspects are the predominant policy objective of IDD provisions on sustainability and transition risks.

Such financial stability-related, future- and long-term-oriented EU Sustainable Finance measures apply to para. 2(a) GATS Annex on Financial Services also because not only urgent measures but also long-lasting policy measures apply. To that effect, the Panel in *Argentina–Financial Services* concluded that measures conducted for prudential reasons under para. 2(a) GATS Annex on Financial Services *"may be urgent measures to confront an imminent risk, temporary or provisional measures, or even permanent (or long-lasting) measures, which might be taken even in the absence of an imminent risk."*[320]

As previously discussed in Sect. 3.2.4.1.1, the protection of investors is not one of the two policy objectives of EU Sustainable Finance. Although it could be viewed as an aspect of the social factor of sustainable development and thus part of that policy objective, it was found not to fall under Art. XIV GATS. Furthermore, however, the protection of investors can be understood to constitute an aspect of financial stability, since significant financial fraud may ultimately pose a threat to financial stability, too. Some of the EU Sustainable Finance measures simultaneously or originally address investor protection alongside for instance information rights and awareness. The question is whether despite this merely parallel addressing of investor protection duties in the same, although amended, substantive regulation the EU Sustainable Finance measure itself can be considered *for prudential reasons* under para. 2 (a) GATS Annex on Financial Services.

Examples for such amended regulations are MiFID II, disclosure and reporting provisions (2.1.6), and fiduciary and advisory provisions (2.1.8). In conclusion, such inclusion of investor protection provisions into para. 2(a) GATS Annex on Financial Services ought to be negated. Otherwise, as argued above (3.2.4.1.1) in relation to

---

[319] Directive 2009/138/EC of the European Parliament and of the Council of 25 November 2009 on the taking-up and pursuit of the business of Insurance and Reinsurance (Solvency II) [2009] OJ L 335/1.

[320] WTO DSB (2015) Argentina – Measures Relating to Trade in Goods and Services, Panel report, para. 7.890; WTO, Analytical Index GATS – Annex on Financial Services (Jurisprudence), pp. 5 et seq.; Cf. Van den Bossche and Zdouc (2017), p. 618; Cf. Martin and Mercurio (2017), p. 88.

investor protection as part of sustainable development, an over-interpretation of the scope of application of Sustainable Finance and para. 2(a) GATS Annex on Financial Services would occur.

An argument in favor of the application of Sustainable Finance under para. 2 (a) GATS Annex on Financial Services is that the two examples given for such prudential reasons are not exhaustive, as the wording of "*such as*" shows. The Panel in *Argentina–Financial Services* came to the same conclusion stating that "*the use of the term 'including' (in Spanish 'entre ellos', in French 'y compris') shows that this is an indicative list.*"[321] Thus, investor protection measures are not immediately an aspect of EU Sustainable Finance measures and thus not prudential reasons under para. 2(a) GATS Annex on Financial Services.

However, the list of prudential reasons given in para. 2(a) GATS Annex on Financial Services is non-exhaustive. Therefore, the question remains whether this clause could apply to EU Sustainable Finance measures that address neither financial stability nor investor protection issues. Instead, EU Sustainable Finance measures that explicitly address Sustainable Finance without also addressing financial stability could also fall under para. 2(a) GATS Annex on Financial Services. Such EU Sustainable Finance measures that neither address financial stability nor investor protection issues are in particular those described in Sect. 2.1 and include the EU GBS, suggested provisions on sustainability ratings, the Climate BMR, and labeling provisions (2.1.2).

There are reasons speaking in favor and against the inclusion of these prudential Sustainable Finance measures described in Sect. 2.1 into the prudential exception of para. 2(a) GATS Annex on Financial Services. In favor of considering all prudential EU Sustainable Finance measures might speak the wording of para. 2(a) GATS Annex on Financial Services, which, as stated above, only gives examples but is not to be understood as exhaustive. However, both of the examples of financial stability and investor protection named therein are closely related to the functioning of the financial market as such. Hence, the functioning of the financial market is the aim. Sustainable Finance, however, inherently tries to alter the way the financial market functions, or *deep re-engineering* as the Commission expressed.[322] Plus, for Sustainable Finance the functioning of the financial market, particularly not the way it functions traditionally, is not the aim but an instrument to further sustainable development. This is exemplified by the debate around short-termism, as discussed in Chap. 2. Thus, there is a thematic difference between measures for prudential reasons and broad Sustainable Finance measures.

Furthermore, para. 2(a) needs to be interpreted contemporarily. What in 1994 has exclusively been viewed from a traditionally medium-term prudential perspective, has changed under influence of sustainable development and long-termism towards a broader understanding of prudential regulation. Taking into account the general

---

[321] WTO DSB (2015) Argentina – Measures Relating to Trade in Goods and Services, Panel report, para. 7.819; Van den Bossche and Zdouc (2017), p. 618.

[322] Cf. Chap. 2; European Commission (2017), p. 9; TEG (2019c), p. 11.

approach to domestic regulation in GATS and the *raison d'être* of para. 2(a) GATS Annex on Financial Services as an exception clause, there is no reason from a prudential perspective for para. 2(a) GATS Annex on Financial Services to only exempt short-term and medium-term prudential measures but not the long-term measures that aim at a more sustainable financial system as a whole—A system, which ideally would decrease the need for many of such prudential measures in the first place. This in turn is contrasted by the danger of para. 2(a) GATS Annex on Sustainable Finance becoming a limitless or at least overly extensive exception for all large-scale financial market regulations, which through para. 2(a) GATS Annex on Financial Services would be automatically exempted from all GATS obligations.

However, with the inclusion of such prudential EU Sustainable Finance measures, not all financial market regulations fall under para. 2(a) GATS Annex on Financial Services, which in turn does not become a limitless exception for all types of large-scale financial market regulations. Instead, the inclusion of Sustainable Finance would accommodate the increasingly important role of sustainable development in international and EU policy-setting. Plus, as outlined above, the wording of para. 2(a) GATS Annex on Financial Services allows for the inclusion of Sustainable Finance as a prudential reason. And finally, the Panel's interpretation of para. 2(a) GATS Annex on Financial Services in *Argentina–Financial Services* in favor of a broad scope with a view to the type of measure to be exempted should also be considered concerning the scope of the prudential reason. Thus, Sustainable Finance measures, which do not explicitly address one of the prudential reasons enumerated in para. 2(a) GATS Annex on Financial Services and described above, may also possess the ability to be exempted thereafter.

Furthermore, para. 2(a) GATS Annex on Financial Services requires that "*[w] here such measures do not conform with the provisions of the [GATS], they shall not be used as a means of avoiding the [WTO] Member's commitments or obligations under the [GATS].*"[323] This clause led to diverging interpretations in the past. It can either be understood as prohibiting all violations of GATS commitments and disciplines—This would mean that this clause would be "*self-canceling*".[324] Or, it can be argued that the clause refers to GATS-inconsistent measures taken in exceptional circumstances only. Such measures would be justified under para. 2 (a) GATS Annex on Financial Services as long as they are not taken solely for protectionist purposes. In favor of this latter understanding speaks the GATS' strong stance on regulatory autonomy, expressed for instance in Recital 4 GATS.[325] In the EU Sustainable Finance measures described in Chap. 2, there is no evidence that

---

[323] Trachtman (1996), p. 71.

[324] Martin and Mercurio (2017), p. 85.

[325] Martin and Mercurio (2017), pp. 81 et seq.; Whereas the latter understanding is certainly more reasonable and widely accepted, the Panel in Argentina-Financial Services derived by stating that para. 2(a) GATS Annex on Financial Services encompasses "*even permanent (or long-lasting) measures, which might be taken even in the absence of an imminent risk*", cf. WTO DSB (2015) Argentina – Measures Relating to Trade in Goods and Services, Panel report, para. 7.890.

such measures have been or are being taken as a means of avoiding the EU's commitments or obligations, in particular those described in Sects. 3.2.1–3.2.3.

Hence, it can be concluded that all EU Sustainable Finance measures taken on grounds of financial stability fall under para. 2(a) GATS Annex on Financial Services and are therefore granted an additional justification in case of violation of a GATS substantive provision.

3.2.5 Conclusion: Legality of Current EU Sustainable Finance under GATS

As the assessment of EU Sustainable Finance measures in this chapter has shown, particularly the *de facto* labeling provisions of the EU GBS and the Climate BMR, the transparency requirements of the Sustainability Disclosures Regulation and the NFR Directive and the fiduciary and advisory duties inherit a potential inconsistency under GATS. The same applies to the underlying categorization instruments—primarily the Taxonomy Regulation but also to dedicated classification systems for instance under the EU GBS, and the ELTIF and EuSEF Regulations.[326] Arguably the largest potential for inconsistency throughout these EU Sustainable Finance measures was found in their assessment under the nondiscrimination standards of Art. II(1) and Art. XIV(1) GATS with a view to the definition of like services and service suppliers and whether a treatment less favorable is taking place in the administration of these measures.

Furthermore, given that EU Sustainable Finance measures explicitly aim at rechanneling private capital as part of a *deep re-engineering of the financial system*[327] the domestic regulation discipline of Art. VI(1) GATS is highly relevant. This applies, in particular, to the requirement of *reasonability* in administration and being *not more burdensome than necessary to ensure the quality of the service*.

Although an outright inconsistency could not be detected under these GATS disciplines—given the uncertainty of a Panel's interpretation of these disciplines—a potential application of the general exception clause of Art. XIV GATS was assessed. General exceptions on environmental measures like Art. XIV(b) GATS thereby apply to EU Sustainable Finance measures closely related to and with the policy objective of environmental protection. The same applies to general exceptions on prudential measures under para. 2(a) GATS Annex on Financial Services for EU Sustainable Finance measures taken in furtherance of financial stability, whereas such measures with the policy objective of sustainable development are justified

---

[326]Regulation (EU) 2015/760 of the European Parliament and of the Council of 29 April 2015 on European long-term investment funds [2015] OJ L 123/98; Regulation (EU) No 346/2013 of the European Parliament and of the Council of 17 April 2013 on European social entrepreneurship funds [2013] OJ L 115/18.

[327]European Commission (2017), p. 9.

under the public morals clause of Art. XIV(a) GATS. In this regard, it can further be noted that there is as of now no WTO jurisprudence on Sustainable Finance measures. The application to Sustainable Finance measures of existing WTO jurisprudence on the likes of sustainability and environmental measures or on financial services can only be undertaken on a case-by-case basis.

Through the assessment of these disciplines, it has been shown that several reoccurring factors render EU Sustainable Finance measures consistent with GATS. First and foremost, the EU increasingly bases its assessment of sustainability on numerical criteria in the form of the Taxonomy Regulation and its technical screening criteria. This makes the substantive EU Sustainable Finance measures more predictable, objective, and transparent.

Another reoccurring element of EU Sustainable Finance legislation is the considerable number of citations of and references to international agreements and reports to which the EU, its institutions, or its specialized agencies themselves contributed. This has proven relevant particularly regarding Art. VI(5)(b) GATS. This approach taken by the EU to collectively address the more recent, broad financial stability legislation and Sustainable Finance measures aimed at fostering sustainable development in this context can also be interpreted to have several structural and policy roots. First, addressing financial stability and financial aspects and fostering sustainable development jointly makes the already existent international institutions tasked with protecting financial stability, such as the FSB, address issues of Sustainable Finance while building upon the EU's long-term experience in sustainable development policy. Second, by interweaving Sustainable Finance measures into the already existing financial legislation,[328] the EU can rely on already existing regulatory frameworks and institutions, which accelerates the implementation of Sustainable Finance and facilitates the transition for market participants. Third, most EU internal financial supervisory institutions as of now deal with investor protection such as the ESAs, or with financial stability requirements such as the ECB and the SRB in the form of capital requirements—by using their expertise and introducing Sustainable Finance into their underlying legislation, the EU can further facilitate the drafting and adoption of Sustainable Finance measures.

Finally, the aforementioned GATS disciplines are also potentially the most relevant when assessing prospective EU Sustainable Finance measures of which the most relevant are discussed in the subsequent Sect. 3.3.

---

[328] Such as investor protection duties, capital requirements, *et cetera*.

3.3 Legality of Prospective EU Sustainable Finance under GATS

The increase in Sustainable Finance legislation and research, as depicted in Chap. 2, demonstrates that the regulatory field of Sustainable Finance both within the EU and at the UN level is in plain development and fast-changing. In light of the deadline for the EU's 2030 sustainability targets fast approaching, a further increase in both quantity and restrictive impact of regulation can be expected. However, in particular the aspect of the restrictive impact of such new regulation is crucial to its consistency under the GATS, as seen in the previous section (3.2). Therefore, this section will assess the legality under GATS of such EU Sustainable Finance legislation, which has either been proposed already or can be expected to soon complement the currently existing EU Sustainable Finance framework.

To assess the restrictive impact of EU Sustainable Finance measures under GATS, examples of prospective measures with comparably high restrictive impact have been chosen. These are namely a prospective compulsory sustainability labeling requirement for all financial services and products (3.3.1), potential additional amendments to the fiduciary, advisory, and product governance duties (3.3.2), and potential sustainability-related border measures (3.3.3). Subsequently, the assessment of these prospective measures is transferred onto a more theoretical level, which enables a higher degree of abstraction and generalization allowing for a less granular assessment of the legality of the concept of Sustainable Finance as such under GATS (3.3.4).

3.3.1 Proposal for Compulsory Labeling

A possible prospective addition to the already existing EU Sustainable Finance measures could be the introduction of compulsory labeling standards. Compulsory labeling provisions mandate financial service suppliers to publish a label even if, or particularly if they or their services do not suffice a certain threshold of sustainability, *ergo* a *non-sustainability label*.

Currently, compulsory labeling requirements only exist concerning such financial services that are advertised as or may lead to the assumption that they promote sustainable investments or carbon emission reduction. An example of such a provision is Art. 9(1)(a), (b), Art. 9(3) and (4) Climate BMR. More broadly, the negative statements required under Art. 1(6) subpara. 1 Climate BMR[329] for benchmark

---

[329] Regulation (EU) 2019/2089, corresponding to Art. 27(2a) subpara. 1 Regulation (EU) 2016/1011 of the European Parliament and of the Council of 8 June 2016 on indices used as benchmarks in financial instruments and financial contracts or to measure the performance of investment funds and amending Directives 2008/48/EC and 2014/17/EU and Regulation (EU) No 596/2014 [2016] OJ L 171/1.

administrators that do not offer EU CTBs or EU PABs could constitute a compulsory label, too. The same conclusion could be made with a view to *comply or explain* similar mechanisms as suggested in the EU GBS. This *per se* would only apply if a bond explicitly describes itself as abiding by the EU GBS rules or calls itself an *EU Green Bond*.[330]

Potential future extensions of such provisions may be twofold. A universal label for all financial services of a certain kind as a sustainability *gradient* could be introduced. This would require unsustainable financial service suppliers to label their products according to the associated degree of sustainability. The other feasible prospective extension towards a compulsory labeling provision is a compulsory sustainability label, which only indicates sustainable financial services. One example of this could be the EU Ecolabel for financial products already discussed above (2. 1.2), if this EU Ecolabel would be compulsory for all sustainable financial services. So far, however, the EU Ecolabel for financial products is only meant to be a voluntary label. This would create peer pressure between different market participants to increase their supply of sustainable financial services.[331]

The question then arises, if and to which degree such prospective EU Sustainable Finance compulsory labeling standards would conflict with the GATS norms discussed in above (3.2). To begin with, compulsory labeling provisions might conflict with Art. VI(5)(a)(ii) GATS as they are no longer *reasonably expectable* given the 2019 update of the EU Schedule on Specific Commitments. Indeed, as described in Sect. 3.2.3.2.2, EU Sustainable Finance legislation under that specific term and the correlating policy concept outlined in Chap. 2 has significantly increased since the March 2018 introduction of the Sustainable Finance Action Plan.[332] Latter outlined the subsequent and most of the currently proposed EU Sustainable Finance measures. Plus, it was issued by the Commission as the main policy-directing organ and thus under Art. VI(5)(a)(ii) GATS is to be deemed *reasonably expectable*.[333] This, however, does not necessarily apply to measures not specified in the Sustainable Finance Action Plan such as those outlined in this chapter.

Furthermore, as sustainable and unsustainable financial services and financial service suppliers are alike according to Art. XVI(1) and Art. II(1) GATS, a label highlighting this *de facto* difference may constitute a treatment less favorable to like

---

[330] Irrespective of whether a bond would be described as an *EU Green Bond*, a positive or negative statement on whether bond abides by the rules set out in the EU GBS would have to be published, cf. HLEG (2018a), pp. 31 et seq., HLEG (2018c), pp. 1 et seqq.

[331] Cf. Sect. 3.2.4.1.4; Cf. Art. 1 and Art. 2(1) Regulation (EC) No 66/2010 of the European Parliament and of the Council of 25 November 2009 on the EU Ecolabel [2009] OJ L 27/1; Cf. JRC (2019), p. 1; Regarding the underlying methodology for a certain term or label already in use in the market, the TEG found that if a methodology is currently not used in consensus in the market, like e.g. a green or brown activity factor, it could not be introduced as mandatory, cf. TEG (2019d), pp. 52, 61 et seq.

[332] European Commission (2018).

[333] Cf. Sect. 3.2.3.2.2.

services or service suppliers. Finally, more restrictive EU Sustainable Finance measures in the form of compulsory labeling standards may not pass the necessity test at the second step of the Art. XIV(a) GATS analysis. Thereby, the *"less restrictive the effects of the measure, the more likely it is to be characterized as 'necessary'."*[334] Thus, more restrictive measures like those described in this chapter are more likely to be considered of a higher degree of trade restrictiveness, whilst not achieving a significantly higher degree of protection for the relevant underlying policy objective.

Therefore, an EU Sustainable Finance measure in the form of a compulsory labeling provision would likely give much more ground to inconsistency under GATS than the existing, voluntary labeling measures and standards (2.1.1, 2.1.4).

3.3.2 Potential Amendments to the Fiduciary, Advisory, and Product Governance Duties

Furthermore, the EU could introduce additional provisions on fiduciary and advisory duties and corporate governance of financial services. As described above (2.1.8), regulations on fiduciary and advisory duties are a core regulatory field in which EU Sustainable Finance provisions are already being introduced. These regulations already in place comprise in particular the MiFID II and IDD provisions and delegated acts.

Such regulations already in place encompass the requirement for a fiduciary and investment adviser to ask the client whether he or she wants to incorporate sustainable investment products into his or her investment strategy. Furthermore, they encompass the requirement of the product manufacturers to always include clients' sustainability preferences into their target market definition under Art. 9(9) MiFID II DelDir,[335] with the respective distributor required to assess whether the actual

---

[334] WTO DSB (2009b) China – Measures Affecting Trading Rights and Distribution Services for Certain Publications and Audiovisual Entertainment Products, Appellate Body report, para. 310; Referring to WTO DSB (2000b) Korea – Measures Affecting Imports of Fresh, Chilled and Frozen Beef, Appellate Body reports, para. 163 and WTO DSB (2007b) Brazil – Measures Affecting Imports of Retreaded Tyres, Appellate Body report, para. 150; Van den Bossche and Zdouc (2017), p. 584.

[335] Commission Delegated Directive (EU) 2017/593 of 7 April 2016 supplementing Directive 2014/65/EU of the European Parliament and of the Council with regard to safeguarding of financial instruments and funds belonging to clients, product governance obligations and the rules applicable to the provision or reception of fees, commissions or any monetary or non-monetary benefits, C/2016/2031 [2017] OJ L 87/500; The Commission Delegated Directive (EU) 2017/593 was further amended by Commission Delegated Directive (EU) 2021/1269 of 21 April 2021 amending Delegated Directive (EU) 2017/593 as regards the integration of sustainability factors into the product governance obligations (Text with EEA relevance) [2021] OJ L 277/137.

individual client falls within the target market given his or her sustainability preferences.

In May and June 2020, the Commission proposed respective amendments to the IDD[336] and amendments to the MiFID II DelReg[337] and MiFID II DelDir[338] concerning compulsory consideration of sustainability preferences in investment advice and in determining the target market. These proposals had already been announced in the Commission's Sustainable Finance Action Plan.[339] ESMA also advised on the inclusion of ESG preferences into the target market definition of Art. 9(9) MiFID II DelDir and the conformity with the target market of Art. 9(11) MiFID II DelDir.[340] The proposals translated into the above-mentioned Commission drafts.

They introduced new definitions of sustainability-related legal terms. For instance, a definition of *sustainability preferences* making reference to the Sustainability Disclosures Regulation for defining the pursued objective of sustainable investments and the promotion of environmental or social characteristics, is set out in Art. 1(1) MiFID II DelReg Draft RTS.[341] This norm also defines *sustainability factors* and *sustainability risks* in reference to the definitions in Art. 2(22) and (24) Sustainability Disclosures Regulation.[342] Further concerning the Sustainability Disclosures Regulation and coherent to Art. 1 MiFID II DelReg Draft RTS, it introduces definitions on *sustainability preferences* and *sustainability factors.*[343]

Under Recital 5 MiFID II DelReg Draft RTS, "*recommendations to clients should reflect both the financial objectives and any sustainability preferences expressed by those clients*" when acting in the best interest of the client. Therefore, sustainability considerations are integrated into the term of *best interest*. The investment firms are further *enabled* "*to ask questions to identify the client's individual sustainability preferences*" in order "*to recommend suitable products to their clients*".[344] Recital 6 MiFID II DelReg Draft RTS further highlights the importance of transparency and information in investment advice and portfolio management with regard to the differentiation between categories of sustainable investment products. This is supplemented by the requirement that "*sustainability preferences should be taken into account in the product oversight and governance process*" set out in the

---

[336] Directive (EU) 2016/97 of the European Parliament and of the Council of 20 January 2016 on insurance distribution (recast) [2016] OJ L 26/19.

[337] European Commission (2020d).

[338] European Commission (2020e).

[339] European Commission (2018), pp. 8 et seq.

[340] ESMA (2019a), pp. 20 et seq.

[341] European Commission (2020d).

[342] European Commission (2020d), Art. 1(1).

[343] European Commission (2020e), Art. 1(1), amending Art. 1 Commission Delegated Directive (EU) 2017/593 of 7 April 2016 supplementing Directive 2014/65/EU of the European Parliament and of the Council with regard to safeguarding of financial instruments and funds belonging to clients, product governance obligations and the rules applicable to the provision or reception of fees, commissions or any monetary or non-monetary benefits, C/2016/2031 [2017] OJ L 87/500.

[344] European Commission (2020d), Recital 5.

MiFID II DelDir Draft RTS[345] and as adopted in the MiFID II DelDir RTS.[346] This particularly applies in respect of the definition of "*the potential target market for each financial instrument and*" the specification of "*the type(s) of client for whose needs, characteristics and objectives, including any sustainability preferences, the financial instrument is compatible.*"[347] This is complemented by the determination "*whether a financial instrument meets the identified needs, characteristics and objectives of the target market*", whereas these characteristics encompass "*the financial instrument's sustainability factors*".[348] To this end, a regular review of the financial instrument is also required.[349] Concerning financial products and services investment firms "*intend to offer or recommend*", they must ensure that these "*are compatible with the needs, characteristics, and objectives, including any sustainability preferences, of an identified target market [. . .]*".[350]

Similar provisions to those set out in the MiFID II DelReg Draft RTS and the MiFID II DelDir RTS have already been introduced in the Sustainability Disclosures Regulation in relation to general disclosures obligations. The peculiarity with these proposals is the fact that they abandon the exclusively profit-oriented understanding of fiduciary and advisory duties by adding a strong sustainability aspect.

Similar rules to those outlined in the MiFID II DelReg were introduced for insurance services for instance in the IDD DelReg.[351]

---

[345] European Commission (2020e), p. 1.

[346] The Commission Delegated Directive (EU) 2017/593 was further amended by Commission Delegated Directive (EU) 2021/1269 of 21 April 2021 amending Delegated Directive (EU) 2017/593 as regards the integration of sustainability factors into the product governance obligations (Text with EEA relevance) [2021] OJ L 277/137.

[347] European Commission (2020e), Art. 1(2), amending Art. Art. 9(9) Commission Delegated Directive (EU) 2017/593.

[348] European Commission (2020e), Art. 1(2), amending Art. Art. 9(11) Commission Delegated Directive (EU) 2017/593; Cf. European Commission (2020e), p. 3.

[349] European Commission (2020e), Art. 1(2), amending Art. Art. 9(14) Commission Delegated Directive (EU) 2017/593; This is accompanied by a requirement for investment firms to "*assess at least whether the product or service remains consistent with the needs, characteristics and objectives, including any sustainability preferences, of the identified target market [. . .]*", cf. European Commission (2020e), Art. 1(3), amending Art. Art. 10(5) Commission Delegated Directive (EU) 2017/593.

[350] European Commission (2020e), Art. 1(3), amending Art. Art. 10(2) Commission Delegated Directive (EU) 2017/593.

[351] Directive (EU) 2016/97 of the European Parliament and of the Council of 20 January 2016 on insurance distribution (recast) [2016] OJ L 26/19; Commission Delegated Regulation (EU) 2017/2359 of 21 September 2017 supplementing Directive (EU) 2016/97 of the European Parliament and of the Council with regard to information requirements and conduct of business rules applicable to the distribution of insurance-based investment products, C/2017/6229 [2017] OJ L 341/8; Commission Delegated Regulation (EU) 2021/1257 of 21 April 2021 amending Delegated Regulations (EU) 2017/2358 and (EU) 2017/2359 as regards the integration of sustainability factors, risks and preferences into the product oversight and governance requirements for insurance undertakings and insurance distributors and into the rules on conduct of business and investment advice for insurance-based investment products (Text with EEA relevance) [2021] OJ L 277/18.

Pre-contractual transparency requirements on how sustainability risks are considered in investment advice and investment decisions of fiduciaries are set out in Art. 6 and Art. 7 Sustainability Disclosures Regulation. This in turn applies to insurance companies, too. In the case of advertising an insurance product as being ESG factor-conducive, there are transparency requirements in Art. 8 Sustainability Disclosures Regulation—or a respective *comply or explain* mechanism in Art. 4 Sustainability Disclosures Regulation. These requirements set out in the Sustainability Disclosures Regulation indeed were originally designed for insurance companies as a 2018 amendment to the IDD DelReg.

Furthermore, financial service suppliers and manufacturers and distributors of financial products are no longer being able to provide these financial services or products to clients if they fall outside the target market under Art. 9(9) MiFID II DelReg. This target market is defined under the MiFID II DelReg *inter alia* considering the sustainability preferences of prospective clients. Offering such a product against a customer's sustainability preferences would subsequently breach the principle of only providing financial services and products according to the client's preferences. Given the importance of fiduciaries and investment advisors to the investment process, by removing the possibility to invest in unsustainable financial products (that for instance offer a higher yield than comparable sustainable financial products), this might create significant amounts of stranded assets. A third country fiduciary would not be allowed to offer a financial product not fitting the sustainability requirements of the target market it was aimed at.

Against this, however, speaks the gravity of the underlying policy objective and the potential effectiveness of the measure at hand. It is particularly important to influence fiduciary duties because of their importance in particular to private investors. Plus, the duty to take into account a customer's sustainability preferences already was in place in respect of their *best interest*. The amendments described above merely clarify this duty. Plus, it is still the customer's independent choice to allow or prohibit investments into unsustainable economic activity, it is merely the duty of the fiduciary to ask for and comply with these preferences.

Furthermore, it can be deduced that the Delegated Regulation highlight very strongly their relation to international agreements and targets. Both refer explicitly to the Paris Agreement, the Commission's Sustainable Finance Action Plan, and the European Green Deal, while also stating that the measures taken are "*in line with the Sustainable Development Goals*".[352] Moreover, the MiFID II DelDir also refers to the Taxonomy Regulation, the Sustainability Disclosures Regulation, and the Climate BMR.[353]

Therefore, taking into account the momentousness of the underlying policy objective and the potential effectiveness of the measures, the amendments to the

---

[352] European Commission (2020d), p. 1; Cf. European Commission (2020d), Recitals 1 to 3; European Commission (2020e), p. 1; Cf. European Commission (2020e), Recitals 1 to 3.
[353] European Commission (2020e), p. 2.

fiduciary, advisory, and product governance duties in MiFID II DelReg and IDD DelReg are not to be deemed of sufficient inconsistency under GATS.

The same applies to prospective EU Sustainable Finance regulation, which might allow fiduciaries to consider ESG factors *independent* from or not exclusively relying on shareholders' or investors' decisions and preferences as discussed in Sect. 2.1.8. Such rules would raise potential legal conflicts in the relation between the customer and the fiduciary. In relation to the potential measure's inconsistency under GATS, the considerations discussed above equally apply. From a trade law perspective, such measures would need to explicitly relate to the international agreements and targets set and approved by the EU.

3.3.3 Proposal for Border Measures

Another proposal for an EU Sustainable Finance measure is the introduction of a border measure. Measures in regulating services are usually domestic measures, governing the offer and provision of services by service providers and to customers already located within, for instance, the EU. Despite these measures potentially creating repercussions on trade in services, they usually do not explicitly address cross-border trade.

A border measure, in turn, would evaluate, categorize, label, reject or tax financial services by third country financial service suppliers entering the EU. Distinctions could be made, for instance, based on the service's underlying score under the Taxonomy Regulation's technical screening criteria. The introduction of border measures originates from the regulation on the import of goods.[354] For this reason, there is considerable GATT-based jurisprudence on such border measures. When applying this GATT-based jurisprudence to a hypothetical border measure for services, one must consider "*the intangible nature of services, their supply through four different modes, and possible differences in how trade in services is conducted and regulated.*"[355]

A border measure in the form of a carbon border tax on trade of goods, a so-called CO_2 *border tax*, was suggested by the HLEG in its Final Report to "*ensure a level playing field, which can be distorted by short-term costs of long-term sustainability-related investments which in other jurisdictions may not be relevant*".[356] So far, though, the Commission has not integrated such trade distortion prevention measures into its action plans or policy proposals. Still, interpretations on border

---

[354] For the sake of completeness, in international investment law, too, border screenings are used to ensure compliance of foreign direct investment (*FDI*) with domestic standards in the host state. In some cases, these screenings have been broadened to include sustainability standards to comply with domestic ESG standards.

[355] WTO DSB (2012) China – Certain Measures Affecting Electronic Payment Services, Panel report, para. 7.698; Cf. WTO (2020f), p. 3.

[356] HLEG (2018a), p. 64.

measures in GATT-based jurisprudence and literature may be indicatory for such border measures on services. In particular, the prevention of trade distortion due to lower sustainability requirements in other jurisdictions has been debated concerning carbon emissions in the context of the EU ETS.[357]

Sustainability screenings, however, do not have to be implemented as border measures. An example of a sustainability screening conducted within the host state is Art. 22 DCI 2006 Regulation[358] governing the Development Cooperation Instrument (*DCI*). It sets out that an *"[a]ppropriate environmental screening shall be undertaken at project level including environmental impact assessment [...] for environmentally sensitive projects."* Thus, the environmental screening is conducted on the project in the host state itself rather than at the border in the form of an import adjustment mechanism.

Sustainability screenings can even be conducted on an exclusively domestic basis. An example of this is EOPIA's proposition of a stewardship program. It would encourage *"adapting investment strategies, for example through exclusions (negative screening), norms-based screening, ESG integration, best-in-class (positive screening), sustainability themed investments or impact investing."*[359] A similar approach was considered by ESMA regarding sustainability in UCITS.[360] Such domestic sustainability screenings will particularly rely on the determinations made by using the Taxonomy Regulation's technical screening criteria.[361]

There have been several ideas and policy recommendations on how to design a border measure against trade distortions due to carbon requirements (*carbon-leakage*). With a view to trade in goods, recommendations focused on how to render the measure GATT-consistent.

Such potential designs of border measures comprise, first, the introduction of border tax adjustments to carbon- or energy-based taxes. Such border tax adjustment may either relate to the consumption of fossil fuels or carbon emissions.[362] Second, border adjustments may be based on a domestic emissions trading scheme like the EU ETS.[363] Third, border measures linked to the carbon emissions of international, cross-territory transport may be introduced. An example of this is France's 2007 proposal for an EU tax on trucks crossing the EU's territory.[364] Finally, a much-debated design is the carbon border adjustment (*CBA*).

---

[357] Cf. e.g. Holzer (2016).

[358] Regulation (EU) No 1905/2006 of the European Parliament and of the Council of 18 December 2006 establishing a financing instrument for development cooperation [2006] OJ L 378/41.

[359] EIOPA (2019), p. 11.

[360] ESMA (2019b), p. 21.

[361] HLEG (2018b).

[362] WTO (2009), p. 100.

[363] WTO (2009), pp. 100 et seq.

[364] WTO (2009), p. 101, fn. 182.

In the European Green Deal,[365] the Commission stated that it *"will propose a carbon border adjustment mechanism, for selected sectors, to reduce the risk of carbon leakage."* As regards the aim of the CBA, the Commission explained that it *"would ensure that the price of imports reflect more accurately their carbon content"*. Further, it clarified that the CBA *"will be designed to comply with World Trade Organization rules and other international obligations of the EU."*[366] In March 2020, the Commission published and consulted an inception impact assessment on the CBA mechanism.[367]

This shows that border carbon measures are not introduced or implemented uniformly but instead can take various regulatory forms and shapes. As stated above, most of these measures are primarily or exclusively applicable to trade in goods. Adding to the issues of implementing such carbon border measures for trade in goods, their implementation for trade in services and particularly trade in financial services raises additional challenges due to their intangibility. Only the CBA will be examined more closely, as it is a border carbon measure *per se* applicable to trade in services. Border measures can further be applied to the export and import of goods and services and they can take a supportive or repressive character. Since the export of goods and services and a supportive character (although measures of *de facto* export subsidies could be challenged under GATT and GATS) exhibit less potential for inconsistency with GATS, a further focus will be placed on *import* measures that have a *repressive* character.[368]

Another question is which consequences would arise in case of noncompliance or poor compliance with the CBA for third country financial services or service suppliers. They could be restricted of access to the market or parts thereof. The former option would resemble the restrictive impact of FDI screenings in international investment law.[369] The latter would be similar to EU Green Bonds or the CBA could merely be a labeling scheme. Finally, the CBA could impose a form of financial adjustment or burden upon noncomplying financial service suppliers.

Apart from the aforementioned practical challenges of introducing a CBA for trade in financial services,[370] such measure would also face legal challenges under WTO law.[371] In a briefing paper of the European Parliament, different forms of a CBA were assessed regarding their consistency with international trade law.[372] It

---

[365] European Commission (2019c).

[366] European Commission (2019c), p. 5.

[367] Cf. European Commission (2020j).

[368] European Parliament (2020), p. 7.

[369] Cf. e.g. Regulation (EU) 2019/452 of the European Parliament and of the Council of 19 March 2019 establishing a framework for the screening of foreign direct investments into the Union [2019] OJ L 79I/1.

[370] For more detail on the practical challenges of implementing CBAs for trade in goods, cf. WTO (2009), pp. 101 et seqq.

[371] For an overview of WTO law consistency of the CBA, cf. Deutscher Bundestag (2018).

[372] Cf. European Parliament (2020).

found that first and foremost, two motives need to be differentiated when assessing a CBA, namely counter-balancing competitive disadvantages and environmental protection.[373] Distortions of competition is not an issue commonly addressed in Sustainable Finance legislation. Thus, to better understand the implications of the introduction of a CBA or comparable measure under GATS, it is helpful to first conduct a brief assessment of such measure under GATT.

Concerning the national treatment standard under Art. III GATT and based on the jurisprudence discussed in Sect. 3.2.2.1 the European Parliament found that two products would be found *like* based on their competitive relationship *"irrespective of their carbon footprint"*.[374] To prevent a subsequent discrimination of two like products with differing carbon footprints, the briefing paper suggests imposing the average carbon price on the product and thus ensuring *"de facto group equality"* with the option of proving that the *de facto* carbon emissions were lower than the EU average.[375] Finally, the paper also proposes establishment of the CBA linked to the *"inputs rather than the final product"*. Thereby, for instance, the energy used in the production would be taxed irrespective of the origin of the product, *ergo* the place of production.[376]

Equally, the European Parliament found that a CBA would discriminate between *like* products from different WTO Members based on the most-favored-nation standard in Art. XIII GATT.[377] In theory, a CBA applied for imports and exports by the respective exporting and importing WTO Members, would balance out any discrimination. In practice, however, exporting CBAs and thus rebates are uncommon and an EU CBA on exports would lead to a discrimination of products from different origins with differing taxation. Pursuant to the European Parliament, this could be solved by discounting carbon taxes already paid in the origin WTO Member from the EU CBA rate.[378] Finally, it also concluded that any origin-based, WTO Member-specific exemption, for example in the form of import duty reductions for products from WTO Members with similar environmental standards—or higher import duties for WTO Members that for instance are not a party to the Paris Agreement—would breach the most-favored-nation standard.[379]

Due to this potential inconsistency of a possible CBA's design, general exceptions under Art. XX GATT may be of relevance. First and foremost, the European Parliament found that EU climate and environmental measures, despite for instance carbon emissions going into the atmosphere and affecting all WTO Members

---

[373] European Parliament (2020), p. 7.

[374] European Parliament (2020), p. 9; For further discussion on a CBA's consistency with GATT, cf. WTO (2009), p. 103.

[375] European Parliament (2020), p. 10.

[376] European Parliament (2020), p. 10.

[377] European Parliament (2020), pp. 6, 10.

[378] European Parliament (2020), p. 10.

[379] European Parliament (2020), pp. 10, 12.

equally, fall under Art. XX(b) and (g) GATT.[380] In respect of the *necessity* requirement, it found that there is a *"close enough nexus between the adjustment on imports
and climate change (e.g. carbon leakage) concerns"* and that there is no less trade-
restrictive measure available. This was because CBAs would not ban trade but
restrict it by charging *"a certain price for embedded carbon"*.[381]

As regards the requirements of the chapeau of Art. XX GATT, the European
Parliament found that a potential CBA, if adjusted by *"the carbon cost already paid
in the country of origin"*, would be *"arguably justified and not arbitrary"*.[382] It
further argues that WTO Members with different carbon emissions or regulations are
WTO Members *"where different 'conditions prevail'"* and thus there might not be a
discrimination, whereas taking into account the jurisprudence on coercive measures
forcing other WTO Members to adopt similar legislation, as discussed in Sect.
3.2.4.1.4.[383]

Finally, the question is whether these findings can be transferred onto a potential
CBA for financial services. First, it needs to be stated that the European Parliament's
findings in its assessment of a CBA under GATT are congruent to the findings in
Sect. 3.2. Hence, they can be transferred onto a CBA for financial services. The
fundamental differences between trade in goods and trade in services, in particular,
"the intangible nature of services",[384] as discussed above, although leading to
practical challenges in implementing such a CBA for financial services, will likely
not result in a Panel's differing conclusion under GATS. For instance, a CBA or
sustainability screening mechanism could theoretically breach the prohibition of an
economic needs test under Art. XVI(2)(a) GATS, if that prohibition would encompass tests based on sustainability considerations. However, a Panel would likely find
that such sustainability-based tests do not fall within the scope of Art. XVI(2)
(a) GATS as discussed in Sect. 3.2.1.1.[385]

Thus, it is hard to conceive how a potential future introduction of a CBA or
comparable sustainability-based border measure for financial services could be
practically designed. Besides, the assessment of the measure's legality highly
depends on the exact specifications of the measure to prevent a violation of GATS
disciplines. Lessons in this regard can be learned from existing and proposed CBAs
and the respective discussions under GATT. Furthermore, these findings concerning

---

[380]European Parliament (2020), pp. 6 et seq., 11.

[381]European Parliament (2020), p. 11.

[382]European Parliament (2020), pp. 6 et seq., 11.

[383]European Parliament (2020), p. 11; The European Parliament also argues that an exemption for
least developed countries is discriminatory but justified as they *"have historically emitted far less
than developed countries"* and it is usual as it is even recognized in the Paris Agreement, cf. *ibid.*

[384]WTO DSB (2012) China – Certain Measures Affecting Electronic Payment Services, Panel
report, para. 7.698; Cf. WTO (2020f), p. 3.

[385]There is, however, a discussion about the consistency with GATS of limiting cross-border
capital movement by so-called *capital controls* as a tool to enhance financial stability and resilience
(and thus under which certain Sustainable Finance measures could potentially fall), cf. Martin and
Mercurio (2017).

the CBA suggest that a CBA for financial services is far more likely to be considered inconsistent with GATS than the domestic measures introduced by the EU so far and discussed above (3.2). Adding to this, border measures like screening and adjustment mechanisms are far more difficult to implement on an ESG basis than a merely carbon-based approach. This is partly indicated by the fact that internally, the EU took long to develop a taxonomy, which in contrast already existed for carbon emissions internationally.

3.3.4 Conclusion: Conceptual Considerations on the Legality of Sustainable Finance under GATS

From the assessment of the three types of possible prospective and under GATS potentially inconsistent EU Sustainable Finance measures discussed above, several deductions can be made.

First, as already found in Sect. 3.2.5, an increased restrictive impact of EU Sustainable Finance legislation may be a viable policy answer to an increasingly pressing policy objective of sustainable development and in particular environmental protection. Under the GATS disciplines, however, such intensification of the restrictive impact needs to be counterbalanced with the urgency of the very policy objective of sustainable development. Further, the legislative structure and administration must suffice the requirements set out in Art. VI(4)(a) to (c) and Art. VI (5) GATS.

This balancing could also be summarized using two factors—proportionality and timing. *Proportionality* entails the balancing of the respective Sustainable Finance measure's necessity and its restrictive impact on trade in financial services and products. Thereby, the broader the scope of application of the measure, the less restrictive the measure must be, examples of which are the EU PAB in contrast to the EU CTB and the EU GBS in contrast to a potential green bond label. *Timing* in turn addresses the time required for market participants to adapt to the measure, the measure's predictability, and simultaneous developments—such as domestic and international Sustainable Finance policy—whereas these three factors interdepend. The more restrictive and the less predictable the measure is to market participants, the more time for implementation and adaption needs to be granted. The Commission's call for long-term signals, its Sustainable Finance road maps, and the intention to prevent stranded assets can be interpreted as an effort to balance its actions by timing its measures.[386]

The restrictive impact of EU Sustainable Finance measures under GATS can be assessed alongside three types of measures. First, measures that offer new and voluntary labels but which through their application put heavy restrictions and requirements on for instance a portfolio's composition. Thereby, the voluntary

---

[386]Cf. e.g. European Commission (2019d), pp. 2 et seqq.

nature balances the high restrictive impact. Examples of this are the EU PAB and EU CTB. Second, measures that apply to a wider group of financial services, which are, however, determined by the financial service supplier's actions and choices. Examples of this are benchmarks claimed to promote sustainability according to Art. 8(1) (b) Sustainability Disclosures Regulation. These measures are compulsory to such service suppliers but are counterbalanced by a low restrictive impact. Third, sustainability-related requirements that apply to all financial services or financial market participants such as disclosure requirements under the Sustainability Disclosures Regulation have a maximum scope of application but a minimum restrictive impact.

Thus, it can be concluded that if this balance is kept, it can convincingly be argued that these measures do not pose unnecessary barriers to trade under the domestic regulation clause of Art. VI(1) and (5) GATS.[387]

Finally, with a view to future WTO jurisprudence and mainly depending on the design of prospective EU Sustainable Finance measures, to a certain extend a reverse assessment is conceivable. This would include examining EU Sustainable Finance measures' treatment of *sustainable* financial services. These measures could be found to be too restrictive on these services, as well as, due to the additional disclosure requirements, on sustainability-related financial services or products or alternative evaluation methods. This would be in addition to the assessment conducted in Sect. 3.2 concerning unsustainable financial services.

Legislation

General Agreement on Tariffs and Trade. 30 October 1947. U.N.T.S. 55 (1950)

Vienna Convention on the Law of Treaties. 23 May 1969. U.N.T.S. 1155 (1969)

United Nations Framework Convention on Climate Change. 9 May 1992. U.N.T.S. 1771 (1992)

Report of the United Nations Conference on Environment and Development, Rio de Janeiro, 3 to 14 June 1992, Annex I, Rio Declaration on Environment and Development. 12 August 1992

Marrakesh Agreement establishing the World Trade Organization. 15 April 1994. U.N.T.S. 1867 (1994)

General Agreement on Tariffs and Trade 1994, Marrakesh Agreement Establishing the World Trade Organization, Annex 1A. 15 April 1994. U.N.T.S. 1867 (1994)

Agreement on Technical Barriers to Trade, Marrakesh Agreement Establishing the World Trade Organization, Annex 1A. 15 April 1994. U.N.T.S. 1867 (1994)

General Agreement on Trade in Services, Marrakesh Agreement Establishing the World Trade Organization, Annex 1B. 15 April 1994. U.N.T.S. 1867 (1994)

---

[387] A similar gradational approach was taken by the TEG regarding *type 1, type 2, and type 3 disclosures*, cf. TEG (2019a), p. 7.

Decision on Trade in Services and the Environment, Uruguay Round ministerial decisions and declarations, Decisions adopted by the Trade Negotiations Committee on 15 December 1993 and 14 April 1994, Final Act Embodying the Results of the Uruguay Round of Multilateral Trade Negotiations. 15 April 1994. U.N.T.S. 1867 (1994)

Understanding on Commitments in Financial Services, Marrakesh Agreement Establishing the World Trade Organization. 15 April 1994

European Communities and their Member States, Schedule of Specific Commitments. 15 April 1994. GATS/SC/31

Decision on Domestic Regulation. 28 April 1999. S/L/70

Regulation (EC) No 1606/2002 of the European Parliament and of the Council of 19 July 2002 on the application of international accounting standards [2002] OJ L 243/1

Regulation (EU) No 1905/2006 of the European Parliament and of the Council of 18 December 2006 establishing a financing instrument for development cooperation [2006] OJ L 378/41

Directive 2007/36/EC of the European Parliament and of the Council of 11 July 2007 on the exercise of certain rights of shareholders in listed companies [2007] OJ L 184/17

Directive 2009/138/EC of the European Parliament and of the Council of 25 November 2009 on the taking-up and pursuit of the business of Insurance and Reinsurance (Solvency II) [2009] OJ L 335/1

Regulation (EC) No 66/2010 of the European Parliament and of the Council of 25 November 2009 on the EU Ecolabel [2009] OJ L 27/1

General Assembly Resolution 66/288, The future we want. 27 July 2012. A/RES/66/288

Consolidated version of the Treaty on European Union [2012] OJ C 326/13

Consolidated version of the Treaty on the Functioning of the European Union [2012] OJ C 326/47

Regulation (EU) No 346/2013 of the European Parliament and of the Council of 17 April 2013 on European social entrepreneurship funds [2013] OJ L 115/18

Regulation (EU) No 575/2013 of the European Parliament and of the Council of 26 June 2013 on prudential requirements for credit institutions and investment firms and amending Regulation (EU) No 648/2012 [2013] OJ L 176/1

Directive 2014/65/EU of the European Parliament and of the Council of 15 May 2014 on markets in financial instruments and amending Directive 2002/92/EC and Directive 2011/61/EU [2014] OJ L 173/349

Directive 2014/95/EU of the European Parliament and of the Council of 22 October 2014 amending Directive 2013/34/EU as regards disclosure of non-financial and diversity information by certain large undertakings and groups [2014] OJ L 330/1

Regulation (EU) No 1286/2014 of the European Parliament and of the Council of 26 November 2014 on key information documents for packaged retail and insurance-based investment products (PRIIPs) [2014] OJ L 352/1

Commission Delegated Regulation (EU) 2015/35 of 10 October 2014 supplementing Directive 2009/138/EC of the European Parliament and of the

Council on the taking-up and pursuit of the business of Insurance and Reinsurance (Solvency II) [2015] OJ L 12/1

Regulation (EU) 2015/760 of the European Parliament and of the Council of 29 April 2015 on European long-term investment funds [2015] OJ L 123/98

Addis Ababa Action Agenda of the Third International Conference on Financing for Development (Addis Ababa Action Agenda), The final text of the outcome document adopted at the Third International Conference on Financing for Development (Addis Ababa, Ethiopia, 13–16 July 2015) and endorsed by the General Assembly in its resolution 69/313 of 27 July 2015. 15 July 2015

General Assembly Resolution 70/1, Transforming our World: The 2030 Agenda for Sustainable Development. 25 September 2015. A/RES/70/1

Directive (EU) 2016/97 of the European Parliament and of the Council of 20 January 2016 on insurance distribution (recast) [2016] OJ L 26/19

Commission Delegated Regulation (EU) 2017/565 of 25 April 2016 supplementing Directive 2014/65/EU of the European Parliament and of the Council as regards organisational requirements and operating conditions for investment firms and defined terms for the purposes of that Directive, C/2016/2398 [2016] OJ L 87/1

Regulation (EU) 2016/1011 of the European Parliament and of the Council of 8 June 2016 on indices used as benchmarks in financial instruments and financial contracts or to measure the performance of investment funds and amending Directives 2008/48/EC and 2014/17/EU and Regulation (EU) No 596/2014 [2016] OJ L 171/1

Trade in Services Agreement (TiSA), Draft Provisions. 21 June 2016

Commission Delegated Directive (EU) 2017/593 of 7 April 2016 supplementing Directive 2014/65/EU of the European Parliament and of the Council with regard to safeguarding of financial instruments and funds belonging to clients, product governance obligations and the rules applicable to the provision or reception of fees, commissions or any monetary or non-monetary benefits, C/2016/2031 [2017] OJ L 87/500

Commission Delegated Regulation (EU) 2017/653 of 8 March 2017 supplementing Regulation (EU) No 1286/2014 of the European Parliament and of the Council on key information documents for packaged retail and insurance-based investment products (PRIIPs) by laying down regulatory technical standards with regard to the presentation, content, review and revision of key information documents and the conditions for fulfilling the requirement to provide such documents [2017] OJ L 100/1

Directive (EU) 2017/828 of the European Parliament and of the Council of 17 May 2017 amending Directive 2007/36/EC as regards the encouragement of long-term shareholder engagement [2017] OJ L 132/1

Commission Delegated Regulation (EU) 2017/2359 of 21 September 2017 supplementing Directive (EU) 2016/97 of the European Parliament and of the Council with regard to information requirements and conduct of business rules applicable to the distribution of insurance-based investment products, C/2017/6229 [2017] OJ L 341/8

Regulation (EU) 2019/452 of the European Parliament and of the Council of 19 March 2019 establishing a framework for the screening of foreign direct investments into the Union [2019] OJ L 79I/1

European Union, Schedule of Specific Commitments. 7 May 2019. GATS/SC/157

Regulation (EU) 2019/876 of the European Parliament and of the Council of 20 May 2019 amending Regulation (EU) No 575/2013 as regards the leverage ratio, the net stable funding ratio, requirements for own funds and eligible liabilities, counterparty credit risk, market risk, exposures to central counterparties, exposures to collective investment undertakings, large exposures, reporting and disclosure requirements, and Regulation (EU) No 648/2012 [2019] OJ L 150/1

Communication, Joint Statement on Services Domestic Regulation. 23 May 2019

Regulation (EU) 2019/1238 of the European Parliament and of the Council of 20 June 2019 on a pan-European Personal Pension Product (PEPP) [2019] OJ L 198/1

Regulation (EU) 2019/2033 of the European Parliament and of the Council of 27 November 2019 on the prudential requirements of investment firms and amending Regulations (EU) No 1093/2010, (EU) No 575/2013, (EU) No 600/2014 and (EU) No 806/2014 [2019] OJ L 314/1

Directive (EU) 2019/2034 of the European Parliament and of the Council of 27 November 2019 on the prudential supervision of investment firms and amending Directives 2002/87/EC, 2009/65/EC, 2011/61/EU, 2013/36/EU, 2014/59/EU and 2014/65/EU [2019] OJ L 314/64

Regulation (EU) 2019/2088 of the European Parliament and of the Council of 27 November 2019 on sustainability-related disclosures in the financial services sector [2019] OJ L 317/1

Regulation (EU) 2019/2089 of the European Parliament and of the Council of 27 November 2019 amending Regulation (EU) 2016/1011 as regards EU Climate Transition Benchmarks, EU Paris-aligned Benchmarks and sustainability-related disclosures for benchmarks [2019] OJ L 317/17

Regulation (EU) 2020/852 of the European Parliament and of the Council of 18 June 2020 on the establishment of a framework to facilitate sustainable investment, and amending Regulation (EU) 2019/2088 [2020] OJ L 198/13

Commission Delegated Regulation (EU) 2021/1253 of 21 April 2021 amending Delegated Regulation (EU) 2017/565 as regards the integration of sustainability factors, risks and preferences into certain organisational requirements and operating conditions for investment firms (Text with EEA relevance) [2021] OJ L 277/1

Commission Delegated Regulation (EU) 2021/1257 of 21 April 2021 amending Delegated Regulations (EU) 2017/2358 and (EU) 2017/2359 as regards the integration of sustainability factors, risks and preferences into the product oversight and governance requirements for insurance undertakings and insurance distributors and into the rules on conduct of business and investment advice for insurance-based investment products (Text with EEA relevance) [2021] OJ L 277/18

Commission Delegated Directive (EU) 2021/1269 of 21 April 2021 amending Delegated Directive (EU) 2017/593 as regards the integration of sustainability factors into the product governance obligations (Text with EEA relevance) [2021] OJ L 277/137

References

Bibliography

Bueren E (2019) Sustainable finance. Zeitschrift für Unternehmens- und Gesellschaftsrecht 48(5): 813–875. https://doi.org/10.1515/zgr-2019-0022. Accessed 19 Dec 2021

Gregersen C et al (2016) Implementation of the 2030 agenda in the European Union: constructing an EU approach to policy coherence for sustainable development. European Centre for Development Policy Management, Discussion Papers 2016(197):1–33. http://ecdpm.org/wp-content/uploads/DP197-Implementation-2030-Agenda-EU-Gregersen-Mackie-Torres-July-2016.pdf. Accessed 8 May 2024

Holzer K (2016) WTO law issues of emissions trading. World Trade Institute, Working Papers 2016(1):1–20. https://boris.unibe.ch/84032/1/WTO%20law%20issues%20of%20emissions%20trading.pdf. Accessed 8 May 2024

Hush ER (2018) Where no man has gone before: the future of sustainable development in the comprehensive economic and trade agreement and new generation free trade agreements. Colum J Environ Law 43(1):93–180. https://ssrn.com/abstract=3373398. Accessed 8 May 2024

Martin AP, Mercurio B (2017) Liberalization commitments, financial stability safeguards and capital controls: practice evolutions from GATS to TPP and megaregional trade agreements. Trade Law Dev 9(1):72–100. http://www.tradelawdevelopment.com/index.php/tld/article/download/9%281%29%20TL%26D%2071%20%282017%29/338. Accessed 8 May 2024

Pauls S (2020) Sustainable development and EU external action. Jean Monnet Papers 2020(1): 1–27. https://www.uni-goettingen.de/de/jean+monnet+papers/594986.html. Accessed 8 May 2024

Sheargold E, Mitchell AD (2016) The TPP and good regulatory practices: an opportunity for regulatory coherence to promote regulatory autonomy? World Trade Rev 15(4):586–612. https://doi.org/10.1017/S1474745616000045

Trachtman J (1996) Trade in financial services under GATS, NAFTA and the EC: a regulatory jurisdiction analysis. Colum J Transnatl Law 34(37):37–122

Trumble WR, Stevenson A (2002) Shorter Oxford English dictionary on historical principles, 5th edn. Oxford University, Oxford

Van den Bossche P, Zdouc W (2017) The law and policy of the World Trade Organization. Text, cases and materials, 4th edn, Cambridge University Press, Cambridge

Documents

Deutscher Bundestag (2018) Wissenschaftliche Dienste, Dokumentation, WTO-Konformität eines Grenzsteuerausgleichs bei nationalen Umwelt- und Klimaschutzmaßnahmen. 9 March 2018. https://www.bundestag.de/resource/blob/550298/73381c7f00dc8c3e70bdbbb68a8e7673/wd-5-035-18-pdf-data.pdf. Accessed 19 Dec 2021

EIOPA (2019) Opinion on Sustainability within Solvency II. 30 September 2019. EIOPA-BoS-19/241. https://www.eiopa.europa.eu/sites/default/files/publications/opinions/2019-09-30_opinionsustainabilitywithinsolvencyii.pdf. Accessed 19 Dec 2021

ESMA (2019a) Final report on integrating sustainability risks and factors in the MIFID II. 3 May 2019. https://www.esma.europa.eu/file/51276/download?token=6b4Tp3Bu. Accessed 19 Dec 2021

ESMA (2019b) Final report on integrating sustainability risks and factors in the UCITS Directive and the AIFMD. 3 May 2019. https://www.esma.europa.eu/file/51275/download?token=laoFYfvk. Accessed 19 Dec 2021

European Commission (2017) Communication from the Commission to the European Parliament, the Council, the European Economic and Social Committee and the Committee of the Regions on the Mid-Term Review of the Capital Markets Union Action Plan. 8 June 2017. COM(2017) 292 final. https://ec.europa.eu/transparency/regdoc/rep/1/2017/EN/COM-2017-292-F1-EN-MAIN-PART-1.PDF. Accessed 19 Dec 2021

European Commission (2018) Communication from the Commission, Action Plan: Financing Sustainable Growth. 8 March 2018. COM(2018) 97 final. https://eur-lex.europa.eu/legal-content/EN/TXT/PDF/?uri=CELEX:52018DC0097&from=EN. Accessed 19 Dec 2021

European Commission (2019b) Communication from the Commission, Guidelines on non-financial reporting: Supplement on reporting climate-related information [2019] OJ C 209/1. https://eur-lex.europa.eu/legal-content/EN/TXT/PDF/?uri=CELEX:52019XC0620(01)&from=EN. Accessed 19 Dec 2021

European Commission (2019c) Communication on The European Green Deal: COM(2019) 640 final, Communication from the Commission to the European Parliament, the European Council, the Council, the European Economic and Social Committee and the Committee of the Regions, The European Green Deal. 11 December 2019. https://ec.europa.eu/info/sites/info/files/european-green-deal-communication_en.pdf. Accessed 19 Dec 2021

European Commission (2019d) Annex to the Communication from the Commission to the European Parliament, the European Council, the Council, the European Economic and Social Committee and the Committee of the Regions, The European Green Deal, Annex, Roadmap and key actions. 11 December 2019. COM(2019) 640 final. https://ec.europa.eu/info/sites/info/files/european-green-deal-communication-annex-roadmap_en.pdf. Accessed 19 Dec 2021

European Commission (2020d) Commission Delegated Regulation (EU) .../...of XXX amending Delegated Regulation (EU) 2017/565 as regards the integration of sustainability factors, risks and preferences into certain organisational requirements and operating conditions for investment firms. 8 June 2020. Ares(2020)2955205. https://ec.europa.eu/finance/docs/level-2-measures/mifid-delegated-act-2018_en.pdf. Accessed 19 Dec 2021

European Commission (2020e) Commission Delegated Directive (EU) .../...of XXX amending Delegated Directive (EU) 2017/593 as regards the integration of sustainability factors and preferences into the product governance obligations. 8 June 2020. Ares(2020)2955234. https://eur-lex.europa.eu/legal-content/EN/TXT/DOC/?uri=PI_COM:Ares(2020)2955234&from=EN. Accessed 19 Dec 2021

European Commission (2020j) Website on the CBA. 4 March 2020. https://ec.europa.eu/info/law/better-regulation/have-your-say/initiatives/12228-Carbon-Border-Adjustment-Mechanism. Accessed 19 Dec 2021

European Parliament (2020) Trade related aspects of a carbon border adjustment mechanism, a legal assessment. https://www.europarl.europa.eu/RegData/etudes/BRIE/2020/603502/EXPO_BRI (2020)603502_EN.pdf. Accessed 8 May 2024

HLEG (2018a) Final report of the High-Level Expert Group on Sustainable Finance. 31 January 2018. https://ec.europa.eu/info/publications/180131-sustainable-finance-report_en. Accessed 19 Dec 2021

HLEG (2018b) Informal supplementary document on sustainable taxonomy. 31 January 2018. https://ec.europa.eu/info/publications/180131-sustainable-finance-report_en. Accessed 19 Dec 2021

HLEG (2018c) Informal supplementary document on green bonds. 31 January 2018. https://ec.europa.eu/info/publications/180131-sustainable-finance-report_en. Accessed 19 Dec 2021

IOSCO (2013) Principles for Financial Benchmarks Final Report. July 2013. FR07/13. https://www.iosco.org/library/pubdocs/pdf/IOSCOPD415.pdf. Accessed 19 Dec 2021

IPCC (2019) Global warming of 1.5°C, An IPCC Special Report on the impacts of global warming of 1.5°C above pre-industrial levels and related global greenhouse gas emission pathways, in the context of strengthening the global response to the threat of climate change, sustainable development, and efforts to eradicate poverty. https://www.ipcc.ch/site/assets/uploads/sites/2/2019/06/SR15_Full_Report_Low_Res.pdf. Accessed 8 May 2024

JRC (2019) Development of EU Ecolabel criteria for Retail Financial Products, Technical Report 2.0, Draft proposal for the product scope and criteria. 20 December 2019. https://susproc.jrc.ec.europa.eu/Financial_products/docs/20191220_EU_Ecolabel_FP_Draft_Technical_Report_2-0.pdf. Accessed 19 Dec 2021

NGFS (2019) First comprehensive report, A call for action – Climate change as a source of financial risk. 17 April 2019. https://www.ngfs.net/en/first-comprehensive-report-call-action. Accessed 19 Dec 2021

TEG (2019a) Report on Climate-related Disclosures. 10 January 2019. https://ec.europa.eu/info/sites/info/files/business_economy_euro/banking_and_finance/documents/190110-sustainable-finance-teg-report-climate-related-disclosures_en.pdf. Accessed 19 Dec 2021

TEG (2019b) Report on EU Green Bond Standard. 18 June 2019. https://ec.europa.eu/info/sites/info/files/business_economy_euro/banking_and_finance/documents/190618-sustainable-finance-teg-report-green-bond-standard_en.pdf. Accessed 19 December 2021

TEG (2019c) Taxonomy technical report. 18 June 2019. https://ec.europa.eu/info/sites/info/files/business_economy_euro/banking_and_finance/documents/190618-sustainable-finance-teg-report-taxonomy_en.pdf. Accessed 19 Dec 2021

TEG (2019d) Final report on climate benchmarks and benchmarks' ESG disclosures. 30 September 2019. https://ec.europa.eu/info/sites/info/files/business_economy_euro/banking_and_finance/documents/190930-sustainable-finance-teg-final-report-climate-benchmarks-and-disclosures_en.pdf. Accessed 19 Dec 2021

United Nations (2015) Central product classification (CPC), Version 2.1. https://unstats.un.org/unsd/classifications/unsdclassifications/cpcv21.pdf. Accessed 8 May 2024

WTO (2009) Trade and climate change, WTO-UNEP Report. https://www.wto.org/english/res_e/booksp_e/trade_climate_change_e.pdf. Accessed 8 May 2024

WTO (2020a) Analytical Index GATS – Preamble (Jurisprudence). https://www.wto.org/english/res_e/publications_e/ai17_e/gats_preamble_jur.pdf. Accessed 8 May 2024

WTO (2020b) Analytical Index GATS – Article II (Jurisprudence). https://www.wto.org/english/res_e/publications_e/ai17_e/gats_art2_jur.pdf. Accessed 8 May 2024

WTO (2020d) Analytical Index GATS – Article XIV (Jurisprudence). https://www.wto.org/english/res_e/publications_e/ai17_e/gats_art14_jur.pdf. Accessed 8 May 2024

WTO (2020e) Analytical Index GATS – Article XVI (Jurisprudence). https://www.wto.org/english/res_e/publications_e/ai17_e/gats_art16_jur.pdf. Accessed 8 May 2024

WTO (2020f) Analytical Index GATS – Article XVII (Jurisprudence). https://www.wto.org/english/res_e/publications_e/ai17_e/gats_art17_jur.pdf. Accessed 8 May 2024

Jurisprudence

WTO DSB (1996) United States – Standards for Reformulated and Conventional Gasoline, Appellate Body report. 29 April 1996. WT/DS2/AB/R

WTO DSB (1997a) European Communities – Regime for the Importation, Sale and Distribution of Bananas, Panel report, 22 May 1997, WT/DS27/R

WTO DSB (1997b) European Communities – Regime for the Importation, Sale and Distribution of Bananas, Appellate Body report, 9 September 1997, WT/DS27/AB/R

WTO DSB (1998) United States – Import Prohibition of Certain Shrimp and Shrimp Products, Appellate Body report, 12 October 1998, WT/DS58/AB/R

WTO DSB (2000a) European Communities – Measures Affecting Asbestos and Products Containing Asbestos, Panel report, 18 September 2000, WT/DS135/R

WTO DSB (2000b) Korea – Measures Affecting Imports of Fresh, Chilled and Frozen Beef, Appellate Body reports, 11 December 2000, WT/DS161/AB/R, WT/DS169/AB/R

WTO DSB (2000c) Argentina – Measures Affecting the Export of Bovine Hides and the Import of Finished Leather, Panel report, 19 December 2000, WT/DS155/R

WTO DSB (2001a) European Communities – Measures Affecting Asbestos and Products Containing Asbestos, Appellate Body report, 12 March 2001, WT/DS135/AB/R

WTO DSB (2001b) United States – Import Prohibition of Certain Shrimp and Shrimp Products, Appellate Body report, 22 October 2001, WT/DS58/AB/RW

WTO DSB (2004a) United States – Measures Affecting the Cross-Border Supply of Gambling and Betting Services, Panel report, 10 November 2004, WT/DS285/R

WTO DSB (2004b) Dominican Republic – Measures Affecting the Importation and Internal Sale of Cigarettes, Panel report, 26 November 2004, WT/DS302/R

WTO DSB (2005) United States – Measures Affecting the Cross-Border Supply of Gambling and Betting Services, Appellate Body report, 7 April 2005, WT/DS285/AB/R

WTO DSB (2006) European Communities – Selected Customs Matters, Appellate Body report, 13 November 2006, WT/DS315/AB/R

WTO DSB (2007a) Brazil – Measures Affecting Imports of Retreaded Tyres, Panel report, 17 June 2007, WT/DS332/R

WTO DSB (2007b) Brazil – Measures Affecting Imports of Retreaded Tyres, Appellate Body report, 3 December 2007, WT/DS332/AB/R

WTO DSB (2009a) Panel Report, China – Measures Affecting Trading Rights and Distribution Services for Certain Publications and Audiovisual Entertainment Products, Panel report, 12 August 2009, WT/DS363/R

WTO DSB (2009b) China – Measures Affecting Trading Rights and Distribution Services for Certain Publications and Audiovisual Entertainment Products, Appellate Body report, 21 December 2009, WT/DS363/AB/R

WTO DSB (2010) Thailand – Customs and Fiscal Measures on Cigarettes from the Philippines, Panel report, 15 November 2010, WT/DS371/R

WTO DSB (2011) United States – Certain country of origin labelling (COOL) requirements, Panel reports, 18 November 2011, WT/DS384/R, WT/DS386/R

WTO DSB (2012) China – Certain Measures Affecting Electronic Payment Services, Panel report, 16 July 2012, WT/DS413/R

WTO DSB (2013) European Communities – Measures Prohibiting the Importation and Marketing of Seal Products, Panel reports, 25 November 2013, WT/DS400/R, WT/DS401/R

WTO DSB (2014) European Communities – Measures Prohibiting the Importation and Marketing of Seal Products, Appellate Body reports, 22 May 2014, WT/DS400/AB/R, WT/DS401/AB/R

WTO DSB (2015) Argentina – Measures Relating to Trade in Goods and Services, Panel report, 30 September 2015, WT/DS453/R

WTO DSB (2016) Argentina – Measures Relating to Trade in Goods and Services, Appellate Body report, 14 April 2016, WT/DS453/AB/R

WTO DSB (2018) European Union and its Member States – Certain Measures Relating to the Energy Sector, Panel report, 10 August 2018, WT/DS476/R

Chapter 4
Propagation and Justification of EU Sustainable Finance Measures through GATS and International Organizations

The preceding Chapters assessed the consistency of EU Sustainable Finance measures in the light of GATS and related disciplines. The question of how a potential inconsistency limits the EU's ability to adopt such regulation internally effectively constitutes a passive approach to the GATS regulatory framework and trade relations in general. There are two proactive policy approaches, which the EU can and does use in the realm of international law and international relations to foster the development of Sustainable Finance.

First, the EU can propagate the concept and policy proposals for Sustainable Finance through international institutions and agreements. This is a feasible policy approach because of the interrelation between international financial markets, Sustainable Finance as a concept, and trade in financial services.[1] Furthermore, as described above, the concept of EU Sustainable Finance is rooted in or strongly influenced by the UN sustainable development agendas.[2] This in turn may lead to the deduction that Sustainable Finance as a policy concept and its implementation shall equally be set and implemented in international fora. This has materialized in multiple initiatives on Sustainable Finance at the international level.[3] Thus, a mere domestic implementation of Sustainable Finance is, similarly to sustainable development, necessary but not sufficient. The conceptual aim of Sustainable Finance—of financing sustainable development—can only be reached if similar policies are implemented by a majority of WTO Members and introduced in all spheres of international cooperation.

For these reasons, this Chapter will examine the propagation of EU Sustainable Finance through the EU's engagement in international organizations, fora, and its external trade relations. Propagation can be understood as a policy approach, which

---

[1]Cf. Chap. 1.
[2]Cf. Sect. 1.1.
[3]Cf. Sect. 4.1.2.

aims at using political, legal, and economic leverage to encourage international institutions and ultimately other WTO Members to adopt a Sustainable Finance policy agenda similar to that of the EU.

Thereby, the underlying *ratio* of the propagation of Sustainable Finance can be described threefold. On the one hand, trade partners ultimately having equal or similar standards will ensure that the provision of sustainable financial services by foreign financial service suppliers within the EU is not diminished by EU Sustainable Finance measures. Due to the similarity in conditions in the host state and home state, there would be no room for a *de facto* discrimination and a potential debate on a better than national treatment. On the other hand, assimilation of sustainability-related conditions in domestic and foreign financial regulatory systems ensures that EU financial service suppliers are not disadvantaged by the stricter EU rules in comparison to their third country counterparts when providing services outside the EU. EU financial service suppliers could then be at the forefront of providing sustainability-related financial services in the states of WTO Members who only recently adopted Sustainable Finance legislation. Finally, the aim of Sustainable Finance policy of fostering sustainable development and ultimately also financial stability can only be reached through international cooperation. The FSB, whose TCFD[4] combines conventional financial stability considerations with Sustainable Finance approaches constitutes an example of such cooperation. This cooperation in turn leads to integration and consolidation of these policy fields.

Effective propagation of Sustainable Finance policy through international cooperation does not only ensure a robust implementation of the concept. It further justifies Sustainable Finance measures and protects domestic policy space, which in the future could be partially contested by claims under the GATS disciplines or bilateral trade agreements.[5] The more the concept of Sustainable Finance and its specific policies is propagated, the less likely such policies are to be contested by other WTO Members equally having adopted such policies.

Such justification, however, can also be achieved legally through explicit policy protection clauses. Such clauses would be especially relevant for the time in which the EU spearheads the global development of Sustainable Finance with its domestic policies. The EU may face contestation by other WTO Members if its Sustainable Finance measures become more restrictive. Thus, this Chapter will also assess the EU's options for introducing policy protection clauses for Sustainable Finance at the different levels of international policy-setting. This is particularly relevant concerning the GATS and TiSA frameworks.[6]

---

[4]Cf. Sects. 2.1.6 and 4.1.2.

[5]With a view to propagating the concept of Sustainable Finance through EU FTAs, cf. Sect. 5.4.

[6]Cf. Sect. 4.2; With a view to justifying and protecting the concept of Sustainable Finance through EU FTAs, cf. Sect. 5.4.

4.1 Propagation through International Organizations

The EU uses international organizations and other bodies of international relations as a key implementation ground for its international propagation of the concept of Sustainable Finance. The EU's approach is twofold.

First, the EU influences macro-political agendas to integrate ambitious sustainability targets, primarily the SDGs. These, in turn, serve as the conceptual aim of domestic policy on Sustainable Finance. Furthermore, these agendas are drafted in a way to comprise a financial perspective to sustainable development as a base for international policy on Sustainable Finance. A brief assessment of this influence will be conducted in Sect. 4.1.1.[7]

Second, the EU is heavily engaged in turning these macro-political agendas into policy at the international level. This is achieved through multiple international fora. An assessment of this commitment will be conducted in Sect. 4.1.2.

4.1.1 Policy-Setting within the UN

To understand the EU Sustainable Finance policy propagation through the UN framework, it is important to also assess the closely related sustainable development policy-setting at the UN level. The EU has been active in the UN policy-setting on sustainable development from early on. Many of the UN's more recent political agendas on sustainable development and climate action are largely rooted in intense political investment by the Commission.[8]

The EU's participation in the drafting of international political agendas on sustainable development and climate action can be understood as an interrelation between two separate phenomena: The EU's increasing internal organizational consolidation and the increase in its external competences through major EU treaties on the one hand and the emancipation and single-mindedness of its external policies on the other hand.

Thus, there are certain internal developments to be acknowledged to better assess the EU's external policies. Under the Amsterdam Treaty's[9] vision of a externally more active EU in international relations and the EU's upcoming enlargement, the EU increased participation in the drafting of international sustainable development conventions. Thereby, its understanding of sustainable development changed from internal policy with external implications, to a policy field largely defined by

---

[7]Policy-setting within the GATS framework and its enhancement process through TiSA are separately addressed in Sect. 4.2.

[8]Pauls (2020), pp. 9 et seqq.

[9]Treaty of Amsterdam, Amending the Treaty on European Union, the Treaties establishing the European Communities and certain related Acts [1997] OJ C 340/1.

international conventions and subsequently reincorporated into internal policies.[10] The EU's increasingly active role in the drafting of international sustainable development agendas becomes even more clear with the revisions undertaken by the Nice Treaty.[11] Pursuant to declaration no. 9 on Art. 175 TEU,[12] the EU shall be taking up a leading role in the negotiation and drafting of international sustainable development and climate action agendas.[13] This declaration of intent in EU primary legislation was made at a time in between the 2000 Millennium Summit and the 2002 Johannesburg Rio+10 World Summit on Sustainable Development.[14] In the following years, the EU's commitment and influence in international political agenda-setting and policy-setting with regard to sustainable development and climate action intensified significantly.

One example of this influence was the EU's stance on the debate whether different strands of sustainable development agendas should be united. Until then, the revision of the MDGs and the post-2015 process had been addressed separately. In advance of the sustainable development Summit,[15] however, those strands were united into a single working strand. Furthermore, the 23rd Conference of the Parties (*COP21*) to the UNFCCC[16] and the 11th Meeting of the Parties to the Kyoto Protocol (*CMP11*) would be jointly held at and as the Paris Summit.[17] In respect of the Paris Summit, the EU is understood to have coordinated and intensively guided the negotiation process.[18] However, also in relation to the other 2015 summits, the EU has strongly influenced the outcome documents by translating its internal aim of leadership in international climate and sustainable development negotiations into the provision of expertise and resources to the negotiations.[19]

A more recent example of this claim for leadership in international climate and sustainability policy-drafting is the European Green Deal.[20] Therein, the Commission pointed out that its climate targets could only be reached in coordination with neighbors and international partners. Furthermore, it determines that the EU would

---

[10] Pauls (2020), p. 9.

[11] Treaty of Nice, Amending the Treaty on European Union, the Treaties establishing the European Communities and certain related Acts [2001] OJ C 80/1–87.

[12] Consolidated version of the Treaty on European Union [2012] OJ C 326/13.

[13] Pauls (2020), p. 10.

[14] The Millennium Summit was held from 6 to 8 September 2000 in New York City, United States; The Rio+10 World Summit on Sustainable Development was held from 26 August to 4 September 2002 in Johannesburg, South Africa; Pauls (2020), p. 10.

[15] The Sustainable Development Summit was held from 25 to 27 September 2015 in New York City, United States.

[16] United Nations Framework Convention on Climate Change. 9 May 1992. U.N.T.S. 1771 (1992).

[17] The UN Climate Change Conference and the 21st Conference of the Parties (COP21; together the *Paris Summit*) were held from 30 November to 12 December 2015 in Paris, France; Pauls (2020), pp. 17 et seq.

[18] Gregersen et al. (2016), p. 7; Gavas (2016), p. 2.

[19] Gregersen et al. (2016), p. 6; Pauls (2020), pp. 17 et seq.

[20] European Commission (2019a).

continue to demonstrate international leadership on climate adaption and climate change mitigation.[21]

Regarding Sustainable Finance, the question arises how the EU's commitment ultimately translated into actual political agendas. Such agendas would recognize the importance of the financial aspect of sustainable development and would create the foundations for Sustainable Finance. There are comparatively few examples, where these financial aspects became part of large-scale political agreements on sustainable development.

One example of such financial provisions in sustainable development agreements is para. 47 'The future we want' Outcome Document. It recognized corporate NFR on sustainability criteria.[22] Another example is the 2030 Agenda's SDG 17. Under SDG 17 (*Revitalize the global partnership for sustainable development*), a subsection on "*finance*" was introduced (SDGs 17.1 to 17.5), with a focus on financing for sustainable development. This subsection particularly encompasses sustainable development in developing and least developed countries, for instance through ODA or investment promotion regimes. More relevant for the broader and global concept of Sustainable Finance are SDGs 17.3 and 17.5. These focus on developing countries.

SDG 17.3 (*Mobilize additional financial resources for developing countries from multiple sources*), although designated for developing countries, in essence, is the same scheme as promoted by EU Sustainable Finance internally. Thus, the mobilization of additional financial resources effectively encompasses the rechanneling of private capital into sustainable investments (in developing counties). Specific EU Sustainable Finance measures covered by this SDG would be social and green bonds.[23] For instance, a market participant located in a developing country would mobilize additional financial resources for sustainable development in that country by issuing bonds that assure fair working and environmental conditions. Read in conjunction with SDG 17.3, SDG 17.5 (*Adopt and implement investment promotion regimes for least developed countries*) can be understood as fostering Sustainable Finance, too. Leveraging and blending schemes such as the EFSD and EFSI effectively constitute such investment promotion regimes.[24]

Considering this inter-WTO Member focus of SDGs 17.3 and 17.5, it is important to differentiate between financing for development and Sustainable Finance. On a broader scale, financing development, and later financing for sustainable development, was addressed only as part of WTO Members' commitments to ODA.[25] This is still represented in SDG 17.2 (*Implement all development assistance*

---

[21] European Commission (2019a), p. 2; Cf. European Commission (2019b), p. 4.

[22] Cf. Recital 11 Directive 2014/95/EU of the European Parliament and of the Council of 22 October 2014 amending Directive 2013/34/EU as regards disclosure of non-financial and diversity information by certain large undertakings and groups [2014] OJ L 330/1.

[23] Such as EU Green Bonds, cf. Sect. 2.1.3.

[24] Cf. Sect. 2.2.

[25] Cf. Sect. 2.2.

commitments). Hence, until recently most of the agreements addressing financing for development are drafted aiming exclusively at the financing through public financial resources. Sustainable Finance, however, as described in Sect. 1.1, has the unique feature of mainly addressing alternative ways of financing sustainable development. An instrument for such financing for development would be rechanneling private capital and creating investment incentives. ODA, hence, is just a minor aspect to be considered under the concept of Sustainable Finance.[26] To understand how Sustainable Finance as a broad concept is being introduced into UN level financing for development agreements, one needs to examine these agreements in more detail. This examination will be conducted in particular with regard to whether these agreements contain the typical Sustainable Finance feature of rechanneling private capital into sustainable investments.

As the outcome document of the first conference on financing for development, the 2002 Monterrey Consensus[27] inherited a strong focus on ODA-based financing for development. However, some aspects of Sustainable Finance were also covered by the Monterrey Consensus.

Para. 10 Monterrey Consensus outlines what it deems to be a critical challenge, namely ensuring "*the necessary internal conditions for mobilizing domestic savings, both public and private [....]*". This thus represents a domestic perspective on financing for development—*or* Sustainable Finance. Furthermore, the provision added an international perspective by calling for "*mobilizing domestic resources [...] and attracting and making effective use of international investment and assistance.*" This was to be achieved by an "*enabling domestic environment*" that "*should be supported by the international community.*" Such efforts supported by the international community would likely encompass measures aimed at creating incentives to private market participants to invest into sustainable economic activity. Para. 10 Monterrey Consensus refers to this as an "*enabling environment*". Such incentivizing measures are those EU Sustainable Finance measures described as *prudential measures* in Sect. 2.1.

A similar approach can be found in para. 17 Monterrey Consensus, which states that it encourages capital market development in favor of "*addressing development financing needs, including the insurance sector and debt and equity markets, that encourage and channel savings and foster productive investments.*" Here, rechanneling capital in favor of sustainable development is explicitly named. Such debt instruments as referred to in para. 17 Monterrey Consensus encompass green bonds.[28] It goes on to state that this "*requires a sound system of [...] transparent regulatory frameworks and effective supervisory mechanisms [...].*" The latter

---

[26] Cf. Chap. 2.

[27] Monterrey Consensus of the International Conference on Financing for Development, The final text of agreements and commitments adopted at the International Conference on Financing for Development Monterrey, Mexico, 18–22 March 2002. 22 March 2002.

[28] Cf. Sect. 2.1.3; In the insurance sector transparency requirements have been developed, cf. Sect. 2.1.6.

sentence accurately fits what the EU considers its supervisory and regulatory regime to be. This points to the congruence between the EU's internal Sustainable Finance policy and its international efforts.

Adding to this, *"the social and economic impact of the financial sector"* is covered by para. 18 Monterrey Consensus. Thereby it focuses on the effect that public and private banks, or cooperation between them can have on the supply of credit and equity financing. Such public-private partnerships have been discussed as an EU Sustainable Finance fiscal instrument.[29] Para. 23 Monterrey Consensus, in turn, addresses corporate governance aspects of *inter alia "banks and other financial institutions"*, which are encouraged *"to foster innovative developmental financing approaches"*. Such development financing approaches would constitute private-sector Sustainable Finance schemes, such as labels or standards, which the EU referenced and encouraged repeatedly in its publications.

Of particular interest for EU Sustainable Finance is para. 25 Monterrey Consensus, since it takes a broader view on *"prudential regulations and supervision"* in an international environment. It sets out *"strengthening prudential regulations and supervision of all financial institutions [. . .] liberalizing capital flows [. . .] consistent with development objectives, and implementation, on a progressive and voluntary basis, of codes and standards agreed internationally, are also important"*. This demonstrated the ambiguity EU Sustainable Finance measures can be viewed to have. On the one hand, the strengthening of prudential regulations and supervision and the adoption of international standards is seen as important. On the other hand, these aims are contrasted with the respective national capacity and the implementation on a voluntary basis. Both of these exceptions were discussed above (Sect. 3.2. 4.1.4) concerning arbitrary discrimination and the conditions prevailing under the chapeau of Art. XIV GATS.

The second conference on financing for development concluded with the adoption of the 2008 Doha Declaration.[30] It added just a few further aspects of Sustainable Finance to the process. For example, para. 8 Doha Declaration declares that *"the necessary enabling environment for mobilizing public and private resources and expanding productive investments"* is required while admitting that *"[g]reater efforts are required to support the creation and sustenance of a conducive environment through appropriate national and international actions"*. Thereby, an *"enabling* and *conducive environment"* effectively equals the *"enabling environment"* as aimed at in para. 10 Monterrey Consensus. Furthermore, the increased efforts the EU undertook in the years following the Doha Declaration can be viewed as an additional or greater effort to mobilize public and private resources for sustainable development.

---

[29] As described in Sect. 2.2; Cf. para. 24 Monterrey Consensus.

[30] Doha Declaration on Financing for Development: Outcome Document of the Follow-up International Conference on Financing for Development to Review the Implementation of the Monterrey Consensus. 9 December 2008.

Plus, clearer than in the Monterrey Consensus, para. 23 Doha Declaration recognizes "*that private international capital flows, particularly foreign direct investment, are vital complements to national and international development efforts*" and that signatories "*will seek to enhance such flows to support development*". As stated already in Sect. 1.1, FDI cannot be considered under financial services as in international trade law and thus is not assessed closer in this book. However, para. 23 Doha Declaration is also applicable to portfolio investments, which in contrast is highly relevant to Sustainable Finance. Enhancing such a portfolio in a way conducive to sustainable development also encompasses the required regulatory changes and incentives embodied in EU Sustainable Finance measures.

In contrast to such private international capital flows and similar to para. 23 Monterrey Consensus, para. 24 Doha Declaration addresses the role ODA, "*guarantees and public-private partnerships, can play [. . .] in mobilizing private flows.*" It further refers to the task of "*multilateral and regional development banks*" to "*facilitate additional private flows to such [developing] countries*". Examples are the EFSD and EFSI funds under the auspices of the EIB described in Sect. 2.2.

The most recent and third conference on financing for development resulted in the adoption of the 2015 AAAA. In line with the SDGs issued the same year, which broadened sustainable development from merely focusing on developing countries to become a global concept, the AAAA did so equally concerning financing for development. Para. 36 AAAA addressed domestic regulation enabling financing for sustainable development internally and externally. It states that signatories "*will develop policies and, where appropriate, strengthen regulatory frameworks to better align private sector incentives with public goals, including incentivizing the private sector to adopt sustainable practices, and foster long-term quality investment.*" This, on the one hand, resembles para. 10 Monterrey Consensus in requiring an enabling environment for private investments. On the other hand, and similar to the approach chosen by many EU Sustainable Finance measures, it focuses on offering incentives to private market participants.

Adding to this, para. 36 AAAA proclaims that signatories "*will continue to promote and create enabling domestic and international conditions for inclusive and sustainable private sector investment, with transparent and stable rules and standards and free and fair competition, conducive to achieving national development policies.*" The AAAA, similar to para. 10 Monterrey Consensus and para. 8 Doha Declaration, thus refers to "*enabling domestic and international conditions*". Although being a broad term for enabling regulatory frameworks, reference to such a concept is a clear statement that signatories are willing to adapt their financial regulations in favor of incentivizing the investment of private capital into financing for sustainable development. At the EU level, the enabling environment described in para. 36 AAAA is very similar to the Commission's European Green Deal statement that the EU is working towards supporting third countries through development cooperation to bridge the funding gap that is at the very heart of Sustainable Finance. It intends to reach this by supporting efforts to improve the investment climate and effectively de-risking sustainable investments, for example through funding guarantees or blended finance.[31]

Adding to these prudential instruments, para. 54 AAAA also references the fiscal instruments described in Sect. 2.2 by stating an *"important use of international public finance, including ODA, is to catalyse additional resource mobilization from other sources, public and private. [...] It can also be used to unlock additional finance through blended or pooled financing and risk mitigation, notably for infrastructure and other investments that support private sector development."* The AAAA thereby recognizes the importance of leveraged finance and guarantee schemes through regional development banks like the EFSI or the EIB.

These examples demonstrate that financing for development agreements indeed interconnect finance and sustainable development. Pre-2015 their primary aim had been to rechannel private capital cross-border into developing countries. Sustainable Finance, however, encompasses not only the rechanneling of private capital as a replacement for ODA but also aims at the domestic implementation of sustainable development.[32] This also takes into account the universal scope of application of the SDGs, as mentioned above. The 2015 AAAA, as has been described, embraced this domestic perspective and broadened the scope of financing for development horizontally to industrialized countries.

Concluding, this means that Sustainable Finance policy is for a large part rooted in international agreements at the UN level, namely, development agreements, sustainable development agreements, and financing for development agreements. Of particular importance for Sustainable Finance can be deemed financing for development agreements. Although financing for development and Sustainable Finance are interlinked, financing for development agreements are still partly based on ODA commitments. Nevertheless, the above analysis has shown that more recent financing for development agreements are increasingly taking into account the role of private capital in development financing. On the one hand, the parallel shift from a mere economic understanding of development towards a sustainability-oriented understanding as sustainable development demonstrates the present-day likeness between the concepts of financing for development and Sustainable Finance. On the other hand, financing for development agreements, too, address prudential regulations and financial supervision and thus coincide with Sustainable Finance's second policy objective of long-term financial stability.

In contrast, despite the relevance of large-scale sustainable development agreements such as the 2030 Agenda as a target-setting policy framework for Sustainable Finance, there are comparatively few examples where Sustainable Finance aspects formed part of such agreements. Therefore, the negotiating and drafting of specific policy guidance and standards on Sustainable Finance through international fora is all the more important as will be discussed in Sect. 4.1.2.

---

[31] European Commission (2019a), p. 22.
[32] Cf. Sects. 1.1, 2.1, and 2.2.

4.1.2   Policy-Setting within International Fora

Fora of international cooperation are currently the epicenter of international Sustainable Finance policy drafting. In recent years, the number of such bodies increased substantially, as did the group of WTO Members and private sector participants contributing to them.

The introduction of Sustainable Finance into international fora thereby, may serve to assure that the EU's efforts of propagating Sustainable Finance globally do not constitute an arbitrary discrimination under the chapeau of Art. XIV GATS. A similar case, as discussed in Sect. 3.2.4.1.4, led to the Appellate Body's conclusion in *US–Shrimp* that a *de facto* coercive implementation requirement for other WTO Members to adopt the same regulations does constitute such arbitrary discrimination. As a solution, the panel suggested *inter alia* the negotiation of bilateral or multilateral agreements.[33]

Therefore, taking into account the developments of EU Sustainable Finance outlined in Chap. 2 and its international trade law implications described in the previous Chapters, two questions arise. First, which channels of influence does the EU have in these international fora? Second, how has the EU's membership in these fora shaped its Sustainable Finance policy?

Turning to the first question, the EU influences the international drafting of Sustainable Finance policy through its memberships, funding memberships, and other forms of participation in these international fora. Not all of these fora are constituted of financial legislative or supervisory bodies but all of them publish relevant and much-referenced material on Sustainable Finance policy.[34] In its Final Report, the Commission's HLEG even explicitly recommended that the EU uses its leverage at the international level to drive Sustainable Finance globally through fora such as the Group of Twenty (*G20*), the Group of Seven (*G7*), the FSB, the UN, IOSCO and the OECD.[35] The HLEG saw for the EU "*a unique opportunity to consolidate its leadership*" in international Sustainable Finance policy drafting through international cooperation.[36] The same was stated by the Commission in its European Green Deal in which it also declared that it is pursuing a global response to climate and sustainability issues through green diplomacy by "*convincing and supporting others to*" promote sustainable development, by using trade and development policies and bilateral and multilateral trade frameworks.[37]

---

[33] WTO DSB (1998) United States – Import Prohibition of Certain Shrimp and Shrimp Products, Appellate Body report, para. 172, 177; Cf. Van den Bossche and Zdouc (2017), pp. 596, 598; Regarding the propagation and justification of EU Sustainable Finance policy through bilateral agreements or EU FTAs, cf. Sect. 5.4.

[34] Cf. Table 4.1.

[35] HLEG (2018), pp. 26, 55, 63 et seq.

[36] HLEG (2018), p. 63.

[37] European Commission (2019a), p. 20.

Table 4.1 List of international fora on sustainable finance with EU participation (alphabetical order)

International forum	Parent organization	EU's role	Thematic scope	Publications
BCBS (Basel Committee on Banking Supervision)	BIS	Membership: ECB, SSM	Supervisory standards	BCBS (2020)
EBRD (European Bank for Reconstruction and Development)	–	Financing Membership: EU, EIB Membership in Environmental and Social Advisory Council: Commission	Financing for development	EBRD (2018)
IASB (International Accounting Standards Board)	–	Membership in IFRS Advisory Council: ECB, ESMA	Accounting standards	Anderson (2019) Hoogervorst (2019) IASB (2024)
IPSF (International Platform on Sustainable Finance)	–	Initiator: Commission Membership: EU Observer: EIB	Taxonomies, disclosures, standards, and labels Build on top of work conducted by EIB, NGFS, and UNEP	IPSF (2019) IPSF (2020a) IPSF (2020b) IPSF (2021a) IPSF (2021b) IPSF (2021c) IPSF (2022a) IPSF (2022b) IPSF (2023a) IPSF (2023b) IPSF (2023c)
LMA (Loan Market Association)	–	Associate Membership: EIB, ESM Courtesy: Commission	Green and sustainable loans	LMA (2018) LMA (2019)
NGFS (Network for Greening the Financial System)	–	Membership: EBA, EIOPA	Climate-related risks	NGFS (2019a) NGFS (2019b) NGFS (2019c) NGFS (2020a) NGFS (2020b)
UN PAGE (Partnership for Action on Green Economy)	UN	Funding Partner: Commission	Sustainability in developing countries	UNEP PAGE (2016)
SFN (Sustainable Finance Network)	IOSCO	Associate Membership: Commission, ESMA	Mapping exercise of domestic and international Sustainable Finance initiatives	SFN (2020)
SFSG (Sustainable		Membership: EU	Stocktaking on Sustainable Finance	

(continued)

Table 4.1 (continued)

International forum	Parent organization	EU's role	Thematic scope	Publications
Finance Study Group)	G20 Secretariat: UNEP		initiatives Voluntary policy recommendations	GFSG (2016) GFSG (2017) SFSG (2018)
SIF (Sustainable Insurance Forum)	Secretariat: UNEP	Membership: EIOPA	Sustainability- and environment-related risks in the insurance sector	SIF (2018) SIF (2017)
TCFD (Task Force on Climate-Related Financial Disclosures)	FSB	Membership: Commission, ECB	Financial disclosures	TCFD (2017) TCFD (2018) TCFD (2019) TCFD (2021) TCFD (2022) TCFD (2023)
UNEP Finance Initiative (Working Group on EU Taxonomy)	UNEP	Observer: Commission, EBA, EIB	EU Taxonomy	–
Working Group Climate Transition Finance	ICMA	Membership: EIB	Green bonds	ICMA (2018a)
Working Group Green Projects Eligibility	ICMA	Membership: EIB	Green taxonomy	–
Working Group Social Bonds	ICMA	Membership: ESM	Social bonds	ICMA (2020) ICMA (2023)
Working Group Sustainability/ KPI-linked bonds	ICMA	Membership: EIB	Sustainability bonds	ICMA (2018b)

Source: Own Research

The memberships in international fora include, in the first place, the Sustainable Finance Study Group (*SFSG*). Originally founded in 2016 as the Green Financing Study Group (*GFSG*), the SFSG is an international research and policy group under the auspices of the G20 with its secretariat at the UNEP. The G20 working group published Synthesis Reports in 2016, 2017, and 2018 with a thematic focus on taking stock of Sustainable Finance, knowledge sharing, and developing voluntary policy tools for participants and for bilateral and multilateral collaboration.[38] The EU is represented through its membership in the SFSG.

Second, the Commission and ESMA hold associate memberships at IOSCO's Sustainable Finance Network (*SFN*). The SFN's thematic scope encompasses a comprehensive mapping exercise of initiatives taken so far or planned by securities

---

[38] GFSG (2016); GFSG (2017); SFSG (2018).

regulators and market participants on Sustainable Finance. It further takes stock of various international initiatives taken by other regional or international organizations. Noteworthily, the Commission's HLEG had recommended influencing IOSCO to incorporate ESG factors into the IOSCO Benchmark Principles,[39] the introduction of reporting requirements of significant benchmark administrators concerning the kind and weighting of the underlying assets, and disclosure requirements for funds, dedicated supervisory standards for ESG-related benchmarks.[40] The SFN published its Final Report in April 2020.[41]

Another international initiative on Sustainable Finance is the independently created Network for Greening the Financial System (NGFS), which is mostly focused on climate-related risks. NGFS published its First Comprehensive Report and a respective Technical Supplement in April and July 2019, respectively. NGFS further published a Sustainable Investment Guide in October 2019.[42] In its First Comprehensive Report, the NGFS outlined major policy proposals that correspond with the relevant EU legislation. For instance, the report stated three major tasks a Sustainable Finance taxonomy needs to accomplish: To prevent greenwashing, to provide criteria for the certification of environmentally sustainable assets, and to facilitate the inclusion of sustainability risks in risk analysis.[43] Membership in the NGFS is extended to central banks, other supervisory authorities, and international organizations. EU institutions holding memberships in NGFS are EBA and EIOPA.[44]

When examining the EU's influence on the international drafting of Sustainable Finance policy, the International Platform on Sustainable Finance (*IPSF*) plays a peculiar role. This is due to the Commission being its initiator, while the EU as a whole holds membership status and the EIB is an observer. IPSF was established in October 2019 to exchange information on *environmentally sustainable finance* in line with the obligations set out in the Paris Agreement and the 2030 Agenda.[45] The creation of a platform on Sustainable Finance acting as a Commission expert group was already outlined in 2018 in Art. 15 of the Commission's Proposal on a Taxonomy Regulation.[46] Instead, however, the Commission initiated the IPSF the same year and therefore replacing the Proposal on a Taxonomy Regulation's domestic approach with an international approach. In Art. 15 Final compromise on a

---

[39] IOSCO (2013).

[40] HLEG (2018), p. 55.

[41] SFN (2020).

[42] NGFS (2019c).

[43] NGFS (2019a), p. 33.

[44] EIOPA (2019c), p. 9; EBA (2019), pp. 64 et seq.

[45] IPSF (2019), p. 1; The IPSF originally consisted of public authorities of the EU, Argentina, Canada, Chile, China, India, Kenya, Morocco and seven observers, which were later joined by Hong Kong, Indonesia, Japan, New Zealand, Norway, Senegal, Singapore, Switzerland and two additional observers, cf. European Commission (2019c); Cf. IPSF (2020a).

[46] Cf. TEG (2019a), p. 28; European Commission (2018).

Taxonomy Regulation,[47] however, the creation of a domestic platform on Sustainable Finance was set out in Art. 20 Taxonomy Regulation.[48] Hereafter, this platform would consist solely of ESA and other EU specialized agencies' representatives and therefore would likely only complement the IPSF.

The IPSF's thematic scope covers policy coordination on taxonomies, disclosures, standards, and labels and builds on work conducted by the EIB, NGFS, and UNEP. The IPSF considers the financial markets to be of core importance in the shift necessary to reach sustainability goals, just like set out in Art. 2.1(c) Paris Agreement and in SDG 17.[49] It sees advantage in including financial markets into the core of the transition policy due to their global nature—alike climate change—and due to them being able to allocate resources cross-border.[50]

Furthermore, the Commission is invested in the work of the Task Force on Climate-Related Financial Disclosures (*TCFD*) created under the auspices of the FSB. As described for the EU level in Sect. 2.1.6, the adoption of a disclosure and reporting framework is paramount to the implementation of Sustainable Finance and also of core focus for TCFD. The TCFD is an industry-led initiative that aims at developing consistent, yet voluntary ESG-related disclosures.[51] The Commission and the ECB are both members of TCFD, which published its TCFD Final Report in June 2017 and its TCFD Status Reports in September 2018 and May 2019, respectively.[52] Further Status Report have been published in 2021, 2022, and 2023.[53] It is to be noted that NGFS members have also *"pledge[d] their support for the recommendations of the [TCFD]"*.[54]

Complementing this, the ECB and ESMA are members of the IASB, which addresses ESG-related accounting standards.[55] The IASB has published an article concerning *"IFRS Standards and climate-related disclosures"*[56] and the IASB chair held a speech on *"what sustainability reporting can and cannot achieve"*.[57] Furthermore, the Loan Market Association (*LMA*) has published the widely referenced Green Loan Principles[58] in December 2018 and the Sustainability Linked Loan

---

[47] European Council (2019).

[48] Regulation (EU) 2020/852 of the European Parliament and of the Council of 18 June 2020 on the establishment of a framework to facilitate sustainable investment, and amending Regulation (EU) 2019/2088 [2020] OJ L 198/13.

[49] IPSF (2019), p. 1; TEG (2019b), p. 13.

[50] IPSF (2019), p. 1.

[51] TCFD (2017), p. iii.

[52] TCFD (2017, 2018, 2019).

[53] TCFD (2021, 2022, 2023).

[54] NGFS (2019a), p. 31.

[55] Cf. Sect. 2.1.6.

[56] Anderson (2019).

[57] Hoogervorst (2019).

[58] LMA (2018).

Principles[59] in March 2019. The EIB and the ESM hold associate memberships, whereas the Commission holds a courtesy membership in the LMA.

Another international association that has worked and published on Sustainable Finance is the International Capital Market Association (*ICMA*). The ICMA has established several working groups on Sustainable Finance-related issues. For instance, the EIB is a member of the Working Group Climate Transition Finance with a thematic scope on climate transition finance through green bonds and the ICMA Green Bond Principles[60] and member of the Working Group Green Projects Eligibility addressing the establishment of a green taxonomy. Furthermore, the EIB is a member of the Working Group Sustainability/KPI-Linked Bonds covering sustainability bonds and the Sustainability Bond Guidelines.[61] The European Stability Mechanism (*ESM*) in turn is a member of the Working Group Social Bonds with a thematic scope covering social bonds and the Social Bond Principles.[62]

Addressing Sustainable Finance in the insurance sector, EIOPA is taking part in the Sustainable Insurance Forum (*SIF*), which has its secretariat with and is convened by the UNEP.[63] The SIF's thematic scope covers strengthening insurance supervisors' and regulators' responses to sustainability challenges and opportunities for the business of insurance. Its focus is on environmental issues such as climate change. The SIF published a paper on "*Sustainable Insurance: The Emerging Agenda for Supervisors and Regulators*"[64] in August 2017 and on "*Climate Change Risks to the Insurance Sector*"[65] in July 2019.

Furthermore, the ECB and the SSM are members of the Basel Committee on Banking Supervision (*BCBS*), which was established under the auspices of the Bank for International Settlements (*BIS*) with a thematic scope regarding coherence in supervisory standards but also regularly addressing Sustainable Finance. The BCBS published a "*survey on current initiatives*"[66] in April 2020.

Another noteworthy channel of influence is the UNEP Finance Initiative (*UNEP FI*) with its Working Group on EU Taxonomy. The UNEP FI was established under the auspices of UNEP and with the Commission, EBA, and the EIB as observers. Its thematic scope covers the provision of a high-level feasibility assessment of the EU taxonomy to core banking products, sharing best practices, and developing use cases where appropriate. It further aims to issue recommendations based on the project findings. Its final report was published in January 2021.[67]

---

[59] LMA (2019).
[60] ICMA (2018a).
[61] ICMA (2018b).
[62] ICMA (2020).
[63] Cf. EIOPA (2019c), p. 10.
[64] SIF (2017).
[65] SIF (2018).
[66] BCBS (2020).
[67] UNEP FI (2021).

Finally, on a broader scale the European Bank for Reconstruction and Development (*EBRD*), of which the EU and the EIB are financing members, has a thematic scope focusing on financing for development. Additionally, the Commission holds membership in its Environmental and Social Advisory Council. The EBRD (co-) published a Sourcebook on EU Environmental Law in March 2010[68] and the Green Economy Transition Handbook in May 2018.[69] Another example of such broadscale initiatives is the UN Partnership for Action on Green Economy (*UN PAGE*), which was established under the auspices of the UN and with the Commission as a *funding partner*. Its thematic focus is on sustainability in developing countries and its main document on Sustainable Finance is its Operational Strategy 2016–2020.[70]

As these remarks on the EU's, its institutions', or its specialized agencies' memberships in these international fora demonstrate, the Commission as the main domestic policy hub for EU Sustainable Finance is not represented in all of these organizations itself. For instance, the EIB is not bound by the Commission's decisions as set out in Art. 282(3)(3) TFEU.[71] However, with a view to the overarching goal of mainstreaming Sustainable Finance into all policy fields of financial regulation, EU institutions and its specialized agencies can equally be expected to apply these standards. As described in Chap. 2, the ESAs, the ECB, EIB, and various other financial supervision, monetary policy, and development assistance agencies have each developed their own Sustainable Finance agendas, mutually referencing these policy proposals.

The following Table 4.1 sets out the EU's participation in these international fora on Sustainable Finance policy, their respective thematic scope, and their relevant publications.

This versatile commitment of the EU's institutions and its specialized agencies in international fora addressing Sustainable Finance leads to the second question, on how the EU's membership in these fora has shaped its Sustainable Finance policy.

This first depends on the EU's incentives to integrate these international policy drafts into its domestic Sustainable Finance agenda. The EU has an interest in *channeling* its policies through international fora and *reintegrate* them into its domestic regulations due to e.g. Art. VI(5)(b) GATS. Domestic regulation such as licensing requirements and technical standards are to be interpreted with the help of international standards adopted by the EU. If those standards are shaped in a way conducive to EU interests and similar to its Sustainable Finance measures, it is less likely, such EU Sustainable Finance measures will be deemed inconsistent with Art. VI(5)(b) GATS.

As regards the influence of international panel publications on internal Sustainable Finance policy, there is insufficient information on the Commission's—and the

---

[68] EIB (2010).

[69] EBRD (2018).

[70] UN PAGE (2016).

[71] Consolidated version of the Treaty on the Functioning of the European Union [2012] OJ C 326/47.

EU's other institutions' and specialized agencies'—internal procedures. Plus, as described above, a variety of different institutions and specialized agencies of the EU is involved in shaping EU Sustainable Finance policy, with a varying combination of representation in these international fora. However, there are two indications of possible channels of influence. First, citations of international fora's publications and agendas in EU Sustainable Finance measures. This has been assessed already in Sect. 3.2.3.2.3 which demonstrated widespread use of referencing international fora' publications and agendas. If, however, such international fora' publications and agendas do not suffice the EU's demands for sustainability, domestically they may be adjusted to EU standards. For instance, the HLEG advises the Commission to revise the IAS Regulation[72] concerning international accounting standards only to be adopted, if they are "*conducive to [. . .] sustainability and long-term investment objectives*" or to conduct IFRS 9 adjustments itself.[73]

A noteworthy example of the re-introduction of policy from the international stage into EU Sustainable Finance measures is the IPSF's work on taxonomies, disclosure rules, sustainability standards, and labels. The Commission claimed it would use it as a reference in developing Sustainable Finance measures.[74] As the Commission regularly references policy recommendations and reports by international fora in which it takes part, the referencing of the IPSF's work should not be surprising. However, as noted above, the IPSF was initiated by the Commission, which also set the IPSF's scope and focus. Therefore, as the IPSF is a platform formed at the initiative of the Commission, its statements can be understood as reflecting or being broadly in line with the Commission's international efforts on Sustainable Finance. Additionally, even the statements by the observers' initiatives can be understood as in line with Commission practice as the IPSF explicitly tries to avoid duplication of work on Sustainable Finance by building on top of the work conducted by the observers.[75] These observers comprise *inter alia* the EIB, the NGFS, and the UNEP, which in turn, as aforementioned, acts as the secretariat to the SFSG.[76] Thus, the NGFS' and the SFSG's work can be understood as incorporated through the IPSF or at least seen as equal to the Commission's work on Sustainable Finance.

Second, an assessment of the timeline regarding the issuance of EU policy and regulation and policy publications by international organizations and panels might shed light on the correlations between the work of international fora and EU Sustainable Finance policy. Annex V summarizes the EU's Sustainable Finance policy publications and the main publications and reports on Sustainable Finance at the international level. The referencing in between these types of publications has

---

[72] Regulation (EC) No 1606/2002 of the European Parliament and of the Council of 19 July 2002 on the application of international accounting standards [2002] OJ L 243/1.

[73] HLEG (2018), p. 58.

[74] European Commission (2019a), p. 22; IPSF (2019), p. 1.

[75] IPSF (2019), p. 1.

[76] Cf. G20 (2018).

been examined above (Sects. 2.1, 3.2.3.2.3). The policy publications demonstrated therein and in Annex V show that the majority of EU Sustainable Finance measures addressed Sustainable Finance issues not only earlier but on a broader scale than the respective international fora's publications. In recent years, however, such international publications are becoming more regular and broader in their respective scope. From these observations, it can be deduced that there is certain reciprocity of influence between Sustainable Finance and international relations. This reciprocity can, again, also be viewed under the light of Art. VII(5)(b) GATS. By influencing the standards of international organizations, which it uses, the EU has more leverage to defend claims of impediments due to licensing and qualification requirements and technical standards.[77]

4.2 Propagation and Justification through the GATS Framework

The concept of Sustainable Finance can also be propagated and justified through the GATS framework, the WTO institutions, or other multilateral negotiations taking place under its auspices.

To better understand the impact and options for the EU to spread and protect EU Sustainable Finance policy and regulation within and through these negotiations, this Chapter will first consider current multilateral negotiations (Sect. 4.2.1). It will discuss the Trade in Services Agreement (*TiSA*),[78] the services domestic regulation negotiations currently underway pursuant to Art. VI(4) GATS, and, finally, potential future additions to the GATS text to that end. Subsequently, unilateral action such as recognition or the modification of a WTO Member's commitments (Sect. 4.2.2), and a potential future TBT Agreement for trade in services (Sect. 4.2.3) will be assessed as feasible instruments for propagation and justification of EU Sustainable Finance policy.

4.2.1   Multilateral Action: GATS and TiSA

Multilateral trade negotiations can refer to the drafting of entirely new agreements potentially based on the GATS and furthering trade liberalization, as additions and specifications to the GATS, or as amendments to the GATS text itself. For the first option concerning the multilateral negotiation of a more integrated trade in services agreement, TiSA is an example. TiSA negotiations started in 2012 with initially

---

[77]Cf. Van den Bossche and Zdouc (2017), p. 537, fn. 339.

[78]Trade in Services Agreement (TiSA), Draft Provisions. 21 June 2016.

sixteen TiSA Parties.[79] The EU, representing the twenty-seven EU Member States, plays an important role in negotiating TiSA.

TiSA has a very similar scope of application to the GATS. For example, TiSA applies *"to measures by [the] Parties affecting trade in services"* under Art. I-1(1) TiSA and categorizes trade in services by using four modes of supply as described in Art. I-1(2) TiSA. A further TiSA provision on the most-favored-nation standard outlines a *"list of MFN exemptions"* and contains a reference to the GATS Annex on Art. II Exemptions.[80] Moreover, rules on market access in Art. I-3 TiSA and on the national treatment standard in Art. I-4 TiSA are similar to those set out in Art. XVI and XVII GATS. Besides, Art. I-5 TiSA on additional commitments mirrors Art. XVIII GATS. Due to these similarities, the findings made in relation to the GATS provisions in the previous Chapters apply to these TiSA provisions, too.

A significant amendment, however, proposed *inter alia* by the EU is the relocation of the right to regulate clause from the general exceptions clause originating from the chapeau of Art. XIV GATS to a novel provision on domestic regulation in the core text of TiSA.[81] Moreover, the EU is one of the TiSA Parties considering the addition of a domestic regulation clause equal to Art. VI(1) GATS requiring Parties to *"ensure that all measures of general application affecting trade in services are administered in a reasonable, objective and impartial manner."* Additionally, Art. VI(2)(a) GATS is reflected in a para. 3 proposed by the EU under the TiSA domestic regulation provision. Finally, Art. I-9 TiSA on general exceptions consists of the same wording as set out in Art. XIV GATS.

Taking into account this *status quo* of TiSA negotiations in particular on market access, most-favored-nation and national treatment standards, the right to regulate, domestic regulation, and general exceptions, it is unlikely that potential future jurisprudence on EU Sustainable Finance's consistency with TiSA disciplines will draw different conclusions from those made under the GATS in Sect. 3.2. However, in addition to its core text, TiSA also elaborates on financial services and domestic regulation, namely in the TiSA Annex on Financial Services[82] and the TiSA Annex on Domestic Regulation.[83] For instance, Art. X.1(1) and (2) TiSA Annex on Financial Services sets out scope of application equaling para. 1(a) and (b) GATS Annex on Financial Services. The same applies to the definition section of Art. X.2 (a) TiSA Annex on Financial Services, which corresponds to the definitions set out in para. 5(a) GATS Annex on Financial Services. However, Art. X.2(d) and (e) TiSA Annex on Financial Services adds a definition of *new financial service*.

---

[79] WTO Members taking part in TiSA negotiations will be referred to as *TiSA Parties*.

[80] The most-favored-nation article is provisionally being referred to as *"Article [...]"* and situated subsequent to Art. I-2 TiSA.

[81] The domestic regulation article is provisionally being referred to as *"Article [...]"* and situated subsequent to Art. I-5 TiSA.

[82] TiSA Annex on Financial Services, Trade in Services Agreement (TiSA), Draft Provisions. 21 June 2016.

[83] TiSA Annex on Domestic Regulation, Trade in Services Agreement (TiSA), Draft Annex on Domestic Regulation. 10 October 2015.

New financial services have already been discussed concerning no. B.7 Understanding on Commitments in Financial Services in Sect. 3.2.1.3.[84] TiSA, however, introduces the definition of and rules on new financial services into the TiSA Annex on Financial Services. This annex, in turn, must be deemed an integral part of the agreement by a TiSA provision equaling Art. XXIX GATS.[85] In the GATS context, new financial services had merely been stated as part of the declaratory Understanding on Commitments in Financial Services. Thus, the inclusion of a new financial services regime into a multilateral trade in services agreement in the form of Art. X.9 TiSA Annex on Financial Services might be a feasible channel of propagating Sustainable Finance.

As stated above, Art. X.2(d) TiSA Annex on Financial Services defines a new financial service as "*a service of a financial nature, including services related to existing and new products or the manner in which a product is delivered, that is not supplied by any financial service supplier in the territory of a Party but which is supplied in the territory of another Party.*" This is the case for novel, sustainable financial instruments that may be developed within the EU and likely do not exist in such form in many other Parties' territories. The EU thus has an interest in securing market access for such sustainable financial services—not only for trade reasons but also for the sake of propagating these novel, sustainable financial services. The requirement set out in Art. X.9 TiSA Annex on Financial Services is limited in a threefold manner. The first precondition is that the host-TiSA Party "*would permit its own like financial services supplier to supply [such service]*". It further states that the supply of a new financial service needs to be permitted only if the supply does not require "*adopting a law or modifying an existing law.*" The host-TiSA Party, however, "*may determine the institutional and juridical form through which the service may be supplied and may require authorization for the supply of the service. Where such authorization is required, a decision shall be made within a reasonable time and the authorization may be refused only for prudential reasons.*" Therefore, the exceptions specified in Art. X.2(d) TiSA Annex on Financial Services give sufficient policy space for potential future sustainability requirements in relation to new financial services in EU Sustainable Finance.

However, whilst the GATS Annex on Financial Services only covers additional rules on domestic regulation and recognition,[86] Art. X.3 TiSA Annex on Financial Services sets out additional regulation on market access commitments in financial services. These commitments, to be included in each TiSA Party's Schedule on Specific Commitments according to Art. I-3 TiSA. particularly cover Mode 1 (*service provision from the territory of one TiSA Party into the territory of any other*

---

[84] With a view to the assessment of provisions on new financial services in EU FTAs, cf. Sect. 5.1.

[85] This Article is provisionally being referred to as "*Article [...]*" and situated subsequent to Article I-10 TiSA.

[86] Cf. para. 2 and 3 GATS Annex on Financial Services.

TiSA Party)[87] and Mode 4 (*presence of natural persons*).[88] It is noteworthy that concerning the latter, the EU opposes the inclusion of "*investment advice to a collective investment scheme located in the Party's territory*" and "*portfolio management services to a collective investment scheme located in the Party's territory [. . .]*". This in turn would mean that measures affecting these particular financial services would not have to be included into a TiSA Party's Schedule on Specific Commitments. Given such lesser protection, the EU can more easily justify its policy in relation to these specific financial services in Sustainable Finance measures.

This, however, only presents a policy space protection aspect of the EU's commitment in the TiSA negotiations. Despite this and the possible propagation of Sustainable Finance through rules on new financial services, the TiSA Annex on Financial Services does not show any efforts on the inclusion of Sustainable Finance clauses. The interpretation of the TiSA Annex on Domestic Regulation, however, might allow for a differing conclusion. For the wording of Art. 1 TiSA Annex on Domestic Regulation, the EU proposes that the TiSA Annex on Financial Services "*applies to measures relating to licensing requirements and procedures, qualification requirements and procedures, and technical standards, affecting trade in services with respect to which a Party has undertaken a commitment under Article I-3 or I-4, subject to any terms, limitations, conditions or qualifications set out in its schedule pursuant to Articles II-1 and II-2.*" Hence, the EU aims at harmonizing the scope of application of TiSA Annex on Financial Services with Art. VI(5) (a) GATS.[89]

This is complemented by Art. 4 TiSA Annex on Domestic Regulation largely equaling Art. VI GATS and explicitly referring to the requirements of Art. VI(4) (a) to (c) GATS. The EU, however, as stated therein, would prefer to spell out "*exact criteria rather than making reference to*" Art. VI(4)(a) to (c) GATS. This would open up a certain negotiation and policy space for possible amendments to the criteria named in Art. VI(a) to (c) GATS through TiSA.[90] Art. 4 TiSA Annex on Domestic Regulation, in turn, already references Art. VI(5)(b) GATS, which requires that the determination of conformity must take into account international standards of relevant international organizations. Hence, the same considerations conducive to EU Sustainable Finance measures discussed in Sects. 3.2.3.2.3 and 4.1 can be consulted. Similarly, Art. X.16 TiSA on prudential measures uses the same wording as para. 2(a) GATS Annex on Financial Services. Due to these similarities and explicit references to the relevant GATS provisions regarding the examination of EU Sustainable Finance measures under Art. 4 TiSA Annex on Domestic Regulation and Art. X.16 TiSA, reference can be made to the considerations in Sects. 3.2.3 and 3.2.4.3.

---

[87] Cf. Art. I-1(2)(a) TiSA.
[88] Cf. Art. I-1(2)(d) TiSA.
[89] Cf. Sect. 3.2.3.2.
[90] Cf. Sect. 3.2.3.2.1.

Instead of the reference to Art. VI(4)(a) to (c) GATS in Art. 4 TiSA Annex on Domestic Regulation, the EU is one of the TiSA Parties proposing an Art. 5 TiSA Annex on Domestic Regulation, which in turn has significant similarities to the requirements set out in Art. VI(4) and (5) GATS. There are, however, several differences. First, Art. 5 TiSA Annex on Domestic Regulation does not require the prior adoption of disciplines by the Council for Trade in Services. This would make Art. 5 TiSA Annex on Domestic Regulation immediately applicable to licensing and qualification requirements and technical standards. Second, Art. 5 TiSA Annex on Domestic Regulation does not contain such restrictions as *not reasonably expectable* or not to *apply in a manner*. This would constitute a wider scope of application to Art. 5 TiSA Annex on Domestic Regulation than the scope set out in Art. VI(4) and (5) GATS. This in turn would theoretically prove detrimental to the interpretation of Sustainable Finance measures under this clause. However, as shown in Sects. 3.2.3.1 and 3.2.3.2.2, these two conditions are not central and not critical to the assessment of EU Sustainable Finance.[91]

Concluding, TiSA negotiations may open up a variety of opportunities to introduce Sustainable Finance into multilateral trade negotiations, especially given the much-criticized lack of addressing sustainable development in TiSA. Sustainable Finance justification provisions could either be incorporated into a prospective TiSA sustainable development chapter—thereby relating Sustainable Finance to the already established concept of sustainable development—or such justification provisions could be added to the TiSA Annex on Financial Services. As regards the propagation of Sustainable Finance, preambulatory reference could be made to the successes made at the international level, for instance by the AAAA. This would draw a connection between domestic Sustainable Finance with its roots in ODA and regional development schemes. This might tilt a Panel's interpretation of TiSA disciplines in favor of a contested Sustainable Finance measure. Finally, a Sustainable Finance clause could be integrated into the exceptions for prudential measures under Art. X.16 TiSA, for instance, using a clarification in a footnote to this provision.

Additionally, the EU could steer the negotiations on services domestic regulation towards the introduction of Sustainable Finance-related language. The EU co-hosts these negotiations replacing the original and stalled Art. VI(4) GATS negotiations on domestic services regulation. The initiative was started by 59 WTO Members at MC11[92] in December 2017 (Sect. 3.2.3.2) and was expected to be finalized at the June 2020 WTO Ministerial Conference (*MC12*), which has been postponed to June 2021.[93] The negotiations on services domestic regulation provide the EU with an opportunity to introduce Sustainable Finance justification and propagation language into the development of disciplines under Art. VI(4) GATS. The current wording of

---

[91] Recognition under Art. I-6 TiSA and Art. X.18 TiSA Annex on Financial Services will be assessed in Sect. 4.2.2.

[92] MC11, as defined in Sect. 3.2.3.2.

[93] Cf. Commission, news archive, http://trade.ec.europa.eu/doclib/press/index.cfm?id=2021.

the Joint Statement on Services Domestic Regulation,[94] however, does not hint towards the particular consideration of, for instance, prudential regulation or sustainable development let alone Sustainable Finance.

Finally, prospective amendments to the GATS text itself would be beneficial to an interpretation conducive to domestic Sustainable Finance measures under the GATS disciplines and the propagation of Sustainable Finance policy towards other WTO Members.

First, a clause stating that *"measures by a [WTO] Member taken in furtherance of Sustainable Finance"* or *"prudential measures by a [WTO] Member taken in furtherance of Sustainable Development"* could be integrated as part and a further example of the *"measures for prudential reasons"* in para. 2(a) GATS Annex on Financial Services. As shown above, para. 2(a) GATS Annex on Financial Services applies to large parts of EU Sustainable Finance legislation, but such clarification would particularly justify those Sustainable Finance measures that do not have a sufficiently close relation to the policy objective of financial stability. Moreover, such an addition to para. 2(a) GATS Annex on Financial Services would guide a Panel's assessment of the GATS disciplines described in Sect. 3.2 and potentially even the prospective EU Sustainable Finance measures described in Sect. 3.3.

Alternatively, an addition to the GATS preamble conducive to Sustainable Finance in a Panel's interpretation of the GATS disciplines could be considered. Such clause may be similar to the *national policy objectives* clause in Recital 4 GATS, for instance: *"Recognizing the right of [WTO] Members to regulate, and to introduce new regulations, on the supply of sustainability-related [financial] services within their territories in order to meet national sustainability objectives [or international sustainability goals]"*. Alternatively, the wording of Recital 4 GATS could be amended, for example stating: *"Recognizing the right of [WTO] Members to regulate, and to introduce new regulations, on the supply of services within their territories in order to meet national policy and sustainability objectives"*.

Furthermore, an addition to Art. XIV(b) GATS could be made to explicitly include environmental measures into its scope of application. Alternatively, an exception could be added for measures aimed at preserving exhaustible natural resources, as there is no equivalent to Art. XX(g) GATT in GATS. However, the Decision on Trade in Services and the Environment in this regard states that *"since measures necessary to protect the environment typically have as their objective the protection of human, animal or plant life or health, it is not clear that there is a need to provide for more than is contained in paragraph (b) of Article XIV"*.[95] Indeed, so far Art. XIV GATS has remained unchanged.[96]

---

[94] Communication, Joint Statement on Services Domestic Regulation. 23 May 2019.

[95] Decision on Trade in Services and the Environment, Whereas, p. 2; Van den Bossche and Zdouc (2017), p. 615.

[96] Van den Bossche and Zdouc (2017), p. 615.

Such additions would not alter the GATS' current system of disciplines but would circumvent regulatory uncertainties by steering a Panel's interpretation of these disciplines in relation to Sustainable Finance measures. It is to be stated, however, that any amendments to GATS are highly unlikely.

Concluding, the EU has the opportunity to use multilateral negotiations in favor of Sustainable Finance measures. With a view to the justification of EU Sustainable Finance measures under TiSA, the assessment of its legality would for large parts mirror the assessment conducted in Sect. 3.2 on GATS, due to the intended similarities between both agreements. In respect of the propagation of Sustainable Finance into multilateral negotiations, the EU has not used TiSA as an opportunity to effectively introduce Sustainable Finance into a multilateral trade framework. Neither have substantive provisions on sustainable development been introduced. This hints at the fact that plurilateral negotiations on matters of trade and sustainable development are difficult. A bilateral negotiation setting, for example through FTAs, is therefore preferable. Furthermore, the EU could work towards a TBT-like agreement for trade in services in order to multilateralize the underlying principles of its Sustainable Finance standards.

Generally, good faith efforts in negotiating multilateral agreements also protect the EU from its Sustainable Finance measures being considered arbitrary or unjustifiable discriminations under the chapeau of Art. XIV GATS, as discussed in Sect. 3.2.4.1.4. The actual conclusion of the respective agreement is not a requirement *per se*, good faith efforts to reach a conclusion suffice, as the Art. 21.5 DSU Appellate Body concluded in *US–Shrimp*.[97]

4.2.2 Unilateral Action: Recognition and Modification of Commitments

Another possible method of propagating the concept and instruments of Sustainable Finance into the GATS regulatory framework is unilateral action through the strategic use of recognition and modification of the Schedule of Commitments.

Recognition is regulated under Art. VII(1) GATS, which instructs that "*a [WTO] Member may recognize the education or experience obtained, requirements met, or licenses or certifications granted in a particular country.*" Thus, through unilateral application or harmonization, the host state can recognize the entirety or parts of the home state's regulatory regime. Concerning EU Sustainable Finance measures, whether certain sustainability requirements are met, or licenses or certifications are granted is of particular relevance.

---

[97]WTO DSB (2001) United States – Import Prohibition of Certain Shrimp and Shrimp Products, Appellate Body report, para. 134; Cf. Van den Bossche and Zdouc (2017), p. 599.

Such *"requirements met, or licenses or certifications granted"* under EU Sustainable Finance cover EU Green Bonds,[98] labeling schemes like the EU Ecolabel for financial products,[99] and the EU PAB and EU CTB benchmark labels.[100] As concluded above, sustainability standards, which in case of noncompliance entirely restrict a financial service supplier's access to a market or market segment, do not yet exist in EU Sustainable Finance legislation. However, as stated above (Sect. 3.2.1), for instance, green bonds do *de facto* restrict access to a market (green bond) segment. Thus, such standards may be understood as a partial licensing of financial services and thus for this purpose fall beneath the definition of *"licenses"* according to Art. VII(1) GATS. Furthermore, certain financial services and their labeling require certification under the applicable EU Sustainable Finance legislation. For instance, EU labeling standards relating to sustainable financial services and financial service suppliers constitute such certification standards in the understanding of Art. VII(1) GATS. The same applies to *"requirements met"*. This broad term encompasses all requirements a financial service supplier is required to abide by, in order to be awarded a certain label or to comply with reporting and disclosure regulations. In any case, the EU Sustainable Finance measures described above are likely to constitute certifications to be granted by an authority to be allowed to be labeled with a certain denomination pursuant to Art. VII(1) GATS.

Regarding these Sustainable Finance measures, para. 3(a) GATS Annex on Financial Services specifies, resembling Art. VII(1) GATS that a *"[WTO] Member may recognize prudential measures of any other country in determining how the [WTO] Member's measures relating to financial services shall be applied. [...]"*.[101] Art. VII(1) GATS adds to this that *"[s]uch recognition, which may be achieved through harmonization or otherwise, may be based upon an agreement or arrangement with the country concerned or may be accorded autonomously."* Thus, recognition can either be achieved through unilateral or multilateral recognition of another WTO Member's licensing standards. With a view to EU Sustainable Finance policy, para. 3(a) GATS Annex on Financial Services thus both protects the unilateral recognition of equal sustainability standards of other jurisdictions and opens a channel for propagating them to other WTO Members. The second question thus is whether the EU has already, or is prospectively likely to enter into bilateral or multilateral agreements or unilaterally recognize another WTO Member's licenses and certifications in relation to Sustainable Finance.

However, neither Art. VII GATS nor the GATS Annex on Financial Services constitute an obligation for recognition of other states' regulatory measures.[102] The EU, nevertheless, may use negotiations on an agreement of reciprocal recognition to incentivize other WTO Members to adopt Sustainable Finance measures. Thus, it

---

[98]Cf. Sect. 2.1.3.

[99]Cf. Sect. 2.1.2.

[100]Cf. Sect. 2.1.4.

[101]Cf. WTO (2020), p. 2.

[102]Trachtman (1996), p. 96.

would ensure compliance of their financial service suppliers with EU Sustainable Finance measures. First and foremost, it is to be stated that the adoption of such recognition agreements is not common in Sustainable Finance measures. So far, the EU has not entered into agreements on the recognition of Sustainable Finance licensing and certification standards with another WTO Member. For the sake of completeness, it shall be noted that the instrument of recognition in itself is limited by the GATS disciplines. In particular, the most-favored-nation standard limits a WTO Member's ability to use recognition as a tool in international trade negotiations.

The tool of recognition under Art. VII(1) GATS is further limited by the "*equal opportunity*" requirement set in Art. VII(2) GATS, which states that a WTO "*Member [...] shall afford adequate opportunity for other interested [WTO] Members to negotiate their accession to such an agreement or arrangement or to negotiate comparable ones with it.*" Thus, the tool of recognition under Art. VII (1) GATS is limited by the requirement of equal opportunity in Art. VII(2) GATS, which in turn can be understood as a limited most-favored-nation standard. Therefore, a WTO Member recognizing another WTO Member's licensing standards is obligated to either ensure the possibility of accession to the bilateral agreement or unilaterally to be equally recognized. This also applies to the prudential carve-out clause set in para. 3(b) GATS Annex on Financial Services, which states that any WTO Member may recognize another WTO Member's prudential measures through recognition as long as it recognizes similar measures by other WTO Members under the most-favored-nation standard.[103] Thus, the EU, concluding such agreements on reciprocal recognition would have to grant the opportunity of accession or similar agreements. However, this would be limited to *comparable* terms and thus would incentivize WTO Members wishing such recognition to adopt similar Sustainable Finance measures.[104]

Similarly, of particular relevance could prove the second sentence of Art. VII (2) GATS, in cases, "*[w]here a [WTO] Member accords recognition autonomously, it shall afford adequate opportunity for any other [WTO] Member to demonstrate that education, experience, licenses, or certifications obtained or requirements met in that other [WTO] Member's territory should be recognized.*". This puts the burden of proof onto the WTO Member seeking recognition by the EU and adds additional incentives to introduce transparent, effective regulation meeting the requirements of EU Sustainable Finance legislation.

Finally, Art. VII(5) GATS instructs that "*[w]herever appropriate, recognition should be based on multilaterally agreed criteria*" established "*in cooperation with relevant intergovernmental and non-governmental organizations*".[105] Such

---

[103] Martin and Mercurio (2017), p. 87.

[104] Trachtman also considered recognition under Art. VII(1) GATS a "*conditional MFN treatment*" or a "*narrower form of integration*" in comparison to Art. V GATS, cf. Trachtman (1996), p. 103.

[105] TiSA recognition requirements such as Art. I-6 TiSA largely equal those described in GATS, namely Art. VII GATS; Art. X.18(a) to (c) TiSA Annex on Financial Services equals the wording of para. 3(a) to (c) GATS Annex on Financial Services.

"*common international standards and criteria for recognition and common international standards for the practice of relevant services trades and professions*" are in extensive use throughout EU Sustainable Finance measures.[106] However, a clearer reference to these standards not only in the preamble of the applicable regulation but also in its implementation might be necessary. So far, EU Sustainable Finance measures mostly use these international standards as a reference point to draft similar domestic regulation. However, except for standards like the IFRS, which are not referenced but incorporated through the IAS Regulation,[107] such inclusions are rare in EU Sustainable Finance legislation.

The need for the use of international standards is also exemplified by the reference to harmonization of licensing and certification standards laid down in Art. VII(1) GATS. Harmonization means the assimilation of two WTO Members' standards. If, however, third countries should be allowed to gain the same recognition through harmonization, ultimately the middle ground for multilateral harmonization would most likely be the standards already set at the UN level. For Sustainable Finance, this means that the use of multilateral standards already in place is conducive to the opportunity for accession to bilateral recognition agreements entered into by the EU.

The same reasoning applies if unilateral recognition by the EU is taken into account. The EU will only apply such unilateral recognition if the other WTO Member's standards are sufficiently similar to the standards applicable within the EU. Because Art. VII(2) GATS requires the EU to then apply the same recognition to other WTO Members with equal domestic standards, the EU is incentivized to not only use international certification and licensing standards within its bilateral recognition agreements but also to draft domestic regulation similar to these standards. For this domestic regulation to still be in line with the EU's internal policy objectives, ensuring international standards are set according to these policy objectives is key. Hence, this hints at the EU's strong commitment to the drafting of international standards on sustainable development in general and Sustainable Finance in specific.

It can be concluded that although Art. VII GATS and the GATS Annex on Financial Services do not constitute an obligation for recognition of other states' regulatory measures, the EU may use negotiations on an agreement of reciprocal recognition to incentivize other WTO Members to adopt Sustainable Finance measures. The adoption of such recognition agreements, however, is not common in Sustainable Finance measures. Further, the "*equal opportunity*" requirement specified in Art. VII(2) GATS is both a limitation to recognition agreements by the EU and a possibility to encourage other jurisdictions to adopt similar sustainability standards. Plus, the EU benefits from its extensive use of "*common international standards and criteria for recognition and common international standards for the*

---

[106]Cf. Sect. 3.2.3.2.3.

[107]Regulation (EC) No 1606/2002 of the European Parliament and of the Council of 19 July 2002 on the application of international accounting standards [2002] OJ L 243/1.

practice of relevant services trades and professions" as required in Art. VII (5) GATS.[108]

Another option for justifying Sustainable Finance policy through GATS could be the modification of the EU's Schedule of Specific Commitments.

As described in Chap. 3, each WTO Member publishes a Schedule of Specific Commitments outlining its commitments in market access, national treatment, and additional commitments pursuant to Art. XX(1) GATS. Art. XXI(1)(a) GATS allows for WTO Members to modify or withdraw such commitments.[109] A modification or withdrawal can be conducted *"at any time after three years have elapsed from the date on which that commitment entered into force".*[110]

The EU originally published its Schedule of Specific Commitments in the aftermath of the Uruguay Round in April 1994.[111] An updated version—a result of the EU's expansion throughout the two preceding decades—was published in May 2019.[112] This 2019 update of its Schedule of Specific Commitments did not introduce limitations or additional commitments relevant to Sustainable Finance policy.[113] The question is whether in the future, given the recent developments in Sustainable Finance both domestically and internationally, a modification of the EU's Schedule of Specific Commitments is in order.

When considering the modification of commitments, a WTO Member must consider several obstacles. The same is true for the EU's possible inclusion of Sustainable Finance-related language into Schedule of Specific Commitments and thus its modification.

Pursuant to Art. XXI(2) GATS, a WTO Member affected by the modification may request compensation. Such *"[c]ompensatory adjustments shall be made on a most-favoured-nation basis".*[114] With a view to EU Sustainable Finance, most large financial institutions and financial market participants potentially affected by such modification are already offering services in the EU. Home states of third-country market participants, therefore, would potentially request compensatory adjustment under Art. XXI(2) GATS.

Due to these compensatory adjustments, a withdrawal or substantial modification of trade in services commitments can be considered rather an exception. For instance, China and Canada, which are among the WTO Members most active in drafting Sustainable Finance policy, supplemented or updated their Schedules of

---

[108]Cf. Sect. 3.2.3.2.3.

[109]The introduction of additional commitments is not covered by Art. XXI GATS under the assumption of *"progressively higher levels of liberalization of trade in services"*, cf. Recital 3 GATS.

[110]Cf. Art. XXI(1)(a) GATS; This is further subject to the notification requirement in Art. XXI(1)(b) GATS.

[111]European Communities and their Member States, Schedule of Specific Commitments. 15 April 1994. GATS/SC/31.

[112]European Union, Schedule of Specific Commitments. 7 May 2019. GATS/SC/157.

[113]Cf. Chap. 3.

[114]Cf. Art. XXI(2)(a) GATS.

Specific Commitments after the introduction of the GATS. None of these updated Schedules of Specific Commitments introduced changes to commitments with regard to financial services and sustainability.

Whilst domestically Canada is active in shaping Sustainable Finance policy,[115] it did not update but only supplement its Schedule of Specific Commitments. Published originally in April 1994[116] with the most recent Supplement in February 1998[117] to the section on financial services, its Schedule on Specific Commitments does not include language specifically beneficial for Sustainable Finance.

China, in turn, was one of the first WTO Members to introduce Sustainable Finance guidelines.[118] Its Schedule of Specific Commitments originates from April 1994, too.[119] In contrast to Canada, it not only supplemented but updated its commitments in February 2002.[120]

For these reasons, unilateral action through modification of the Schedule of Specific Commitments may not be an effective way of justifying EU Sustainable Finance policy. Multilateral action through the instruments described above, in turn, offers the possibility of propagation of Sustainable Finance. It effectively serves to facilitate trade in sustainable financial services rather than to restrict market access and national treatment for trade in unsustainable financial services.

4.2.3   Technical Barriers to Trade

Finally, the experiences made from the negotiation of and jurisprudence stemming from the Agreement on Technical Barriers to Trade (*TBT Agreement*)[121] may prove helpful in a potential negotiation of a similar agreement for trade in financial services or addition of similar disciplines into the GATS or EU FTA frameworks. This would in turn also strongly influence the propagation and justification of EU Sustainable Finance measures.

The TBT Agreement itself is not applicable to trade in financial services since services, in general, are not covered as per Art. 1.3 TBT Agreement and the opening paragraph of TBT Agreement Annex 1. However, the drafting of an agreement similar to the TBT Agreement for trade in services has previously been discussed.[122]

---

[115] Cf. e.g. Government of Canada (2019).

[116] Government of Canada (1994).

[117] Government of Canada (1998).

[118] Cf. e.g. People's Bank of China (2016).

[119] People's Republic of China (1994).

[120] People's Republic of China (2002).

[121] Agreement on Technical Barriers to Trade, Marrakesh Agreement Establishing the World Trade Organization, Annex 1A. 15 April 1994. U.N.T.S. 1867 (1994).

[122] Cf. Hoekman and Mavroidis (2015).

The TBT Agreement or its Standards Code[123] and the principles they promote, in contrast, may be relevant to a proportionality examination of domestic regulation under Art. VI(4)(b) GATS and prospective negotiations on Sustainable Finance in multilateral services trade agreements. After all, GATS was drafted under the influence and bearing the experience of GATT.[124]

First, it is to be noted that Art. VI(4)(b) GATS in preventing *unnecessary barriers to trade in services* and requiring for domestic legislation to be *not more burdensome than necessary to ensure the quality of the service* as discussed in Sect. 3.2.3.2.1 is similar to certain requirements under the TBT Agreement and its Standards Code. For instance, para. E Standards Code describes an obligation for WTO Members to prevent their standards from *"creating unnecessary obstacles to international trade"* while according to para. F Standards Code they *"shall use [international standards], or the relevant parts of them, as a basis for the standards"* they develop if available and appropriate. Additionally, para. I Standards Code clearly states that domestic standards should rather be based on the performance of products than on their design and descriptive characteristics.[125] Translating these requirements into terms of trade in services, Sustainable Finance measures would be within the scope of international standards if they refer to the relevant underlying's performance in relation to, for example, UN-level agreements on sustainable development. They would further need to base their standards of identifying such performance on available international standards.

Another example of international trade in goods norms, similar to the requirements outlined in Art. VI(4) GATS, is Art. 2.2 TBT Agreement. As part of the Uruguay Round's Final Act, the TBT Agreement has a much broader backing by WTO Members than the Standards Code set in its Annex 3 due to the latter's voluntary nature. Art. 2.2 TBT Agreement states that standards set by national regulation fulfilling a legitimate policy objective, as defined therein, may not be *"more restrictive to trade than necessary"* to fulfill these policy objectives. According to Art. 2.5 TBT Agreement, if a regulatory standard aims to achieve such policy objectives described in Art. 2.2 TBT Agreement and is *"in accordance with relevant international standards"*, it is deemed not to be an unnecessary obstacle to trade in goods.[126] This mirrors the indicative relationship between Art. VI(5)(b) and (4)(b) GATS, with the proportionality exam thereunder conducted in light of the EU's use of and compliance with international standards. Thus, the rationale of Art. 2.5 TBT Agreement translated to Art. VI(5)(b) GATS would mean that the domestic application of international standards would not just indicate but

---

[123] Code of Good Practice for the preparation, adoption and application of standards, Agreement on Technical Barriers to Trade, Annex 3, Marrakesh Agreement Establishing the World Trade Organization, Annex 1A. 15 April 1994. U.N.T.S. 1867 (1994).

[124] Trachtman (1996), pp. 87 et seq.

[125] Trachtman (1996), p. 87.

[126] Trachtman (1996), p. 87.

predetermine consistency with the requirements set out in Art. VI(5)(a)(i) and (ii) GATS.

Hence, although the regulations on proportionality in the Standards Code and the TBT Agreement are not directly applicable to trade in services, they do demonstrate that WTO Members submitting to such discipline show an acceptance of international standards. This in turn requires proportionality in their application. In a bilateral context, this would translate into equivalence between the host state's and home state's norms to the end that if equivalence or a state of sufficient similarity exists, there is no necessity for the application of host state regulation on the matter.[127] Thus, the material application of international standards under Art. VI (5) GATS is not only a guiding principle but rather needs to be understood as a mechanism favoring equivalence and preventing duplication.[128] The aim of avoiding such duplication would thus be conducive to the propagation of Sustainable Finance through international trade law.

A final similarity between the TBT Agreement and many of the EU Sustainable Finance measures introduced so far is their respective scope of application. Pursuant to the definition of standards in TBT Agreement Annex 1.2, a standard is a *"document [. . .], that provides, for common and repeated use, rules, guidelines and characteristics [. . .], with which compliance is not mandatory."*[129] The same applies to EU Sustainable Finance standards such as the EU GBS or the EU PAB or EU CTB, which pose voluntary *self-regulatory* standards. However, as the necessity of introducing the TBT Agreement has shown, even voluntary standards can create sufficient pressure on market participants to participate in the standard. This then can lead to a *de facto* compulsory regulation and thus needs international harmonization through, for instance, the TBT Agreement.[130] Although an agreement on technical barriers to trade does not exist for standards in trade in services, the TBT Agreement is an important sign of international recognition of the issue of potential adverse impacts of domestic standards on trade. This might have implications for future negotiation of comparable clauses for trade in services. Plus, the TBT Agreement thereby differentiates between a compulsory technical regulation and a voluntary standard.[131] This differentiation is of utmost importance when analyzing EU Sustainable Finance measures such as sustainability labels. This can be seen in the considerations made concerning a proposal for compulsory labeling provisions in Sect. 3.3.1.

Although Art. VI(5)(b) GATS states that *"international standards of relevant international organizations applied by that [WTO] Member"* shall be used in *"determining whether a [WTO] Member is in conformity with the obligation under*

---

[127]Cf. e.g. Art. 2.7 TBT Agreement and para. H Standards Code; Cf. Trachtman (1996), p. 88.

[128]Cf. e.g. para. H Standards Code.

[129]Cf. Van den Bossche and Zdouc (2017), p. 886.

[130]Cf. Van den Bossche and Zdouc (2017), p. 886.

[131]Van den Bossche and Zdouc (2017), pp. 886, 891; Therein: WTO DSB (2002) *European Communities – Trade Description of Sardines*, Appellate Body report, para. 176.

paragraph 5(a)",[132] the TBT Agreement takes a much stronger stance on the adoption of such international standards by requiring WTO Members to issue notifications in case of introduction of a technical requirement inconsistent with international standards.[133] Such a notification requirement could be introduced into the GATS agreement, too.

4.3   Conclusion: Effective Channels of Propagation and Justification

Despite the consistency of EU Sustainable Finance under GATS not being self-evident, its potential for inconsistency under GATS so far remains low as concluded in Sects. 3.2.5 and 3.3.4. Taking into account the forward-looking nature of Sustainable Finance as a concept, this Chapter discussed the possibilities international organizations, panels, and the GATS framework pose to Sustainable Finance from a proactive point of view.

As summarized in Sect. 4.1, the EU does actively incorporate Sustainable Finance policy into the international fora it is taking part in. Their close thematic focus on Sustainable Finance or fine thematic granularity, however, comes at the cost of their decisions' binding character. The fine thematic granularity can be exemplified by the BCBS' and NGFS' work on climate-related financial risks or the mapping exercises by SFN and SFSG. As such, these fora do not settle for declarations of intent concerning the furtherance of sustainability and financial stability, the kind of which can usually be found in preambulatory clauses. The international fora' publications described in Sect. 4.1.2, however, are regularly to be understood as policy recommendations and research. They lack binding character for the respective participants, let alone for non-participants.

To enhance effectiveness, a forum to address Sustainable Finance must be found that keeps the thematic focus while producing binding guidelines.

Section 4.2 discussed such a forum in the form of the GATS framework. It showed that despite the GATS norms' binding character the options for propagation and justification through the GATS framework are limited. In particular, the proactive approach chosen for the EU's work in international fora did not resonate in its TiSA negotiation positions. Therefore, GATS did not prove itself as an effective channel for propagating and justifying EU Sustainable Finance policy. This is due to two reasons. First, its high-level approach. Financial services provisions such as those set out in the GATS Annex on Financial Services lack sufficient granularity. Sufficient granularity is a precondition for introducing specific justification provisions for Sustainable Finance. Second, the large number of GATS signatories hinders a substantive amendment conducive to EU Sustainable Finance policy.

---

[132] Cf. Sect. 3.2.3.2.3; Cf. Van den Bossche and Zdouc (2017), p. 537, fn. 339.

[133] Hoekman and Mavroidis (2015), pp. 4, 11.

FTAs may constitute a viable policy alternative to multilateral approaches examined in Sects. 4.1 and 4.2. As bilateral agreements, they resemble GATS in respect of their binding character. Simultaneously, recent FTAs exhibit a similar granularity as provided by the publications of international fora. For these reasons, EU FTAs may function as potential channels of justifying and propagating Sustainable Finance through international trade law. The following Chapter will transpose the *de lege lata* assessment of Sects. 3.2 and 3.3 into the legal framework of EU FTAs. This is complemented by possible and actual channels of propagation and justification of EU Sustainable Finance in Sect. 5.4.

Legislation

United Nations Framework Convention on Climate Change. 9 May 1992. U.N.T.S. 1771 (1992)

General Agreement on Tariffs and Trade 1994, Marrakesh Agreement Establishing the World Trade Organization, Annex 1A. 15 April 1994. U.N.T.S. 1867 (1994)

Agreement on Technical Barriers to Trade, Marrakesh Agreement Establishing the World Trade Organization, Annex 1A. 15 April 1994. U.N.T.S. 1867 (1994)

Code of Good Practice for the preparation, adoption and application of standards, Agreement on Technical Barriers to Trade, Annex 3, Marrakesh Agreement Establishing the World Trade Organization, Annex 1A. 15 April 1994. U.N.T.S. 1867 (1994)

General Agreement on Trade in Services, Marrakesh Agreement Establishing the World Trade Organization, Annex 1B. 15 April 1994. U.N.T.S. 1867 (1994)

Decision on Trade in Services and the Environment, Uruguay Round ministerial decisions and declarations, Decisions adopted by the Trade Negotiations Committee on 15 December 1993 and 14 April 1994, Final Act Embodying the Results of the Uruguay Round of Multilateral Trade Negotiations. 15 April 1994. U.N.T.S. 1867 (1994)

Understanding on Commitments in Financial Services, Marrakesh Agreement Establishing the World Trade Organization. 15 April 1994

European Communities and their Member States, Schedule of Specific Commitments. 15 April 1994. GATS/SC/31

Treaty of Amsterdam, Amending the Treaty on European Union, the Treaties establishing the European Communities and certain related Acts [1997] OJ C 340/1

Treaty of Nice, Amending the Treaty on European Union, the Treaties establishing the European Communities and certain related Acts [2001] OJ C 80/1–87

Monterrey Consensus of the International Conference on Financing for Development, The final text of agreements and commitments adopted at the International Conference on Financing for Development Monterrey, Mexico, 18–22 March 2002. 22 March 2002

Regulation (EC) No 1606/2002 of the European Parliament and of the Council of 19 July 2002 on the application of international accounting standards [2002] OJ L 243/1

Doha Declaration on Financing for Development: Outcome Document of the Follow-up International Conference on Financing for Development to Review the Implementation of the Monterrey Consensus. 9 December 2008

General Assembly Resolution 66/288, The future we want. 27 July 2012. A/RES/66/288

Consolidated version of the Treaty on European Union [2012] OJ C 326/13

Consolidated version of the Treaty on the Functioning of the European Union [2012] OJ C 326/47

Directive 2014/95/EU of the European Parliament and of the Council of 22 October 2014 amending Directive 2013/34/EU as regards disclosure of non-financial and diversity information by certain large undertakings and groups [2014] OJ L 330/1

Addis Ababa Action Agenda of the Third International Conference on Financing for Development (Addis Ababa Action Agenda), The final text of the outcome document adopted at the Third International Conference on Financing for Development (Addis Ababa, Ethiopia, 13–16 July 2015) and endorsed by the General Assembly in its resolution 69/313 of 27 July 2015. 15 July 2015

General Assembly Resolution 70/1, Transforming our World: The 2030 Agenda for Sustainable Development. 25 September 2015. A/RES/70/1

TiSA Annex on Domestic Regulation, Trade in Services Agreement (TiSA), Draft Annex on Domestic Regulation. 10 October 2015

Directive (EU) 2016/97 of the European Parliament and of the Council of 20 January 2016 on insurance distribution (recast) [2016] OJ L 26/19

Trade in Services Agreement (TiSA), Draft Provisions. 21 June 2016

TiSA Annex on Financial Services, Trade in Services Agreement (TiSA), Draft Provisions. 21 June 2016

Communication, Joint Statement on Services Domestic Regulation. 23 May 2019

Regulation (EU) 2019/2033 of the European Parliament and of the Council of 27 November 2019 on the prudential requirements of investment firms and amending Regulations (EU) No 1093/2010, (EU) No 575/2013, (EU) No 600/2014 and (EU) No 806/2014 [2019] OJ L 314/1

Regulation (EU) 2020/852 of the European Parliament and of the Council of 18 June 2020 on the establishment of a framework to facilitate sustainable investment, and amending Regulation (EU) 2019/2088 [2020] OJ L 198/13

References

Bibliography

Anderson N (2019) IFRS Standards and climate-related disclosures. In: IASB, In Brief, Climate-related and other emerging risks disclosures: Assessing financial statement materiality.

28 November 2019. https://cdn.ifrs.org/-/media/feature/news/2019/november/in-brief-climate-change-nick-anderson.pdf?la=en. Accessed 19 Dec 2021

Gavas M (2016) The European Union's global strategy: putting sustainable development at the heart of EU external action. European Think Tanks Group. https://www.die-gdi.de/uploads/media/ETTG_Briefs.2.pdf. Accessed 8 May 2024

Gregersen C et al (2016) Implementation of the 2030 Agenda in the European Union: Constructing an EU approach to Policy Coherence for Sustainable Development. In: European Centre for Development Policy Management, Discussion Papers 2016(197):1–33. http://ecdpm.org/wp-content/uploads/DP197-Implementation-2030-Agenda-EU-Gregersen-Mackie-Torres-July-2016.pdf. Accessed 8 May 2024

Hoekman B, Mavroidis PC (2015) A technical barriers to trade agreement for services? In: European University Institute, Global Governance Programme Working Papers 2015(25):1–18. https://scholarship.law.columbia.edu/cgi/viewcontent.cgi?article=3374&context=faculty_scholarship. Accessed 8 May 2024

Martin AP, Mercurio B (2017) Liberalization commitments, financial stability safeguards and capital controls: practice evolutions from GATS to TPP and Megaregional Trade Agreements. In: Trade, Law and Development 9(1):72–100. http://www.tradelawdevelopment.com/index.php/tld/article/download/9%281%29%20TL%26D%2071%20%282017%29/338. Accessed 8 May 2024

Pauls S (2020) Sustainable Development and EU External Action. In: Jean Monnet Papers 2020(1):1–27. https://www.uni-goettingen.de/de/jean+monnet+papers/594986.html. Accessed 8 May 2024

Trachtman J (1996) Trade in financial services under GATS, NAFTA and the EC: a regulatory jurisdiction analysis. Columbia J Transnatl Law 34(37):37–122

Van den Bossche P, Zdouc W (2017) The law and policy of the World Trade Organization. Text, cases and materials, 4th edn. Cambridge University Press, Cambridge

Documents

BCBS (2020) Climate-related financial risks: a survey on current initiatives. https://www.bis.org/bcbs/publ/d502.pdf. Accessed 8 May 2024

EBA (2019) EBA Report on undue short-term pressure from the financial sector on corporations. 18 December 2019. https://eba.europa.eu/file/461440/download?token=gM-ur7b2. Accessed 8 May 2024

EBRD (2018) Green Economy Transition Handbook, Implementing the EBRD Green Economy Transition, Version 2. https://www.ebrd.com/cs/Satellite?c=Content&cid=1395250280926&pagename=EBRD%2FContent%2FdownloadDocument. Accessed 8 May 2024

EIB (2010) Sourcebook on EU Environmental Law. https://www.eib.org/attachments/strategies/sourcebook_on_eu_environmental_law_en.pdf. Accessed 8 May 2024

EIOPA (2019c) Opinion on Sustainability within Solvency II. 30 September 2019. https://www.eiopa.europa.eu/document/download/d5ae4db7-cc30-40db-ad5e-045876e3c7b3_en?filename=Opinion%20on%20Sustainability%20within%20Solvency%20II%20%28EIOPA-BoS-19/241%29%E2%80%8B. Accessed 18 Oct 2024

European Commission (2018) Proposal for a Regulation of the European Parliament and of the Council on the establishment of a framework to facilitate sustainable investment. 24 May 2018. COM(2018) 353 final. https://ec.europa.eu/transparency/regdoc/rep/1/2018/EN/COM-2018-353-F1-EN-MAIN-PART-1.PDF. Accessed 19 Dec 2021

European Commission (2019a) Communication on The European Green Deal: COM(2019) 640 final, Communication from the Commission to the European Parliament, the European Council, the Council, the European Economic and Social Committee and the Committee of the Regions, The European Green Deal. 11 December 2019. https://ec.europa.eu/info/sites/info/files/european-green-deal-communication_en.pdf. Accessed 19 Dec 2021

European Commission (2019b) Website on the IPSF. https://ec.europa.eu/info/business-economy-euro/banking-and-finance/sustainable-finance/international-platform-sustainable-finance_en. Accessed 19 Dec 2021

European Commission (2019c) Annex to the Communication from the Commission to the European Parliament, the European Council, the Council, the European Economic and Social Committee and the Committee of the Regions, The European Green Deal, Annex, Roadmap and key actions. 11 December 2019. COM(2019) 640 final. https://ec.europa.eu/info/sites/info/files/european-green-deal-communication-annex-roadmap_en.pdf. Accessed 19 Dec 2021

European Council (2019) Proposal for a Regulation of the European Parliament and of the Council on the establishment of a framework to facilitate sustainable investment, approval of the final compromise text. 17 December 2019. COM (2018) 353 final. https://data.consilium.europa.eu/doc/document/ST-14970-2019-ADD-1/en/pdf. Accessed 19 Dec 2021

G20 (2018) Sustainable Finance Study Group Document Repository. https://unepinquiry.org/g20greenfinancerepositoryeng/

GFSG (2016) G20 Green Finance Synthesis Report. 5 September 2016. http://unepinquiry.org/wp-content/uploads/2016/09/Synthesis_Report_Full_EN.pdf. Accessed 19 Dec 2021

GFSG (2017) G20 Green Finance Synthesis Report 2017. July 2017. http://unepinquiry.org/wp-content/uploads/2017/07/2017_GFSG_Synthesis_Report_EN.pdf. Accessed 19 Dec 2021

Government of Canada (1994) Schedule of Specific Commitments. 15 April 1994. GATS/SC/16. https://docs.wto.org/dol2fe/Pages/SS/directdoc.aspx?filename=Q:/SCHD/GATS-SC/SC16.pdf&Open=True. Accessed 19 Dec 2021

Government of Canada (1998) Schedule of Specific Commitments, Supplement 4. 26 February 1998. GATS/SC/16/Suppl.4. https://docs.wto.org/dol2fe/Pages/SS/directdoc.aspx?filename=Q:/SCHD/GATS-SC/SC16S4.pdf&Open=True. Accessed 19 Dec 2021

Government of Canada (2019) Final Report of the Expert Panel on Sustainable Finance, Mobilizing Finance for Sustainable Growth. 14 June 2019. https://publications.gc.ca/collections/collection_2019/eccc/En4-350-2-2019-eng.pdf. Accessed 18 Oct 2024

HLEG (2018) Final report of the High-Level Expert Group on Sustainable Finance. 31 January 2018. https://ec.europa.eu/info/publications/180131-sustainable-finance-report_en. Accessed 19 Dec 2021

Hoogervorst H (2019) Speech: IASB Chair on what sustainability reporting can and cannot achieve, 2 April 2019. https://www.ifrs.org/news-and-events/2019/04/speech-iasb-chair-on-sustainability-reporting/. Accessed 19 Dec 2021

IASB (2024) International Financial Reporting Standards. https://www.ifrs.org/issued-standards/. Accessed 19 Dec 2021

ICMA (2018a) Green Bond Principles, Voluntary Process Guidelines for Issuing Green Bonds. 14 June 2018. https://www.icmagroup.org/assets/documents/Regulatory/Green-Bonds/June-2018/Green-Bond-Principles%2D%2D-June-2018-140618-WEB.pdf. Accessed 19 Dec 2021

ICMA (2018b) Sustainability Bond Guidelines. June 2018. https://www.icmagroup.org/assets/documents/Regulatory/Green-Bonds/Sustainability-Bonds-Guidelines-June-2018-270520.pdf. Accessed 19 Dec 2021

ICMA (2020) Social Bond Principles, Voluntary Process Guidelines for Issuing Social Bonds. 9 June 2020. https://www.icmagroup.org/assets/documents/Regulatory/Green-Bonds/June-2020/Social-Bond-PrinciplesJune-2020-090620.pdf. Accessed 26 May 2024

ICMA (2023) Social Bond Principles, Voluntary Process Guidelines for Issuing Social Bonds. 22 June 2023. https://www.icmagroup.org/assets/documents/Sustainable-finance/2023-updates/Social-Bond-Principles-SBP-June-2023-220623.pdf. Accessed 26 May 2024

IOSCO (2013) Principles for Financial Benchmarks Final Report. July 2013. FR07/13. https://www.iosco.org/library/pubdocs/pdf/IOSCOPD415.pdf. Accessed 19 Dec 2021

IPSF (2019) Joint Statement on the International Platform on Sustainable Finance (IPSF). 18 October 2019. https://ec.europa.eu/info/sites/info/files/business_economy_euro/banking_and_finance/documents/191018-international-platform-sustainable-finance-joint-statement_en.pdf. Accessed 19 Dec 2021

IPSF (2020a) Factsheet: International platform on sustainable finance. 25 March 2020. https://ec.europa.eu/info/sites/info/files/business_economy_euro/banking_and_finance/documents/200325-international-platform-sustainable-finance-factsheet_en.pdf. Accessed 19 Dec 2021

IPSF (2020b) Annual report 2020. October 2020. https://finance.ec.europa.eu/document/download/32694a61-2cf9-45a8-9637-4bf0573bed6a_en?filename=international-platform-sustainable-finance-annual-report-2020_en.pdf. Accessed 26 May 2024

IPSF (2021a) Annual report 2021. 4 November 2021. https://finance.ec.europa.eu/document/download/d45218ff-26f9-4977-81a8-c1ccc4c1db98_en?filename=211104-ipsf-annual-report_en.pdf. Accessed 26 May 2024

IPSF (2021b) Common Ground Taxonomy Instruction Report. 4 November 2021. https://finance.ec.europa.eu/document/download/cb2aef5e-25f4-43d5-91a2-61f0039c1693_en?filename=211104-ipsf-common-ground-taxonomy-instruction-report-2021_en.pdf. Accessed 26 May 2024

IPSF (2021c) Report on ESG disclosure. 4 November 2021. https://finance.ec.europa.eu/document/download/3295cbdd-cb0c-4e34-b4a3-00974cb0a6bd_en?filename=211104-international-platform-sustainable-finance-cop26-statement_en.pdf. Accessed 26 May 2024

IPSF (2022a) Annual report 2022. 9 November 2022. https://finance.ec.europa.eu/document/download/9db9aca1-9044-4112-8fd6-c3d71f3d5a63_en?filename=221109-ipsf-annual-report_en.pdf. Accessed 26 May 2024

IPSF (2022b) Report on transition finance. 9 November 2022. https://finance.ec.europa.eu/document/download/80a3510e-2ac1-4229-9583-98e95d76f718_en?filename=221109-international-platform-sustainable-report-transition-finance_en.pdf. Accessed 26 May 2024

IPSF (2023a) Annual report 2023. 4 December 2023. https://finance.ec.europa.eu/document/download/cb307a8e-8b9a-4360-8dff-64110a6187d9_en?filename=231204-ipsf-annual-report_en.pdf. Accessed 26 May 2024

IPSF (2023b) Report on social bonds. 4 December 2023. https://finance.ec.europa.eu/document/download/9d8bfe51-3969-4e3d-8369-a73c1f7cf941_en?filename=231204-ipsf-social-bonds-report_en.pdf. Accessed 26 May 2024

IPSF (2023c) Interim report on implementing transition finance principles. 4 December 2023. https://finance.ec.europa.eu/document/download/f332838d-a5da-4279-8986-dbb38a212432_en?filename=231204-ipsf-transition-finance-interim-report_en.pdf. Accessed 26 May 2024

LMA (2018) Green Loan Principles, Supporting environmentally sustainable economic activity. December 2018. https://www.lma.eu.com/application/files/9115/4452/5458/741_LM_Green_Loan_Principles_Booklet_V8.pdf. Accessed 19 Dec 2021

LMA (2019) Sustainability Linked Loan Principles. March 2019. https://www.icmagroup.org/assets/documents/Regulatory/Green-Bonds/LMASustainabilityLinkedLoanPrinciples-270919.pdf. Accessed 19 Dec 2021

NGFS (2019a) First comprehensive report, A call for action – Climate change as a source of financial risk. 17 April 2019. https://www.ngfs.net/en/first-comprehensive-report-call-action. Accessed 19 Dec 2021

NGFS (2019b) First comprehensive report A call for action – Climate change as a source of financial risk, Technical Supplement. 23 July 2019. https://www.ngfs.net/en/technical-supplement-first-ngfs-comprehensive-report. Accessed 19 Dec 2021

NGFS (2019c) Technical document, A sustainable and responsible investment guide for central banks' portfolio management. 17 October 2019. https://www.ngfs.net/sites/default/files/medias/documents/ngfs-a-sustainable-and-responsible-investment-guide.pdf. Accessed 19 Dec 2021

NGFS (2020a) Annual Report 2019. March 2020. https://www.ngfs.net/sites/default/files/medias/documents/ngfs_annual_report_2019.pdf. Accessed 19 Dec 2021

NGFS (2020b) Guide for Supervisors Integrating climate-related and environmental risks into prudential supervision. May 2020. https://www.ngfs.net/sites/default/files/medias/documents/ngfs_guide_for_supervisors.pdf. Accessed 19 Dec 2021

People's Bank of China (2016) Press Release, The People's Bank of China and six other agencies jointly issue Guidelines for Establishing the Green Financial System. 1 September 2016. http://www.pbc.gov.cn/en/3688110/3688172/3712407/index.html. Accessed 19 Dec 2021

People's Republic of China (1994) Schedule of Specific Commitments. 15 April 1994. GATS/SC/ 19. https://docs.wto.org/dol2fe/Pages/SS/directdoc.aspx?filename=Q:/SCHD/GATS-SC/SC1 9.pdf&Open=True. Accessed 19 Dec 2021

People's Republic of China (2002) Schedule of Specific Commitments. 14 February 2002. GATS/ SC/135. https://docs.wto.org/dol2fe/Pages/SS/directdoc.aspx?filename=Q:/SCHD/GATS-SC/ SC135.pdf&Open=True. Accessed 19 Dec 2021

SFN (2020) Sustainable Finance and the Role of Securities Regulators and IOSCO, Final Report. 14 April 2020. https://www.iosco.org/library/pubdocs/pdf/IOSCOPD652.pdf. Accessed 19 Dec 2021

SFSG (2018) Sustainable Finance Synthesis Report. July 2018. http://unepinquiry.org/wp-content/ uploads/2018/11/G20_Sustainable_Finance_Synthesis_Report_2018.pdf. Accessed 19 Dec 2021

SIF (2017) Sustainable Insurance, The Emerging Agenda for Supervisors and Regulators. August 2017. https://www.unepfi.org/psi/wp-content/uploads/2017/08/Sustainable_Insurance_The_ Emerging_Agenda.pdf. Accessed 19 Dec 2021

SIF (2018) Issues Paper on Climate Change Risks to the Insurance Sector. July 2018. https://www. insurancejournal.com/research/app/uploads/2018/08/IAIS_and_SIF_Issues_Paper_on_Cli mate_Change_Risks_to_the_Insurance_Sector_-1.pdf. Accessed 19 Dec 2021

TCFD (2017) Final Report, Recommendations of the Task Force on Climate-related Financial Disclosures. 15 June 2017. https://www.fsb-tcfd.org/wp-content/uploads/2017/06/FINAL-201 7-TCFD-Report-11052018.pdf. Accessed 19 Dec 2021

TCFD (2018) 2018 Status Report. 17 September 2018. https://www.fsb-tcfd.org/wp-content/ uploads/2018/08/FINAL-2018-TCFD-Status-Report-092518.pdf. Accessed 19 Dec 2021

TCFD (2019) 2019 Status Report. 31 May 2019. https://www.fsb-tcfd.org/wp-content/uploads/201 9/06/2019-TCFD-Status-Report-FINAL-053119.pdf. Accessed 19 Dec 2021

TCFD (2021) 2021 Status Report. 14 October 2021. https://www.fsb.org/wp-content/uploads/ P141021-1.pdf. Accessed 26 May 2024

TCFD (2022) 2022 Status Report. 13 October 2022. https://www.fsb.org/2022/10/2022-tcfd-status-report-task-force-on-climate-related-financial-disclosures/. Accessed 26 May 2024

TCFD (2023) 2023 Status Report. 12 October 2023. https://www.fsb.org/wp-content/uploads/ P121023-2.pdf. Accessed 26 May 2024

TEG (2019a) Report on EU Green Bond Standard. 18 June 2019. https://ec.europa.eu/info/sites/ info/files/business_economy_euro/banking_and_finance/documents/190618-sustainable-finance-teg-report-green-bond-standard_en.pdf. Accessed 19 Dec 2021

TEG (2019b) Taxonomy Technical Report. 18 June 2019. https://ec.europa.eu/info/sites/info/files/ business_economy_euro/banking_and_finance/documents/190618-sustainable-finance-teg-report-taxonomy_en.pdf. Accessed 19 Dec 2021

UN PAGE (2016) Operational Strategy 2016-2020. 2016. https://www.un-page.org/files/public/ page_operational_strategy_2016-2020_web_0.pdf. Accessed 19 Dec 2021

UNEP FI (2021) Testing the application of the EU Taxonomy to core banking products, High level recommendations. January 2021. https://www.unepfi.org/publications/banking-publications/ testing-the-application-of-the-eu-taxonomy-to-core-banking-products-high-level-recommenda tions/. Accessed 19 Dec 2021

WTO (2020) Analytical Index GATS – Article VII (Practice). https://www.wto.org/english/res_e/ publications_e/ai17_e/gats_art7_oth.pdf. Accessed 8 May 2024

Jurisprudence

WTO DSB (1998) United States – Import Prohibition of Certain Shrimp and Shrimp Products, Appellate Body report, 12 October 1998, WT/DS58/AB/R

WTO DSB (2001) United States – Import Prohibition of Certain Shrimp and Shrimp Products, Appellate Body report, 22 October 2001, WT/DS58/AB/RW

Chapter 5
Propagation and Justification of EU Sustainable Finance Measures through EU FTAs

Previous Chapters have adopted a multilateral perspective on EU Sustainable Finance's consistency when assessing the EU's obligations under GATS. This is to be complemented with a bilateral perspective adopted in this Chapter. As the EU enters into bilateral agreements with other WTO Members, it could be restricted from adopting certain Sustainable Finance measures. For this assessment, two regimes can be considered—namely, bilateral investment treaties (*BITs*) and free trade agreements (*FTAs*).[1]

BITs usually apply only to foreign direct investment (*FDI*). Particularly with a view to market access, FDI will usually remain unaffected by EU Sustainable Finance measures. Those measures considered in Chap. 2 exclusively address the provision of financial services. Financial services constitute, if anything, the provision of portfolio investments. Portfolio investments are regularly excluded from BITs. Thus, BITs do not apply to EU Sustainable Finance measures.

FTAs, in contrast, are bilateral agreements addressing disciplines and rights in international trade in goods and services. The services disciplines in FTAs resemble those set out in GATS. Thereby, the trade in services provisions in FTAs and in GATS interact. Under GATS, a favorable treatment granted by one WTO Member to another is to be extended, on the same terms, to all others, too. This stems from the most-favored-nation standard discussed in Sect. 3.2.2. Set out in Art. II(1) GATS,[2] it requires that services and service suppliers from another WTO Member shall be treated "*no less favourable than [. . .] like services and service suppliers of any other country.*" Hence, a preferential treatment applied only to selected WTO Members constitutes discrimination and is thus inconsistent with GATS.

Exempt from this principle is the possibility of entering into *regional trade agreements*. Art. V(1) GATS states that the GATS requirements including to

---

[1] FTAs, as defined in Sect. 1.2.

[2] An equivalent requirement for trade in goods is set in Art. I(1) GATT.

© The Author(s), under exclusive license to Springer Nature Switzerland AG 2024
S. N. Pauls, *EU Sustainable Finance and International Trade Law*, EYIEL Monographs - Studies in European and International Economic Law 37, https://doi.org/10.1007/978-3-031-73853-1_5

most-favored-nation standard do not apply to such agreements given a *"substantial sectoral coverage"* and the *"elimination of substantially all discrimination"*.[3] Hence, a preferential treatment based on a regional trade agreement does not violate Art. II(1) GATS. As such it is another exception to the substantive GATS provisions.[4] The term regional trade agreements used in Art. V(1) GATS is not accurate insofar as most of current FTAs are not *regional* but *transregional*.[5] Therefore, this book will refer to regional trade agreements in general terms as FTAs.

FTAs represent economic integration and additional liberalization disciplines for trade in services. These disciplines usually surpass those of GATS and are referred to as *WTO plus*. The additional disciplines effectively further restrict the parties' respective policy space and are counterbalanced with additional exceptions. This restriction of policy space through FTAs may have implications for the assessment of EU Sustainable Finance measures under international trade law.

Within the EU legal system and following the December 2009 application of the Lisbon Treaty,[6] the Commission was assigned the competence for the negotiation of FTAs based on explicit and implicit competence norms pursuant to Art. 216(1) TFEU.[7] Furthermore, the Lisbon Treaty clarified the EU's role as a subject of international law in Art. 47 TEU.[8] This significant addition to the external competences of the Commission coincided with its increased efforts in international sustainable development policy-drafting.[9]

Currently, the EU has FTAs with seventy-eight WTO Members in place, FTAs with twenty-four WTO Members currently being adopted or ratified, and six FTAs in negotiation.[10] Analyzing each of these agreements individually would not only surpass the scope of this book but it is also not necessary to understand the consistency of EU Sustainable Finance measures under the EU FTAs. This is due to the fact that the different types of EU FTAs regularly set out comparable provisions or references to GATS allowing for an assessment of EU Sustainable Finance measures in a conceptual manner. This is particularly the case with regard to the prospective measures discussed in Sect. 3.3. Moreover, the EU FTAs can broadly be subdivided into *first-generation* FTAs, more comprehensive economic partnership agreements (*EPAs*), and finally *new generation* FTAs.

---

[3]Cf. Art. V(1)(a) and (b) GATS; Cf. Van den Bossche and Zdouc (2017), pp. 689 et seq.

[4]Van den Bossche and Zdouc (2017), p. 671.

[5]Van den Bossche and Zdouc (2017), p. 672.

[6]Treaty of Lisbon amending the Treaty on European Union and the Treaty establishing the European Community [2007] OJ C 306/1.

[7]Consolidated version of the Treaty on the Functioning of the European Union [2012] OJ C 326/47.

[8]Art. 47 Consolidated version of the Treaty on European Union [2012] OJ C 326/13 states that the *"Union shall have legal personality."*

[9]As described in more detail in Sect. 4.1.1.

[10]Cf. European Commission (2024); Therefore, the EU surpasses the average of thirteen FTAs per WTO Member, cf. Van den Bossche and Zdouc (2017), p. 674.

First-generation FTAs were negotiated up until the early 2000s and exhibit a limited scope of policy fields. They include provisions on trade in goods such as customs regulations and subsidies. They mostly refer to the GATS for the definition and application of trade disciplines like the most-favored-nation, national treatment, or domestic regulation standards. Concerning financial services this particularly applies to the GATS Annex on Financial Services.

An example of a first-generation FTA is the economic partnership agreement between the EU and Mexico (*EU-Mexico FTA*)[11] signed in December 1997. The EU-Mexico FTA consists of only seventeen pages with a mere four articles on trade in goods and services.[12] Art. 6 EU-Mexico FTA determines Art. V GATS as the main reference point for drafting a trade framework under Art. 4 EU-Mexico FTA.[13] Due to this systemic use of references to the GATS provisions, first-generation FTAs like the EU-Mexico FTA are unlikely to enable a conclusion different from that made in Sect. 3.2.5 concerning the consistency of EU Sustainable Finance under GATS. Therefore, a potential inconsistency of EU Sustainable Finance measures under such first-generation FTAs will not be examined further.

EPAs, in turn, are substantially more comprehensive. They cover trade and development relationships between the EU and WTO Members in the Africa, Caribbean, and Pacific regions. As long-term partnership agreements, they cover a wide range of policy fields. This includes the development of the financial services sector and particularly the banking sector in the respective partner country. Therefore, these EPAs might be relevant for the assessment of EU Sustainable Finance measures under the EU's external trade relations.

Even further, new generation FTAs usually do not only contain an investment chapter. They often also cover competition issues and sections on *trade and environment* or *trade and development*. These new generation FTAs initiate a consolidation process of the Commission's drafting of future EU FTAs. The 2011 EU-South Korea FTA[14] can be considered the EU's first new generation FTA. Further examples are the 2012 EU-Colombia-Peru FTA[15] and the 2012

---

[11] Economic Partnership, Political Coordination and Cooperation Agreement between the European Community and its Member States, of the one part, and the United Mexican States, of the other part [2000] OJ L 276/45.

[12] Namely Art. 4–6 EU-Mexico FTA.

[13] Even the provision laid down in Art. 16(1) EU-Mexico FTA addressing cooperation in the financial services sector states that this cooperation needs to be in accordance with the GATS.

[14] Council Decision of 16 September 2010 on the signing, on behalf of the European Union, and provisional application of the Free Trade Agreement between the European Union and its Member States, of the one part, and the Republic of Korea, of the other part, Commission's statements, Free trade Agreement between the European Union and its Member States, of the one part, and the Republic of Korea, of the other part, Protocol concerning the definition of 'originating products' and methods of administrative cooperation, Protocol on mutual administrative assistance in customs matters, Protocol on cultural cooperation [2011] OJ L 127/1.

[15] Trade Agreement between the European Union and its Member States, of the one part, and Colombia and Peru, of the other part [2012] OJ L 354/3.

EU-Central America Association Agreement.[16] In the following Chapters, the EU-CARIFORUM EPA, CETA, and the international agreements relating to the UK's withdrawal from the EU will be used as examples of an EPA and new generation EU FTAs.

The EU-CARIFORUM EPA is a trade agreement between the EU and the Caribbean Forum (*CARIFORUM*) signed in October 2008.[17] The CARIFORUM is a subdivision of the Organisation of African, Caribbean, and Pacific States and consists of fifteen states.[18] The EU-CARIFORUM EPA covers a *Trade Partnership for Sustainable Development*, trade in goods, investment, trade in services, and e-commerce. It further contains rules on current payments and capital movement, dispute avoidance and settlement, general exceptions, and institutional provisions. Although investments are named in EU-CARIFORUM EPA part two (*Trade and trade-related matters*), title two (*Investment, trade in services and e-commerce*), investments do only relate to FDI insofar as a commercial presence is created.[19]

The Comprehensive Economic and Trade Agreement (*CETA*)[20] is a trade and investment agreement between the EU and Canada. It was signed in October 2016 and provisionally applied from September 2017. CETA covers trade in goods, non-tariff barriers, trade in services, and FDI protection.[21]

A more recent and noteworthy EU FTA was negotiated as part of the UK withdrawal from the EU. Following its formal announcement of 29 March 2017, the UK left the EU and European Atomic Energy Community (*Euratom*) effective 31 January 2020. After several rounds of negotiation, on 17 October 2019, the EU and the UK reached the Withdrawal Agreement.[22] The Withdrawal Agreement initiated a transition period until 31 December 2020. Shortly before the end of this transition period, on 30 December 2020, the EU and the UK signed the post-

---

[16] Agreement establishing an Association between the European Union and its Member States, on the one hand, and Central America on the other [2012] OJ L 346/3; Cf. European Commission (2017) Report from the Commission to the European Parliament, the Council, the European Economic and Social Committee and the Committee of the Regions on Implementation of Free Trade Agreements. 9 November 2017. COM(2017) 654 final, p. 38.

[17] Economic Partnership Agreement between the CARIFORUM States, of the one part, and the European Community and its Member States, of the other part [2008] OJ L 289/3.

[18] CARIFORUM members: Antigua and Barbuda, Bahamas, Barbados, Belize, Dominica, Dominican Republic, Grenada, Guyana, Haiti, Jamaica, St. Kitts and Nevis, St. Christoph and Nevis, St. Lucia, St. Vincent and the Grenadines, Suriname, and Trinidad and Tobago; To the latter seven, the EU-CARIFORUM EPA is not yet applicable.

[19] Cf. EU-CARIFORUM EPA Chapter Two (*Commercial presence*).

[20] Comprehensive Economic and Trade Agreement (CETA) between Canada, of the one part, and the European Union and its Member States, of the other part [2017] OJ L 11/23.

[21] Chapter eight (*Investment*), however, is not covered by the provisional application of CETA.

[22] Agreement on the withdrawal of the United Kingdom of Great Britain and Northern Ireland from the European Union and the European Atomic Energy Community [2019] OJ C 384I/1.

transition period Trade and Cooperation Agreement (*TCA*), which was published in April 2021.[23] This effectively constitutes the most recent of EU FTAs.[24]

Hence, the UK withdrawal process produced two international agreements, the Withdrawal Agreement and the TCA. Both and in particular TCA Annex 3 are potentially relevant for the above assessment of EU Sustainable Finance legislation. Thereby, these agreements potentially inhibit similarities and differences to the other FTAs under consideration, the EU-CARIFORUM EPA and CETA.

With a view to the Withdrawal Agreement, the consistency of EU Sustainable Finance provisions can briefly be summarized as follows. Under Art. 50 TEU the TEU, the TFEU and the EU level 2 legislation cease to apply by the end of the transition period and thus from 1 January 2021. This includes all EU Sustainable Finance legislation discussed in Chap. 2 such as the Taxonomy Regulation, the Climate BMR,[25] and the SFDR. An exception to this is Art. 138 Withdrawal Agreement. It renders certain EU law applicable even after 31 December 2020. This is in particular if it was introduced in relation to the implementation of the EU multiannual financial framework (*MFF*) 2014–2020.[26] The MFF 2014–2020 is set out in the MFF Regulation.[27] The MFF 2014–2020 does not include specific provisions on Sustainable Finance apart from funding provisions on the EFSI and EFSD[28] and general provisions on sustainable development.[29] Apart from this exception, the Withdrawal Agreement does not state any specific provisions immediately relevant for Sustainable Finance legislation. It thus does not allow for a differing conclusion compared to the one made under GATS (Chap. 3). Of the two

---

[23] Trade and Cooperation Agreement between the European Union and the European Atomic Energy Community, of the one part, and the United Kingdom of Great Britain and Northern Ireland, of the other part [2021] OJ L 149/10.

[24] European Commission, Proposal for a Council Decision on the signing, on behalf of the Union, and on provisional application of the Trade and Cooperation Agreement between the European Union and the European Atomic Energy Community, of the one part, and the United Kingdom of Great Britain and Northern Ireland, of the other part, and of the Agreement between the European Union and the United Kingdom of Great Britain and Northern Ireland concerning security procedures for exchanging and protecting classified information. 25 December 2020. COM(2020) 855 final; The draft TCA, its Annexes, and the respective Euratom Agreement are retrievable under https://ec.europa.eu/info/publications/draft-eu-uk-trade-and-cooperation-agreement-accompany ing-acts_en. Accessed 19 December 2021.

[25] Regulation (EU) 2019/2089 of the European Parliament and of the Council of 27 November 2019 amending Regulation (EU) 2016/1011 as regards EU Climate Transition Benchmarks, EU Paris-aligned Benchmarks and sustainability-related disclosures for benchmarks [2019] OJ L 317/17.

[26] Art. 138(2)(a) Withdrawal Agreement.

[27] Regulation (EU, Euratom) 2018/1046 of the European Parliament and of the Council of 18 July 2018 on the financial rules applicable to the general budget of the Union, amending Regulations (EU) No 1296/2013, (EU) No 1301/2013, (EU) No 1303/2013, (EU) No 1304/2013, (EU) No 1309/ 2013, (EU) No 1316/2013, (EU) No 223/2014, (EU) No 283/2014, and Decision No 541/2014/EU and repealing Regulation (EU, Euratom) No 966/2012 [2018] OJ L 193/1.

[28] Cf. e.g. Recital 151 Regulation (EU, Euratom) 2018/1046.

[29] Cf. e.g. Art. 271(13) and Recital 212 Regulation (EU, Euratom) 2018/1046.

international agreements associated with the UK's withdrawal from the EU, only the TCA will be assessed in the following Chapters.

Considering the EU FTAs described above and their relation to GATS through Art. V(1) GATS, this Chapter aims to discuss several questions. Given the additional disciplines on trade in services usually outlined in FTAs, how does the consistency under the respective EU FTA compare to the consistency under GATS? Are these additional disciplines sufficiently counterbalanced by respective exceptions applicable to Sustainable Finance? Do these exceptions and other rules in these EU FTAs allow for additional policy space for future EU Sustainable Finance measures?

In this regard, Sect. 5.1 assesses the consistency of the EU Sustainable Finance measures described in Chap. 2 and Sect. 3.3 under the trade in services disciplines in the above EU FTAs. Subsequently, Sect. 5.2 describes the environmental and sustainable development chapters in these EU FTAs. It examines the feasibility of applying these chapters to trade in financial services in general and to EU Sustainable Finance measures in specific. Following this, Sect. 5.3 assesses the potential application of sustainability and prudential carve-out clauses on EU Sustainable Finance measures. Thereby, Sect. 5.3 largely follows the structure of the relevant Art. XIV GATS general exceptions described in Sects. 3.2.4.1.1 and 3.2.4.1.3. The same applies to the para. 2(a) GATS Annex on Financial Services prudential exception examined in Sect. 3.2.4.3. Finally, Sect. 5.4 describes the actual and possible channels of influence regarding the propagation and justification of EU Sustainable Finance measures through the EU FTAs, comprising the TCA.

5.1 Trade in Service Disciplines in EU FTAs

As described in Sect. 3.2, GATS sets out disciplines regulating trade in services such as market access, national treatment and most-favored-nation treatment. Given the interaction and similarities between GATS and bilateral FTAs mentioned in the previous Chapter, do the conclusions drawn on EU Sustainable Finance measures under GATS (Sect. 3.2.5) apply to the same assessment under the trade in services disciplines in EU FTAs?

To this end, the consistency of EU Sustainable Finance under the trade in services disciplines in EU FTAs will be examined in this Chapter. In addition to the EU Sustainable Finance measures examined in Sect. 3.2, particular focus will be on the prospective EU Sustainable Finance measures described in Sect. 3.3.

5.1.1 Scope of Application of EU FTAs

First, the scope of application of the EU FTAs in with a view to that of EU Sustainable Finance measures needs to be examined. This is parallel to the approach taken in Sect. 3.1.

The EU-CARIFORUM EPA sets its scope of application on financial services in Art. 103 EU-CARIFORUM EPA as part of EU-CARIFORUM EPA Section Five (*Financial Services*).[30] First, the application of the EPA's rules on financial services is limited to liberalized services.[31] Art. 103.2 EU-CARIFORUM EPA defines financial services by applying a similar structure to para. 5 GATS Annex on Financial Services.[32] It uses, however, an exhaustive instead of a non-exhaustive enumeration of different activities that constitute financial services. The division into the sections *Insurance and insurance-related services* and *Banking and other financial services (excluding insurance)* and their respective scope and wording further mirror para. 5 GATS Annex on Financial Services. This includes the definition of *financial service supplier* and the exclusion of *public entities*. Thus, as regards the EU-CARIFORUM EPA's scope of application on Sustainable Finance measures, reference can be made to the considerations in Sect. 3.1.

CETA's scope of application, in turn, is considerably more complex to define. Similar to the matter of whether international investment law is applicable to EU Sustainable Finance measures,[33] the question arises whether CETA's chapter eight (*Investment*) applies to financial services. Different from the considerations made in relation to international investment law, CETA Chapter Eight does cover some aspects apart from FDI. For instance, under Art. 8.1 CETA[34] an "*investment means every kind of asset that an investor owns or controls, directly or indirectly [. . .]*". Art. 8.1 CETA follows by listing possible forms of investments. One of these forms are "*bonds, debentures and other debt instruments of an enterprise*" and thus a policy field covered by EU Sustainable Finance measures.[35] However, Art. 8.3.1 CETA, by defining the "*relation to other chapters*", states that CETA Chapter Eight "*does not apply to measures adopted or maintained by a Party to the extent that the measures apply to investors or to their investments covered by Chapter Thirteen (Financial Services). [. . .]*".[36]

The same question arises in view of CETA Chapter Nine (*Cross-border trade in services*). Its scope of application set in Art. 9.1.1 CETA is very broad and covers "*(a) the production, distribution, marketing, sale, and delivery of a service; (b) the purchase of, use of, or payment for, a service; and, (c) the access to and use of, in connection with the supply of a service, services which are required to be offered to the public generally.*" This broad scope of application would cover EU Sustainable Finance measures. However, like Art. 8.3.1 CETA, Art. 9.1.2 CETA states that CETA Chapter Nine "*does not apply to a measure affecting: [. . .] financial services*

---

[30] Cf. EU-CARIFORUM EPA Chapter Five (*Regulatory framework*).

[31] Cf. Art. 103(1) EU-CARIFORUM EPA, which makes reference to EU-CARIFORUM EPA chapters Two, Three, and Four.

[32] Cf. Sect. 3.1.

[33] Cf. Sect. 3.1.

[34] Cf. CETA Chapter Eight (*Investment*), Section A (*Definitions and Scope*).

[35] Cf. e.g. green bonds in Sect. 2.1.3.

[36] For the relation between CETA Chapters eight and thirteen, cf. Art. 13.2.2 CETA.

as defined in Article 13.1 (Definitions); [...]." In contrast, CETA Chapter Ten (*Temporary entry and stay of natural persons for business purposes*) applies to the temporary entry and stay of natural persons in relation to financial services.[37] CETA Chapter Ten will not be assessed in further detail at this point due to the low potential for inconsistency of EU Sustainable Finance measures under GATS Mode 4.

CETA Chapter Thirteen (*Financial services*) can be applied to EU Sustainable Finance measures. The definitions of a *"financial service"* and a *"financial service supplier"* resemble para. 4 GATS Annex on Financial Services.[38] In coherence with Art. 10.6.3 CETA, CETA Chapter Thirteen only applies to GATS modes 1 to 3.[39] These modes as described therein are examples of cases in which EU Sustainable Finance might affect trade in financial service. The CETA modes cover *"(a) financial institutions of the other Party; (b) an investor of the other Party, and an investment of that investor, in a financial institution in the Party's territory; and (c) cross-border trade in financial services."* Thereby, the cross-border supply of a financial service comprises the supply *"(a) from the territory of a Party into the territory of the other Party; or (b) in the territory of a Party by a person of that Party to a person of the other Party; but does not include the supply of a service in the territory of a Party by an investment in that territory".[40]* Therefore, the considerations made in Sect. 3.1 in respect of the GATS modes of supply can be transferred onto the assessment of the EU Sustainable Finance measures under CETA.

CETA Chapter Twelve (Domestic regulation) is incorporated into CETA Chapter Thirteen via Art. 13.2.6 CETA. There are certain exemptions, namely *"licensing requirements, licensing procedures, qualification requirements or qualification procedures [...] pursuant to a non-conforming measure maintained by the European Union, as set out in its Schedule to Annex I, to the extent that such measure relates to financial services"* according to Art. 13.2.7.b CETA. Adding to this, Art. 13.10.1 and 2 CETA exempt in particular *"an existing non-conforming measure that is maintained by a Party"* from CETA Chapter Thirteen's scope of application. As most EU Sustainable Finance measures and in particular, those referred to in Sect. 3.3 had not been introduced by the date of CETA's provisional application, this exception will not be considered in more detail.

With a view to the TCA's application to EU Sustainable Finance measures, sustainable financial services would need to fall in the scope of the TCA. First of all, from an international trade law perspective, the TCA constitutes an EU FTA just as CETA and the EU-CARIFORUM EPA. Many of the TCA's provisions are particularly similar to those set out in these earlier EU FTAs. Thereby, financial services are governed by several parts of the TCA. Most relevant are TCA

---

[37] Cf. Art. 10.6.3 CETA.

[38] Cf. Art. 13.1 CETA.

[39] Cf. Art. 13.2.1 CETA.

[40] Art. 13.1 CETA.

Section Five and TCA Annex 3.[41] Provisions potentially relevant for EU Sustainable Finance include other chapters of TCA Title Two (*Services and investment*).

The scope for TCA Section Five (*financial services*) is defined in Art. SERVIN.5.37 TCA. It applies to several chapters under TCA Title Two (*services and investment*).[42] The TCA provisions on cross-border trade in services, domestic regulation, and provisions of general application apply to financial services regulation in general and Sustainable Finance legislation.[43] The definition of financial services, financial service suppliers, and new financial services in Art. SERVIN.5.38 TCA closely resembles para. 5 GATS Annex on Financial Services.[44] Hence, certain parts of the TCA apply to financial services.

TCA Annex 3 sets out a *Joint Declaration on Financial Services Regulatory Cooperation*, which calls for the TCA parties to "*establish structured regulatory cooperation on financial services*". The TCA Annex 3 itself, however, does not provide for rules or declarations on Sustainable Finance or its policy objectives of furthering sustainable development and financial stability. Financial stability is only mentioned as part of "*market integrity and investor protection*" in para. 1 Joint Declaration on Financial Services Regulatory Cooperation. These areas, as discussed in Sect. 3.2.4.1.1 are not to be considered part of Sustainable Finance.

In contrast, more relevant both to Sustainable Finance legislation and to financial services regulation, in general, is para. 2 Joint Declaration on Financial Services Regulatory Cooperation. It sets out that by March 2021 "*a Memorandum of Understanding establishing the framework for this cooperation*" will be agreed upon. In January 2021 ESMA published the first of such *Memoranda of Understanding*.[45] One of the outstanding Memoranda of Understanding may include criteria for equivalence decisions on Sustainable Finance legislation.[46]

Therefore, financial services are indeed covered by the TCA but specific rules governing trade in financial services between the TCA parties are yet to be decided

---

[41]TCA Annex 3 consists of thirteen Joints Declarations and two Draft Protocols; In this Chapter reference is made exclusively to the *Joint Declaration on Financial Services Regulatory Cooperation between the European Union and the United Kingdom*.

[42]Pursuant to Art. SERVIN.5.37 TCA these are TCA Chapter One (*General provisions*), TCA Chapter Two (*Investment liberalisation*), TCA Chapter Three (*Cross-border trade in services*), TCA Chapter Four (*Entry and temporary stay of natural persons for business purposes*), and TCA Section One (*Domestic regulation*) and TCA Section Two (*Provisions of general application*) of TCA Chapter Five (*Regulatory framework*).

[43]Cf. European Commission (2020).

[44]Cf. Sects. 3.1 and 3.2.1.3.

[45]Cf. FCA (2021a, b, c, d).

[46]The equivalence decisions taken so far, however, indicate that focus will be put on equivalence under the European Market Infrastructure Regulation 648/2012, the Central Securities Depositories Regulation 909/2014, and Regulation (EU) 2016/1011 of the European Parliament and of the Council of 8 June 2016 on indices used as benchmarks in financial instruments and financial contracts or to measure the performance of investment funds and amending Directives 2008/48/EC and 2014/17/EU and Regulation (EU) No 596/2014 [2016] OJ L 171/1, cf. e.g. HM Treasury (2020).

upon. Plus, these rules will not entirely cover market access and equivalence. Financial services are exempted from many of the trade in services provisions, such as the most-favored-nation standard. Regarding sustainable financial services, however, for the subsequent assessment also some general TCA provisions are of relevance.

These include references to one of the underlying policy objectives of Sustainable Finance in the TCA preamble, namely ESG-based sustainable development. With a view of the social sphere, the TCA preamble stresses *"commitment [. . .] to human rights"* and *"to uphold [the TCA parties'] respective high levels of protection in the areas of labour and social standards"*. Regarding the environmental sphere of sustainable development, the TCA parties commit *"to the fight against climate change"* and *"to uphold their respective high levels of protection in the areas of environment [and] the fight against climate change [. . .]"*. Similar to the *"enabling domestic environment"* envisaged in para. 10 Monterrey Consensus,[47] the trade provisions set in the TCA are understood to ensure *"a predictable commercial environment that fosters trade and investment"* and that therefore is *"conducive to sustainable development in its economic, social and environmental dimensions"*. Although these extracts of the TCA preamble do not exhibit an immediate connection to Sustainable Finance, the TCA underlines the supreme importance of sustainability-oriented policy-drafting. This fact in turn ensures an interpretation and application of the agreement conducive to Sustainable Finance.

Furthermore, Art. OTH.3 et seqq. TCA outline the TCA's general relation to GATT and GATS. For instance, the TCA establishes a free trade area between the TCA parties as provided in Art. V GATS. Under Art. OTH.4 TCA, the TCA *"[p]arties affirm their rights and obligations with respect to each other under the WTO Agreement and other agreements to which they are party."* This means that under the TCA the EU is also bound by its commitments made for instance by its signature of the Understanding on Commitments in Financial Services.[48] The same applies to the application of WTO jurisprudence to the TCA's interpretation provided for in Art. OTH.4a TCA. This is also highlighted in the TCA preamble which references the *"respective rights and obligations under the Marrakesh Agreement [. . .] and other multilateral and bilateral instruments of cooperation"*.

5.1.2　Market Access

Furthermore, resembling Art. XVI(1) GATS, both the EU-CARIFORUM EPA and CETA cover provisions on market access in their relevant chapters on financial services. This is particularly relevant since such bilateral agreements as the

---

[47]Cf. Sect. 4.1.1.
[48]Cf. Sect. 3.2.1.3.

EU-CARIFORUM EPA and CETA function as an Art. V(1) GATS exception to the market access obligations under GATS.

The EU-CARIFORUM EPA differentiates between commercial presence[49] and cross-border supply of services.[50] Concerning market access, both chapters use equal language requiring that the parties "*shall accord to commercial presences and investors of the other Party a treatment no less favourable than that provided for in the specific commitments contained in Annex IV*".[51] Art. 13.6.1 CETA in contrast specifies those measures prohibited under CETA's market access discipline using the same wording as Art. XVI(2)(a) to (f) GATS.[52] For further market access disciplines, Art. 13.6.2 incorporates Art. 8.4.2 CETA.

Similarly, in respect of the cross-border supply of financial services, Art. 13.7.1 CETA incorporates Art. 9.6 CETA into CETA Chapter Thirteen. Measures prohibited under the Art. 9.6 CETA market access provision are neither to be adopted or maintained under Art. 13.7.3 CETA. Insofar, there are only negligible and merely technical differences to those requirements discussed in Sect. 3.2.1. The conclusions made therein apply to the market access provisions in EU-CARIFORUM EPA and CETA, too.

Finally, both the EU-CARIFORUM EPA and CETA comprise rules on *new financial services*. Insofar, both agreements use similar language. Art. 106 EU-CARIFORUM EPA and Art. 13.14.1 CETA state that parties "*shall permit a financial service supplier of the other Party to provide any new financial service*" while limiting this requirement to such new financial services that would also be permitted to the host party's financial service suppliers. Art. 13.1 CETA defines new financial services as "*a financial service that is not supplied in the territory of a Party but that is supplied in the territory of the other Party and includes any new form of delivery of a financial service or the sale of a financial product that is not sold in the Party's territory*". As already discussed in Sect. 3.2.1.3, new sustainable and new unsustainable financial services do fall under the definition of new financial services. However, EU Sustainable Finance measures do not restrict the former and do not withhold the permission to supply the latter. Therefore, although applicable, EU Sustainable Finance measures do not constitute a violation of the new financial services clauses in Art. 106 EU-CARIFORUM EPA and Art. 13.14.1 CETA.

Under Art. 106 EU-CARIFORUM EPA and Art. 13.14.2 CETA, a potentially required authorization "*may only be refused for prudential reasons*". This in turn means that an EU Sustainable Finance measure denying or limiting authorization based on sustainability considerations is inadmissible. The subsumption of EU Sustainable Finance measures under the term of "*prudential measures*" has already been assessed in Sect. 3.2.4.3 regarding the exception clause for measures for prudential reasons in para. 2(a) GATS Annex on Financial Services. This

---

[49] EU-CARIFORUM EPA Chapter Two (*Commercial presence*).

[50] EU-CARIFORUM EPA Chapter Three (*Cross-border supply of services*).

[51] Art. 67.1 and Art. 76.1 EU-CARIFORUM EPA.

[52] Cf. Sect. 3.2.1.

subsumption led to the conclusion that all EU Sustainable Finance measures taken on grounds of financial stability fall under the exemption for prudential measures of para. 2(a) GATS Annex on Financial Services. There are significant similarities in wording and the resemblance in structure between the market access clauses in the EU-CARIFORUM EPA and CETA, on the one hand, and the market access provision in Art. XVI(1) GATS, on the other hand. Therefore, these findings can be applied in a similar way to Art. 106 EU-CARIFORUM EPA and Art. 13.14.1 CETA.

Regarding the TCA, chapters applicable to financial services include provisions on market access in TCA Title Two. Art. SERVIN.2.2(a) and (b) TCA resembles the enumeration of prohibited measures and limitations set out in Art. XVI(2)(a) to (f) GATS. Art. SERVIN.2.2 TCA constitutes the market access standard for TCA Chapter Two (*investment liberalisation*). This TCA Chapter, as described above, applies to financial services regulation under Art. SERVIN.5.37 TCA.

The market access standard of Art. SERVIN.3.2(a) and (b) TCA in TCA Chapter Three (*cross-border trade in services*), in turn, is less ample and only covers the equivalent of Art. XVI(2)(a) to (c) and (e) GATS.[53] Both provisions, however, cover the GATS market access standards under which certain EU Sustainable Finance measures are more likely to be deemed inconsistent, namely Art. XVI(2) (a) and (b) GATS. A further, more detailed differentiation between the TCA provisions is not required. Plus, due to its wording, the TCA's market access standard would most likely lead to the same conclusion as the one found in Sect. 3.2.1.1.

Regarding new financial services, Art. SERVIN.5.42 TCA compares to No. B.7 Understanding on Commitments in Financial Services, Art. 106 EU-CARIFORUM EPA, and Art. 13.14.1 CETA. Therefore, the considerations made in Sect. 3.2.1.3 can be applied to the assessment of EU Sustainable Finance measures under Art. SERVIN.5.42 TCA.

5.1.3 Nondiscrimination Standards

Furthermore, the EU-CARIFORUM EPA and CETA contain regulations on the most-favored-nation and national treatment standards. Art. 68.1 EU-CARIFORUM EPA concerning commercial presence and Art. 77.1 EU-CARIFORUM EPA concerning other modes of supply of services do both constitute national treatment provisions and were drafted similar in wording to Art. XVII(1) GATS.

Equally, Art. 70.1.a EU-CARIFORUM EPA introduces the most-favored-nation standard for the *commercial presence* mode of supply of a service and Art. 79 EU-CARIFORUM EPA does so for other such modes of supply. However,

---

[53] Recital 10 TCA further recognizes "*the need to ensure an open and secure market [. . .] through addressing unjustified barriers to trade and investment*" and thus resembles no. B.10 Understanding on Commitments in Financial Services, cf. Sect. 3.2.1.2.

Art. 79.1 EU-CARIFORUM EPA uses as the treatment of comparison "*the most favourable treatment applicable to like services and services suppliers of any third country with whom it concludes an economic integration agreement after the signature of [the EU-CARIFORUM EPA]*". Thus, although the wording again is similar to that of the GATS provision, in contrast to Art. II(1) GATS, Art. 79.1 EU-CARIFORUM EPA requires most-favored-nation treatment only in relation to other EPAs. This can be understood as a result of the EPA's comprehensiveness.

Similarly, the TCA sets out the most-favored-nation standard in Art. SERVIN.2.4 TCA with respect to establishment and operation. Although differing in wording, in its content it corresponds to Art. II(1) GATS. Due to its nature as a cross-border trade in services provision Art. SERVIN.3.5 TCA does not differentiate between establishment and operation. Apart from this, it resembles Art. SERVIN.2.4 TCA and hence Art. II(1) GATS.

Excluded from this most-favored-nation standard pursuant to Art. SERVIN.2.4 (3)(b) and Art. SERVIN.3.5(2)(b) TCA are "*measures providing for recognition, including the recognition of the standards or criteria for the authorisation, licencing, or certification [. . .], or the recognition of prudential measures as referred to in paragraph 3 of the GATS Annex on Financial Services.*" Therefore, Art. SERVIN.2.4(3)(b) and Art. SERVIN.3.5(2)(b) TCA allow for measures excluded from para. 3 GATS Annex on Financial Services. This allows for easier recognition of Sustainable Finance measures of other WTO Members as it does not breach the most-favored-nation standard of Art. SERVIN.2.4 TCA.[54]

As regards the cross-border supply of financial services, Art. 13.7.1 CETA incorporates Art. 9.3 CETA setting out the national treatment standard into CETA Chapter Thirteen. Art. 13.7.2 CETA specifies that the "*treatment accorded by a Party to its own service suppliers and services under Article 9.3.2 [. . .] means treatment accorded to its own financial service suppliers and financial services*". Art. 13.3 CETA incorporates the national treatment obligations for investments set out in Art. 8.6 CETA into CETA Chapter Thirteen and thus creates a bridge between financial services disclosures on the one hand and the investment regime on the other hand. Finally, Art. 13.7.4. and Art. 13.4 CETA incorporate through Art. 9.5 and Art. 8.7 CETA, respectively, most-favored-nation treatment obligations into CETA Chapter Thirteen.

In TCA Chapters Two and Three also include the national treatment standard. Whereas Art. SERVIN.2.3(2) TCA adds a sub-national perspective to the national treatment standard, Art. SERVIN.3.4(4) TCA clarifies that it shall not be understood to the effect that a TCA party would have to "*compensate for inherent competitive disadvantages which result from the foreign character of the relevant services or services suppliers.*" This relates to the discussion on better than national treatment in Sect. 3.2.1.2. This clarification clause inversely means that the TCA parties seem to see a possible obligation for such compensation under the GATS national treatment standard.

---

[54]Cf. Sect. 4.2.2.

The wording of the most-favored-nation and national treatment standards in the EU-CARIFORUM EPA and CETA closely resemble the GATS national treatment and most-favored-nation standards of Art. XVII(1) and Art. II(1) GATS, respectively. The same applies as regards the *like situations* and *treatment no less favourable* components in Art. SERVIN.2.4(3)(b) and Art. SERVIN.3.5(2) (b) TCA. Therefore, the conclusions drawn in Sect. 3.2.2 with regard to *like services and service suppliers* and *treatment no less favourable* can be restated can be adapted to the provisions at hand.

However, moving beyond the regulatory scope of Art. XVII(1) and Art. II(1) GATS, TCA Chapters Two and Three include further provisions on non-conforming measures. Most notably, Art. SERVIN.2.7(4) TCA exempts information requirements from the most-favored-nation and national treatment standards under TCA Chapter Two, "*provided that it does not constitute a means to circumvent that Party's obligations under those Articles.*" This can be understood to equal the *arbitrary discrimination* provision in the chapeau of Art. XIV GATS.[55] Art. SERVIN.2.7 and Art. SERVIN.3.6(2) TCA further exempt such measures from the market access, national treatment, and most-favored-nation standards in TCA Chapters Two and Three introduced in relation to a sector or activity listed in TCA Annex SERVIN-2 (*future measures*).

First, para. 2 TCA Annex SERVIN-2 clarifies that the reservations made therein "*are without prejudice to the rights and obligations of the Parties under GATS.*" This means that the conclusions drawn in Chap. 3 are also relevant to the TCA parties' trade in sustainable financial services. Further exempt from "*prudential regulations harmonised at European Union level*" and "*[w]ith respect to financial services*" are "*branches established directly in a Member State by a non-European Union financial institution*" are exempt.[56] However, they "*may be required to satisfy a number of specific prudential requirements such as, in the case of banking and securities, separate capitalisation and other solvency requirements and reporting and publication of accounts requirements*" under para. 13 TCA Annex SERVIN-2. Although not specifically aimed at justifying sustainability-related measures, this exception could therefore apply to the EU Sustainable Finance measures described in Sects. 2.1.6 and 2.1.7.

Concerning financial services, the EU made reservations in the TCA Annex SERVIN-2. Regarding EU Sustainable Finance measures in particular EU Reservation no. 16 is of relevance. Therein the "*EU reserves the right to adopt or maintain any measure*" with a view to investment liberalization and cross-border trade in services. Regarding the latter, the EU reserves "*the right to adopt or maintain any measure with respect to the cross-border supply of all financial services*". The counter-exceptions stipulated thereinafter are not relevant to Sustainable Finance measures. The EU further exempts *Banking and other Financial Services* in EU Reservation no. 16. Existing measures named therein include the UCITS Directive

---

[55] Cf. Sect. 3.2.4.1.4.
[56] Cf. para. 13 TCA Annex SERVIN-2.

and the AIFM Directive.[57] The other exemptions set in EU Reservation no. 16, however, are not immediately relevant to EU Sustainable Finance measures. Concerning financial services, the UK, however, made reservations in the TCA Annex SERVIN-2. UK Reservation no. 9 thereby equals EU Reservations no. 16. The existing measures named under *Banking and other financial services* in UK Reservation no. 9, however, have no relevance with regard to EU Sustainable Finance measures.

Hence, these additional provisions in TCA Chapters Two and Three do not require the assessment's conclusion to deviate from that reached about Art. SERVIN.2.4(3)(b) and Art. SERVIN.3.5(2)(b) TCA.

5.1.4   Domestic Regulation

EU FTAs regularly outline provisions on domestic regulation. For instance, both the EU-CARIFORUM EPA and CETA comprise rules on *effective and transparent regulation*, which in parts closely resemble Art. VI(1) GATS. For instance, Art. 13.11.1 CETA calls on each party to "*ensure that all measures of general application to which this Chapter applies are administered in a reasonable, objective, and impartial manner*". Art. 105.1 and 2 EU-CARIFORUM EPA instead offers a more detailed description of what must be understood under "*effective and transparent regulation*", particularly concerning the administrative process. Art. 13.11.2 CETA offers such details with a view to the administrative process under CETA. Regarding these general rules on domestic regulation, the conclusions drawn in Sect. 3.2.3.1 apply.

Domestic regulation, however, is also addressed in further detail in TCA Section One (*domestic regulation*) of chapter five (*regulatory framework*). These provisions on domestic regulation apply to financial services according to Art. SERVIN.5.37 TCA. In general terms, TCA Section One applies to cross-border trade in services as specified in Art. SERVIN.5.1(1) TCA. However, the relevant regulatory and implementing technical standards set out in Art. SERVIN.5.9 TCA are excluded from its scope of application.[58] Therefore, the group of EU Sustainable Finance measures most relevant to the assessment under international trade law and as discussed in Sect. 3.2.3.2 is exempt from the domestic regulation provisions in TCA Section One.

Further provisions on domestic regulation are set out in TCA Title Eleven (*Level playing field for open and fair competition and sustainable development*), which demonstrates from a regulatory perspective the close relationship between "*open and fair competition*",[59] the stability of the financial system, and sustainable

---

[57]Cf. Sect. 2.2.
[58]Cf. Art. SERVIN.5.1(1) TCA; Cf. Sect. 3.2.3.2.
[59]Cf. Art. 1.1(1) TCA Title Eleven.

development. To the latter trade is to be *"conducive"*,[60] whereas fair competition commitments can only be met *"by contributing to sustainable development"*.[61] The TCA parties further commit *"to promote the development of international trade [. . .] in a way that contributes to the objective of sustainable development"* and to achieve climate neutrality.[62] This provision thus resembles Art. 22.3.2 CETA in its connection between international trade and sustainable development. It thus is equally conducive to the assessment of trade in sustainable financial services and EU Sustainable Finance measures.

Adding to this, Art. 1.2(1) TCA Title Eleven sets out a partial regulatory carve-out clause under which TCA parties' policy space is protected—if these policies are in line with the respective TCA party's *"international commitments, including its commitments under this Title."* It further includes the precautionary approach under which a measure is not to be prevented solely on grounds of lack of scientific evidence.[63] Inversely this means that EU Sustainable Finance's underlying policy objective of environmental protection is *a maiore ad minus* exemptible due to the immense scientific proof of climate change and environmental degradation.

Art. 1.2(3) TCA Title Eleven states that measures for environmental or labor protection potentially affecting trade, *"relevant, available scientific and technical information, international standards, guidelines and recommendations"* shall be taken into account. This requirement resembles the criteria set out in Art. VI (4) GATS. The conclusions drawn in Sect. 3.2.3.2 in this regard can be transferred to the assessment of EU Sustainable Finance measures under Art. 1.2(3) TCA Title Eleven.

TCA Chapter Six (*Labour and social standards*) sets out labor and social principles and an obligation of non-regression.[64] Although contributing to the social factors of ESG-based sustainable development as one of the two core underlying policy objectives of Sustainable Finance, the provisions set out in TCA Chapter Six neither facilitate the justification or propagation of EU Sustainable Finance—nor do they establish its inconsistency. Merely Art. 6.2(4) TCA Chapter Six does state that the TCA parties *"strive to increase their respective labour and social levels of protection"*.

Simultaneously, TCA Chapter Seven (*Environment and climate*) covers standards on *"environmental levels of protection"* and *"climate levels of protection"*[65] and thus another factor of Sustainable Finance. Art. 7.2(1) and (5) TCA Chapter Seven, too, includes a non-regression obligation on those levels of protection and a statement that the TCA parties *"strive to increase their respective environmental levels of protection or their respective climate level of protection"*.

---

[60] Cf. Art. 1.1(1) TCA Title Eleven.

[61] Cf. Art. 1.1(4) TCA Title Eleven.

[62] Cf. Art. 1.1(2) and (3) TCA Title Eleven.

[63] Cf. Art. 1.2(2) TCA Title Eleven.

[64] Cf. Art. 6.1 TCA Chapter Six.

[65] Cf. Art. 7.1(1) and (3) TCA Chapter Seven, respectively.

An increase in such levels of protection, however, must practically be accompanied by measures ensuring the financing of such sustainable economic activities. Art. 7.2 (1) and (5) TCA can thus be construed to support measures of EU Sustainable Finance policy.[66]

The environmental and climate principles in Art. 7.4(1) TCA refer to international agreements on environmental protection or climate action. These are namely *"the Rio Declaration on Environment and Development [...] and in multilateral environmental agreements, including in the [...] UNFCCC"*.[67] Particular reference is *inter alia* made to *"the principle that environmental protection should be integrated into the making of policies"*.[68] Art. 7.4 TCA(1) therefore is applicable to EU Sustainable Finance measures. On the one hand, they are based on international environmental agreements as described in Sect. 3.2.3.2.3. On the other hand, EU Sustainable Finance measures, as concluded in Sect. 2.4, merely introduce sustainability considerations into already existing financial regulation.

Similarly, TCA Chapter Eight (*Other instruments for trade and sustainable development*) refers to *"the Agenda 21 and the 1992 Rio Declaration [..., 'The future we want' Outcome Document], and the UN 2030 Agenda [...] and its Sustainable Development Goals."*[69] With a view to multilateral climate action agreements Art. 8.5(1) TCA references the Paris Agreement. All of these documents are referenced in EU Sustainable Finance measures.[70] In concordance with Art. 7.4 (1) TCA, Art. 8.1(1) TCA equally refers to enhancing *"the integration of sustainable development, notably its labour and environmental dimensions, in the Parties' trade and investment relationship"* as its objective.

Whereas Art. 8.3 TCA focuses on multilateral labor standards and agreements, Art. 8.4 TCA addresses multilateral environmental agreements recognizing *"the importance [...] of the UN Environment Programme (UNEP) and multilateral environmental governance and agreements as a response of the international community to global or regional environmental challenges and stress the need to enhance the mutual supportiveness between trade and environment policies, rules and measures."*[71] Thereby, the connection drawn between trade and environmental measures resembles the provision in Art. 24.4.1 CETA and is potentially conducive to EU Sustainable Finance measures as discussed in Sect. 5.2. This is also supported by Art. 8.4(2) TCA committing the TCA parties to *"effectively implementing the multilateral environmental agreements [...] that it has ratified in its law and practices"* as EU Sustainable Finance measures explicitly aim to implement and

---

[66] A further issue covered by Art. 7.3 TCA Chapter Seven is carbon pricing, which is also relevant in the context of the EU ETS. They will, however, not be discussed in further detail as the EU ETS does not constitutes integral part of EU Sustainable Finance, cf. Sect. 3.3.3.

[67] Cf. Art. 7.4(1) TCA.

[68] Cf. Art. 7.4(1)(a) TCA.

[69] Cf. Art. 8.1(1) TCA.

[70] Cf. Sect. 3.2.3.2.3.

[71] Cf. Art. 8.4(1) TCA.

finance in particular the environmental goals set at the international level.[72] The TCA sets out similar provisions concerning trade and climate change.[73]

Apart from these domestic regulation standards, CETA further sets out regulatory cooperation provisions in CETA Chapter Twenty-one (*Regulatory cooperation*). Therein Art. 21.3 CETA states that the objectives of this cooperation are *inter alia* to "*contribute to the protection of human life, health or safety, animal or plant life or health and the environment by [. . .] leveraging international resources [. . .] contributing to the base of information used by regulatory departments to identify, assess and manage risks*".[74] Such general statements of intent on the use of regulatory cooperation may on the one hand limit a party's regulatory autonomy even without entailing harmonization.[75] On the other hand, it indicates the direction regulatory cooperation is expected to be developed towards. This direction is conducive to EU Sustainable Finance measures, although in this respect, Art. 21.3 CETA asserts no immediate legal obligation or right.

Furthermore, in the Understanding on the Dialogue on the Regulation of the Financial Services Sector in CETA Annex 13-C the "*commitment to strengthening financial stability*" is reaffirmed. A "*dialogue on the regulation of the financial services sector within the Financial Services Committee*" shall be instated. This dialogue "*shall be based on the principles and prudential standards agreed at the multilateral level.*" Similarly, Art. 6 EU-CARIFORUM EPA contains a clause on the Cooperation in international fora "*where issues relevant to this partnership are discussed*". The domestic regulation clauses in the EU-CARIFORUM EPA and CETA are therefore negligible in comparison to the GATS disciplines set out in Sect. 3.2.3. Instead, much of the domestic regulation regime under these EU FTAs is subject to further regulatory cooperation and dialogue between the respective parties. Such regulatory cooperation mechanisms could prove pivotal to evolving regulatory and policy fields such as Sustainable Finance while at the same time assure increased flexibility in the adaption of the necessary definitions and standards.

In the TCA such regulatory cooperation is provided for *inter alia* in Art. 8.4 (5) TCA, which requires the TCA parties to "*work together on trade-related aspects of environmental policies and measures, including in multilateral fora*". Such cooperation *inter alia* shall cover "*the impact of environmental law and standards on trade and investment; or the impact of trade and investment law on the environment*" and "*other trade-related aspects of multilateral environmental agreements, including their protocols, amendments and implementation.*"[76] The same cooperation in international fora is set out in Art. 8.5(3) TCA concerning climate action and in Art. 8.9(2)(d) TCA regarding trade and investment favoring sustainable development. This envisaged cooperation of TCA parties on international fora is coherent

---

[72] Cf. Sect. 3.2.3.2.3.

[73] Cf. Art. 8.5(2) TCA.

[74] Sheargold and Mitchell (2016), p. 596.

[75] Sheargold and Mitchell (2016), p. 601.

[76] Cf. Art. 8.4(5) TCA.

with the EU's commitment in such fora as outlined in Sect. 4.1.2 and thus conducive to both the justification and the propagation of EU Sustainable Finance policy.[77]

Art. 8.9(2)(c) TCA further states that the TCA parties *"shall continue to promote [. . .] trade in goods and services that contribute to enhanced social conditions and environmentally sound practices, including [. . .] fair and ethical trade schemes and eco-labels"*. Although this constitutes only a declaration of intent rather than an obligation, Art. 8.9(2)(c) TCA will guide the conclusion that voluntary eco-labels such as the EU Ecolabel for financial products are not only consistent with the TCA parties' obligations under the TCA but mutually accepted and intentional.[78]

Finally, both the EU-CARIFORUM EPA and CETA contain rules on recognition. Art. 85 EU-CARIFORUM EPA covers the recognition of necessary qualifications and professional experience. Art. 13.5.1 CETA, in turn, has significant similarities to the wording used in para. 3(a) GATS Annex on Financial Services and addresses the recognition of prudential measures. Further, it is to be noted that the most-favored-nation standard outlined in Art. 79.3 EU-CARIFORUM EPA *"shall not apply to treatment granted [. . .] under measures providing for recognition of qualifications, licenses or prudential measures in accordance with Article VII of the GATS or its Annex on Financial Services [. . .]"*.[79] The ramifications of the instrument of recognition with a view to the propagation of EU Sustainable Finance measures have been discussed in Sect. 4.2.2.

5.2 Sustainability and Environmental Chapters and Obligations in EU FTAs

EU EPAs and new generation EU FTAs usually comprise extensive rules on environmental protection or other aspects of sustainability. These chapters usually precede the section on general trade in services disciplines in the EU FTAs. As such, they either apply to all sections of the FTA or only to certain parts of it. In any case, environmental provisions in EU FTAs offer an important frame for the interpretation of the substantive norms of the respective agreement.

This interpretation aid is of particular avail with a view to EU Sustainable Finance under EU FTAs. The trade in financial services rules in EU FTAs, much like the corresponding GATS provisions, are rather vague and require extensive interpretation. Guiding this interpretation within a framework of sustainability provisions, may also impact the consistency of EU Sustainable Finance provisions under EU FTAs. As EU FTAs offer increasingly detailed provisions on environmental

---

[77] Art. 8.4(6) TCA further clarifies that cooperation pursuant to Art. 8.4(5) TCA may include *"technical exchanges, exchanges of information and best practices, research projects, studies, reports, conferences and workshops"*.

[78] Cf. Sects. 3.2.2.2 and 3.2.3.1.

[79] Art. 79.3 EU-CARIFORUM EPA.

protection and sustainability than GATS, they may justify EU Sustainable Finance policy more effectively, too. This is particularly relevant, given the close relation between EU Sustainable Finance on the one hand and sustainable development or environmental provisions on the other hand.[80]

Therefore, this Chapter will demonstrate the *prima facie* applicability of sustainability provisions on trade in service in general and trade in financial services in specific. This is to show how sustainability or the concept of sustainable development and trade in financial services are interconnected in EU FTAs. It will further provide the base for the considerations on the applicability of sustainable development and environmental exceptions and carve-outs.[81]

EU-CARIFORUM EPA part one (*Trade partnership for sustainable development*) sets out a partnership whose objectives according to Art. 1.a EU-CARIFORUM EPA are poverty reduction "*consistent with the objective of sustainable development, the Millennium Development Goals and the Cotonou Agreement*". Art. 1.f EU-CARIFORUM EPA specifies that the partnership is "*taking into account [the parties'] respective levels of development and consistent with WTO obligations [...]*." Art. 3.1 to Art. 3.3 EU-CARIFORUM EPA further detail the EPA's understanding of sustainable development.[82] However, the EU-CARIFORUM EPA does not provide for sector-specific rules on sustainable development such as for trade in financial services. Thus, the Trade Partnership for Sustainable Development is applicable by its scope to EU Sustainable Finance measures but does not provide for more detailed disciplines.

CETA in turn does not restrict the concept of sustainable development to a separate agreement between the parties but incorporates it into its various sectoral parts. Recital 6 Preamble CETA highlights the right to regulate sustainability-related policy objectives in domestic regulation and the "*flexibility to achieve legitimate policy objectives, such as public health, safety, environment, public morals and the promotion and protection of cultural diversity*". More specifically concerning the concept of sustainable development, the CETA Preamble states that the parties are committing "*to promote sustainable development and the development of international trade in such a way as to contribute to sustainable development in its economic, social and environmental dimensions*".[83] The CETA Preamble thus highlights the interconnection between sustainable development and trade under the agreement.

CETA Chapter Twenty-two (*Trade and sustainable development*), in its Art. 22.1.1 CETA refers to multiple international sustainable development

---

[80] Cf. Sect. 3.2.4.

[81] Cf. Sect. 5.3.

[82] Pursuant to Art. 2.1 EU-CARIFORUM EPA, it further "*is based on the Fundamental Principles as well as the Essential and Fundamental Elements of the Cotonou Agreement [...]*".

[83] Recital 9 CETA.

agreements, *inter alia* the Rio Declaration and the Agenda 21.[84] Its aim is *"to contribute to the objective of sustainable development, for the welfare of present and future generations"*. With regard to Sustainable Finance and trade in financial services, this demonstrates the close relationship discussed in Sect. 3.2.3.2.3 that international trade law and sustainable development agreements as policy frameworks for international standards inhibit. Art. 22.1.2 CETA even highlights *"the benefit of considering trade-related labour and environmental issues as part of a global approach to trade and sustainable development."* Consequentially, the provisions of CETA Chapters twenty-three and twenty-four *"are to be considered in the context of"* these approaches. Hence, sustainable development and environmental protection both must be integrated into the interpretation of the trade in financial services obligations described in Sect. 5.1. This is in contrast to the GATS disciplines, which despite the similarities to the EU FTA obligations described above do not outline any general rule-of-interpretation based on sustainable development.

Art. 22.1.3.d CETA sets out two clear but voluntary aims of the CETA parties. First, CETA Chapters twenty-three and twenty-four shall be introduced in a manner promoting *"the full use of instruments, such as impact assessment and stakeholder consultations, in the regulation of trade, labour and environmental issues"*. Second, market participants are encouraged *"to develop and implement practices that contribute to the achievement of sustainable development goals [. . .]"*. EU Sustainable Finance can be understood to fall under the wording of Art. 22.1.3.d CETA as it encourages financial market participants to invest in sustainable economic activities.

Pursuant to Art. 22.3.2 CETA *"each Party shall strive to promote trade and economic flows and practices"* conducive to sustainable development *inter alia* by the use of four instruments, which each are integral aspects of EU Sustainable Finance. The first of these instruments is the encouragement of developing and using *"voluntary schemes relating to the sustainable production of goods and services, such as eco-labelling and fair-trade schemes"*. An example of such voluntary schemes is the EU Ecolabel for financial products (Sect. 2.1.2), and the EU GBS (Sect. 2.1.3). Further instruments comprise to encourage *"the development and use of voluntary best practices of corporate social responsibility by enterprises, such as those in the OECD Guidelines for Multinational Enterprises [. . .]"* and to promote *"the development, the establishment, the maintenance or the improvement of environmental performance goals and standards"*. Such corporate governance guidelines, best practices, and environmental goals and standards are used in EU Sustainable Finance as described above (Sect. 2.1.9). Finally, the instruments outlined in Art. 22.3.2 CETA include the encouragement of the *"integration of sustainability considerations in private and public consumption decisions"*. This has been addressed *inter alia* in Sect. 2.1.6 under the phenomenon of short-termism. Thus, Art. 22.3.2 CETA serves as an indication that such measures are not only

---

[84]Report of the United Nations Conference on Environment and Development, Rio de Janeiro, 3 to 14 June 1992, Annex II, Agenda 21. 12 August 1992.

destined to be in line with CETA's substantive provisions but their mutual introduction is indeed encouraged.

Adding to this, CETA includes declarations of intend with a view to the cooperation on trade supporting sustainable development in Art. 22.3.1 CETA and on environmental issues in Art. 24.12.1 CETA. Latter highlights the cooperation on several policy fields affecting EU Sustainable Finance measures including the "*activity in international fora dealing with issues relevant for both trade and environmental policies, including in particular the WTO [. . .]*". Further cooperation is set out with a view to "*the trade impact of environmental regulations and standards as well as the environmental impact of trade and investment rules including on the development of environmental regulations and policy*". Finally, the cooperation is set to comprise "*trade and investment in environmental goods and services [. . .] and [. . .] exchange of views on the relationship between multilateral environmental agreements and international trade rules.*" This for the first time highlights the interrelation between trade, trade law, and environment or sustainable development in general and the respective international fora. Although Art. 22.3.1 CETA and Art. 24.12.1 CETA does not allow for or require a shift in the interpretation of the substantive CETA obligations, they do show a shift in the common understanding of the parties concerning the relevance and importance of said interrelation.

A partially more restrictive scope of application is constituted in Art. 24.1 CETA, which defines *environmental law* for CETA Chapter Twenty-four (*Trade and environment*) as a measure, "*the purpose of which is the protection of the environment, including the prevention of a danger to human life or health from environmental impacts, such as*" emission control and reduction measures. It can be argued that the prevention, for example, of carbon emissions is the eventual goal of EU Green Bonds as one of the EU Sustainable Finance measures. The question thus is whether the link between emission reduction and EU Green Bonds is sufficiently close to qualify as a *purpose* in terms of Art. 24.1 CETA. The actual and immediate carbon emission reduction happens through the companies issuing these bonds or more precisely the specific activities the capital deriving from the issuance of EU Green Bonds are invested into. Indeed, this indirect approach aiming at influencing in particular private investor's decision-making towards investments into more sustainable economic activities is inherent to EU Sustainable Finance measures. Interpreted in conjunction with the above findings on the CETA Preamble and Art. 22.3.2 and Art. 24.2 CETA has to be found to cover also those EU Sustainable Finance measures only mediately aiming at carbon emission reduction and environmental protection.

In Art. 24.2 CETA, the parties stress the relation between environmental protection as an integral aspect of sustainable development and international environmental agreements. Art. 24.4.1 CETA further elaborates on this relation and stresses "*the need to enhance the mutual supportiveness between trade and environment policies, rules, and measures*". Although Sustainable Finance measures are not explicitly mentioned, Art. 24.4.1 CETA adds to the norms guiding the interpretation of trade in sustainable financial services as aiming to be conducive to sustainable development.

Similar support for this interpretation is given by Art. 24.9.1 CETA stating that the parties will aim to *"facilitate and promote trade and investment in environmental goods and services, including through addressing the reduction of non-tariff barriers related to these goods and services."* Art. 24.9.2 CETA adds to this by stating that the *"Parties shall, consistent with their international obligations, pay special attention to facilitating the removal of obstacles to trade or investment in goods and services of particular relevance for climate change mitigation [...]"*. On the one hand, this might not directly apply to EU Sustainable Finance measures since the instruments used therein promote sustainable economic activities but not necessarily environmental services. On the other hand, Art. 24.9 CETA shows an aspect not yet addressed in EU Sustainable Finance legislation, namely the further removal of obstacles to market access for sustainable financial services. This particularly comprises pro-active measures, instead of only hindering market access for unsustainable financial services.

Finally, Art. 24.8 CETA requires trade-restrictive measures to be based on scientific and technical information, as long as the lack of such is not *"used as a reason for postponing cost-effective measures to prevent environmental degradation"*. As outlined in Sect. 3.2.3.2.1, EU Sustainable Finance measures and their administrative and consultation processes are usually informed by scientific and technical information.

It thus can be concluded that new generation EU FTAs and EU EPAs may vary in their inclusion of a sustainable development chapter and its respective application to Sustainable Finance measures and their binding legal nature. In the case of the EU-CARIFORUM EPA, the Trade Partnership for Sustainable Development applies to EU Sustainable Finance measures while not providing for more detailed disciplines on trade in financial services. In contrast to the EU-CARIFORUM EPA and GATS, in CETA sustainable development serves as an interpretation tool for the provisions in the substantive chapters, whereby the EU Sustainable Finance measures do fall under CETA Chapter Twenty-two (*Trade and development*). Those EU Sustainable Finance measures aimed specifically at carbon emission reduction are further covered by CETA Chapter Twenty-four (*Trade and environment*). This is relevant for certain prospective EU Sustainable Finance measures such as the carbon border adjustment discussed in Sect. 3.3.3.

Similar to the sustainability and environmental provisions in the EU-CARIFORUM EPA and CETA, the TCA outlines such rules in TCA Chapters Six (*Labour and social standards*), Seven (*Environment and climate*), and Eight (*Other instruments for trade and sustainable development*), as described in Sect. 5.1.4.

For these environmental and sustainability chapters to serve as a justification tool for Sustainable Finance measures, specifically, the legally binding carve-outs set out therein and in the trade in financial services sections would need to apply to EU Sustainable Finance measures.

5.3   Application of Sustainability and Prudential Carve-Outs

In general terms, FTAs set out additional liberalization commitments compared to those agreed in GATS. To avoid misuse of these commitments, these liberalization commitments are counterbalanced with right to regulate clauses, so-called *carve-outs*. Such carve-outs may cover a broad range of national policy objectives.[85] They may also specifically justify environmental or prudential policy.[86] In particularly latter provisions are of relevance when considering Sustainable Finance measures. Contrasting their respective GATS equivalents, policy carve-outs in FTAs are usually more detailed than, for instance, those set out in Art. XIV GATS. The higher detail corresponds to the additional liberalization commitments made in an FTA.

These general considerations can be projected onto the specific carve-out provisions in EU FTAs. Supplementing the sustainability and environmental provisions in the EU-CARIFORUM EPA, CETA and the TCA the sustainability and prudential carve-outs for measures otherwise inconsistent with the obligations set out in these FTAs might apply to EU Sustainable Finance measures. The structure of such carve-outs as a counter-exception to otherwise inconsistent measures resembles the GATS provisions on general exceptions assessed in Sect. 3.2.4. These comprise in particular Art. XIV GATS and para. 2(a) GATS Annex on Financial Services.

The first type of such policy protection clauses are general exception clauses. For instance, Art. 224.1 EU-CARIFORUM EPA sets out a general exception clause while reflecting the wording of Art. XIV GATS including the requirements of the chapeau of not constituting "*a means of arbitrary or unjustifiable discrimination*" or "*a disguised restriction on trade*". There are only a few changes to the wording of the clause in comparison to Art. XIV GATS, which stems from the fact that Art. 224 EU-CARIFORUM EPA is applicable not only to trade in services but to "*trade in goods, services or establishment*". Adding to this, EU-CARIFORUM EPA only refers to the parties of the EU-CARIFORUM EPA and not to the WTO Members. Likewise, due to the similarities with Art. XIV GATS, the conclusions concerning EU Sustainable Finance measures made in Sect. 3.2.4.1 can be transferred to Art. 224 EU-CARIFORUM EPA.

Similarly, Art. 28.3.2 CETA comprises general exceptions *inter alia* with a view to CETA Chapter Nine (*Cross-Border Trade in Services*), chapter ten (*Temporary Entry and Stay of Natural Persons for Business Purposes*), chapter twelve (*Domestic Regulations*), and chapter thirteen (*Financial Services*). It covers CETA's provisions on financial services and therefore applies to EU Sustainable Finance measures under the regulations discussed in Sect. 5.1. This application is, however, under the precondition that the measure meets the requirements of Art. XIV(a) to (c) GATS. Given the respective reproduction of Art. XX GATT's wording in Art.

---

[85] Such as Recital 4 GATS, cf. Sect. 3.2.4.2.

[86] Such as Art. XIV(b) GATS and para. 2(a) GATS Annex on Financial Services, cf. Sects. 3.2.4.1.3 and 3.2.4.3; Cf. Hush (2018), p. 96.

28.3.1 CETA for the CETA Chapters on trade in goods, which in contrast to Art. 28.3.1 CETA makes explicit reference to the GATT, this may lead to the conclusion that WTO jurisprudence like the *US–Shrimp* case is to be considered when interpreting Art. 28.3.1 CETA.[87] Art. 24.2.4 CETA even explicitly stipulates that the *"Parties acknowledge their right to use Article 28.3 [...] in relation to environmental measures, including those taken pursuant to multilateral environmental agreements to which they are party."* As a additional exception to those set out in GATS, Art. 24.2.4 CETA would relevant for a possible prospective compulsory labeling provision as described in Sect. 3.3.1. Hence, explicitly basing such measure on multilateral agreements would lower its potential for inconsistency with regard to the substantive provisions in EU FTAs discussed in Sect. 5.1.

General exceptions are further outlined in title twelve TCA (*Exceptions*). Art. EXC.1(1) TCA incorporates Art. XX GATT into TCA Title Twelve and applies to the interpretation *inter alia* of TCA Chapter Two (*Investment liberalisation*). Art. EXC.1(2) TCA sets out that nothing in TCA Title Two (*Services and Investment*) *"shall be construed to prevent the adoption or enforcement by either Party of measures [...] necessary to protect public security or public morals or to maintain public order"* or *"necessary to protect human, animal or plant life or health"*. This strongly resembles Art. XIV(a) and (b) GATS as assessed in Sects. 3.2.4.1.1 and 3.2. 4.1.3.[88] Such measures protecting *"human, animal or plant life or health"* pursuant to Art. EXC.1(3)(a) TCA explicitly encompass *"environmental measures, which are necessary to protect human, animal or plant life and health"*. EU Sustainable Finance measures aimed at financing environmental protection and climate action, as discussed in Sect. 3.2.4.1.3 constitute such environmental measures *necessary* to protect human, animal or plant life or health. This conclusion due to Art. EXC.1(3) (a) TCA can be transferred onto the assessment of EU Sustainable Finance measures under the TCA. This is underlined by the EU Sustainable Finance measures being based on international environmental agreements, as discussed in Sect. 3.2.3.2.3. Such *"measures taken to implement multilateral environmental agreements can fall [...] under"* the Art. 1(2) TCA exception.

EU FTAs regularly also include specific exception clauses for financial regulation, which in turn could apply to EU Sustainable Finance measures. For example, adding to the general exception clause in Art. 224 EU-CARIFORUM EPA, Art. 70.3 EU-CARIFORUM EPA constitutes a financial services exception to the most-favored-nation standard for commercial presence set out in Art. 70.1 EU-CARIFORUM EPA. Equally, Art. 79.3 EU-CARIFORUM EPA introduces such exceptions to the most-favored-nation obligations for other modes of supply of services. Art. 70.3 and Art. 79.3 EU-CARIFORUM EPA further exempt

---

[87] Hush (2018), p. 129; Cf. the jurisprudence discussed in Sect. 3.2.4.1.

[88] With regard to the Chapeau of Art. XIV GATS the Art. EXC.1(2) TCA exception, too, is under the condition *"that such measures are not applied in a manner which would constitute a means of arbitrary or unjustifiable discrimination between countries where like conditions prevail, or a disguised restriction on investment liberalization or trade in services"*.

"measures providing for recognition of qualifications, licences or prudential measures in accordance with Article VII of the GATS or its Annex on Financial Services [. . .]". Art. 70.3 and Art. 79.3 EU-CARIFORUM EPA thus refer to Art. VII GATS and the GATS Annex on Financial Services.[89] Prudential carve-outs referenced in Art. 70.3 and Art. 79.3 EU-CARIFORUM EPA are likely to comprise para. 2 (a) GATS Annex on Financial Services.[90] Therefore, the findings made in Sect. 3. 2.4.3 can be transferred to the EU Sustainable Finance measures under the EU-CARIFORUM EPA at hand.

Similar to these financial regulation exception clauses, new generation EU FTAs may also set out carve-out clauses for measures for prudential reasons. One example of such a clause is Art. 104.1 EU-CARIFORUM EPA, which underlines that parties *"may adopt or maintain measures for prudential reasons"*. These prudential reasons comprise *"(a) the protection of investors, depositors, policy-holders or persons to whom a fiduciary duty is owed by a financial service supplier; (b) ensuring the integrity and stability of their financial system."* As discussed in Sect. 3.2.1.1, investor protection is closely related to and financial stability can be understood to be an aspect of Sustainable Finance. Therefore, such EU Sustainable Finance measures with sufficiently close relation to financial stability may be exempted from the EU-CARIFORUM EPA's substantial obligations according to Art. 104.1 EU-CARIFORUM EPA.

Similar to Art. 104.1 EU-CARIFORUM EPA, Art. 13.16.1 CETA as well contains a carve-out clause but limits it to *"reasonable measures for prudential reasons"*. Reasonability as a precondition to the consistency of a services regulation can also be found in Art. VI(1) GATS. As discussed in Sect. 3.2.3.1, reasonability therein refers *"to notions such as 'in accordance with reason', 'not irrational or absurd', 'proportionate', 'having sound judgement', 'sensible', 'not asking for too much', 'within the limits of reason, not greatly less or more than might be thought likely or appropriate', 'articulate'"*.[91] It is not apparent why and how the reasonability requirement under Art. 13.16.1 CETA would have to be interpreted substantially different from Art. VI(1) GATS. Hence, the Art. 13.16.1 CETA reasonability requirement can be deemed to be met regarding the currently existing EU Sustainable Finance measures. In addition to this reasonability test, Art. 13.16.1.b CETA introduces *"the maintenance of the safety, soundness, integrity, or financial responsibility of a financial institution, cross-border financial service supplier, or financial service supplier"* as a further option under which an exception is granted, in addition to the two requirements already stated in Art. 104.1 EU-CARIFORUM EPA. On the one hand, the *"safety [. . .] of a [. . .] financial service supplier"* can be understood to be an expression of financial stability. The fact, that in Art. 13.16.1 CETA, too, the

---

[89] Recognition pursuant to Art. VII GATS with regard to EU Sustainable Finance measures will further be considered in Sect. 4.2.2.

[90] Cf. Sect. 3.2.4.3.

[91] WTO DSB (2004) Dominican Republic – Measures Affecting the Importation and Internal Sale of Cigarettes, Panel report, para. 7.385; Cf. Van den Bossche and Zdouc (2017), p. 508.

option of financial stability is named separately, however, leads to the conclusion
that safety must rather be understood as referring to the individual stability of the
financial service supplier. This in turn is similar to investor protection rules and thus
instead of constituting an aspect of Sustainable Finance, it is merely related to the
regulations EU Sustainable Finance is implemented into.

In this regard, CETA Annex 13-B (Understanding on the Application of Articles
13.16.1 and 13.21) must further be considered, which in general terms states that the
*"Parties recognise that prudential measures strengthen domestic financial systems,
[. . .] and promote international financial stability by facilitating better-informed
lending and investment decisions"*. More precisely, para. 8(a) CETA Annex 13-B
contains high-level principles preserving the right of the respective party to *"determine its own appropriate level of prudential regulation [. . .] and enforce measures
that provide a higher level of prudential protection than those set out in common
international prudential commitments"*. Such prudential regulation exceeding the
international prudential commitments of the EU can be seen in the prudential EU
Sustainable Finance measures introducing sustainable development-related criteria
into financial regulation while maintaining a sufficiently close relation to financial
stability.[92] Such measures add a sustainable development perspective to the conventional understanding of the scope of financial stability and thus exceeding the
common international prudential commitments. Such EU Sustainable Finance measures thus would be covered by the prudential exception of Art. 13.16.1 CETA
pursuant to para. 8(a) CETA Annex 13-B.

Para. 8(e) CETA Annex 13-B further exempts from Art. 13.16.1 CETA measures
that are *"applied in a manner which would constitute a means of arbitrary or
unjustifiable discrimination between investors in like situations, or a disguised
restriction on foreign investment"*. Hence, a *"measure is deemed to meet the
requirements of Article 13.16.1 if it is [. . .] in line with international prudential
commitments that are common to the Parties"*. The first requirement of not constituting an arbitrary or unjustifiable discrimination of like investors or a disguised
restriction on foreign investment has already been discussed with regard to EU
Sustainable Finance in Sect. 3.2.4.1.4. More relevant, however, is the notion that
the criterion of being in line with international prudential commitments shows the
importance of international fora like the FSB and the EU's commitments and
efforts in introducing Sustainable Finance into these fora, as has been discussed
in Sect. 4.1.2.[93]

Art. 13.16.3 CETA goes further by allowing the parties to introduce prudential
measures that *"prohibit a particular financial service or activity. Such a prohibition
shall not apply to all financial services or to a complete financial services
sub-sector, such as banking"*. This exception is applicable as long as the measure
does not breach the most-favored-nation or national treatment standards set out in
Art. 13.3 and Art. 13.4 CETA and described in Sect. 5.1. This carve-out for a

---

[92] Cf. Sect. 3.2.4.3.

[93] Cf. Martin and Mercurio (2017), pp. 96 et seq.

prudential prohibition would be in particular relevant if a sustainability screening as described in Sect. 3.3.3 would be introduced not only as a carbon border adjustment but also with the possibility of a prohibition of noncompliant financial services.

A prudential carve-out clause is also set out in Art. SERVIN.5.39 TCA. It specifies that the TCA shall not *"prevent a Party from adopting or maintaining measures for prudential reasons"*. These prudential reasons include investor protection and the integrity and stability of the financial system. Art. SERVIN.5.39 TCA thus resembles para. 2(a) GATS Annex on Financial Services and the EU FTA examples, namely Art. 106 EU-CARIFORUM EPA and Art. 13.14.2 CETA.[94]

Besides, new generation EU FTAs usually comprise general *right to regulate* and *levels of protection* clauses. For the EU to promote sustainable development through FTAs preserving its right to regulate is one of the tools to do so.[95] This is exemplified by the relevant CETA Chapters twenty-two (*Trade and sustainable development*) and twenty-four (*Trade and environment*).[96] Thereby, the right to regulate clauses in CETA are based on the fundamental approach set out in Recital 6 Preamble CETA. It outlines CETA's aim for preserving the CETA parties' *"flexibility to achieve legitimate policy objectives, such as public health, safety, environment, public morals and the promotion and protection of cultural diversity"*.[97] With a view to the potential relevance of Recital 6 Preamble CETA for EU Sustainable Finance measures, reference is made to the arguments and considerations made in Sect. 3.2.4.2 in respect of Recital 4 GATS.

Another example of such right to regulate clauses is set out in TCA Title Ten (*Good Regulatory Practices and Regulatory Cooperation*), which contains an exception from its regulatory scope as to not *"requiring a Party to [. . .] take actions that would undermine or impede the timely adoption of regulatory measures to achieve its public policy objectives"*.[98] Art. GRP.1(2)(b) TCA thus is protecting national policy objectives. EU Sustainable Finance measures may fall under such national policy objectives, as discussed in Sect. 3.2.4.2 with a view to Recital 4 GATS. Art. GRP.1(2)(b) TCA, however, is legally binding, whereas the GATS preambulatory clause lacks such binding effect.[99] In contrast, Art. GRP.1(2)(b) TCA is only applicable to TCA Title Ten. This is complemented by the exception set out in Art. GRP.1(3) TCA. Although also restricted to the application of TCA Title Ten, it preserves *"the right of a Party to define or regulate [. . .] its public policy objectives in areas such as [. . .] human, animal or plant life and health, and animal*

---

[94]This includes the restriction of otherwise inconsistent measures to *"not be used as a means of avoiding the Party's commitments or obligations under the [TCA]"*, cf. Art. SERVIN.5.39 TCA.

[95]Hush (2018), p. 113.

[96]Cf. Hush (2018), p. 123.

[97]Cf. Hush (2018), p. 136.

[98]Cf. Art. GRP.1(2)(b) TCA.

[99]The TCA also includes a preambultory clause in Recital 7 TCA resembling Recital 4 GATS as it recognizes *"the Parties' respective autonomy and rights to regulate within their territories in order to achieve legitimate public policy objectives such as the protection and promotion of public health, [. . .] safety, the environment including climate change, public morals [. . .]"*.

welfare; [...] environment including climate change; [...] integrity and stability of the financial system, and protection of investors; [...]'. Insofar, the conclusion drawn from the assessment of EU Sustainable Finance measures under Art. XIV and Recital 4 GATS, and para. 2(a) GATS Annex on Financial Services can be restated.[100]

Consistently, Art. 23.2 CETA recognizes *"the right of each Party to set its labor priorities, to establish its levels of labor protection and to adopt or modify its laws and policies accordingly in a manner consistent with its international labor commitments"*.[101] First, it is to be noticed that labor standards as a core social safeguard are an expression of just one of the three ESG factors, despite the Art. 23.2 CETA's title reading sustainable development. Thus, Art. 23.3 CETA cannot be considered a policy protection clause for all EU Sustainable Finance measures. Vice versa, the question arises whether Art. 23.2 CETA covers EU Sustainable Finance measures explicitly referring to such labor standards. This is the case for instance with Art. 3 (a) to (d) Taxonomy Regulation, which refers to international labor standards. As described above (Sect. 2.1.1), it defines ecologically sustainable economic activities as being *inter alia* respective of the minimum safeguards deriving from the ILO conventions as of Art. 18 Taxonomy Regulation.[102] Art. 3 Taxonomy Regulation, therefore, makes direct reference to international labor standards and thus falls within the wording of Art. 23.2 CETA, indeed. However, the referencing of international labor standards is not one of the provisions in the EU Sustainable Finance measures likely to be contested under WTO law, in contrast to the provisions discussed in Sect. 3.2. Therefore, although Art. 23.2 CETA would serve as a policy protection clause for provisions such as Art. 3 Taxonomy Regulation, such justification is not required for these provisions.

Likewise, new generation EU FTAs may include provisions justifying levels of environmental protection. For instance, through Art. 24.3 CETA each party's right is protected with a view to *"environmental priorities, [...] levels of environmental protection"* and the adoption of correspondent legal provisions *"in a manner consistent with the multilateral environmental agreements to which it is party [...]'*. Parties are further encouraged to assure that these provisions *"provide for and encourage high levels of environmental protection, and shall strive to continue to improve such laws and policies and their underlying levels of protection."*[103] Therefore, Art. 24.3 CETA functions not only as a right to regulate clause for environmental measures but also as a statement of intent: that a high level of protection is not only feasible but welcome and encouraged. In relation to EU Sustainable Finance, Art. 24.3 CETA thus protects the EU's right to modify its

---

[100] This includes the provision that *"[r]egulatory measures shall not constitute a disguised barrier to trade"*, which thus resembles the *"disguised restriction on trade in services"* prohibition in the chapeau of Art. XIV GATS, cf. Sect. 3.2.4.1.4.

[101] A similar *rebalancing* clause is set out in Art. 9.4 TCA.

[102] Bueren (2019), p. 858.

[103] Cf. Art. 24.3 CETA.

financial services regulations in a manner conducive to environmental protection. However, it also obligates the EU to take these measures following international environmental agreements. The EU complies with this obligation by extensively referencing international climate and sustainable development agreements as described in Sect. 3.2.3.2.3.

Similarly, para. 12(c) TCA Annex SERVIN-2 further clarifies that *inter alia* such measures *"seeking to ensure the conservation and protection of natural resources and the environment"* do not breach the market access standards described in Sect. 5.1.2. Keeping in mind the examples enumerated subsequent thereof, it can rather be argued that cases such as the EU ETS were intended to fall under this provision and not Sustainable Finance measures.

Therefore, it can be concluded that if EU Sustainable Finance measures would be deemed inconsistent with the requirements set out in the respective EU FTA, particularly new generation FTAs include exceptions and policy protection clauses applicable to Sustainable Finance. Whereas the EU FTAs discussed herein do not comprise a specific exception for Sustainable Finance measures, in this regard exception clauses may apply from both the realms of prudential and environmental regulation.

5.4   Propagation and Justification through EU FTAs

As demonstrated in Chap. 4, the EU propagates the concept of Sustainable Finance through various fora and multilateral agreements.[104] This also includes introducing policy protection clauses for Sustainable Finance at the different levels of international policy-setting. This form of influencing international policy-setting on Sustainable Finance can also be transferred onto bilateral relations. The above-discussed EU FTAs—CETA, the EU-CARIFORUM EPA, and the TCA—are examples of such bilateral agreements.

The EU could use these FTAs, first, to justify its Sustainable Finance policy and, second, to propagate the concept across and through its bilateral trade partners. Third, a similar approach could be adopted with a view to the EU's multilateral development agreements *inter alia* governing ODA and its own development assistance schemes, such as the EDF, the DCI, and the ENI.[105]

To this end, further clauses could be introduced aimed at justifying EU Sustainable Finance policy as part of ongoing or prospective EU FTA negotiations. This is, in particular, relevant for the more recent and comprehensive new generation FTAs. Protecting EU Sustainable Finance policy space through the introduction of new

---

[104] Cf. Sect. 4.3.

[105] Although these agreements do not constitute EU FTAs, due to the trade-related aspects incorporated in them and the similarities between FTAs and development schemes the propagation through them will be discussed in this Chapter.

FTA clauses is particularly necessary with a view to possible future and more restrictive measures described in Sect. 3.3. Plus, there is a significant difference between introducing Sustainable Finance provisions into the GATS framework as discussed in Sect. 4.2 and including them into FTAs. This is due to the FTAs' bilateral nature, which encourages a mutually beneficial solution and which, as a result, can be sought more easily than through multilateral GATS negotiations.[106]

A clause specifying the applicable law with a view to Sustainable Finance could be introduced into prospective EU FTAs. Such a clause may instruct that the strictest of either of the parties' Sustainable Finance standards is taken as the reference when determining, for instance, *de facto* barriers to trade in financial services. This would not only justify the EU Sustainable Finance policy as it is but encourage the respective trade partner to introduce similar or more ambitious Sustainable Finance measures than the EU. The introduction of a clause specifying the applicable law thus is also a tool for propagating Sustainable Finance.

Such a clause could be complemented by a provision that introduces a Sustainable Finance measure into the FTA itself—such as a border screening arrangement. Similar provisions like FDI screenings are common in bilateral investment agreements (*BITs*). However, due to the differing nature of financial services and the various practical challenges in the introduction of such measures on a domestic level as discussed in Sect. 3.3.3, the drafting of an EU FTA clause including such a measure on a bilateral basis is unlikely in the medium term.

Furthermore, the introduction of additional clauses justifying EU Sustainable Finance policy could address the problem of subjectivity of a Panel's ruling on the appropriateness of a Sustainable Finance measure. This could be tackled by either taking into account the policy objective of the measure, as was done by the Panel in *Argentina–Financial Services* with a view to prudential objectives. Alternatively, clearer language could be introduced into the respective FTA. Furthermore, like in the EU-Singapore FTA,[107] the GATS Annex on Financial Services could be incorporated into the FTA or a *joint determinations* mechanism could be introduced into the agreement.[108]

Such joint determinations concerning the parties' understanding of Sustainable Finance policy would also address the timeliness of measures and thus when such Sustainable Finance measures become inequitable or too burdensome. As shown in *Argentina–Financial Services*, parties, and the Panel, may develop different understandings, which in turn could be addressed by introducing interpretation mechanisms such as *joint determinations*.[109] Similar to the introduction of a joint determinations mechanism into an EU FTA might be to work towards bilateral declarations by the contracting parties in order to create a mutual understanding of

---

[106] Hush (2018), p. 153.

[107] Free Trade Agreement between the European Union and the Republic of Singapore [2019] OJ L 294/3.

[108] Martin and Mercurio (2017), pp. 89 et seq.

[109] Martin and Mercurio (2017), pp. 89 et seq.

certain terms of the FTA. This may lead to terms like *sustainable development* to encompass *Sustainable Finance*, or terms like *prudential regulation* to also comprise *Sustainable Finance* measures aimed at financial stability.[110] Such legal clarity would circumvent many of the uncertainties accompanying the interpretation and application of the provisions discussed in Sect. 3.2 to EU Sustainable Finance measures.

Furthermore, EU FTAs could refer to international prudential agreements. For instance, a clause similar to para. 8(e) CETA Annex 13-B[111] could be added to future EU FTAs. By referring to international prudential agreements it would for instance ensure that Sustainable Finance measures meeting or exceeding these commitments are in line with the FTA's obligations.

Prospective EU FTAs could further contain regulatory cooperation clauses explicitly outlining the policy objective of contributing to Sustainable Finance. Such a clause could be drafted similar to Art. 21.3 CETA, which states that the "*objectives of regulatory cooperation include to [. . .] contribute to the protection of human life, health or safety, animal or plant life or health and the environment [. . .]*".[112] Art. 21.3 CETA further lists policy instruments by which the stated objectives are to be achieved. Either a general reference to the mobilization of "*additional financial resources for developing countries from multiple sources*" as stated in SDG 17.3[113] or a specific reference to some of the EU Sustainable Finance measures discussed in Chap. 2 could be added to this clause.

Furthermore, dedicated carve-outs for Sustainable Finance measures could be introduced into future EU FTAs. For instance, Art. 15.5 and Art. 15.15 CETA encompasses such carve-outs for financial services measures concerning prudential regulation. Further, the inclusion of dedicated dispute settlement mechanisms for financial services could be beneficial to the justification of Sustainable Finance policy through the use of dedicated prudential carve-outs for sustainable financial services. This would prevent these services, for instance, from falling under the investment section of an FTA and thus losing access to the aforementioned carve-outs. CETA outlines such a dedicated arbitral system for financial services comprising the Financial Services Committee.[114] Alternatively, such carve-outs could be inserted into both, the financial services section and the investment section of the FTA.[115] An inclusion could also be conducted by referencing the investment chapter

---

[110]Cf. UN PAGE (2018), p. 30; However, there are differing opinions on whether the inclusion of Sustainable Development in FTAs is beneficial or detrimental to Sustainable Development and in particular environmental protection, cf. Hush (2018), p. 152.

[111]Cf. Sect. 5.3.

[112]Sheargold and Mitchell (2016), p. 590.

[113]As discussed in Sect. 4.1.1.

[114]Cf. Art. 13.18 CETA.

[115]Martin and Mercurio (2017), pp. 78 et seqq.; In contrast, the EU-Singapore FTA, while incorporating a Chapter on financial services with a prudential carve-out for financial stability in Art. 8.50 EU-Singapore FTA, that Chapter is a of the services chapter. Thus, if a financial services dispute is brought forward by an investor it would fall under the investment Chapter of the

carve-outs for sustainable financial services in the financial services sections of EU FTAs. Art. 13.2.4 CETA is an example of such referencing.

Furthermore, para. 2(a) GATS Annex on Financial Services could be incorporated by reference similar to Art. 70.3 and Art. 79.3 EU-CARIFORUM EPA. This would introduce a dedicated financial services exception into the FTA, which could in turn also explicitly exempt Sustainable Finance measures.

Finally, specific sustainable development targets also covering Sustainable Finance could be integrated into EU FTAs. *Hush* thus suggests lexical changes to FTA clauses that require parties to achieve certain sustainable development targets instead of using the vague language of sustainable development methodology obligations.[116] However, there have been concerns that including sustainable development into FTAs might increase inefficiencies due to it being difficult to quantify and monitor. *Hush*, however, argues that including sustainable development not only does not mandate specific actions but also gives the implementing party a certain discretion in choosing the respective instrument to enact the sustainable development policy target in good faith.[117] Now it could be argued that Sustainable Finance provisions as a mere implementation instrument of an FTA's sustainable development targets are covered by this margin of discretion. Including specific Sustainable Finance clauses into an FTA would therefore be detrimental to the FTA's flexibility. However, if Sustainable Finance measures are eventually found not to fall under the common understanding of a conventional sustainable development provision,[118] a specification in this regard through a dedicated FTA clause would be necessary. Plus, a more specific FTA clause on Sustainable Finance decreases the likelihood of conflict between the parties, especially in such sensitive areas as financial legislation.[119]

With a view to the TCA, consultations under TCA Chapter Nine (*Horizontal and institutional provisions*) may open policy space for the EU to propagate EU Sustainable Finance policy through further negotiations. These consultations may in particular refer to TCA Chapters Seven (*Environment and climate*) and Eight (*Other instruments for trade and sustainable development*).[120]

Second, the future (re)negotiation of EU FTAs could be used as a channel to propagate Sustainable Finance policy. So far, there are no specific provisions on the propagation of Sustainable Finance in the EU FTAs.[121] However, the Commission

---

EU-Singapore FTA, which does not include a prudential carve-out, cf. Martin and Mercurio (2017), pp. 91 et seq.

[116] Hush (2018), p. 154.

[117] Hush (2018), p. 153.

[118] This is in contrast to the findings made in Sect. 5.3.

[119] Hush (2018), p. 153; It is also to be duly noted that with a view to trade and investment partnerships, UN Environment and International Institute for Sustainable Development (*IISD*) published a Sustainability Toolkit for Trade Negotiators, cf. https://www.iisd.org/toolkits/sustainability-toolkit-for-trade-negotiators/. Accessed 26 May 2024; Cf. UN PAGE (2018), p. 7.

[120] Cf. in particular Art. 9.1(1) TCA.

[121] As discussed in Sect. 5.2.

states that it is pursuing a global response to climate and sustainability issues through green diplomacy by means of trade and development policies and bilateral and multilateral frameworks.[122] Furthermore, the EU claims that it will use its expertise to engage in the creation of regional strategies.[123] Thereby, the Commission is working towards the creation of *green alliances*, particularly in its relations with Latin America, the Caribbean, Asia, and the Pacific, while also integrating green transition into its extensive diplomatic relationships with Africa and China.[124] The creation of green alliances could then be used to alter existing trade agreements in view of the sustainability of the service traded, for instance regarding the trade in financial services. Finally, the Commission also claims to put focus on Sustainable Finance in its international initiatives with third countries, while including climate policy considerations into all EU external action.[125]

The UK withdrawal from the EU provides for a useful case study on the introduction of language conducive to the propagation of EU Sustainable Finance into the negotiation of EU FTAs. As a consequence of the vague language of the Withdrawal Agreement and in absence of a post-transition FTA, the UK Government and the UK Financial Conduct Authority (*FCA*) had continued to participate in the elaboration and implementation of EU Sustainable Finance legislation and standards even after its formal withdrawal announcement in March 2017.

In July 2019, the UK Government subsequently initiated its own policy framework on Sustainable Finance by publishing the UK Green Finance Strategy.[126] The much-anticipated document commits *"to at least match the ambition of the [. . .] Sustainable Finance Action Plan"*.[127] The same was voiced by the FCA.[128] This demonstrates a form of policy goal transferral and can be understood to the effect that EU targets pursued through Sustainable Finance are to be adopted at least to the same extent in the UK post-Brexit. Given the discussion concerning Art. VII (1) GATS in Sect. 4.2.2, this would justify the EU's domestic implementation of Sustainable Finance policy—The UK having similar standards on Sustainable Finance would likely not contest those of the EU. Equally, the UK Government's commitment to equal Sustainable Finance targets renders the EU's ambitions on the propagation of the concept redundant. It needs to be highlighted, however, that the UK Green Finance Strategy only refers to the 2018 Sustainable Finance Action Plan,[129] whereas the Commission already consults on the renewed Sustainable Finance Strategy and targets are likely to shift (Sect. 2.3). In the future, other

---

[122] European Commission (2019a), p. 20.

[123] European Commission (2019a), p. 20.

[124] European Commission (2019a), p. 20 et seq.; European Commission (2019b), p. 4.

[125] European Commission (2019a), p. 21.

[126] HM Government (2016).

[127] HM Government (2016), p. 26.

[128] FCA (2019), p. 22.

[129] European Commission (2018).

channels of influence would need to be considered for the effective propagation of Sustainable Finance to the UK as one of the EU's major trading partners.

On the other hand, the UK Green Finance Strategy highlights the possibility of *"onshoring"* the EU's proposals of the Sustainable Finance Action Plan into UK legislation.[130] This is in particular stated regarding disclosures, benchmarks, and the EU taxonomy. The FCA, too, stated that it will *"[e]ngage and consider the proposals of the European Commission's Sustainable Finance Action Plan"*.[131] Therefore, EU policy targets will likely be transferred not only into UK legislation but also specific EU legislation. While the regulatory similarity between for instance the Taxonomy Regulation and its UK counterpart is certainly instrumental to the cross-border financial markets, it also gives the EU another channel of influence for the propagation of Sustainable Finance post-Brexit.

This is also demonstrated in the UK Government and the FCA further sharing the EU's ambition to *"[d]rive action through international collaboration"*[132] and to promote *"globally consistent standards"*.[133] Likewise, the UK Government has built up its channels of influence on international Sustainable Finance policy-setting for instance by chairing the International Organization for Standardization's (*ISO*) Technical Committee on Sustainable Finance.[134] On the other hand, the UK will join the Commission's IPSF.[135]

Adding to this and potentially more relevant to Sustainable Finance, Art. SERVIN.5.41 TCA states that the TCA parties endeavor to implement and apply *"internationally agreed standards in the financial services sector for regulation and supervision"*. This includes *inter alia* standards by the G20, the FSB, the BCBS, and IOSCO. These international fora are currently at the forefront of developing Sustainable Finance policy guidance in their respective fields of expertise (Sect. 4.1.2). Through Art. SERVIN.5.41 TCA their publications, although not constituting an obligation, are likely to be implemented both in the EU and UK.

The EU could further propagate Sustainable Finance by a *de facto* continued influence on the UK's adoption of its Sustainable Finance standards. This could be achieved through the adoption of legislation and technical standards outlined in the Sustainable Finance Strategy but not fully adopted yet. One example of such *de facto* continued influence could be the adoption of the technical screening criteria for the Taxonomy Regulation. The Taxonomy Regulation itself is not applicable within the UK from 1 January 2021. The fact that, for instance, the Taxonomy Regulation has not been mentioned in Art. 138(2) Withdrawal Agreement as applicable after the transition period, is thought to be due to the EU taxonomy as a basic framework not

---

[130]HM Government (2016), p. 26.

[131]FCA (2019), p. 22.

[132]HM Government (2016), p. 27.

[133]FCA (2020).

[134]HM Government (2016), p. 26; Cf. ISO (2018).

[135]Cf. E3G (2020); IPSF, as defined in Sect. 4.1.2.

yet having had technical screening criteria. These were only proposed and consulted in December 2020, as described in Sect. 2.1.1.[136]

Third, the EU could propagate Sustainable Finance policy through the framework of its multilateral development agreements such as the EDF, DCI, and the European Neighbourhood Instrument (*ENI*).[137] The legal texts carrying these frameworks do not contain Sustainable Finance provisions. However, similar to the evolution of financing for development outcome documents,[138] the EDF, DCI, and ENI might shift to a broader understanding of financing for development to comprise further aspects of Sustainable Finance. It is, however, to be duly stated that there is no need for a Sustainable Finance policy protection clause in these multilateral development agreements since these agreements address substantially more disciplines governing the regulatory frameworks in the EU's partner countries. In contrast, these agreements could play a pivotal role in propagating Sustainable Finance in the EU Neighbourhood and throughout developing countries. Even more so, since the 2030 Agenda, in contrast to the MDGs, does not focus on developing countries but is universally applicable to all UN Member States. Equally, Sustainable Finance is not just a concept to finance development in developing countries but, ideally, a concept addressed to all UN Member States, to finance all sustainable development efforts globally.

Concluding, EU FTAs could be amended or renegotiated taking into account the above examples of clauses. Such provisions would both justify and propagate EU Sustainable Finance policy. The approaches exemplified above should be implemented given the current design of such agreements and similar clauses on sustainable development already included. Therefore, Sustainable Finance justification clauses may rather be designed in a legally binding manner, for instance in the form of specific exemptions. Propagation clauses, in turn, would rather take the form of soft law, non-binding declarations of intent. Either way, the increased introduction of Sustainable Finance clauses into the EU's bilateral agreements would accommodate the similarity in nature between the concepts of Sustainable Finance, sustainable development, international financial markets, and cross-border trade in financial services as discussed in Chap. 1.

---

[136] Cf. FT (2020).

[137] The ENI was established through Regulation (EU) No 232/2014 of the European Parliament and of the Council of 11 March 2014 establishing a European Neighbourhood Instrument [2014] OJ L 77/27.

[138] As discussed in Sect. 4.1.1.

5.5   Conclusion: EU FTAs as a Channel of Propagation and Justification

The currently applied EU Sustainable Finance measures are within the limitations set out in the EU FTAs. This conclusion can be based on the same considerations as under the GATS disciplines in Sect. 3.2. This is in particular due to the substantially similar wording and the occasionally explicit reference to the GATS disciplines in the EU FTAs discussed.

Furthermore, EU FTA chapters on sustainable development and the environment are for a large part applicable to financial services regulation. These chapters are thus insofar also relevant for the interpretation and the determination of the consistency of EU Sustainable Finance measures under the EU FTA disciplines.

Adding to this, general exception clauses and sustainable development and environmental right to regulate clauses, as mostly set out in aforementioned EU FTAs chapters on sustainability and the environment, apply to a large extend to EU Sustainable Finance measures. Such exception or right to regulate clauses may be necessary in cases of inconsistency under the EU FTA disciplines on trade in financial services. This might occur in respect of prospective EU Sustainable Finance measures like those described in Sect. 3.3. Adding to this, the prudential right to regulate clauses in EU FTAs apply to EU Sustainable Finance measures to the extent determined in Sect. 3.2.4.3. In particular, the TCA domestic regulation standards include multiple provisions applicable to EU Sustainable Finance measures and conducive to justifying them. This refers to the TCA provisions concerning the connection between international trade and sustainable development and those supporting environmental, climate action, and financial stability measures.

In Sect. 4.3 it has been argued that contrasting the assessment of EU Sustainable Finance's potential inconsistency, EU FTAs also inhibit the creative potential for designing binding legal provisions conducive to the propagation of Sustainable Finance. This approach was chosen in Sect. 5.4. With regard to the TCA, although for the EU there is certainly not as much policy ground to be gained from active propagation of its Sustainable Finance framework, the approach and seriousness of introducing sustainability into UK financial regulation post-Brexit may very well vary from the one taken by the EU. However, the aim of achieving a level playing field—an aim that was found to be generally applicable to the regulation of sustainable financial services and is pursued by both the EU and the UK—indicates there will not be a significant discrepancy between their respective approaches to Sustainable Finance.[139] Second, throughout the implementation period of the Withdrawal Agreement the UK and particularly the FCA instated separate policy roadmaps on Sustainable Finance.[140]

---

[139]Cf. Sect. 5.1.4.

[140]Cf. Sect. 5.1.4.

Negotiations under the respective EU FTA may further constitute a channel of propagation for EU Sustainable Finance policy. An example of this is the review of the TCA parties' respective *"legal framework relating to trade in services and investment, including"* the TCA itself as provided for in Art. SERVIN.1.4 TCA could function as a process to introduce Sustainable Finance explicitly into the TCA framework. It states that such review shall be conducted *"[w]ith a view to introducing possible improvements to the provisions of this Title, and consistent with their commitments under international agreements"*. However, the review process is not applicable *"with respect to financial services"* according to Art. SERVIN.1.4 (a) TCA. For the utility of including Sustainable Finance language immediately into the TCA, reference is made to the considerations under EU FTAs in Sect. 5.4.

Therefore, EU FTAs can be effective tools in steering the interpretation of trade in services disciplines in a manner conducive to the protection of policy space for the adoption and implementation of Sustainable Finance legislation.

Legislation

United Nations Framework Convention on Climate Change. 9 May 1992. U.N.T.S. 1771 (1992)

Report of the United Nations Conference on Environment and Development, Rio de Janeiro, 3 to 14 June 1992, Annex I, Rio Declaration on Environment and Development. 12 August 1992

Report of the United Nations Conference on Environment and Development, Rio de Janeiro, 3 to 14 June 1992, Annex II, Agenda 21. 12 August 1992

Marrakesh Agreement establishing the World Trade Organization. 15 April 1994. U.N.T.S. 1867 (1994)

General Agreement on Tariffs and Trade 1994, Marrakesh Agreement Establishing the World Trade Organization, Annex 1A. 15 April 1994. U.N.T.S. 1867 (1994)

General Agreement on Trade in Services, Marrakesh Agreement Establishing the World Trade Organization, Annex 1B. 15 April 1994. U.N.T.S. 1867 (1994)

Understanding on Commitments in Financial Services, Marrakesh Agreement Establishing the World Trade Organization. 15 April 1994

Economic Partnership, Political Coordination and Cooperation Agreement between the European Community and its Member States, of the one part, and the United Mexican States, of the other part [2000] OJ L 276/45

Monterrey Consensus of the International Conference on Financing for Development, The final text of agreements and commitments adopted at the International Conference on Financing for Development Monterrey, Mexico, 18–22 March 2002. 22 March 2002

Treaty of Lisbon amending the Treaty on European Union and the Treaty establishing the European Community [2007] OJ C 306/1

Economic Partnership Agreement between the CARIFORUM States, of the one part, and the European Community and its Member States, of the other part [2008] OJ L 289/3

Council Decision of 16 September 2010 on the signing, on behalf of the European Union, and provisional application of the Free Trade Agreement between the European Union and its Member States, of the one part, and the Republic of Korea, of the other part, Commission's statements, Free trade Agreement between the European Union and its Member States, of the one part, and the Republic of Korea, of the other part, Protocol concerning the definition of 'originating products' and methods of administrative cooperation, Protocol on mutual administrative assistance in customs matters, Protocol on cultural cooperation [2011] OJ L 127/1

Directive 2011/61/EU of the European Parliament and of the Council of 8 June 2011 on Alternative Investment Fund Managers and amending Directives 2003/41/EC and 2009/65/EC and Regulations (EC) No 1060/2009 and (EU) No 1095/2010 [2011] OJ L 174/1

Agreement establishing an Association between the European Union and its Member States, on the one hand, and Central America on the other [2012] OJ L 346/3

Trade Agreement between the European Union and its Member States, of the one part, and Colombia and Peru, of the other part [2012] OJ L 354/3

Consolidated version of the Treaty on European Union [2012] OJ C 326/13

Consolidated version of the Treaty on the Functioning of the European Union [2012] OJ C 326/47

Regulation (EU) No 232/2014 of the European Parliament and of the Council of 11 March 2014 establishing a European Neighbourhood Instrument [2014] OJ L 77/27

Directive 2014/91/EU of the European Parliament and of the Council of 23 July 2014 amending Directive 2009/65/EC on the coordination of laws, regulations and administrative provisions relating to undertakings for collective investment in transferable securities (UCITS) as regards depositary functions, remuneration policies and sanctions [2014] OJ L 257/186

General Assembly Resolution 70/1, Transforming our World: The 2030 Agenda for Sustainable Development. 25 September 2015. A/RES/70/1

Regulation (EU) 2016/1011 of the European Parliament and of the Council of 8 June 2016 on indices used as benchmarks in financial instruments and financial contracts or to measure the performance of investment funds and amending Directives 2008/48/EC and 2014/17/EU and Regulation (EU) No 596/2014 [2016] OJ L 171/1

Comprehensive Economic and Trade Agreement (CETA) between Canada, of the one part, and the European Union and its Member States, of the other part [2017] OJ L 11/23

Regulation (EU, Euratom) 2018/1046 of the European Parliament and of the Council of 18 July 2018 on the financial rules applicable to the general budget of the Union, amending Regulations (EU) No 1296/2013, (EU) No 1301/2013, (EU) No 1303/2013, (EU) No 1304/2013, (EU) No 1309/2013, (EU) No 1316/2013,

(EU) No 223/2014, (EU) No 283/2014, and Decision No 541/2014/EU and repealing Regulation (EU, Euratom) No 966/2012 [2018] OJ L 193/1

Free Trade Agreement between the European Union and the Republic of Singapore [2019] OJ L 294/3

Agreement on the withdrawal of the United Kingdom of Great Britain and Northern Ireland from the European Union and the European Atomic Energy Community [2019] OJ C 384I/1

Regulation (EU) 2019/2089 of the European Parliament and of the Council of 27 November 2019 amending Regulation (EU) 2016/1011 as regards EU Climate Transition Benchmarks, EU Paris-aligned Benchmarks and sustainability-related disclosures for benchmarks [2019] OJ L 317/17

Regulation (EU) 2020/852 of the European Parliament and of the Council of 18 June 2020 on the establishment of a framework to facilitate sustainable investment, and amending Regulation (EU) 2019/2088 [2020] OJ L 198/13

European Commission, Proposal for a Council Decision on the signing, on behalf of the Union, and on provisional application of the Trade and Cooperation Agreement between the European Union and the European Atomic Energy Community, of the one part, and the United Kingdom of Great Britain and Northern Ireland, of the other part, and of the Agreement between the European Union and the United Kingdom of Great Britain and Northern Ireland concerning security procedures for exchanging and protecting classified information. 25 December 2020. COM(2020) 855 final

Trade and Cooperation Agreement between the European Union and the European Atomic Energy Community, of the one part, and the United Kingdom of Great Britain and Northern Ireland, of the other part [2021] OJ L 149/10

References

Bibliography

Bueren E (2019) Sustainable finance. Zeitschrift für Unternehmens- und Gesellschaftsrecht 48(5): 813–875. https://doi.org/10.1515/zgr-2019-0022. Accessed 19 Dec 2021

FT (2020) UK delays pledge to follow EU green finance rules post-Brexit. 6 June 2020. https://www.ft.com/content/f1623027-26fb-4d73-8161-19e40f1f7eb2. Accessed 19 Dec 2021

Hush ER (2018) Where no man has gone before: the future of sustainable development in the comprehensive economic and trade agreement and new generation free trade agreements. Columbia J Environ Law 43(1):93–180. https://ssrn.com/abstract=3373398. Accessed 8 May 2024

Martin AP, Mercurio B (2017) Liberalization commitments, financial stability safeguards and capital controls: practice evolutions from GATS to TPP and megaregional trade agreements. Trade Law Dev 9(1):72–100. http://www.tradelawdevelopment.com/index.php/tld/article/download/9%281%29%20TL%26D%2071%20%282017%29/338. Accessed 8 May 2024

Sheargold E, Mitchell AD (2016) The TPP and good regulatory practices: an opportunity for regulatory coherence to promote regulatory autonomy? World Trade Rev 15(4):586–612. https://doi.org/10.1017/S1474745616000045

Van den Bossche P, Zdouc W (2017) The law and policy of the World Trade Organization. Text, cases and materials, 4th edn. Cambridge University Press, Cambridge

Documents

E3G (2020) Press Release, UK to work with EU to harmonize approach to investment taxonomies. 10 November 2020. https://www.e3g.org/news/uk-to-work-with-eu-to-harmonise-approach-to-investment-taxonomies/. Accessed 19 Dec 2021

European Commission (2017) Report from the Commission to the European Parliament, the Council, the European Economic and Social Committee and the Committee of the Regions on Implementation of Free Trade Agreements. 9 November 2017. COM(2017) 654 final. https://eur-lex.europa.eu/legal-content/EN/TXT/PDF/?uri=CELEX:52017DC0654&from=HU. Accessed 27 May 2024

European Commission (2018) Communication from the Commission, Action Plan: Financing Sustainable Growth. 8 March 2018. COM(2018) 97 final. https://eur-lex.europa.eu/legal-content/EN/TXT/PDF/?uri=CELEX:52018DC0097&from=EN. Accessed 19 Dec 2021

European Commission (2019a) Communication on The European Green Deal: COM(2019) 640 final, Communication from the Commission to the European Parliament, the European Council, the Council, the European Economic and Social Committee and the Committee of the Regions, The European Green Deal. 11 December 2019. https://ec.europa.eu/info/sites/info/files/european-green-deal-communication_en.pdf. Accessed 19 Dec 2021

European Commission (2019b) Annex to the Communication from the Commission to the European Parliament, the European Council, the Council, the European Economic and Social Committee and the Committee of the Regions, The European Green Deal, Annex, Roadmap and key actions. 11 December 2019. COM(2019) 640 final. https://ec.europa.eu/info/sites/info/files/european-green-deal-communication-annex-roadmap_en.pdf. Accessed 19 Dec 2021

European Commission (2020) Questions & Answers: EU-UK Trade and Cooperation Agreement. 24 December 2020. https://ec.europa.eu/commission/presscorner/detail/en/qanda_20_2532. Accessed 19 Dec 2021

European Commission (2024) Website on current EU FTAs. https://ec.europa.eu/trade/policy/countries-and-regions/negotiations-and-agreements/#_in-place. Accessed 19 Dec 2021

FCA (2019) Climate Change and Green Finance, Summary of responses and next steps. Feedback to DP18/8. 16 October 2019. https://www.fca.org.uk/publication/feedback/fs19-6.pdf. Accessed 19 Dec 2021

FCA (2020) Richard Monks, Director of Strategy, FCA, Speech at SRI Services and Partners Good Money Week panel discussion, https://www.fca.org.uk/news/speeches/building-trust-sustainable-investments. Accessed 19 Dec 2021

FCA (2021a) Memorandum of Understanding concerning consultation, cooperation and the exchange of information between ESMA and the UK Financial Conduct Authority. https://www.esma.europa.eu/sites/default/files/library/mou_esma-uk_fca_on_consultation_cooperation_and_exchange_of_information.pdf. Accessed 19 Dec 2021

FCA (2021b) Multilateral Memorandum of Understanding concerning consultation, cooperation and the exchange of information between each of the EEA competent authorities and the UK Financial Conduct Authority. https://www.esma.europa.eu/sites/default/files/library/mmou_eu-uk_fca_on_consultation_cooperation_and_exchange_of_information.pdf. Accessed 19 Dec 2021

FCA (2021c) Multilateral Memorandum of Understanding between ESMA and the Bank of England to set out arrangements for cooperation on the monitoring and supervision of CCPs established in the UK. https://www.esma.europa.eu/sites/default/files/library/esma70-152-2 531_esma-boe_mou_on_uk_ccps.pdf. Accessed 19 Dec 2021

FCA (2021d) Memorandum of Understanding related to ESMA's Monitoring of the Ongoing Compliance with Recognition Conditions by CSDs established in the United Kingdom of Great Britain and Northern Ireland, cf. https://www.esma.europa.eu/sites/default/files/library/ esma70-153-236_esma-boe_mou_on_uk_csd_recognition.pdf. Accessed 19 Dec 2021

HM Government (2016) Green Finance Strategy, Transforming Finance for a Greener Future. 16 July 2016. https://assets.publishing.service.gov.uk/government/uploads/system/uploads/ attachment_data/file/820284/190716_BEIS_Green_Finance_Strategy_Accessible_Final.pdf. Accessed 19 Dec 2021

HM Treasury (2020) Policy paper, equivalence decisions for the EEA States. 9 November 2020. https://www.gov.uk/government/publications/hm-treasury-equivalence-decisions-for-the-eea-states-9-november-2020/hm-treasury-equivalence-decisions-for-the-eea-states-9-novem ber-2020. Accessed 19 Dec 2021

ISO (2018) Technical Committees. ISO/TC 322. Sustainable finance. 2018. https://www.iso.org/ committee/7203746.html. Accessed 19 Dec 2021

UN PAGE (2018) International Investment Agreements and Sustainable Development: Safeguarding Policy Space and Mobilizing Investment for a Green Economy. https://www. greengrowthknowledge.org/sites/default/files/downloads/resource/international_investment_ agreements_sustainable_development_1.pdf. Accessed 8 May 2024

Jurisprudence

WTO DSB (2004) Dominican Republic – Measures Affecting the Importation and Internal Sale of Cigarettes, Panel report, 26 November 2004, WT/DS302/R

Chapter 6
Concluding Remarks

International trade law poses certain limitations and offers various opportunities to EU Sustainable Finance measures affecting third country financial services and service suppliers. Through the three-step approach—definition of scope, assessment of legality, and identification of channels of propagation and justification—chosen for this book, a set of recurring questions could be identified: Are EU Sustainable Finance measures *de facto* discriminatory? Do prudential or sustainable development carve-outs apply? What role do international agreements and policy-setting in international fora play? This book intended to contribute to answering these questions.

The ample scope of the GATS disciplines results in the difficulty of defining both their application and a potential violation through EU Sustainable Finance measures. Given that the existing WTO jurisprudence does not explicitly address the issue of Sustainable Finance and given the current impasse in the appointment of new Appellate Body members,[1] the Appellate Body's interpretation and handling of the new interdisciplinary regulatory field of Sustainable Finance is anything but predetermined. Instead, it is very much subject to analysis on a case-by-case basis. This case-by-case approach, as discussed in Sect. 3.3.4, could overall be guided by *proportionality* and *timing*. Both these factors are sufficiently embraced by current EU Sustainable Finance legislation, which, given such similar interpretation by a Panel, is thus to be found within the confinements of GATS.

EU FTAs, in this book represented by the EU-CARIFORUM EPA, CETA, and the TCA, in contrast to GATS and due to their bilateral nature, may offer a more detailed regulatory field for Sustainable Finance legislation. Matters of Sustainable Finance not addressed explicitly in these agreements. Yet, they address, in detail, the interrelation and thematical cluster of financing for development, sound financial

---

[1] For an overview of this impasse, cf. Stewart (2020).

© The Author(s), under exclusive license to Springer Nature Switzerland AG 2024
S. N. Pauls, *EU Sustainable Finance and International Trade Law*, EYIEL
Monographs - Studies in European and International Economic Law 37,
https://doi.org/10.1007/978-3-031-73853-1_6

services regulation, mainstreaming of sustainable development, and financial stability. This has consequently a strong influence on the assessment of Sustainable Finance legislation under EU FTAs. In this respect, EU Sustainable Finance legislation, as demonstrated in Chap. 2, covers a vast regulatory field and policy space. This again leads to the conclusion that only an assessment on a case-by-case basis of each EU Sustainable Finance provision under the respective EU FTA may allow for a conclusion on its consistency.

In this respect, it also needs to be emphasized that Sustainable Finance policy and legislation are at an early stage of development—both at the EU and international level. As demonstrated in Sect. 2.3, many of the announced EU Sustainable Finance measures are still undergoing the legislative process at various stages. However, policy publications like the Commission's Sustainable Finance Action Plan[2] or the European Green Deal[3] offer insight into what future measures are to be expected. Advances in Sustainable Finance legislation by other WTO Members amplify this notion.[4] As part of the propagation of Sustainable Finance, they may culminate in a dynamic effectively influencing WTO jurisprudence and the drafting of FTAs. Therefore, this book can only offer a first, initial, interpretation of Sustainable Finance legislation under GATS and the EU FTAs. Prospective developments of this regulatory field may result in an increased potential for inconsistency of these provisions.

It can, however, also be argued that Sustainable Finance is too broad of a concept to be defined with sufficient granularity and to be regulated in the macro-regulatory context of FTAs. This assumption is contrasted by the concept's close ties to its roots—sustainable development, financing for development, and financial stability, all of which are well established in international trade law. Underlining the interrelation with these roots would make future WTO jurisprudence on the consistency of Sustainable Finance measures more predictable. Although not explicitly named therein, most recent EU FTAs—like CETA and the TCA—draw a connection between measures regulating financial services, sustainable development, and prudential regulation.

However, international trade law and relations must not only be interpreted under the notion of limitation by GATS and EU FTAs. Instead, or arguably primarily, they can be seen as channels for the propagation of Sustainable Finance. As demonstrated in Chap. 4 and Sect. 5.4, such channels comprise general sustainable development negotiations and policy-setting in international fora, the GATS framework, and EU FTAs. The interrelation between Sustainable Finance, sustainable development, and prudential cooperation enables the international community to benefit from the collective experience of having successfully navigated the latter topics. This capacity is magnified through the regularly broad participation in sustainable development

---

[2]European Commission (2018).

[3]European Commission (2019).

[4]For an overview of current Sustainable Finance initiatives by other WTO Members, cf. SFSG (2018) and SFN (2020).

agreements on the one hand. On the other hand, the binding character of international prudential cooperation is conducive to the propagation of Sustainable Finance policy.[5]

Thereby, justification and propagation of Sustainable Finance are interlinked.[6] Policy protection and justification clauses incentivize the adoption of similar legislation by the trade partner. Propagation of Sustainable Finance eventually leads to a reduction of the potential inconsistency of Sustainable Finance measures and thus reduces the need for policy protection clauses in the first place.

Through the assessment of a possible propagation of Sustainable Finance by the EU, channels of influence on the policy of international fora could be identified. Whilst the Commission itself is not always represented in these fora, various EU specialized agencies are. However, the fora's preliminary and final policy recommendations and reports have been systematically referenced and substantially incorporated into the Commission's policy publications and legislative proposals. Given the EU's influence on international policy-setting at the levels described, this referencing can be interpreted as a reintroduction of EU-influenced international Sustainable Finance policy back into EU Sustainable Finance policy. The form of and reasons for this reintroduction have been discussed in Sect. 4.1.2.

In the future, further research would be necessary to assess prospective EU Sustainable Finance legislation – with a particular focus on future WTO jurisprudence addressing the threshold between sustainable development and prudential regulation. Furthermore, given the trend of addressing international trade law and international investment law jointly in the EU's new generation FTAs, a comprehensive analysis of prospective EU Sustainable Finance legislation could be of additional value.

On a larger scale, the role and treatment of Sustainable Finance measures in international trade law may stand as an example of a novel policy field accruing from developments in international climate action and sustainable development agreements. Given the impasse in the negotiations on domestic regulation and the Appellate Body,[7] the GATS framework might not be the primary international forum of development, cooperation, and policy-setting for Sustainable Finance. Instead, the example of Sustainable Finance shows that such development can more efficiently take place in specialized multilateral fora. This also allows such concepts to be spread or propagated through these fora and their participating parties and thus reach a more efficient implementation of the SDGs and climate change mitigation targets. Or, in other words, these fora in the future will likely play an even greater role in the development of Sustainable Finance policy. This would take account of the international nature of financial markets. Hence, international financial markets need international policy solutions and, in the Commission's own

---

[5]Cf. Sect. 4.3.
[6]Cf. Chap. 4.
[7]Cf. Sect. 4.2.1; Cf. above.

words, *"[r]eorienting private capital to more sustainable investments requires a comprehensive shift in how the financial system works."*[8]

Legislation

General Agreement on Trade in Services, Marrakesh Agreement Establishing the World Trade Organization, Annex 1B. 15 April 1994. U.N.T.S. 1867 (1994)

Economic Partnership Agreement between the CARIFORUM States, of the one part, and the European Community and its Member States, of the other part [2008] OJ L 289/3

Comprehensive Economic and Trade Agreement (CETA) between Canada, of the one part, and the European Union and its Member States, of the other part [2017] OJ L 11/23

European Commission, Proposal for a Council Decision on the signing, on behalf of the Union, and on provisional application of the Trade and Cooperation Agreement between the European Union and the European Atomic Energy Community, of the one part, and the United Kingdom of Great Britain and Northern Ireland, of the other part, and of the Agreement between the European Union and the United Kingdom of Great Britain and Northern Ireland concerning security procedures for exchanging and protecting classified information. 25 December 2020. COM(2020) 855 final

References

Stewart TP (2020) WTO Appellate Body Impasse – How and Why. https://currentthoughtsontrade.com/2020/01/30/wto-appellate-body-impasse-how-and-why/. Accessed 19 Dec 2021

Documents

European Commission (2018) Communication from the Commission, Action Plan: Financing Sustainable Growth. 8 March 2018. COM(2018) 97 final. https://eur-lex.europa.eu/legal-content/EN/TXT/PDF/?uri=CELEX:52018DC0097&from=EN. Accessed 19 Dec 2021

European Commission (2019) Communication on The European Green Deal: COM(2019) 640 final, Communication from the Commission to the European Parliament, the European Council, the Council, the European Economic and Social Committee and the Committee of the Regions, The European Green Deal. 11 December 2019. https://ec.europa.eu/info/sites/info/files/european-green-deal-communication_en.pdf. Accessed 19 Dec 2021

---

[8]European Commission (2018), p. 1.

SFN (2020) Sustainable Finance and the Role of Securities Regulators and IOSCO, Final Report. 14 April 2020. https://www.iosco.org/library/pubdocs/pdf/IOSCOPD652.pdf. Accessed 19 Dec 2021

SFSG (2018) Sustainable Finance Synthesis Report. July 2018. http://unepinquiry.org/wp-content/uploads/2018/11/G20_Sustainable_Finance_Synthesis_Report_2018.pdf. Accessed 19 Dec 2021

Annex

General Agreement on Trade in Service (Extract)[1]

Members,

Recognizing the growing importance of trade in services for the growth and development of the world economy;

Wishing to establish a multilateral framework of principles and rules for trade in services with a view to the expansion of such trade under conditions of transparency and progressive liberalization and as a means of promoting the economic growth of all trading partners and the development of developing countries;

Desiring the early achievement of progressively higher levels of liberalization of trade in services through successive rounds of multilateral negotiations aimed at promoting the interests of all participants on a mutually advantageous basis and at securing an overall balance of rights and obligations, while giving due respect to national policy objectives;

Recognizing the right of Members to regulate, and to introduce new regulations, on the supply of services within their territories in order to meet national policy objectives and, given asymmetries existing with respect to the degree of development of services regulations in different countries, the particular need of developing countries to exercise this right;

Desiring to facilitate the increasing participation of developing countries in trade in services and the expansion of their service exports including, inter alia, through the strengthening of their domestic services capacity and its efficiency and competitiveness;

---

[1] See https://www.wto.org/english/docs_e/legal_e/26-gats_01_e.htm.

Taking particular account of the serious difficulty of the least-developed countries in view of their special economic situation and their development, trade and financial needs;
Hereby agree as follows:

Part I: Scope and Definition

Article I: Scope and Definition

1. This Agreement applies to measures by Members affecting trade in services.
2. For the purposes of this Agreement, trade in services is defined as the supply of a service:

   (a) from the territory of one Member into the territory of any other Member;
   (b) in the territory of one Member to the service consumer of any other Member;
   (c) by a service supplier of one Member, through commercial presence in the territory of any other Member;
   (d) by a service supplier of one Member, through presence of natural persons of a Member in the territory of any other Member.

3. For the purposes of this Agreement:

   (a) "measures by Members" means measures taken by:

       (i) central, regional or local governments and authorities; and
       (ii) non-governmental bodies in the exercise of powers delegated by central, regional or local governments or authorities;

   In fulfilling its obligations and commitments under the Agreement, each Member shall take such reasonable measures as may be available to it to ensure their observance by regional and local governments and authorities and non-governmental bodies within its territory;

   (b) "services" includes any service in any sector except services supplied in the exercise of governmental authority;
   (c) "a service supplied in the exercise of governmental authority" means any service which is supplied neither on a commercial basis, nor in competition with one or more service suppliers.

Part II: General Obligations and Disciplines

Article II: Most-Favoured-Nation Treatment

1. With respect to any measure covered by this Agreement, each Member shall accord immediately and unconditionally to services and service suppliers of any other Member treatment no less favourable than that it accords to like services and service suppliers of any other country.

2. A Member may maintain a measure inconsistent with paragraph 1 provided that such a measure is listed in, and meets the conditions of, the Annex on Article II Exemptions.
3. The provisions of this Agreement shall not be so construed as to prevent any Member from conferring or according advantages to adjacent countries in order to facilitate exchanges limited to contiguous frontier zones of services that are both locally produced and consumed.

Article III: Transparency
1. Each Member shall publish promptly and, except in emergency situations, at the latest by the time of their entry into force, all relevant measures of general application which pertain to or affect the operation of this Agreement. International agreements pertaining to or affecting trade in services to which a Member is a signatory shall also be published.
2. Where publication as referred to in paragraph 1 is not practicable, such information shall be made otherwise publicly available.
3. Each Member shall promptly and at least annually inform the Council for Trade in Services of the introduction of any new, or any changes to existing, laws, regulations or administrative guidelines which significantly affect trade in services covered by its specific commitments under this Agreement.
4. Each Member shall respond promptly to all requests by any other Member for specific information on any of its measures of general application or international agreements within the meaning of paragraph 1. Each Member shall also establish one or more enquiry points to provide specific information to other Members, upon request, on all such matters as well as those subject to the notification requirement in paragraph 3. Such enquiry points shall be established within two years from the date of entry into force of the Agreement Establishing the WTO (referred to in this Agreement as the "WTO Agreement"). Appropriate flexibility with respect to the time-limit within which such enquiry points are to be established may be agreed upon for individual developing country Members. Enquiry points need not be depositories of laws and regulations.
5. Any Member may notify to the Council for Trade in Services any measure, taken by any other Member, which it considers affects the operation of this Agreement.

Article III bis: Disclosure of Confidential Information
[...]

Article IV: Increasing Participation of Developing Countries
[...]

Article V: Economic Integration

1. This Agreement shall not prevent any of its Members from being a party to or entering into an agreement liberalizing trade in services between or among the parties to such an agreement, provided that such an agreement:

    (a) has substantial sectoral coverage(1), and

    (b) provides for the absence or elimination of substantially all discrimination, in the sense of Article XVII, between or among the parties, in the sectors covered under subparagraph (a), through:

      (i) elimination of existing discriminatory measures, and/or

      (ii) prohibition of new or more discriminatory measures,

    either at the entry into force of that agreement or on the basis of a reasonable time-frame, except for measures permitted under Articles XI, XII, XIV and XIV bis.

2. In evaluating whether the conditions under paragraph 1(b) are met, consideration may be given to the relationship of the agreement to a wider process of economic integration or trade liberalization among the countries concerned.

3. (a) Where developing countries are parties to an agreement of the type referred to in paragraph 1, flexibility shall be provided for regarding the conditions set out in paragraph 1, particularly with reference to subparagraph (b) thereof, in accordance with the level of development of the countries concerned, both overall and in individual sectors and subsectors.

    (b) Notwithstanding paragraph 6, in the case of an agreement of the type referred to in paragraph 1 involving only developing countries, more favourable treatment may be granted to juridical persons owned or controlled by natural persons of the parties to such an agreement.

4. Any agreement referred to in paragraph 1 shall be designed to facilitate trade between the parties to the agreement and shall not in respect of any Member outside the agreement raise the overall level of barriers to trade in services within the respective sectors or subsectors compared to the level applicable prior to such an agreement.

5. If, in the conclusion, enlargement or any significant modification of any agreement under paragraph 1, a Member intends to withdraw or modify a specific commitment inconsistently with the terms and conditions set out in its Schedule, it shall provide at least 90 days advance notice of such modification or withdrawal and the procedure set forth in paragraphs 2, 3 and 4 of Article XXI shall apply.

6. A service supplier of any other Member that is a juridical person constituted under the laws of a party to an agreement referred to in paragraph 1 shall be entitled to treatment granted under such agreement, provided that it engages in substantive business operations in the territory of the parties to such agreement.

7. (a) Members which are parties to any agreement referred to in paragraph 1 shall promptly notify any such agreement and any enlargement or any

significant modification of that agreement to the Council for Trade in Services. They shall also make available to the Council such relevant information as may be requested by it. The Council may establish a working party to examine such an agreement or enlargement or modification of that agreement and to report to the Council on its consistency with this Article.

(b) Members which are parties to any agreement referred to in paragraph 1 which is implemented on the basis of a time-frame shall report periodically to the Council for Trade in Services on its implementation. The Council may establish a working party to examine such reports if it deems such a working party necessary.

(c) Based on the reports of the working parties referred to in subparagraphs (a) and (b), the Council may make recommendations to the parties as it deems appropriate.

8. A Member which is a party to any agreement referred to in paragraph 1 may not seek compensation for trade benefits that may accrue to any other Member from such agreement.

Article V bis: Labour Markets Integration Agreements
[...]

Article VI: Domestic Regulation

1. In sectors where specific commitments are undertaken, each Member shall ensure that all measures of general application affecting trade in services are administered in a reasonable, objective and impartial manner.

2. (a) Each Member shall maintain or institute as soon as practicable judicial, arbitral or administrative tribunals or procedures which provide, at the request of an affected service supplier, for the prompt review of, and where justified, appropriate remedies for, administrative decisions affecting trade in services. Where such procedures are not independent of the agency entrusted with the administrative decision concerned, the Member shall ensure that the procedures in fact provide for an objective and impartial review.

(b) The provisions of subparagraph (a) shall not be construed to require a Member to institute such tribunals or procedures where this would be inconsistent with its constitutional structure or the nature of its legal system.

3. Where authorization is required for the supply of a service on which a specific commitment has been made, the competent authorities of a Member shall, within a reasonable period of time after the submission of an application considered complete under domestic laws and regulations, inform the applicant of the decision concerning the application. At the request of the applicant, the competent authorities of the Member shall provide, without undue delay, information concerning the status of the application.

4. With a view to ensuring that measures relating to qualification requirements and procedures, technical standards and licensing requirements do not constitute unnecessary barriers to trade in services, the Council for Trade in Services

shall, through appropriate bodies it may establish, develop any necessary disciplines. Such disciplines shall aim to ensure that such requirements are, inter alia:

(a) based on objective and transparent criteria, such as competence and the ability to supply the service;

(b) not more burdensome than necessary to ensure the quality of the service;

(c) in the case of licensing procedures, not in themselves a restriction on the supply of the service.

5. (a) In sectors in which a Member has undertaken specific commitments, pending the entry into force of disciplines developed in these sectors pursuant to paragraph 4, the Member shall not apply licensing and qualification requirements and technical standards that nullify or impair such specific commitments in a manner which:

(i) does not comply with the criteria outlined in subparagraphs 4(a), (b) or (c); and

(ii) could not reasonably have been expected of that Member at the time the specific commitments in those sectors were made.

(b) In determining whether a Member is in conformity with the obligation under paragraph 5(a), account shall be taken of international standards of relevant international organizations(3) applied by that Member.

6. In sectors where specific commitments regarding professional services are undertaken, each Member shall provide for adequate procedures to verify the competence of professionals of any other Member.

Article VII: Recognition

1. For the purposes of the fulfilment, in whole or in part, of its standards or criteria for the authorization, licensing or certification of services suppliers, and subject to the requirements of paragraph 3, a Member may recognize the education or experience obtained, requirements met, or licenses or certifications granted in a particular country. Such recognition, which may be achieved through harmonization or otherwise, may be based upon an agreement or arrangement with the country concerned or may be accorded autonomously.

2. A Member that is a party to an agreement or arrangement of the type referred to in paragraph 1, whether existing or future, shall afford adequate opportunity for other interested Members to negotiate their accession to such an agreement or arrangement or to negotiate comparable ones with it. Where a Member accords recognition autonomously, it shall afford adequate opportunity for any other Member to demonstrate that education, experience, licenses, or certifications obtained or requirements met in that other Member's territory should be recognized.

3. A Member shall not accord recognition in a manner which would constitute a means of discrimination between countries in the application of its standards or criteria for the authorization, licensing or certification of services suppliers, or a disguised restriction on trade in services.

4. Each Member shall:

    (a) within 12 months from the date on which the WTO Agreement takes effect for it, inform the Council for Trade in Services of its existing recognition measures and state whether such measures are based on agreements or arrangements of the type referred to in paragraph 1;

    (b) promptly inform the Council for Trade in Services as far in advance as possible of the opening of negotiations on an agreement or arrangement of the type referred to in paragraph 1 in order to provide adequate opportunity to any other Member to indicate their interest in participating in the negotiations before they enter a substantive phase;

    (c) promptly inform the Council for Trade in Services when it adopts new recognition measures or significantly modifies existing ones and state whether the measures are based on an agreement or arrangement of the type referred to in paragraph 1.

5. Wherever appropriate, recognition should be based on multilaterally agreed criteria. In appropriate cases, Members shall work in cooperation with relevant intergovernmental and non-governmental organizations towards the establishment and adoption of common international standards and criteria for recognition and common international standards for the practice of relevant services trades and professions.

Article VIII: Monopolies and Exclusive Service Suppliers
[…]

Article IX: Business Practices
[…]

Article X: Emergency Safeguard Measures
[…]

Article XI: Payments and Transfers
[…]

Article XII: Restrictions to Safeguard the Balance of Payments
[…]

Article XIII: Government Procurement
[…]

Article XIV: General Exceptions
Subject to the requirement that such measures are not applied in a manner which would constitute a means of arbitrary or unjustifiable discrimination between countries where like conditions prevail, or a disguised restriction on trade in services, nothing in this Agreement shall be construed to prevent the adoption or enforcement by any Member of measures:

(a) necessary to protect public morals or to maintain public order;
(b) necessary to protect human, animal or plant life or health;

(c) necessary to secure compliance with laws or regulations which are not inconsistent with the provisions of this Agreement including those relating to:

   (i) the prevention of deceptive and fraudulent practices or to deal with the effects of a default on services contracts;

  (ii) the protection of the privacy of individuals in relation to the processing and dissemination of personal data and the protection of confidentiality of individual records and accounts;

 (iii) safety;

(d) inconsistent with Article XVII, provided that the difference in treatment is aimed at ensuring the equitable or effective imposition or collection of direct taxes in respect of services or service suppliers of other Members;

(e) inconsistent with Article II, provided that the difference in treatment is the result of an agreement on the avoidance of double taxation or provisions on the avoidance of double taxation in any other international agreement or arrangement by which the Member is bound.

Article XIV bis: Security Exceptions
[. . .]

Article XV: Subsidies
[. . .]

Part III: Specific Commitments

Article XVI: Market Access
1. With respect to market access through the modes of supply identified in Article I, each Member shall accord services and service suppliers of any other Member treatment no less favourable than that provided for under the terms, limitations and conditions agreed and specified in its Schedule.
2. In sectors where market-access commitments are undertaken, the measures which a Member shall not maintain or adopt either on the basis of a regional subdivision or on the basis of its entire territory, unless otherwise specified in its Schedule, are defined as:

(a) limitations on the number of service suppliers whether in the form of numerical quotas, monopolies, exclusive service suppliers or the requirements of an economic needs test;

(b) limitations on the total value of service transactions or assets in the form of numerical quotas or the requirement of an economic needs test;

(c) limitations on the total number of service operations or on the total quantity of service output expressed in terms of designated numerical units in the form of quotas or the requirement of an economic needs test;

(d) limitations on the total number of natural persons that may be employed in a particular service sector or that a service supplier may employ and who are necessary for, and directly related to, the supply of a specific service in the form of numerical quotas or the requirement of an economic needs test;

(e) measures which restrict or require specific types of legal entity or joint venture through which a service supplier may supply a service; and

(f) limitations on the participation of foreign capital in terms of maximum percentage limit on foreign shareholding or the total value of individual or aggregate foreign investment.

Article XVII: National Treatment

1. In the sectors inscribed in its Schedule, and subject to any conditions and qualifications set out therein, each Member shall accord to services and service suppliers of any other Member, in respect of all measures affecting the supply of services, treatment no less favourable than that it accords to its own like services and service suppliers.

2. A Member may meet the requirement of paragraph 1 by according to services and service suppliers of any other Member, either formally identical treatment or formally different treatment to that it accords to its own like services and service suppliers.

3. Formally identical or formally different treatment shall be considered to be less favourable if it modifies the conditions of competition in favour of services or service suppliers of the Member compared to like services or service suppliers of any other Member.

Article XVIII: Additional Commitments

Members may negotiate commitments with respect to measures affecting trade in services not subject to scheduling under Articles XVI or XVII, including those regarding qualifications, standards or licensing matters. Such commitments shall be inscribed in a Member's Schedule.

Part IV: Progressive Liberalization

Article XIX: Negotiation of Specific Commitments

[. . .]

Article XX: Schedules of Specific Commitments

1. Each Member shall set out in a schedule the specific commitments it undertakes under Part III of this Agreement. With respect to sectors where such commitments are undertaken, each Schedule shall specify:

(a) terms, limitations and conditions on market access;

(b) conditions and qualifications on national treatment;

(c) undertakings relating to additional commitments;
(d) where appropriate the time-frame for implementation of such commitments; and
(e) the date of entry into force of such commitments.

2. Measures inconsistent with both Articles XVI and XVII shall be inscribed in the column relating to Article XVI. In this case the inscription will be considered to provide a condition or qualification to Article XVII as well.
3. Schedules of specific commitments shall be annexed to this Agreement and shall form an integral part thereof.

Article XXI: Modification of Schedules
[...]

Part V: Institutional Provisions

Article XXII: Consultation
[...]

Article XXIII: Dispute Settlement and Enforcement
[...]

Article XXIV: Council for Trade in Services
1. The Council for Trade in Services shall carry out such functions as may be assigned to it to facilitate the operation of this Agreement and further its objectives. The Council may establish such subsidiary bodies as it considers appropriate for the effective discharge of its functions.
2. The Council and, unless the Council decides otherwise, its subsidiary bodies shall be open to participation by representatives of all Members.
3. The Chairman of the Council shall be elected by the Members.

Article XXV: Technical Cooperation
[...]

Article XXVI: Relationship with Other International Organizations
[...]

GATS Annex on Financial Services

1. Scope and Definition

(a) This Annex applies to measures affecting the supply of financial services. Reference to the supply of a financial service in this Annex shall mean the supply of a service as defined in paragraph 2 of Article I of the Agreement.

(b) For the purposes of subparagraph 3(b) of Article I of the Agreement, "services supplied in the exercise of governmental authority" means the following:

  (i) activities conducted by a central bank or monetary authority or by any other public entity in pursuit of monetary or exchange rate policies;

  (ii) activities forming part of a statutory system of social security or public retirement plans; and

  (iii) other activities conducted by a public entity for the account or with the guarantee or using the financial resources of the Government.

(c) For the purposes of subparagraph 3(b) of Article I of the Agreement, if a Member allows any of the activities referred to in subparagraphs (b)(ii) or (b)(iii) of this paragraph to be conducted by its financial service suppliers in competition with a public entity or a financial service supplier, "services" shall include such activities.

(d) Subparagraph 3(c) of Article I of the Agreement shall not apply to services covered by this Annex.

2. Domestic Regulation

(a) Notwithstanding any other provisions of the Agreement, a Member shall not be prevented from taking measures for prudential reasons, including for the protection of investors, depositors, policy holders or persons to whom a fiduciary duty is owed by a financial service supplier, or to ensure the integrity and stability of the financial system. Where such measures do not conform with the provisions of the Agreement, they shall not be used as a means of avoiding the Member's commitments or obligations under the Agreement.

(b) Nothing in the Agreement shall be construed to require a Member to disclose information relating to the affairs and accounts of individual customers or any confidential or proprietary information in the possession of public entities.

3. Recognition

(a) A Member may recognize prudential measures of any other country in determining how the Member's measures relating to financial services shall be applied. Such recognition, which may be achieved through harmonization or otherwise, may be based upon an agreement or arrangement with the country concerned or may be accorded autonomously.

(b) A Member that is a party to such an agreement or arrangement referred to in subparagraph (a), whether future or existing, shall afford adequate opportunity for other interested Members to negotiate their accession to such agreements or arrangements, or to negotiate comparable ones with it, under circumstances in which there would be equivalent regulation, oversight, implementation of such regulation, and, if appropriate, procedures concerning the sharing of information between the parties to the agreement or arrangement. Where a Member accords recognition autonomously, it shall afford adequate opportunity for any other Member to demonstrate that such circumstances exist.

(c) Where a Member is contemplating according recognition to prudential measures of any other country, paragraph 4(b) of Article VII shall not apply.

4. Dispute Settlement

Panels for disputes on prudential issues and other financial matters shall have the necessary expertise relevant to the specific financial service under dispute.

5. Definitions

For the purposes of this Annex:

(a) A financial service is any service of a financial nature offered by a financial service supplier of a Member. Financial services include all insurance and insurance-related services, and all banking and other financial services (excluding insurance). Financial services include the following activities:
Insurance and insurance-related services

  (i) Direct insurance (including co-insurance):
   (A) life
   (B) non-life
  (ii) Reinsurance and retrocession;
  (iii) Insurance intermediation, such as brokerage and agency;
  (iv) Services auxiliary to insurance, such as consultancy, actuarial, risk assessment and claim settlement services.

Banking and other financial services (excluding insurance)

  (v) Acceptance of deposits and other repayable funds from the public;
  (vi) Lending of all types, including consumer credit, mortgage credit, factoring and financing of commercial transaction;
  (vii) Financial leasing;
  (viii) All payment and money transmission services, including credit, charge and debit cards, travellers cheques and bankers drafts;
  (ix) Guarantees and commitments;
  (x) Trading for own account or for account of customers, whether on an exchange, in an over-the-counter market or otherwise, the following:

   (A) money market instruments (including cheques, bills, certificates of deposits);
   (B) foreign exchange;
   (C) derivative products including, but not limited to, futures and options;

(D) exchange rate and interest rate instruments, including products such as swaps, forward rate agreements;

(E) transferable securities;

(F) other negotiable instruments and financial assets, including bullion.

(xi) Participation in issues of all kinds of securities, including underwriting and placement as agent (whether publicly or privately) and provision of services related to such issues;

(xii) Money broking;

(xiii) Asset management, such as cash or portfolio management, all forms of collective investment management, pension fund management, custodial, depository and trust services;

(xiv) Settlement and clearing services for financial assets, including securities, derivative products, and other negotiable instruments;

(xv) Provision and transfer of financial information, and financial data processing and related software by suppliers of other financial services;

(xvi) Advisory, intermediation and other auxiliary financial services on all the activities listed in subparagraphs (v) through (xv), including credit reference and analysis, investment and portfolio research and advice, advice on acquisitions and on corporate restructuring and strategy.

(b) A financial service supplier means any natural or juridical person of a Member wishing to supply or supplying financial services but the term "financial service supplier" does not include a public entity.

(c) "Public entity" means:

(i) a government, a central bank or a monetary authority, of a Member, or an entity owned or controlled by a Member, that is principally engaged in carrying out governmental functions or activities for governmental purposes, not including an entity principally engaged in supplying financial services on commercial terms; or

(ii) a private entity, performing functions normally performed by a central bank or monetary authority, when exercising those functions.

Understanding on Commitments in Financial Services

Participants in the Uruguay Round have been enabled to take on specific commitments with respect to financial services under the General Agreement on Trade in Services (here in after referred to as the "Agreement") on the basis of an alternative approach to that covered by the provisions of Part III of the Agreement. It was agreed that this approach could be applied subject to the following understanding:

(i) it does not conflict with the provisions of the Agreement;

(ii) it does not prejudice the right of any Member to schedule its specific commitments in accordance with the approach under Part III of the Agreement;

(iii) resulting specific commitments shall apply on a most-favoured-nation basis;
(iv) no presumption has been created as to the degree of liberalization to which a
      Member is committing itself under the Agreement.

Interested Members, on the basis of negotiations, and subject to conditions and
qualifications where specified, have inscribed in their schedule specific commitments conforming to the approach set out below.

A. Standstill
Any conditions, limitations and qualifications to the commitments noted below
shall be limited to existing non-conforming measures.

B. Market Access
Monopoly Rights

1. In addition to Article VIII of the Agreement, the following shall apply:

Each Member shall list in its schedule pertaining to financial services existing
monopoly rights and shall endeavour to eliminate them or reduce their scope.
Notwithstanding subparagraph 1(b) of the Annex on Financial Services, this
paragraph applies to the activities referred to in subparagraph 1(b)(iii) of the
Annex.

Financial Services purchased by Public Entities

2. Notwithstanding Article XIII of the Agreement, each Member shall ensure
   that financial service suppliers of any other Member established in its territory
   are accorded most-favoured-nation treatment and national treatment as regards
   the purchase or acquisition of financial services by public entities of the
   Member in its territory.

Cross-border Trade

3. Each Member shall permit non-resident suppliers of financial services to
   supply, as a principal, through an intermediary or as an intermediary, and
   under terms and conditions that accord national treatment, the following
   services:
   (a) insurance of risks relating to:

      (i) maritime shipping and commercial aviation and space launching and
          freight (including satellites), with such insurance to cover any or all of
          the following: the goods being transported, the vehicle transporting
          the goods and any liability arising therefrom; and
      (ii) goods in international transit;

   (b) reinsurance and retrocession and the services auxiliary to insurance as
       referred to in subparagraph 5(a)(iv) of the Annex;
   (c) provision and transfer of financial information and financial data
       processing as referred to in subparagraph 5(a)(xv) of the Annex and
       advisory and other auxiliary services, excluding intermediation, relating

to banking and other financial services as referred to in subparagraph 5(a) (xvi) of the Annex.

4. Each Member shall permit its residents to purchase in the territory of any other Member the financial services indicated in:

(a) subparagraph 3(a);
(b) subparagraph 3(b); and
(c) subparagraphs 5(a)(v) to (xvi) of the Annex.

Commercial Presence

5. Each Member shall grant financial service suppliers of any other Member the right to establish or expand within its territory, including through the acquisition of existing enterprises, a commercial presence.

6. A Member may impose terms, conditions and procedures for authorization of the establishment and expansion of a commercial presence in so far as they do not circumvent the Member's obligation under paragraph 5 and they are consistent with the other obligations of the Agreement.

New Financial Services

7. A Member shall permit financial service suppliers of any other Member established in its territory to offer in its territory any new financial service.

Transfers of Information and Processing of Information

8. No Member shall take measures that prevent transfers of information or the processing of financial information, including transfers of data by electronic means, or that, subject to importation rules consistent with international agreements, prevent transfers of equipment, where such transfers of information, processing of financial information or transfers of equipment are necessary for the conduct of the ordinary business of a financial service supplier. Nothing in this paragraph restricts the right of a Member to protect personal data, personal privacy and the confidentiality of individual records and accounts so long as such right is not used to circumvent the provisions of the Agreement.

Temporary Entry of Personnel

9. (a) Each Member shall permit temporary entry into its territory of the following personnel of a financial service supplier of any other Member that is establishing or has established a commercial presence in the territory of the Member:

(i) senior managerial personnel possessing proprietary information essential to the establishment, control and operation of the services of the financial service supplier; and
(ii) specialists in the operation of the financial service supplier.

(b) Each Member shall permit, subject to the availability of qualified personnel in its territory, temporary entry into its territory of the following personnel associated with a commercial presence of a financial service supplier of any other Member:

    (i) specialists in computer services, telecommunication services and accounts of the financial service supplier; and

    (ii) actuarial and legal specialists.

Non-discriminatory Measures

10. Each Member shall endeavour to remove or to limit any significant adverse effects on financial service suppliers of any other Member of:

(a) non-discriminatory measures that prevent financial service suppliers from offering in the Member's territory, in the form determined by the Member, all the financial services permitted by the Member;

(b) non-discriminatory measures that limit the expansion of the activities of financial service suppliers into the entire territory of the Member;

(c) measures of a Member, when such a Member applies the same measures to the supply of both banking and securities services, and a financial service supplier of any other Member concentrates its activities in the provision of securities services; and

(d) other measures that, although respecting the provisions of the Agreement, affect adversely the ability of financial service suppliers of any other Member to operate, compete or enter the Member's market;

provided that any action taken under this paragraph would not unfairly discriminate against financial service suppliers of the Member taking such action.

11. With respect to the non-discriminatory measures referred to in subparagraphs 10(a) and (b), a Member shall endeavour not to limit or restrict the present degree of market opportunities nor the benefits already enjoyed by financial service suppliers of all other Members as a class in the territory of the Member, provided that this commitment does not result in unfair discrimination against financial service suppliers of the Member applying such measures.

C. National Treatment

1. Under terms and conditions that accord national treatment, each Member shall grant to financial service suppliers of any other Member established in its territory access to payment and clearing systems operated by public entities, and to official funding and refinancing facilities available in the normal course of ordinary business. This paragraph is not intended to confer access to the Member's lender of last resort facilities.

2. When membership or participation in, or access to, any self-regulatory body, securities or futures exchange or market, clearing agency, or any other organization or association, is required by a Member in order for financial service suppliers of any other Member to supply financial services on an equal basis with financial service suppliers of the Member, or when the Member provides directly or indirectly such entities, privileges or advantages in supplying financial services, the Member shall ensure that such entities accord national treatment to financial service suppliers of any other Member resident in the territory of the Member.

D. Definitions

1. A non-resident supplier of financial services is a financial service supplier of a Member which supplies a financial service into the territory of another Member from an establishment located in the territory of another Member, regardless of whether such a financial service supplier has or has not a commercial presence in the territory of the Member in which the financial service is supplied.

2. "Commercial presence" means an enterprise within a Member's territory for the supply of financial services and includes wholly- or partly-owned subsidiaries, joint ventures, partnerships, sole proprietorships, franchising operations, branches, agencies, representative offices or other organizations.

3. A new financial service is a service of a financial nature, including services related to existing and new products or the manner in which a product is delivered, that is not supplied by any financial service supplier in the territory of a particular Member but which is supplied in the territory of another Member.

Printed by Printforce, the Netherlands